Activism and Post-activism

Activism and Post-activism

Korean Documentary Cinema, 1981–2022

Jihoon Kim

OXFORD
UNIVERSITY PRESS

Oxford University Press is a department of the University of Oxford. It furthers the University's objective of excellence in research, scholarship, and education by publishing worldwide. Oxford is a registered trade mark of Oxford University Press in the UK and certain other countries.

Published in the United States of America by Oxford University Press
198 Madison Avenue, New York, NY 10016, United States of America.

© Oxford University Press 2024

All rights reserved. No part of this publication may be reproduced, stored in a retrieval system, or transmitted, in any form or by any means, without the prior permission in writing of Oxford University Press, or as expressly permitted by law, by license, or under terms agreed with the appropriate reproduction rights organization. Inquiries concerning reproduction outside the scope of the above should be sent to the Rights Department, Oxford University Press, at the address above.

You must not circulate this work in any other form and you must impose this same condition on any acquirer.

Library of Congress Cataloging-in-Publication Data
Names: Kim, Jihoon, author.
Title: Activism and post-activism :
Korean documentary cinema 1981 to 2022 / Jihoon Kim.
Description: New York, NY : Oxford University Press, 2024. |
Includes bibliographical references and index.
Identifiers: LCCN 2023039551 (print) | LCCN 2023039552 (ebook) |
ISBN 9780197760420 (paperback) | ISBN 9780197760413 (hardback) |
ISBN 9780197760444 (epub)
Subjects: LCSH: Documentary films—Korea (South)—History and criticism. |
Documentary films—Social aspects—Korea (South) |
Social change in motion pictures. | Social problems in motion pictures.
Classification: LCC PN1995.9.D6 K4764 2024 (print) |
LCC PN1995.9.D6 (ebook) | DDC 791.43/6095195—dc23/eng/20231004
LC record available at https://lccn.loc.gov/2023039551
LC ebook record available at https://lccn.loc.gov/2023039552

DOI: 10.1093/oso/9780197760413.001.0001

This book was supported by the Ministry of Education of the Republic of Korea and the National Research Foundation of Korea (NRF-2020S1A6A4040617).

For Lee Sun Joo,
Who dreams of a better cinema, life, and society together

Contents

Acknowledgments	*ix*
Note on Romanization and Translations	*xi*

Introduction: The Double Helix   1

PART I. ACTIVISM

1. **The Development of the Activist Tradition in the 1980s and 1990s**   33

2. **Twenty-First-Century Activist Documentaries: Three Traditional Issues**   61

3. **New Social Movements and Alternative Media Practices**   88

PART II. POST-ACTIVISM

4. **The Personal Turn: Domestic Ethnography, the Essay Film, Reenactment**   127

5. **The Audiovisual Turn: From *hyŏnjang* to Memoryscape**   166

6. **The Archival Turn: Memory Wars and Materialist Historiography**   192

7. **The Digital Turn: Seeking Truth Differently**   220

Epilogue   250

Notes	*263*
Index	*299*

Acknowledgments

I started to write this first-ever English-language monograph on the beginning, development, and divergences of South Korean documentary films and videos in the nongovernmental and noncorporate sectors in 2017. This was driven by my awareness that unless I did, they would remain uncharted in anglophone academia and cinephile culture for many years to come. With this book, Korean documentary cinema finally has its own history, which is doubtless open to revision, critique, and expansion by future scholars. Besides my unwavering thanks to my family members, including my wife, Lee Sun Joo, who is a devoted cinephile and scholar dedicated to the history of Korean cinema, my sincere gratitude particularly goes to all the local filmmakers, artists, activists, critics, and scholars, including those who generously shared their materials. It is indeed they that have written this history on their own terms. I also send my gratitude to my esteemed editor, Norman Hirschy, two anonymous reviewers for their generous support for this book, and to my research assistant, Kim Yong-jin, who helped me complete its index.

Portions of chapter 5 are excerpts from "The Audiovisual Turn of Recent Korean Documentary Cinema: The Time-Image, Place, and Landscape," published in *Positions: Asia Critique* 30.1 (February 2022): 189–216, reprinted by permission of Duke University Press; parts of chapter 6 appeared as "The Uses of Found Footage and the 'Archival Turn' of Recent Korean Documentary," *Third Text* 34.2 (2020): 231–254, reprinted by permission of Taylor & Francis Ltd; and two sections in chapter 7 were published as "The Subjunctive Mode, CGI, and Digital Editing: Documentaries on the Yongsan Massacre and the Sewol Ferry Disaster," *Concentric: Literary and Cultural Studies* 48.1 (March 2022): 85–113.

Note on Romanization and Translations

All Korean names of filmmakers, authors, and places have been romanized using the Revised Romanization of Korean. All Korean common nouns, Korean pronunciation of titles of films, videos, and scholarly works, and Korean pronunciation of organization names and laws translated into English have been romanized using the McCune-Reischauer system. Following Korean custom, surnames precede given names, excluding names of filmmakers and authors who are based in foreign countries. All translations from Korean into English are mine unless otherwise specified.

Introduction

The Double Helix

Two Documentaries on Women Workers

Directed by Lee Hye-ran, a member of the collective Feminist Video Activism WOM (Yŏsŏng yŏngsang chiptan Um, hereafter abbreviated as WOM; see also chapter 3), *We Are Not Defeated* (*Uridŭrŭn chŏngŭip'ada*, 2006, 105 min.) is a milestone among Korean documentaries about the history of the labor movements led by women workers (*yŏgong*) in the 1970s.[1] The film's protagonists are former female factory workers at Dongil Textile, one of the leading firms that exported low-cost products based on the exploitation of their cheap labor (figure I.1). The former female workers were also subject to the structural gender discrimination, which included the company's deeply ingrained patriarchal norm and the low wages of women compared to those of the male counterparts. In response to the workers' desire to write the history of their heated struggles (*t'ujaeng*), including a nude demonstration, to establish a female-led union against the company's oppression from 1976 to 1978, Lee interviewed a dozen of their leaders, who were living in different regions after the company fired them in 1978. In so doing, she also documented the leaders' regular meetings during their ongoing fight for reinstatement. Built on Lee's intimate relationship with the leaders, their vocal utterances foreground a rich array of personal memories and feelings, including their different motivations to join the company, their pains from its violent repression of their strikes and sit-ins, and their dissident voices against the masculine hierarchy of the factory. Positioning the leaders as *uri* (we), Lee's voice-over interweaves a tapestry of the testimonies that represent them as working-class women charged with energies of resistance and solidarity.

By privileging the speech acts of the marginalized subjects as the primary resource for positing the female workers' activism as the collective action opposing labor and gender inequalities, the film inherits a prevalent tradition of Korean independent documentary cinema. The activist tradition emerged in the early 1980s to partake of and document people's struggles

---

Activism and Post-activism. Jihoon Kim, Oxford University Press. © Oxford University Press 2024.
DOI: 10.1093/oso/9780197760413.003.0001

Figure I.1 *We Are Not Defeated* (Lee Hye-ran, 2006)
Image courtesy: Feminist Video Activism WOM.

for democratization and labor rights against the oppressive power of military dictatorship and the corporate power of unequal labor-management relations. Since then, the tradition has legitimized itself as an alternative form of filmmaking for urgent intervention in social problems and protests. Such leading practitioners of Korean independent documentary as Kim Dongwon, Byun Young-joo, and Hong Hyung-sook, based in the small film production collectives that they led, marked the now-canonical political and aesthetic trend of Korean independent documentary. Their films established the camera's *hyŏnjang* (on-the-spot) witnessing of ongoing events and the director's immediate conversation with the social actors as fundamental to documentary filmmaking's commitment to engaging social movements and issues and making truth claims. In this sense, Nam Inyoung and Chris Berry characterize the activist aesthetics and politics of the Korean independent documentary as exemplifying the "committed documentary"[2] or "socially engaged documentary."[3] To borrow the words of Thomas Waugh, the pioneers of the activist tradition fulfilled the idea of commitment as a "declaration of solidarity with the goal of radical socio-political transformation," a desire to make films "not only about people engaged in [the political] struggles but also *with* and *by* them as well."[4]

Meanwhile, *Factory Complex* (*Wirogongdan*, 2014/2015, 103 min.), whose single-channel installation version won the Silver Lion at the 2015 Venice Biennale, brings together interviews with sixty-six female former and current workers, covering the period from Korea's industrialization to its contemporary neoliberal economic system. The subjects' testimonies, too, bear witness to the harsh and exploitative labor conditions in the textile and garment factories in the 1970s and 1980s (including Dongil Textile) and the electronics and heavy industries (Kiryung Electronics and Hanjin Heavy Industries in the 2000s), their strikes against these conditions, and the companies' suppression of their struggles, such as mass dismissal and physical violence. In parallel to those interviews, some contemporary female workers tell viewers about the fatal impacts of the semiconductor industry on its laborers, including stories of the Samsung Semiconductor workers who died of leukemia, as well as about affective traumas of service workers in shopping marts, call centers, and airlines. These workers' voices across different generations are assembled to constitute audiovisual testimonial scenes of the social suffering caused by the capitalist exploitations of the past and present. The scenes richly supplement the official history of labor movements in Korea, in which women have been relegated to the periphery despite their indisputable contributions to advancing labor conditions and democratizing work,[5] with the workers' personal experiences and anecdotes.

However, Im Heung-soon, the film's director as well as an artist, is ultimately more interested in exploring the indescribable pain and sorrow of the workers as *individuals*, rather than, as in the case of *We Are Not Defeated*, in representing them as the *collective* working-class subject armored with resistance and coalition.[6] This is initially evident in Im's deliberately close attention to the women's tears during his interviews, which are loosely linked in an episodic manner unlike *We Are Not Defeated* that chronologically unfolds the progression and consequence of the struggles at Dongil Textile. What encapsulate this is legendary trade union activist Kim Jin-suk (born in 1960), who drew nationwide attention with her 309-day sit-in atop a crane in 2011 against Hanjin Heavy Industries and Construction, which fired her in 1986.[7] The close-up of her face in tears, which condenses her ineffable mourning of fellow workers who died during the long fights against the company, exceeds the articulated tone of her testimony. Im's emphasis upon the workers' corporeal and affective dimensions is also the case with two formal devices distinct from the primacy of interviews in *We Are Not Defeated*: autonomous landscape imagery and reenactment. Im's camera poetically observes the past and present landscapes of the workplaces, while occasionally embodying the viewpoint of the workers, which shows their poor and overpopulated quarters that are now abandoned. The spectral persistence of the female workers' pain, sacrifice, and loss in the landscape images of the present collaborates with various uses of reenactment. Besides Im's documentation of a theatrical play in which now-old former female workers perform their experiences of harsh labor conditions, strikes, and the companies' brutal oppression, what is noticeable in this film is several vignettes in which young female actors in a do-rag or blindfold silently stand or roam through some of the natural or artificial landscapes. In relation to the testimony of the worker who tells about her pitiful experience of sleeping in the cramped dormitory, viewers see an unknown girl in a blindfold standing in the dormitory of the present—a fantasmatic, spectral stand-in for those who suffered there. The interplay of testimony, landscape imagery, and reenactment is also evident in the sequence with Lee Chong-gak, a female worker of Dongil Textile who also appeared in *We Are Not Defeated*. Her testimony offers a vivid description of routinized night shifts, darkness, dust, smells, and the furious noise of machines. During her testimonial act, images of the company's buildings and barbwire fences are perceived as ruins within which workers' physical and psychic pain are buried yet still persist. Lee's account of how noisy the factory was ("The noise from the machines was so loud that we used whistles to communicate") is accompanied by a surreal close-up of two girls masking their faces with white do-rags. With inserted beeps, the gestures of the two workers facing and whispering to each other render the corporeal and affective elements of Lee's testimony phantasmatically visible (figure I.2).

Im's aesthetic deployment of landscape imagery and reenactment in *Factory Complex* could be ascribed to his background, distinct from the collective production of *We Are Not Defeated*. Having worked on a series of artistic

Figure I.2 *Factory Complex* (Im Heung-soon, 2014/2015)
Image courtesy: Im Heung-soon and Bandal Doc.

projects that documented the precarious lives of evictees' communities or immigrant workers by employing activist videos, video diaries, and photographs from the late 1990s to the middle of the next decade, Im has expanded his artistic exploration of disenfranchised subjects in Korean society into the tumultuous history of its ideological, political, and economic conflicts by venturing into feature-length documentary and video installation since the late 2000s.[8] His artistic direction has been known to represent post-*minjung* art, an artistic movement that emerged in the late 1990s as a consequence of the critical reflection on *minjung* art (*minjung misul*) in the 1980s. As part of the surge of social movements against military dictatorship and for democratization, *minjung* art aimed to represent the life and spirit of *minjung* (meaning "common people" oppressed in the sociopolitical system) to awaken them as a collective subject for social change.[9] Overcoming *minjung* art's dogmatic rejection of modernist art as "formalist" and its failure to accommodate the social and cultural changes after democratization in the 1990s, the post-*minjung* generation of artists, in the words of artist and critic Park Chan-kyong who represented this tendency, became preoccupied with the "question of how to maintain its local and critical interests while embracing the tradition of the international avant-garde."[10] In this regard, *Factory Complex* attests to Im's effort to negotiate his commitment to the life and psyche of female workers with his exploration of the medium and aesthetics of art. As he remarks in his conversation with Park, "My role is to graft social documentary with media art."[11]

The double projection of *We Are Not Defeated* and *Factory Complex*, which share the same social subjects and their corresponding issues but which are distinct in documentary form, aesthetics and discourse, and mode of production, serves as the opening sequence of this book. These films represent two broad tendencies of the South Korean documentary cinema practiced by individual directors as well as activists (*hwaltongga*) and collectives (*chiptan*) during about the last four decades: *We Are Not Defeated* represents the *activist* tradition since the early 1980s, whereas *Factory Complex* falls within the *post-activist* turns of the twenty-first century, which include a variety of nonfiction film and video works aimed to expand the thematic, formal, and aesthetic components of documentary cinema in favor of overcoming and renewing the tradition. Surveying the forty-year development of South Korean documentary cinema with the intersection of documentary studies, Korean studies, and local documentary discourse, this book argues that what is unique and particular about its history is the intensive and compressed coevolution of these two tendencies.

Making the tripartite connections between the sociopolitical history of South Korea, documentary's aesthetics and politics, and the shifting

6 Introduction

institutional and technological conditions of documentary production and distribution, *Activism and Post-activism: Korean Documentary Cinema, 1981–2022* is the first English-language monograph dedicated to nonfiction film- and video-making in the nongovernmental and noncorporate—including personal and independent—sectors of South Korean cinema and media. Primary relying on ethnographical interviews, Young-a Park's *Unexpected Alliances* (2014) is a valuable book-length study on this subject insofar as it positions the mobilizations and alliances of independent filmmakers and activists (including the pioneering Kim Dong-won) in the Korean film in- dustry within the context of Korea's political transition from the 1980s' mil- itary dictatorship to the postauthoritarian regimes in the late 1990s and early 2000s. But it does not consult the concepts and methods of documen- tary film, much less textual and aesthetic analysis.[12] *Movie Minorities* (2021), coauthored by Hye Seung Chung and David Scott Diffrient, significantly draws critical attention to several documentaries on long-term political prisoners, disabled persons, and migrant workers in the twenty-first century, including Kim's *Repatriation* and Yi Seung-jun's *Planet of Snail* (see chapter 2). However, the book's methodological insistence on textual analysis does not substantially illustrate its argument that "the medium of motion pictures has played an important role in solidifying social movements within discrete, identity-based categories while universalizing the experiences of different ac- tivist communities."[13] Also, the book's narrow selection of films, determined by the criterion of the presence of human rights policies and discourses, does not adequately show a larger political, aesthetic, and institutional ecosystem of documentary films and videos that has exponentially grown in the twenty- first century, much less a number of documentaries whose discourse does not necessarily dovetail with humanitarian and social movement purposes de- spite their attention to disenfranchised subjects.

As a comprehensive historiography of the Korean documentary cinema since the early 1980s and a critical map of its dynamic divergence since the beginning of the twenty-first century, *Activism and Post-activism* updates local documentary studies' periodization of its development into three periods: first, the "enlightenment period" (*kyemongchŏk shigi*) from the 1980s to the mid-1990s, marked by activist filmmaking's aspiration to enlighten *minjung* as collective participants in democratization movements and labor struggles; second, the "reflexive period" (*sŏngch'alchŏk shigi*) from the late 1990s to the mid-2000s, in which filmmakers became aware of documen- tary as representation and their status as directors (*kamdok*); and finally, the "aesthetic period" (*mihakchŏk shigi*) from the late 2000s, in which modes of filmmaking other than the participatory mode have rigorously been explored on the basis of "grappling with not only 'what to film' but also 'how to film.'"[14] While identifying the formal and epistemological distinctions between twenty-first century Korean documentary films and their activist precursors, this periodization risks bypassing the consistency and transformation of the activist tradition throughout forty years, as well as the extent to which the latter two ages have inherited and refashioned the tradition's preoccupation with society, politics, and individuals in history, as evidenced by *Factory Complex*. Amending the rigidity of this distinction that tends to prioritize differences between the three periods, the book places equal emphasis on activist and post-activist documentaries, characterizing their dialectical coevolution as a master narrative of South Korean documentary cinema.

Activism

The book's Part I, comprising three chapters, offers a comprehensive history of South Korean social change documentaries since the early 1980s in terms of their activist tradition. The local master narrative of the development of Korean documentary cinema, which has resonated with the conventional historiography of democratization in contemporary Korea, has often employed the term activism unquestionedly and homogeneously, cementing it as a token of its political and aesthetic authenticity (*chinchŏngsŏng*). This suggests the demand for a more systematic account of what activism has been in Korean documentary cinema. Bearing in mind what has been agreed in the rich studies on alternative and activist media,[15] I define the activist tradition as a diverse set of nonfiction film and video practices that share three components. First, the tradition has been premised on its participation in social movements and problems, as well as its commitment to their sites and social actors. Second, it has utilized media technologies, regardless of whether it be 16 mm or Super 8 mm film, analog video, or digital devices, to develop alternative modes of production and distribution outside mainstream media apparatuses, including the state-sponsored and public nonfiction media. And finally, it has advocated such values as democracy, equity, progressiveness, and rights against the state-driven or corporate-friendly dominant ideologies and citizenship, therefore responding to and organizing counterpublics—workers, the urban poor, sexual minorities, and others—that "differ markedly in one way or another from the premises that allow the dominant culture to understand itself as a public."[16] The consistency and development of the tradition throughout the last four decades is a key distinctiveness of South Korean documentary cinema. As critic Lee Seung-min summarizes, activism has

8 Introduction

been a "determining identity of Korean documentary cinema since its emergence in the 1980s, inasmuch as it has functioned through *yŏndae* (solidarity) with *hyŏnjang* (spot) both as *sahoe undong* (social movement) for revealing social problems and as *taean maech'e* (alternative media) to the broadcasting and press operated for the top-down communication of state ideologies."[17] Drawing on Korean studies on the political, economic, and societal transformations of the society since the 1980s, my writing in Part I focuses on the ways in which the tradition has engaged and mirrored key social movements and issues during the last four decades. Simultaneously, I also illuminate the shifting yet firm intersections of historical events and the tradition's production, distribution, and aesthetics.

Chapter 1 chronicles the development of the activist tradition from the early 1980s to the late 1990s. The 1980s is the founding decade of South Korean nonfiction film and video practices in the noncorporate and nongovernmental sectors, the period of Presidents Chun Doo-hwan's (1980–1988) and Roh Tae-woo's (1988–1993) military dictatorship. The May 18 Gwangju Democratic Uprising (Kwangju minjuhwa hangjaeng) in 1980, a mass protest in the city of Gwangju against the martial law imposed by then Major General Chun, was a watershed moment in the history of the struggles for democratization after the end of the Korean War. Despite its failure, with military troops' massacre of participants and innocent citizens, the protest ignited a heated wave of social movements by student protesters, intellectuals, peasants, workers, and evictees from urban redevelopment towns against political and societal oppressions and for democracy, to the point of forming *undongkwŏn* (which refers to those who are in the "movement sphere") as the "zeitgeist of the 1980s."[18] Influenced by the radical social theories such as "dependency/world system theory, neo-Marxist theories, Marxism-Leninism, and Maoism," which "swept through the movement's leadership,"[19] cinephile students and intellectuals formed university cine-clubs and film collectives, establishing their activities of film production, studies, and screening as "film movement" (*yŏnghwa undong*). Against Hollywood's imperialism and the Korean mainstream cinema's commercialist escape from social reality, *yŏnghwa undong* established cinema as a revolutionary tool for *minjung* as a collective subject for social change. In order to practice that idea, the clubs and collectives deployed communal production (*kongdong jejak*) in opposition to the apprenticeship system of the Korean film industry with Super 8 mm and 16 mm film cameras or lightweight video cameras that galvanized the low cost and amateur modes of filming, circulating their films and videos via community screening (*kongdongch'e sangyŏng*) at universities, labor unions, factories, and other social spaces outside the institutionalized movie theaters.

Built upon this alternative mode of production and distribution and the ideology of cinema as social movement, the clubs and collectives laid the groundwork for the activist tradition of Korean documentary cinema. Translating the influences of the radical film movements in Latin America, France, and other countries into their different experiments in filmmaking, the actors of *yŏnghwa undong* explored the idea of *kirok yŏnghwa* (documentary film) and *kirok yŏngsang* (document visual) as documenting the struggles of evictees and workers and fostering their class consciousness for social reform (*sahoe byŏnhyŏk*), in a way that went against the mainstream media censored by the authoritarian government. Although the nonfiction films and videos of the period did not advance to full-fledged documentary, they nonetheless contributed to heralding *minjung* and their *hyŏnjang* as two major concepts charged with both political and aesthetic underpinnings in Korean documentary cinema.

In the 1990s, Korean nonfiction media activism innovated in dealing with new societal challenges after the end of military dictatorship. The June Democratic Struggle (Yuwŏl minju hangjaeng) in 1987, a massive protest that achieved the direct election system, and the advent of civilian government (*munmin jŏngbu*) with the election of President Kim Young-sam (1993–1998), brought about the decline of the mass, militant protests and the rise of the civil movement (*shimin undong*). As Cho Hee-yeon writes, the civil movement "could be defined as a non-radical, mostly liberal [movement] aimed to driving the democratic reform and rationalization of the post-dictatorship era."[20] The growing irrelevance of mass and militant mobilization against the dictatorship as its common target enabled civil society groups to "face their most serious identity crisis under a democratic government."[21] This crisis, however, also allowed the civil movement to engage gender/economic inequities, environmental issues, and the human rights (*in'gwŏn*) of the marginalized subjects outside the *minjung*-oriented paradigm of the 1980s social movements. Supported by the new nonprofit organizations that advocated their demands for apology and redress by the Japanese and Korean governments, such as the Korean Council for Justice and Remembrance (Chŏngdaehyŏp, later renamed as Chŏngŭi kiŏk yŏndae, founded in 1990, hereafter "Korean Council") and the Human Rights Movement Sarangbang (In'gwŏn undong sarangbang, founded in 1990, hereafter "Sarangbang"), the subjects were former comfort women (*wianbu*), whose enforced sex slavery by the Japanese imperialist regime became publicized thanks to their painstaking effort to break the long-term silencing of their experiences,[22] and the victims (*hisaengja*) of the Cold War, such as the long-term prisoners and the bereaved families (*yugajok*) of those who were killed by the state violence and

10 Introduction

atrocities during the Cold War and authoritarian periods. The pioneering activists Kim Dong-won, Hong Hyung-sook, and Byun Young-joo revised their previously militant practice in a way that responded to this societal change, embracing as their subjects not only the urban poor and labor issues but also the state and ideological violence of the colonial and Cold War eras. More than maintaining their bond with the social movements and their advocacy for democracy, human rights, and equality, their films also signaled the activist tradition's shifting interest from the struggles in the present to the historical past that demands the revelation of truth and trauma, and from *minjung* as a collective subjectivity to the bodies and voices of *kaein* (individual). This shift also entailed the practitioners' long-term commitment to their social subjects in lieu of immediate reporting on in-progress struggles in the 1980s, thus updating the supremacy of *hyŏnjang* with observational and participatory filming akin to the models of direct cinema and cinéma-vérité, as Chris Berry and Nam Inyoung comment in their takes on Kim's films. Aided by the practitioners' growing self-consciousness of themselves as *kamdok* (director) and their endeavors to update the production system and to maintain the alternative strategies of distribution and exhibition, the activist tradition in the 1990s evolved into *tongnip tak'yumentŏri* (independent documentary) as an institutionalized mode of nonfiction film and video practice against state censorship and commercial cinema. Also contributing to this formation were the practitioners' exposure to foreign documentaries and the establishment of film festivals, including Busan International Film Festival (BIFF) in 1996, as a platform for showcasing their outputs. For both allowed the practitioners to nurture their consciousness of a documentary film as an artwork (*chakp'um*) and of their relationship to social actors.

Chapter 2 discusses a set of twenty-first-century documentaries on the three traditional subjects inherited from the activist tradition of the 1980s and 1990s: state and ideological violence, labor issues, and disenfranchised subjects (urban poor, evictees, disabled persons, and animals). The issue of state and ideological violence has been in sync with the political regime change between Presidents Kim Dae-jung (1998–2003), Roh Moo-hyun (2003–2008), and Moon Jae-in (2017–2022), all of whom represented the liberal democracy bloc tied to the agents of democratization (*minjuhwa*) in the 1980s, and Presidents Lee Myung-bak (2008–2013) and Park Geun-hye (2013–2017), supported by the anticommunist, conservative bloc and the generation of Korea's dramatic industrialization (*sanŏp'wa*) during the military dictatorship of President Park Chung-hee (1961–1979). The governments of Kim and Roh sponsored the civil movement for uncovering the truth of the atrocities by state authorities during the periods of the Cold War and military dictatorship, including the Korean War and the Jeju April Third Incident (Sasam sagŏn, see chapter 5), and for restoring the honor of their victims, with the legislation of special acts in the early 2000s and the establishment of the Truth and Reconciliation Commission (Chinshilgwa hwahae wiwŏnhoe) in 2005.[23] The efforts to pursue historical justice as a way of approximating democracy, however, were challenged during the regimes of Presidents Lee and Park by the "New Right" ideology that glamorized the legacy of Park Chung-hee as Korea's national hero,[24] and by the rise of *chongbuk* (pro–North Korea) ideology, a variation of postwar Korea's deep-seated anticommunist ideology which stigmatizes not only suspected agents of North Korea but also anyone who is sympathetic to or willing to work with North Korea. As Namhee Lee rightly points out, the politics of *chongbuk* functioned to "discredit groups or individuals associated with the previous governments of Kim Dae-jung and Roh Moo-hyun."[25] Indeed, the issues of state and ideological violence do more than point to the increasingly sharp ideological dichotomy between *chinbo* (progressive) and *posu* (conservative) as a major aspect of the twenty-first-century political domain. They have also been situated within the larger historical and mnemonic battlefield surrounding several key historical events of the twentieth century. For instance, the issue of Japan's military sexual slavery triggered the conflict between activists who erected and protected a *sonyŏsang* ("Statue of a Girl for Peace": a bronze statue of a girl comfort woman) in front of the Japanese embassies in Korea and overseas in 2011 and right-wing, pro-Japanese historians and groups who objected to the monuments.[26] Similarly, the May 18 Gwangju Uprising, which became a national memorial day in 1997, has been thrown into conflicts between the democratization bloc, which commemorated it as the Gwangju Democratization Movement and demanded further investigation of its hidden truth, and the neoconservative politicians and groups who have downplayed it as a "riot" (*p'oktong*) agitated by North Korean special agents. All these tensions valorize, as a key issue of twenty-first-century Korean society, the politics of memory, or what historian Lim Jie-hyun has called "memory war" (*kiŏk chŏnjaeng*). By this Lim means not only the ongoing battle between victims and perpetrators, as evidenced by the still unending struggle of the former comfort women, but also the situation that "people's critical attitude toward the forgetting and distortion of the past has become more sensitive than ever."[27] In this context, documentarians who take as their subject the social movements or incidents associated with the state and ideological violence are seen to engage the memory wars surrounding it. Based on their awareness of the persistence of the Cold War and the authoritarian regime in the postdictatorial period, these directors have deepened the activist tradition by propelling truth-finding (*chinsang*

12 Introduction

gyumyŏng) about past injustices, by retrieving the testimonies of the victims' families and survivors, and by investigating the suppressive impacts of anti-communist and *chongbuk* ideologies on the individual's political, social, and psychic dimensions.

The issues of labor and urban eviction in the twenty-first century are linked largely to the process of economic and societal neoliberalization that began with the transition to democracy in the late 1980s, and most saliently to the post–International Monetary Fund (IMF) system since the 1997 monetary crisis. As Namhee Lee persuasively demonstrates in her recent book, the socioeconomic policies of the governments in the 1990s, evidenced by President Kim Young-sam's inaugural announcement of building a *sin Hanguk* (New Korea) through *segyehwa* (globalization), were marked by the "conflation of neoliberal measures with the democratization process."[28] This suggests that neoliberalism's emphasis upon deregulation, free markets, and growth was perceived and promoted as an alternative to the previous authoritarian style and even to the *minjung*-oriented paradigm of the 1980s. The drive to neoliberalization was amplified in the Kim Dae-jung government, which embraced it as a key strategy for overcoming the 1997 monetary crisis, which marked a crucial break with Korea's previous economic and societal systems as it propelled the decisive shift to neoliberal capitalism. There have been many accounts that tease out its key consequences, such as the increase in irregular jobs (*pijŏnggyujik*), income and property polarization (*yanggŭk'wa*), job insecurity (*koyong buran*), and the intensification of competition for limited economic opportunities.[29] All these consequences are attributed to a new economic system that has facilitated the deregulation of decision-making and capital investment by transnational corporations and chaebols (conglomerates) and enhanced labor market flexibility since the late 1990s. These new policies or strategies signaled a notable break from the economic system of modern Korea, as evidenced by the new patterns of social inequality in the labor market,[30] and by the increasing differentiation of laborers into regular workers in the public sector and large firms and irregular (temporary and part-time) workers who lack the same degree of job security.[31] From another perspective, however, the neoliberalization of economy and society also means that labor issues, which were a major agenda of the 1980s *minjung* movement, have been diversified and even deteriorated with the combination of traditional labor-management conflicts and union-busting activities with the new challenges to laborers and unions, such as mass dismissal, privatization, and the precarity of irregular workers.[32] The interplay of state and corporate powers, too, has produced not only evictees and the urban poor but also small-scale business owners whose shops were demolished by urban gentrification. Documentarians in twenty-first-century Korea have engaged new types of social struggle by irregular workers and the victims of gentrification while also investigating the double consequences of the neoliberal reform, that is, the persistence of social inequalities before the IMF crisis and the proliferation of new crises. At the same time, they also have expanded their scope into other disenfranchised subjects, such as the disabled and animals, in dialogue with the growth of social movements aimed to advocate for their rights and demands.

Chapter 3 discusses another set of documentaries that aim to participate in new social movements of the twenty-first century and also identifies new activist nonfiction practices reflective of their characteristics. The movements, which gained momentum in the public sphere of the 2010s, are the feminist and LGBT movements and the regional environmental activism against the state-driven economic or military infrastructure. Both were ignited in the twenty-first-century society, in which diverse groups of social subjects irreducible to the monolithic conception of *minjung* have claimed their rights—not only political rights, workers' rights, human rights, and the right to live, but also women's rights, sexual minority rights, animal rights, and environmental rights—with various organizations, mobilizations, alliances, actions, and interactions.[33] Bearing in mind the diversification of claimed rights, Sun-chul Kim labels twenty-first-century Korean society as a "social movement society," highlighting the pervasiveness of social protests, which take forms different from the hierarchically organized mass protest, traverse both online and offline spaces, and involve various groups and citizens unassimilable into a coherent entity.[34] Shin Jin-wook, too, argues for the decentralization of social movements since the late 2000s, characterized by the "emergence of independent networks and political participation by citizens who do not identify themselves with particular camps in institutional politics and organized civil society."[35] A major practice that has encapsulates these decentralized social movements is undoubtedly the "candlelight protest" (*chotbul siwi*), a nonviolent practice of resistance in which "citizens hold lit candles instead of throwing stones or Molotov cocktails, and participate in more spontaneous and individual forms of protest than organizational mobilizations by activist groups."[36] Often voluntarily organized via the internet and small-scale groups and mediated by the interplay of social media and live broadcasting, these street protests have collected the common contentious voices of people from different social backgrounds, including younger generations, for teenage girls killed by US armored vehicle in 2002, against the import of American beef in 2008, and notably against the Park Geun-hye government in 2016 and 2017.

14 Introduction

In this context, the environmental movement in several regions since the early 2010s and the third generation of the feminist movement since the mid-2010s have created new dynamics in Korean society, as both have raised their urgent issues (sexual violence and discrimination, structural gender inequity, misogyny, and environmental crises) not only in organized rallies and actions but also in citizens' everyday life and culture. Considering this new dynamics of civic participations, I employ Michael Hardt and Antonio Negri's idea of the multitude (*tajung*). Hardt and Negri define the multitude as a formation of the common distinct from the people, the masses, and the working class, in that it is "composed of innumerable *internal differences that can never be reduced to a unity or a single identity*—different cultures, races, ethnicities, genders, and sexual orientations; different forms of labor; different ways of living; different views of the world; and different desires."[37] The documentaries that engage feminist, queer, and environmental issues accordingly veer toward representing these diverse subjects, their different identities and stories, and their different strategies of resistance and coalition, thus reflecting the ways in which the activist tradition of the twenty-first century articulates the social changes demanded by *tajung*.

While this social multiplicity challenges the unitary conception of *minjung* and its assumption of a shared, single identity, twenty-first-century Korean society has also validated that "the internal differences of the multitude must discover *the common* that allows them to communicate and act together."[38] A prominent case in point is the Candlelight Protests from October 2016 to March 2017 against the political corruption of the Park Geun-hye government, its structural failure to manage social and ideological problems, and its anachronistic attempts to turn the society upside down and return to the disciplinary governmentality of the authoritarian age. One of these attempts was the "blacklist scandal," in which the government listed and discriminated against artists and cultural workers (including many independent filmmakers) for public funding and exhibition whose works it believed were nonconformist, leftist, or harmful to the government's maintenance.[39] Enormous nationwide rallies composed of myriad individuals and many social groups different in interests and identity were sparked by the "common" awareness that we live in a post-traumatic society, namely, one after the Sewol Ferry Disaster in April 16, 2014, that claimed 304 deaths. The disaster was an event of media witnessing in which not only activists but also ordinary citizens watched the Park administration's malfunctional efforts to rescue the sinking ferry and its passengers in real time. As scholars have pointed out, the disaster motivated various agents, including ordinary citizens, to participate in candlelight vigils and demonstrations wearing the yellow ribbon (which became a widespread symbol of hopes for return of the passengers). For it generated a collective sense of grief, mourning, fragility, and anger, which were intensified by the administration's media control and its uncooperative treatment of bereaved families and civic groups concerned with finding the truth about the disaster and punishing those who were responsible for the blunders.[40] In these contexts, chapter 3 introduces migratory-grassroots activism and issue-based omnibus documentaries as two alternative activist nonfiction practices attuned to the commonality of the multitude. Apart from updating the alternative mode of production in the activist tradition, these two practices reflect both the multiplicity of *tajung* and their alliance with the common, in that they are based on a diversity of subjects and styles and the horizontal connection of shorts compiled in a single film. Along with these two practices, former journalists and broadcast producers have amplified the alternative production and distribution of activist media since the 2010s with alternative journalism documentaries that reveal the political injustices of the right-wing regimes and their press control.

Throughout chapters 2 and 3, I suggest that the templates of *hyŏnjang*-oriented aesthetics and interviews have consistently remained the activist representational strategies of political resistance to engage marginalized subjects, to communicate their emotions, and to raise public awareness. Just as the realist attention to the lifeworld and the site of struggles enables viewers to perceive diverse social problems as issues in the present tense, so does the presence of talking heads empower the marginalized subjects with political agency, presenting them as individuals marked by their memories and feelings and identifying them as the multitude that shares a common experience. Along with these two, twenty-first-century activist documentaries have realized the four political potentials of social change documentary that Angela J. Aguayo has neatly stipulated: "representing social change," "speaking for social change," "collaborating for social change," and "engaging in social change."[41] This means that the activist documentaries produced and circulated during the last two decades have been devoted to producing historical or present-tense documentations of struggles, to speaking for the marginalized, to enhancing collective awareness of their problems, and to promoting solidarity between filmmakers, activists, social actors, and audiences. These four potentials testify to the extent to which twenty-first-century Korean documentary cinema has productively nurtured its activist tradition by offering the alternative public sphere of views, opinions, and voices that resists the state-sponsored discourse and mass media in pursuit of political democracy, social equality, and economic justice.

Unlike the situation of the 1980s and 1990s, the continual prevalence of the activist tradition in the twenty-first century is considerably indebted to the

16 Introduction

interplay of the alternative media movement and governmental patronage. The cultural policy of the liberal democracy governments from 1998 to 2008 facilitated the institutionalization of independent film, which in turn offered a relatively solid industrial ground for social change documentaries. In 1999, the Kim Dae-jung government transformed the previously state-sponsored Korean Motion Picture Promotion Corporation (Yŏnghwa jinhŭng gongsa) into the Korean Film Council (KOFIC: Yŏnghwa jinhŭng wiwŏnhoe) as a quasi-governmental organization comprising nine film professionals from different private sectors, including independent film and media activism. The council's first members (1999–2002) developed the "Master Plan for the Promotion of Korean Films" in 2000, and its second set of members (2002–2005) created the Subcommittee for Film Public Policy to secure a public and diverse film culture.[42] Based on these two institutional developments, KOFIC in the early and mid-2000s offered a series of institutional and infrastructural supports for national arthouse and independent cinema: they included financial support programs for the production of independent films (for documentary films in 2006 and for feature-length narrative films in 2008) and for their theatrical release, as well as venues and institutions, such as the opening of Indiespace in 2007, a theater exclusively devoted to independent films. Aside from these infrastructural and institutional supports, the growth of civil society in the postauthoritarian climate encouraged requests for public access to media services as part of strengthening democratization starting from the late 1990s. As Kim Ji-hyun writes, the idea of public access heralded by the alternative media movement in the early 2000s "enabled socially disenfranchised subjects to directly participate in the process of media production, so that they would make their own images, raise issues of their community, and organize and strengthen and it."[43] Mediact (Midiaekt'ŭ), founded in 2002, was the result of the demands for public access and participation that were made by the civil society and the independent film scene. Equipped with tools for digital shooting and postproduction, the media center has enabled both professional filmmakers and amateur citizens to produce their own audiovisual content and has also held education and workshop programs to promote the public's media literacy and participatory practice. With this dual effort for production and education, the center has been a key springboard for the practices of numerous activists and documentarians who aspired to mobilize communities, to engage and advocate the issues of disenfranchised subjects, or to achieve media democracy. Their collectives as well as individual directors have contributed not only to consolidating and innovating social change documentaries but also to diversifying the forms and aesthetics of documentary that transcend the confines of the activist mode. The latter aspect is indeed in parallel to the post-activist turns that this book investigates in Part II.

Post-activism

The Description of Bankruptcy (*P'asanŭi kisul*, 2006, 61 min.), the feature-length debut of director Lee Kang-hyun (1975–2023), gained critics' attention due to its formal and aesthetic distinctions from activist documentaries on the issues of labor and economy. Lee's fragmentary montage does more than include seemingly disparate materials, encompassing CCTV footage of a man who attempted to commit suicide on a subway track, a video record of a family whose properties are seized due to bankruptcy, home videos of the family's happy moments, laborers in transportations and various workplaces, and recordings of a radio broadcast that collects small stories of everyday life. Combined with the intermittent insertion of black screens between two adjacent shots, the montage offers a formal and aesthetic equivalent to liquidation and fragmentation that the neoliberal socioeconomic system imposes on subjects with its ubiquitous yet unequal distribution of inequality and precarity. This editing also corresponds to another distancing yet powerful device that Lee employs to portray interviews with women who are irregular workers faced with bankruptcy due to the IMF crisis: extreme close-ups of the women's faces and lips, which starkly contrast with the centrality and visibility of talking heads in many documentaries. This seemingly uncomfortable device draws viewers' attention to the extent to which the neoliberal system has not only marginalized the women but also made them "fragmented" subjects who are everywhere in the society but have not been organized in a collective voice. Here it becomes evident that Lee's strategies of montage and cinematography, a sort of directorial self-consciousness, aim to provide an aesthetic and structural critique of the post-IMF crisis in ways that are distinct from the politico-aesthetic paradigm of the activist tradition.

Part II of this book consists of four chapters, each of which identifies a notable tendency of the twenty-first-century post-activist documentary practices illustrated by *The Description of Bankruptcy*. I define post-activism as a dialectic of departure and inheritance, namely, of the formal, aesthetic, epistemological and discursive breaks from the activist tradition and its renewals. The formal and aesthetic distinctions of post-activism are obvious in four types of documentary films that have grown over more than two decades: variants of personal documentary and the documentaries based on

18 Introduction

reenactment (chapter 4), experimental documentaries that take places and landscapes as their aesthetic object of investigation (chapter 5), films mobilized by the extensive use of archival footage (chapter 6), and the nonfiction works that capitalize on the capacities of digital postproduction and virtual reality (VR) (chapter 7). Without jettisoning the contexts of the social events or issues that they address, Part II prioritizes the importance of formal and textual analysis of the films that represent the four types, with the concepts of Western documentary studies and the theories of Marianne Hirsch (postmemory), Gilles Deleuze (time-image), and Walter Beniamin (materialist historiography) that I consider as reflecting local documentary criticism and as substantive in explaining their aesthetic and political implications.

Throughout Part II, I employ the term "turn" in its four chapters to underline the shifts in documentary production toward increasing concerns with the filmmaker-as-I, audiovisual qualities of space and landscape images, archival documents, and digital technologies in a manner akin to the terminology of "turns" in arts, humanities, and social sciences, such as the "visual turn" and the "cultural turn."[44] The four modes of documentary practice depart from the emphasis upon *hyŏnjang* as the activist tradition's hallmark of political authenticity and truth claims. This entails discursive effects dislodged not only from the omnipotent narration of the films and videos in 1980s and 1990s and its imperatives to enlightenment and reform, but also from the cause-and-effect and problem-solution schemes of the activist tradition and its enunciation of consciousness-raising, empowerment, and solidarity. Local documentary criticism in the early 2000s anticipated the post-activist turns of Korean independent documentary. Critic and scholar Kim Sunah observed in 2000 the growing disappearance of the propagandistic, realist documentary storytelling from independent documentary production, which suggested that "our time is no longer dominated or controlled by a single superior voice and its transcendental position."[45] Similarly, Nam Inyoung wrote in 2003 that the emergence of self-reflexive, first-person documentaries in the early 2000s stemmed from "directors' from-the-scratch exploration of what is truth and how it can be contained," and that "reality in documentary cinema is constructed by peculiar conventions of representation—not that which exists outside representation."[46]

The new ramifications of Korean documentary filmmaking in the twenty-first century, evinced by Kim and Nam, recall what Michael Renov has referred to as the "post-verité" tendency, namely, the dramatic growth of personal documentary filmmaking after the dominance of direct cinema in the 1960s. By this term, Renov means not simply the aesthetic and epistemological departure of personal documentary filmmaking from the objectivist assumptions of direct cinema, but also the ways in which this filmmaking responded to key social and cultural changes of the period, including the emphasis on the politics of the everyday and the interrogations of identity, subjectivity, and private histories and memories.[47] Given that a number of post-activist films aim to investigate the "identity, subjectivity, and private memories" haunted by Korea's ruptured historical pasts, they also resonate with what Linda Williams has termed the "New Documentary." As she observes from the films that attest to that trend since the late 1980s with the uses of reenactment and fiction, "While traumatic events of the past are not available for representation by any simple or single 'mirror with a memory'—in the *vérité* sense of capturing events as they happen—they do constitute a multifaceted receding horizon which [the] films powerfully evoke."[48] Despite their affinities with the North American nonverité modes of documentary since the 1970s, there has been little verified influence of foreign films and documentarians on directors' adoption of the post-activist modes, unlike the influence of Shinsuke Ogawa on Kim Dong-won and Byun Young-ioo in the early 1990s. It is nonetheless possible to single out several institutional and discursive contexts for their prosperity in the twenty-first century: the entrance of nonactivist professionals from various backgrounds into documentary production (broadcast producers, popular documentarians, young directors who pursued the MFA degree at foreign universities, and the artists such as Im Heung-soon, Park Chan-kyung, Kelvin Kyung Kun Park, and Jung Yun-suk, all of whom have presented their documentary films and installations both in movie theaters and inside the gallery walls); the growth and increase of film festivals as the platform both for exhibiting documentarians' own outputs and for their encounters with various foreign classical and contemporary documentaries; the development of local documentary studies and criticism since the early 2000s, which have applied Bill Nichols's classification of expository, poetic, observational, participatory, reflexive, and performative documentaries,[49] as well as the concepts of postdocumentary, reenactment, essay film, and so on; and the operation of paper and online journals dedicated to timely criticism of independent films, including the quarterly *Tongnip yŏnghwa* (Independent film, 1999–present) published by the Association of Korean Independent Film and Video (see chapter 1).

Besides these contexts, a prominent driving force of the post-activist practices is the shift of the practitioners' identity and self-consciousness from *hwaltongga* (activist) to *kamdok* (director) from the mid-1990s, as many local commentators have commonly pointed out since the beginning of the century. Documentary discourse in the early twenty-first century evaluated the various modes of the director's self-inscription in the film text, from on-screen or

20 Introduction

off-screen interview to first-person narration and to self-exposure as a character, expressing "the reflexive filmmaker-I beyond her functional roles as interlocutor and reporter . . . who is able to document not only *hyŏnjang* but also excluded identities and memories."[50] Lee Seung-min in the late 2010s noted that a key index of changes in the twenty-first century documentary is the rise of the director as *kaein* (individual), a development that derived from the "self-reflection of documentary cinema as 'genre' and 'artwork.'"[51] The emphasis upon *kamdok* as a linchpin of the post-activist documentaries implies that their relationship to the activist tradition is by no means one-dimensional. As Young-a Park rightly observes, the independent films labeled "individual films" (*kaein yŏnghwa*) and "personal/private films" (*sajŏk yŏnghwa*) in the early 2000s emerged in spite of the dominant tendency within the activist-oriented groups "to dismiss 'personal' topics as 'apolitical,'" in contrast to the film activism in the 1980s and 1990s where "such a dichotomy between the personal and the political was clear."[52] While the development of those films has in some senses reflected the shifting agency of documentary production from *chpitan* to *kaein*, the post-activist films also have increasingly made their claim to political and ethical legitimacy while also expanding the formal and aesthetic boundaries of Korean documentary cinema.

The maturation of the director's "personal" subjectivity and consciousness has been in close dialogue with his or her interest in another implication of the "personal," which means *kaein* in history. Herein lies a crucial way in which post-activist documentaries emerged from the efforts to critically reflect on the activist tradition and renew its politics in aesthetic forms. On a thematic level, post-activist films in the twenty-first century have not only extended documentary's subject matter into the everyday life of *kaein* (including the director's self), his or her surrounding space, and his or her memory and imagination: they have also addressed the very subjects of the activist tradition. A major subject that many of the films engage and investigate is indeed individuals upon whom state and ideological violence has been inflicted in Korea's postcolonial age. More than validating their overlap with the activist documentaries, a profound achievement of the post-activist documentaries lies in their endeavors to explore the individuals' pain and traumatic memories in ways that cannot be articulated by the discourses of truth and reconciliation, legal evidentiality, human rights, victimhood (*hisaengjasŏng*), empowerment, or solidarity, all of which have been demanded by a diverse array of "memory activism" practices since the 1990s that have aimed to intervene in the sites and victims of the political and ideological tragedies encompassing the April Third Incident, the Korean War, and the human rights violations during the Cold War and authoritarian eras. Kim Dong-ryung and Park Kyoung-tae, codirectors of *The Pregnant Tree and the Goblin* (see chapter 4) who have long been committed to reclaiming the previously untold painful stories of former sex workers in Korea's US military camptowns (*kijich'on*), epitomize this awareness in their production note on the film, which was published on the occasion of the film's theatrical release in January 2022.

> It is hypocritical to say that healing is possible when the painful subject subsists. The only thing that heals is the guilt that outsiders had. . . . The babbling screams bear such various tales, yet only the women of the kind can understand the language and respond with silence. To record the stories that are not allowed to them, to show the truth as it is, fantasy is required.[53]

The two directors' comment does more than suggest that the interview, as a key methodology of the activist-oriented oral history (*kusulsa*) and documentary, is a political and discursive construction although it aspires to retrieve stories of the subjects that were marginalized, erased, and silenced. It also underscores that the interview's underlying imperatives—to validate the subjects' victimhood and to establish their testimonial act as a stepping stone for their political subjectivization and solidarity—do not always lead them to utter their other stories, including the affective, corporeal, and mnemonic repercussions of their pains and traumas, which circumvent the (chrono)logical link between past and present.[54] In this regard, many post-activist documentaries discussed in Part II experiment with wide-ranging nonverité devices not only to craft their artifact as artwork based on the self-consciousness of *kamdok* but also to devise alternative approaches to documentary interrogation and storytelling beyond the discourses of memory activism—for instance, the fantasy that Kim and Park activate in their film. The latter aspect is genuinely what makes post-activism a process of reconfiguring activism, rather than entirely departing from it.

Chapter 4, "The Personal Turn," investigates a group of first-person films that have foregrounded the personal view as integral to documentary's construction of reality and history since the 2000s. Starting with refiguring the "personal documentary" (*sajŏk tak'yumentŏ-ri*) in the early 2000s as a multilayered concept constituted by transitions to personalized video technologies, to individuals and their microhistories, and to practitioners' awareness of themselves as *kamdok* and of their work as personal expression, this chapter moves on to first-person documentaries on a director's family (i.e., "domestic ethnographies") and essay films as two major trends. These two modes, I argue, proclaim their political legitimacy against the activist downplaying of personal film as "apolitical" by expressing "personal" elements—the

22   Introduction

director's reflection, her everyday reality, and her intimate others—as deeply intertwined with the public, political, and historical. In this view, the dominance of domestic ethnographies has been a key specific aspect of Korean first-person documentaries due to women filmmakers' feminist awareness of the family (*kajŏng*) as the community where patriarchal, Confucianist-oriented values, including the subordination of women to the father, are being dismantled and nevertheless have still had lingering effects. It was also thanks to recognition of the urgency of the family, in the sense that, in the words of prominent anthropologist Heonik Kwon, "family relations are important vectors in understanding the decomposition of the bipolar world not merely because these relations are an elementary constituent of civil society . . . but above all because during the Cold War they were actually a vital site of political control and ideological oppression."[55] The filmmakers' awareness of the latter, as well as their experimentations with nonverité devices encompassing the exposures of the filmmaker-I, reenactment, and the complex overlapping of past and present, runs in parallel to that of many young artists and writers in the twenty-first century—the "postmemory" generation of practitioners who have ventured into nonconventional styles and representational strategies based on their distance from the first-order memory of the generation who directly experienced the traumatic events of modern Korea.[56] The domestic ethnographies' attempt to dissolve the boundaries between the personal and the public is also the case with the essay film that has been gaining popularity since the 2010s, in that the films of Kim Eung-su and Kelvin Kyung Kun Park offer profound and rich reflections on the colonial and postcolonial history of industrialization and on recent public events from their personal viewpoints. The correspondence between the emphasis upon the creativity of *kamdok* and the interest in exploring *kaein* is also evident in the growing employment of reenactment during the last two decades, as it has the effect of approximating the latter's subjective dimensions of pain and trauma and thereby connecting the personal to the political and historical.

Chapter 5, "The Audiovisual Turn," discusses several documentary films that portray and investigate places and landscapes related to Korea's social reality or a personal or collective memory of its past with the use of poetic and aesthetic techniques to highlight the visual and auditory qualities of their images. The emergence of these experimental documentaries falls under several interconnected political and cultural contexts in the twenty-first century, such as the burgeoning of memory activism in conjunction with the climate of truth and reconciliation, the increasing construction of memorials, monuments, and museums aimed to commemorate the tragedies of the Cold War and military dictatorship, and the investigation of land as a historical and geopolitical site.[57] Here I elaborate on Deleuze's idea of the transition from the movement-image to the time-image in order to demonstrate the ways in which the poetic and aesthetic techniques mark a break with the activist tradition's expository or didactic voice-over, its cause-and-effect or problem-solution narrative scheme, and its synchronicity of sound and image. My inquiry into their time-images of the place and landscape highlights a key epistemological shift of the post-activist mode, from *hyŏnjang* as a site of struggle in the present tense to "memoryscape" marked by the spectral persistence of past memories in the present space, where their trace is often perceived, paradoxically, as invisible. By exploring and expressing the material, corporeal, and mnemonic aspects of memoryscapes, the documentaries refresh the ways of representing the workplace, the urban ruin as the remnant of redevelopment, and the historical landscape coupled with the ideological violence or trauma of modernization in post-liberation Korea, all of which are the subjects of the activist tradition.

Chapter 6, "The Archival Turn," attends to several documentaries of the 2010s that investigate and rework archival footage of the distant or recent histories of Korea. Apart from the contexts that informed the films of the audiovisual turn, the documentaries discussed in this chapter engage a series of "memory wars" in twenty-first-century Korean society. Broadly, the scenes of the wars can be found not only in the contestation of memories connected to the events of state violence and crime, such as the Gwangju Uprising, but also in the present political and ideological suppressions or societal contradictions that directors perceive as the recurrence of the past. These contexts, as well as the increasing availability and accessibility of archival photos, films, and videos thanks to digitization and the construction of public archives in both online and offline spaces of museums and institutions, have cultivated the directors' awareness of the archival document as more than a resource for illustrating political discourse—namely, as embattled material that reveals its internal fissures and thus subject to different approaches and interpretations.[58] In this regard, the document activates the alternative historiography inasmuch as the past inscribed in it is summoned up from the present's perspective. Drawing on Benjamin's idea of "materialist historiography" in light of its emphasis upon the dialectical encounter between past and present and its implications for archival film practice, I argue that extensive use of found footage allows filmmakers to develop modes of documentary filmmaking—compilation documentary, essay film, and investigative documentary—other than the participatory mode of the activist tradition. The filmmakers' appropriation, reassessment, and manipulation of the footage are then intended to unveil and deconstruct its intended meanings and aesthetic effects and to

24 Introduction

endow it with a new historical perspective in relation to directors' engagement with the politics of the present. Again, this signals another way that twenty-first-century Korean documentary cinema both transcends and renovates the activist tradition.

Chapter 7, "The Digital Turn," examines the impacts of digital technologies on the epistemological and aesthetic changes of post-activist documentary cinema. It appears to be logical that the activist tradition, which had adopted analog video as its master medium efficient for production and distribution in the 1980s, incorporated digital video at the turn of the twenty-first century. Apart from this transition, however, this chapter tracks the applications of digital technologies to other purposes than making *hyŏnjang*-oriented social change documentary, from the uses of lo-fi visual effects for parody and satire in the early 2000s to VR and subjunctive documentaries in the 2010s. Unlike the postmodern epistemological critique that champions the strategies of reenactment, docufiction, and performativity in the North American documentary scene of the 1980s and 1990s in recognition of the constructedness of truth and the artificiality of reality,[59] the documentaries that attest to the digital turn, I argue, spring from directors' desire to seek truth differently than has the activist tradition in its realistic reliance on the authenticity of the photographic image. As in the case of its previous three chapters, the three trends of digital documentary in this chapter turn out to have renewed the ways of experiencing the activist tradition's traditional issues, such as the persistence of the authoritarian ideologies, military violence and its spectral presence in *kijich'on* and the DMZ (Demilitarized Zone), and a couple of major social incidents in the twenty-first century, the Yongsan Massacre (see chapter 6) and the Sewol Ferry Disaster.

The Double Helix

Overall, this book argues that another substantial specificity of twenty-first-century South Korean documentary cinema has been the synergetic empowerment of the activist and post-activist tendencies. Throughout Part I, readers will notice that a number of practitioners in different generations, including such veterans as Kim Dong-won, Hong Hyung-sook, and Byun Young-joo, have contributed to enriching the activist tradition by venturing into the formal and aesthetic elements of the post-activist turn, based on their personal awareness as *kamdok*. Just as nonactivist directors have elaborated upon these elements to investigate the profundity of *kaein* in history and the spatiotemporal complexity of *hyŏnjang* as alternative ways of engaging the social issues common to films of the activist tradition, so have many activist directors matured their political reflection and cinematic expression in ways that are not totally assimilated into the discourses of social movement for human rights, solidarity, and truth-finding. In this sense, the activist and post-activist tendencies are not two mutually exclusive categories: rather, these two, in their productive intersections, have formed a double helix of Korean documentary cinema, in which its politics and aesthetics have dynamically been negotiated. Before moving on to Part I, I briefly explicate three contexts of the ecosystem that has made possible the coevolution of activism and post-activism, as well as their categorical porosity. This also help readers to eschew understanding these two tendencies as the simple binary oppositions of production and reception.

With their programs for production, screening, and public forum, film festivals have had a significant influence on diversifying the forms, aesthetics, and critical discourses of Korean documentary cinema. As demonstrated by the Hubert Bals Fund and CineMart in the International Film Festival Rotterdam (IFFR), for instance, many film festivals worldwide have functioned as producer by offering financial support for the production of specific film projects and for the publicity and circulation of their outcomes.[60] Following BIFF's Busan Promotion Plan (since 1998), Asian Project Market, and Asian Cinema Fund, all of which were modeled after IFFR's cases, several other film festivals in Korea have been offering support or incubating programs in the forms of funds for development, production, postproduction, project pitching, producer-investor matching, and awards. These include the Documentary Okrang Culture Award (since 2002) of the Seoul International Women's Film Festival (SIWFF, since 1997), the Jeonju Project Market at Jeonju International Film Festival (JIFF, since 2000), and the DMZ Industry at DMZ International Documentary Film Festival (DMZDocs, since 2009), an international documentary-oriented film festival in South Korea comparable to the International Documentary Film Festival Amsterdam (IDFA), to name just a few. Aside from the activities of these international film festivals, I would underline the way in which a few other low-budget film festivals less known to international film culture have played a vital role in fostering the diverse ecosystem of Korean documentary films. They include Indie Forum (see chapter 1, since 1996), the Seoul Independent Documentary Film Festival (SIDOF, 2001–2020), a festival committed to discovering new documentary films with its catchphrase "Experiment, Progress, Communication"; the Seoul International New Media Festival (NeMaf, since 2000), a festival dedicated to the screening and exhibition of politically alternative and experimental films, videos, and installations; and the Seoul Independent Film Festival (SIFF, since

26 Introduction

2002), the biggest outlet for cataloging year-round independent films and promoting solidarity of independent filmmakers. These diverse and overlapping platforms that have coexisted with BIFF, JIFF, and DMZDocs, I argue, have formed a kind of local documentary film festival circuit, as most of the films that I discuss in this book have been circularly exposed to programmers, critics, and audiences from one festival to the next. To be sure, the concept of a film festival circuit has largely been applied to the network of international film festivals across the globe, as it indicates their coordination in circulating, exhibiting, and distributing films. While the concept has been thought of as a "global network" that "constitutes the exhibition dates of most independent films in the first-run venues of the world market,"[61] I contend that it is also productively applied to the ecosystem of local film festivals that share specific interests in programming and discourse-formation. For instance, SIDOF has presented special screening and forum programs in dialogue with the formal, thematic, and political changes of the local documentary scene, from personal documentary and the essay film (in 2016) to activism (in 2017) to the "postmemory" documentaries made by the generation of young filmmakers (in 2018). It should be also noted that, however, the operation of film festivals, particularly the large-scale international events, has been influenced by the policies of the central and municipal governments that financially and administratively undergird them. A case in point is the incident relating to BIFF's selection of *The Truth Shall Not Sink with the Sewol* (*Taibing bel*, 2014, 77 min., see chapter 3), caused by the festival organizers' rejection of the Busan Metropolitan Government's demand that it cancel screenings. The festival subsequently underwent financial and administrative crises during the Park Geun-hye regime in exchange for its insistence on the independence of selection and programming from political interests, which was supported by the boycotts of high-profile filmmakers and foreign film festival professionals.[62]

Another platform for both activist and post-activist documentaries is the movie theater. Unlike the activist films and videos in the twentieth century that were circulated outside the movie theater (with an exception of Byun Young-joo's "comfort women" trilogy), independent documentarians and collectives have combined their traditional community screening model with theatrical release since the early 2000s. Besides KOFIC's public funding programs for the production, distribution, and marketing of independent and arthouse films since the late 1990s, several distribution companies devoted to these films, including Indiestory and Cinemadal, have also contributed to establishing the synergy of community screening and theatrical release. Examples of this synergy are *Repatriation* (23,496 attendances), which won the Freedom of Expression Award at the Sundance Film Festival in 2004 and was extended KOFIC's

Table I.1 Number of Theatrically Released Korean Documentary Films from 2000 to 2020

2000	2001	2002	2003	2004	2005	2006	2007	2008	2009	2010
1	1	1	2	1	3	2	3	11	10	19

2011	2012	2013	2014	2015	2016	2017	2018	2019	2020	
24	23	25	30	23	30	32	30	38	25	

Source: Korean Film Commission, Integrated Box Office (KOBIS), https://www.kobis.or.kr/kobis/busin ess/stat/boxs/findYearlyBoxOfficeList.do.

support, Indiestory's distribution, community screenings of Kim's production collective (Docu Purn), and the regional paid community screenings before theatrical release of *Our School* (*Uri hakkyo*, Kim Myung-joon, 2006, 131 min., 34,439 attendances), a film about the lives of ethnic Korean students in a pro–North Korean high school in Japan.[63] As demonstrated in Table I.1, the number of theatrically released documentary films has increased to two digits since the late 2000s. Perhaps this change could be ascribed to the commercial successes of three top-grossing documentaries. They include *Old Partner* (*Wŏnangsori*, Lee Chung-ryoul, 2008, 75 min., 2,962,897 attendances),[64] a moving story about the slow rural life of an elderly farmer and his forty-year partnership with a cow, *My Love, Don't Cross That River* (*Nima, kŭ kangŭl kŏnnŏji mao*, 2014, 85 min., 4,801,257), which follows a couple who share intimate moments after seventy-six years of marriage, and *Our President* (*No Muhyŏnyipnida*, Lee Chang-jae, 2017, 110 min., 1,854,867), a quasi-biographical nonfiction film that covers the election campaign of President Roh Moo-hyun. The twenty-first-century documentary scene has also witnessed the growth of popular documentaries that encompass humanitarian or political figures, nature and wildlife, Christianity, pop music, and so on.[65] Although I do not underestimate the films' industrial and popular impact, this book firmly focuses on the political and aesthetic landscape of twenty-first-century activist and post-activist documentary films, many of which have brought activists and disenfranchised subjects associated with social movements and the general public to the movie theater. Despite their relative shortage of commercial value, they are profoundly critical to understanding twenty-first-century Korean documentary cinema as a collection of both artworks and nonfiction artifacts inseparable from Korea's historical reality.

It is also significant that the subject matter, both state and ideological violence that originated in Korea's ruptured history, and several key social events in the twenty-first century, has allowed directors to take varying approaches to documentary production, to the degree that reality and history are perceived

28   Introduction

as demanding no privileged access and articulation. The Sewol Ferry Disaster is a watershed event that attests to the multiplicity of these approaches. Arousing public feelings of grief, fragility, compassion, mourning, and anger, it had immense impact on the social movement of the mid-2010s: not only did it transform bereaved families into active subjects who questioned and resisted the state with a legislative struggle and staged sit-ins, rallies, and the performance of songs and plays based on the stories of their lost members,[66] but it sparked a nationwide surge of memory activism, in which yellow as the "color of dissent" and such slogans as "The truth does not sink" (*chinshirŭn ch'immorhaji annŭnda*) were "circulated and recirculated in layered metaphorical assemblages that constituted new forms of public memory and new practices of political mobilization."[67] As discussed in chapter 3, many documentarians participated in that activism not only by portraying and assisting the interconnected networks of solidarity and sympathy among activists, bereaved families, and ordinary citizens, but also by positing their act of documenting as archiving the subjects' bodies and voices, as well as the monuments and memorabilia of the disaster. This archival activism, however, could not only be achieved with filming *hyŏnjang* of the subjects' direct action. The truth behind the disaster, perceived as both elusive (in terms of its real causes) yet grave (in terms of its devastating effects), also propelled documentarians to investigate and replay its audiovisual records from various sources, to contemplate the site where it took place, and to reconstruct what could have happened with hypotheses and inferences aided by digital visualizations used to substitute for the lack of decisive visible evidence. These are the ways that both activism and post-activism have converged in their common politics of memory and temporality, or their impetus to render the traumatic recent past as ongoing in the present tense.

Let me recapitulate the overlapping of activism and post-activism by briefly discussing Yi Seung-jun's twenty-nine-minute *In the Absence* (*Pujaeŭi kiŏk*, 2018), the first Korean documentary film nominated for an Oscar (Best Documentary [short subject] in 2020). The film is post-activist in its institutional and technological aspects. Yi was a former TV producer who directed documentaries on disenfranchised subjects, such as disabled persons (*Planet of Snail* [2011, see chapter 2]) and a North Korean refugee (*Shadow of Flowers* [*Kŭrimjakkot*, 2019, 107 min.]), and the film's circulation was not limited to community screenings for bereaved families and activists but extended across international documentary film festivals (such as IDFA and DOC NYC in 2017) and the YouTube channel of the *New Yorker*, which had received more than sixteen million views as of October 6, 2023.[68] Yi's motivation for making the film is grounded in his awareness that "if there is still broadly rooted pain in there, then we need to go back to the time when the pain had begun."[69] This drive to memory activism stemmed from Yi's empathy with the bereaved families' pain against those who disliked talking about the tragedy and downplayed it as a kind of "car accident," including the supporters of President Park Geun-hye and her conservative party. Accordingly, the film was produced in dialogue with the families' struggles for truth-finding and punishment of the persons who were in charge of the belated rescue operation and its improper information control. What further demonstrates Yi's link to activism is the vast array of audiovisual materials he collected (broadcast news footage; conversations between the officials of Blue House [the presidential office], the Ministry of Maritime, the National Coast Guard, and the crew of the ferry; its dash-cam footage; the cellphone videos shot by victims during the sinking) from a variety of sources, including the 4.16 Solidarity Media Committee (see chapter 3), and the association of the bereaved families that granted Yi permission to use the victims' videos.[70]

Its activist motivation and production processes notwithstanding, *In the Absence* clearly demarcates itself from the traditional activist practices on aesthetic and epistemological levels. The film puts forward its argument that "it was not an accident but an incident that was caused by the systemic human frailty, corruption and the incompetence of the government."[71] This argument, however, is made primarily neither by the on-the-spot filming of the families' protests on the street nor by the omniscient voice-over that would awaken viewers to what they could have not known about the tragedy and the government's mishandling of the incident. Instead of these two devices, Yi's meticulous investigation and editing of the audio recordings and video footage positions them within the timeline of the incident, juxtaposed with testimonies of families and the civilian divers who voluntarily rescued the bodies and belongings of its victims, and with expository intertitles overlaid with the landscape of the sea where the ferry sank (figure I.3). This archival approach, which I will discuss in chapter 6, is certainly intended to reconstruct the disaster as it happened, by giving the viewers an experience of what was really going on on April, 16, 2014. This immersive experience, however, further suggests that the disaster was more than a catastrophic event the government's mishandling of which was responsible for the deaths and the pain of the victims' families: it was the kind of event that compelled a filmmaker to develop new ways of constructing public memories, an event whose witnessing via televisual and digital liveness places audiences in a position beyond their immediate perception of the world. More than provoking audiences' moral powerlessness and their sense of responsibility, the documentaries that deal with this type of event strive to employ strategies that offer a witnessing of what we have witnessed, so that they transport their experience of the past into the living

Figure I.3 *In the Absence* (Yi Seung-jun, 2018)

present, and that some materials claim the persistence of what audiences did not see, or, what the dead saw and recorded (the videos taken by the victims). This is the reason that *In the Absence*'s use of records as its organizing material, which is distinct from the verité aesthetic, powerfully persuades viewers that we still need to watch what we have already watched, or to recall the "memory of the absence" (this is the meaning of the film's original Korean title), without necessarily relying on its persuasive or augmentative rhetorical devices. Yi's insertion of poetic landscape images, the tranquil sea shot from above and the obscure waters filmed from below, expresses memory as persisting in the world that we now live in, although the world looks as though the disaster had not happened, and the truth of the disaster still remains to be discovered. His treatment of the natural environments as memoryscapes accords with the documentaries of the "audiovisual turn" in chapter 5.

The book's epilogue furnishes two afterthoughts on Korean documentary cinema over the last forty years. The first recapitulates the idea of post-activist turns in terms of the shifting constellation of aesthetics and politics. If this reflects the internally dynamic processes of differentiation and border-crossing in Korean nonfiction film and video practices, the second presents my prospect for future inquiry into the external boundaries of Korean documentary cinema as a specific construct of national cinema in terms of its transnational encounters and diasporic drifting, with several examples of Korean diaspora filmmakers and the films that trace and reconstruct the inter-Asian network of common yet differing experiences.

PART I
ACTIVISM

1

The Development of the Activist Tradition in the 1980s and 1990s

Introduction

Documentary films of a nation-state do not have a single history; rather, they have multiple, interrelated histories given their distinctive practices of production and exhibition, as well as their underlying ideology. South Korean documentary films and videos are not an exception in this regard, although they share documentary cinema's functions of registering reality, producing information and knowledge, and offering viewers particular perspectives on the world and history. Since South Korea's liberation from Japan in 1945, there have been two nonfiction modes of filmmaking practiced by two official or public apparatuses, to both of which the term *kirok yŏnghwa* (*kirok* means "document," while *yŏnghwa* indicates both "film" and "cinema") has been applied.[1] The first includes newsreels, short and feature-length nonfiction films, animated shorts, and docudramas made by state-sponsored institutions and private film production companies for communicative, educational, propagandistic, and promotional uses. Based on the concept of *munhwa yŏnghwa* (culture film), which originated in the Japanese importation of German *Kulturfilm* during the Occupation, the film department in the Bureau of Public Information after the establishment of the South Korean government in 1948, which was later extended into National Film Production Agency (NFPA: Kungnib yŏnghwa jejakso) in 1961,[2] was committed to the production of these nonfiction artifacts that propagated anticommunist and developmentalist ideologies, educated laws and governmental policies, and informed people of the ideas, lifestyles, and moral codes of modernization.[3] Apart from this state-sponsored production based on the institutional and legal supports during the President Park Chung-hee regime (1961–1979), former members of NFPA ran a number of private film production companies in the 1970s that were devoted to films used for commercials and the publicity of regional tourism and policies. During this period, however, *munhwa yŏnghwa* faced a powerful alternative—the second mode of public

Activism and Post-activism. Jihoon Kim, Oxford University Press. © Oxford University Press 2024.
DOI: 10.1093/oso/9780197760413.003.0002

34 Activism

documentary practice: the popularization of television sets in the 1970s promoted the growth of broadcast documentary (*pangsong tak'yumentŏri*), the production of which started in 1962 with the first airing by the public broadcasting corporation Korean Broadcasting System (KBS). As a result, broadcast documentary gradually took over the functions of *munhwa yŏnghwa*, whose screening had been mandated in commercial movie theaters (before the showcase of a main feature) and local community centers (which often required a portable 16 mm projector).

While these two public-based modes of documentary undoubtedly await their own historiography, this brief summary suggests that from 1948 to the late 1970s there was no established mode of documentary cinema distinct from them in the private sectors of filmmaking—much less in Chungmuro (a central district of Seoul), the former headquarters of the Korean film industry. A few exceptions were experimental shorts that filmmakers made personally with a Super 8 mm or 16 mm camera. They include *2 Minutes 40 Seconds* (*2pun 40ch'o*, 1975, 10 min.) and *Colors of Korea* (*Saekdong*, 1976, 7 min.) by Han Ok-hee, a key member of the women's avant-garde film collective Khaidu (K'aitu) who employed associative montage to express her fascination with Korea's traditional culture and its rapid modernization,[4] and *Seoul 7000* (*Sŏul 7000*, Kim Hong-joon and Hwang Joo-ho, 1976, 7 min.), an 8 mm personal portrait of a day of Seoul that reminds one of the European city symphony shorts in the 1920s and 1930s. Although they deserve to be viewed as experimental documentary from today's perspective given their manipulative techniques to represent reality afresh, the films were not produced by way of documentary as a genre circumscribed by its conventions, its discourse, its modes of production and exhibition, and its intended audience (as both viewers and the subjects that documentarians address and engage). In this regard, it is correct to label the films—to use Tom Gunning's words—as "documentary before documentary."[5] It is due to the existence of *munhwa yŏnghwa* and *pangsong tak'yumentŏri* as two viable modes of nonfiction media practice before the 1980s that a history of South Korean documentary cinema in the private, particularly independent, sectors starts from the early 1980s.

This chapter overviews the first twenty years of the history in terms of the formation of the activist tradition in South Korean documentary cinema. The Gwangju Uprising did more than fuel a continual wave of university students' dissident protests for democracy against the dictatorship of the New Military (*Sin'gunbu*) government (1980–1988): it also became "a watershed for political activists in 'discovering' the importance of the media."[6] Among them were university students who were cinephiles and who became cognizant of film as a tool for expressing political dissent, engaging the lives and problems of peasants, workers, and urban evictees, and enlightening their class consciousness for social change. Their groups, both university cine-clubs and film production collectives, embarked upon the nongovernmental and nonbroadcast practice of fiction and nonfiction filmmaking, establishing their mission as *yŏnghwa undong* (film movement). Besides pointing to the foundational bond between cinema and social movements, the first section of this chapter characterizes the collectives' nonfiction artifacts in terms of how *yŏnghwa undong* formed three components of the activist tradition: its alternative modes of production and exhibition as distinct from the state-sponsored nonfiction apparatuses and commercial cinema, *minjung* (people) as the subject that it aspired to engage and enlighten, and experiments with documenting reality. Identifying these components, I also argue that the artifacts should be viewed as *kirok yŏngsang* (document visuals) rather than full-fledged documentary films. That is, it was from the early 1990s that the nonfiction practices of *yŏnghwa undong* became transformed into documentary (*kirok yŏnghwa* or *tak'yument'ŏri*) as a distinctive genre. The second section of this chapter tracks down the evolution of the early film activism into independent documentary (*tongnip tak'yument'ŏri*), an institutionalized mode of nonfiction film and video practices founded upon their orientation toward being independent from state power and commercial capital. In so doing, the section makes clear several social and institutional contexts that contributed to the formation of independent documentary, such as the transition to civil society (*simin sahoe*) after the end of the military dictatorship, the transformation of local film culture, and the growth of film festivals. This will lead to explaining how these contexts enabled participants of the 1980s *yŏnghwa undong* to reform its strategies of production, representation, and distribution, based on their changing self-identity as directors (*kamdok*) and in dialogue with the shifting social movements and the marginalized subjects that they advocated.

The 1980s: *yŏnghwa undong*, *minjung*, and Experiments with *kirok yŏngsang*

Two groups were crucial in the origin of 1980s film activism: first, Yalrashung (Yallasyŏng), a cine-club founded at Seoul National University in 1979 that paved the way for other university cine-clubs in Seoul during the 1980s; and second, the Seoul Film Collective (SFC: Sŏul yŏnghwa chiptan, 1982–1986), a collective formed by the alumni of Yalrashung and others who were interested in cinema as art and its function of articulating social commentary by audiovisual means. Stimulated by the Gwangju Uprising and inspired by

36 Activism

Marxist social theory (for the revolution of the working class) and antiimperialist nationalism as two ideological foundations of the student movement, the two collectives established *yŏnghwa undong* as their mission. In the words of Kim Hong-joon, who belonged to both groups, *yŏnghwa undong* meant that cinema should "participate in reality" and that film production should be based on "communal production" (*kongdong chejak*) because it was believed to "provide the opportunity to experience and experiment with the life of community (*kongdongch'e*)."[7] These two ideological directions of film movement were driven by members' penchant for alternatives to Hollywood cinema's commercialism and escapism, and by the impact of the *minjung* culture movement in the 1980s, a sum of cultural and artistic practices that aimed to address, participate in, and construct *minjung* endowed with a coherent and unified political subjectivity. As Namhee Lee explains in her seminal work on the movement, "Meaning 'common people' as opposed to elites and leaders or even the educated or cultured, *minjung* came to signify those who are oppressed in the sociopolitical system but who are capable of rising up against it."[8] The two groups' pursuit of "small film" (*chakŭn yŏnghwa*) was realized with their communal production of many short films about workers, peasants, and the urban poor, on the one hand, with the opening of a nonauthorized film festival that eventually led to the manifestation of its concept in 1984 ("Small Film Festival"), on the other. The concept of small film laid the groundwork for the modes of production and exhibition in the activist practices of the decade that followed. For it referred to more than 16 mm and 8 mm film technologies distinct from the 35 mm format of commercial film industry, namely, an ideological construct that championed a kind of "open cinema that offers critical viewpoints on reality and its future-oriented alternative."[9]

Kukpung (*Kukp'ung*, 1981), arguably the first nonfiction artifact based on the communal production system of *yŏnghwa undong*, is a seventeen-minute film for which members of Yalrashung juxtaposed the 8 mm record of Kukpung in May 1981 (a large-scale culture festival organized by the New Military government for the purpose of defusing people's interest in politics) with postsynchronized voices of its participants and local pop songs. The collective's early interest in documenting the lives of *minjung* evident in *Kukpung* was later extended into two 8 mm nonfiction films designed to agitate fellow students about the need for social revolution in 1984. *Galileans of This Land* (*I ttangŭi kallilli saramdŭl*, 30 min.) records the struggles of evictees in a neighborhood of Seoul, and *Twenty-Five Years of Democratization Struggles* (*Minjuhwa t'ujaeng 25nyŏn*, 30 min.) takes on the form of reportage that summarizes the history of student prodemocracy movements from the April

19 Revolution (which ended the dictatorship of President Rhee Syngman in 1960) to university demonstrations in the early 1980s.[10] By documenting the scenes of the struggles and holding screenings in and outside universities, Yalrashung, SFC, and other university cine-clubs during the New Military regime aimed to raise critical consciousness of progressive intellectuals, university students, and *minjung*, interpellating them as subjects of social reform and democracy. It is significant to note, however, that this political direction did not result in a unified form of documentary cinema. Instead, the nonfiction artifacts of *yŏnghwa undong* sprang from various interconnected experiments with the forms of alternative cinema and *kirok yŏngsang*.

Pannori Arirang (*P'annori arirang*, 1982), a film SFC produced on 8 mm, has long been known as "the first documentary film that was made outside the mainstream media including the Chungmuro studio and broadcasting corporations"[11] before the recent local rediscovery of *Kukpung*. The film reconstructs a *madanggŭk* (a reinvented traditional Korean folk theater), *On the Pannori Arirang Hill*, that Theater Yeonwoo performed from May 20 to 25, 1982, juxtaposing the footage and stills of the live stage with the behind-the-scene record of rehearsals. According to Park Kwang-soo, a leading figure in SFC at that time (who would later lead the Korean New Wave cinema in the late 1980s), the eighteen-minute film was a kind of étude rather than a full-fledged filmic work, based on his connection with the troupe. Despite this provisional aspect, *Pannori Arirang* has been regarded as "a unique film distinct from other [activist-oriented] documentaries in the 1980s and early 1990s . . . due to *its evocation of documentary structure and its 'reflexive attitude' towards the meaning of art in the reality of the time*."[12] This evaluation centers on the film's strategies to make visible the whole process of the play and create a sound-image disjunction. Both strategies, I argue, testify to early activist nonfiction not as a homogeneous mode of filmic practice but as a hybrid of heterogeneous cinematic and cultural influences. The first strategy is akin to the self-reflexive device frequently employed in the films of French *nouvelle vague* and New German Cinema to draw viewers' attention to the process of filmmaking. These two foreign influences were shared by certain members of SFC as cinephiles who were frequent visitors of the French Institute and the Goethe Institute in Seoul in the 1970s and early 1980s.[13] The exposure of the process was then read as creating the "distanciation effect diverged from the viewer's immersive identification with a film's protagonist in the traditional cinema."[14] Strengthening this effect, the film's postsynchronization dissonance between sound and image originated from SFC's reference to the Third Cinema that its members carefully studied during their activities of filmmaking and seminars. This is evident in the film's dubbed soundtrack,

38 Activism

comprising audiences' reactions to the play and the troupe's discussion of its achievements and limitations. The soundtrack recalls Third Cinema's experimentation with postsynchronization as a way of innervating viewers' active meaning-making of a film's text. What is interesting in those two strategies is that SFC grafted these transnational influences of nonrealistic, quasi-Brechtian cinema with the ideal of *minjung* culture in the group's cinematic rearticulation of *madangguk*, a form that cultural activists of the *minjung* movement "envisioned not only as a new form of theater but also as a new form of community based on the shared experience of work and play."[15] This accords with the activists' embrace of the decolonialization movement in the Third World, through which indigenous culture was believed to serve as a "cultural resistance to . . . the commercially marketed, mass-produced culture of the West."[16]

Water Utilization Tax (*Surise*, Hong Ki-seon, 1983, 35 min.) reconstructs the struggle of the tenant farmers of the Gurye county in Jollanam-do Province against the government's to[-down policy for them to pay water taxes with their produce from November 1983 to January 1984. In response to the then growing indigenous farmers' movement against the Land Reform Guild's bureaucratic operation and its excessive demand for taxes,[17] the members of SFC embarked upon the film's production based on their shared belief in "film's values for pedagogy and documentation."[18] In so doing, the collective aspired to extend the idea of communal production, formerly articulated by the dialogical relationship between producers and viewers in *Pannori Arirang*, into making the film with the farmers so that they would be the subjects of its production and reception. However, the unexpected situation of the location compelled the members to change the film's original production plan, instead intermixing newspaper clippings, still images of the struggles, reenactment sequences of indigenous rituals played by the farmers themselves, and the postsynchronized soundtrack of interviews, folk songs, and a female voice-over narration that explains the economic and local contexts of the struggles. The film received a negative response from SFC's internal evaluation: "The film does not deeply convey the farmers' pain and their battles in the movement because its representation is limited to a plain commentary on the event and thus does not inscribe the keen sense of its *hyŏnjang*."[19] During the last few years, however, young critics have reevaluated it as a primitive case of the essay film or, more precisely, the "pamphlet" film that offer viewers a propagandistic discourse on reality with its dialogic blending of reports, documents, analyses, and slogans.[20] In line with this, I would clarify that the "pamphlet" film should be read as reflecting SFC's inclination to the Third Cinema. In their seminal manifesto, Fernando Solanas and Octavio Getino proposed to develop new forms of cinematic practice that existed at the margins of the mainstream film, as strategies to promote people's participation in the production and consumption of a film for the purpose of bridging art and politics: "The man of the *third cinema*, be it *guerrilla cinema* or a *film act*, with the infinite categories that they contain (film letter, film poem, *film essay*, *film pamphlet*, *film report*, etc.) above all counters the film industry of a cinema of characters with one of the themes, that of individuals with that of masses, that of the author with that of the operative group."[21] In experimenting with the format of the pamphlet film, *Water Utilization Tax* also expresses SFC's quasi-anthological interest in the farmers' indigenous culture in that it includes several postsynchronized folk songs juxtaposed with the footage of their use of fire to exterminate harmful insects and strengthen their communal solidarity. This formal heterogeneity and functional multiplicity tempts me to propose an alternative view to the standardized, partially romanticized, assumption on the origin of Korean independent documentary as unilaterally converging in the on-the-spot realism of cinéma-vérité and the cinema for the disenfranchised. This view also echoes Hieyoon Kim's recent revisionist take on the way that local critics and filmmakers legitimized the SFC and other film collectives in the 1980s as the pioneers of independent cinema in the late 1990s and early 2000s. As she persuasively writes, this self-historiography of independent cinema has tended to glorify the SFC's experiments with a new cinema "as a homogeneous force that yielded its vision of poor as victims of capitalist developmentalism under autocratic rule... without attending to the SFC's multifaceted struggles, particularly its reflexive engagement with its positionality and sustainability."[22]

The aesthetic and rhetorical heterogeneity evident in *Pannori Arirang* and *Water Utilization Tax*, which Young-a Park could describe as "extreme[ly] eclectic,"[23] was rooted in SFC's translation and appropriation of various radical cinemas as alternatives to the imperialist cinematic model of Hollywood and the commercialized film industry of Chungmuro. The influences of the Third Cinema, which included the Bolivian Ukamau Film and the Brazilian Cinema Novo, were undoubtedly most conspicuous, as evidenced by SFC's publication of two edited collections that attested to its activist aspiration of integrating film theory and practice: *Toward a New Cinema* (*Saeroun yŏnghwarŭl wihayŏ*, 1983) and *Theory of Film Movement* (*Yŏnghwa undongnon*, 1985). After translating foreign texts on the different branches of the New Latin American cinema, the Free Cinema in the UK, the French New Wave, the New German Cinema for the former, the collective included translations of Solanas and Getino's "Toward a Third Cinema"(1969) and excerpts from Teshome Gabriel's *Third Cinema in the Third World* (1982) in the latter. These

40 Activism

references to the Third Cinema were extended into SFC's pursuit for *yŏllyŏjin yŏnghwa* (opened cinema) in two senses. First, as Jang Sun-woo, who later became another key director of the Korean New Wave, declared in his manifesto published in *Toward a New Cinema*, *yŏllyŏjin yŏnghwa* serves as an alternative to the "closed" Western bourgeois mode of film production and reception in that it proposes to blend Italian Neorealism's use of the camera as an "observer" and "witness" of reality with the folk traditions of Korean performance and oral art, including *madanggŭk*, through which "the camera is capable of participating in and playing with its object."[24] Second, it also entails SFC's adoption of communal production in which "art production and reception are enmeshed."[25] For SFC, this meant not merely group authorship and small films that manifest the anticapitalist mode of cinematic production but also dissolution of the boundary between a film's producers and its audiences, in contrast to Hollywood's interpellation of the latter as passive consumer of movies as commodity.[26] Again, the group regionalized the influence from the Third Cinema by incorporating the culture of *minjung* where creators and audiences could be conjoined.[27] This negotiation of the traditional and the foreign in the concept of communal production required the collective-based film movement to "be faithful to the historical consciousness, idea, and sentiment of the *minjung* community and participate in the community's *hyŏnjang*" through "reinventing its practitioner as the community's member."[28]

Indeed, SFC's practice of communal production and its ideological aspiration to participate in *hyŏnjang* also enabled its members to be interested in the postwar documentaries of the West. *Toward a New Cinema* included excerpts from Erik Barnouw's *Documentary: A History of the Non-fiction Film* (1974), in which he posits three functions of documentary cinema as "observer," "catalyst," and "guerrilla."[29] The members' roundtable discussion published in the book demonstrates that the traditions of Free Cinema, direct cinema, cinéma-vérité formed the nascent idea of documentary cinema as opposed to the two existing modes of nonfiction filmmaking in the official apparatuses. The panelists envisioned that the traditions would inspire filmmakers "to immediately report the ordinary life of *minjung* . . . beyond television news and *munhwa yŏnghwa* whose screening [was] mandatory in theaters."[30] In order to continue its search for communal production of "films for democracy and for the solution of the problems in this land," SFC was later reformed into the Seoul Visual Collective (SVC: Sŏul yŏngsang chiptan) in 1986 in order expand its scope of *yŏnghwa undong* into "all visual media encompassing photos, slides, video, and film."[31]

The Gwangju Uprising also paved the way for the alternative production and distribution of nonfiction artifacts with video technology. Due to the

The Development of the Activist Tradition   41

New Military government's media censorship, Korea's local presses were not permitted to do on-the-scene reporting on the uprising and the military troop's brutal suppression of it. Only a few journalists from foreign presses (in West Germany, Japan, and the United States) bypassed the troops' blockage of Gwangju and infiltrated the city, producing their reports. The scenes of the reports became a source material for so-called "Gwangju Video," four versions of edited video produced by the Catholic associations in Gwangju and Japan and by the Korean immigrants living in the three countries (for this reason, they are distinct not simply in the production country but also in the language of narration). The videos were imported to Korea, illegally duplicated, and disseminated by human rights priests and activists, and screened at universities and churches from 1985 to 1987, having a notable impact on the growth of the political rallies during that time.[32]

It was indeed Kim Dong-won, then an assistant director in the apprentice system of Chungmuro, who made the first step toward video activism with his *Sanggye-dong Olympics* (*Sanggye-dong ollimp'ik*, 1988, 27 min.).[33] It documents struggles of the tenants against eviction due to the large-scale demolition and beautification of dilapidated houses in the old towns of Seoul in preparation for the 1988 Seoul Olympics. The work has already been discussed in existing English-language studies on Korean documentary cinema and independent film, so it is sufficient to briefly recapitulate the ways in which it has been accepted as the "prototype of activist video."[34] The film identified evictees (*chŏlgŏmin*) and the urban poor (*toshi pinmin*) as the first type of disenfranchised, marginalized subjects that the activist tradition of Korean documentary cinema has later engaged; Kim's filming of the tenants was triggered by the recommendation of a foreign Catholic father who had supported their struggles, so his practice validates Korean activist documentary's advocacy for social movements. His use of the video camera as a tool to film the tenants while living among them for five years not only fulfilled activism's demand for a newsreel that would make public their precarious lives neglected by mainstream news outlets, but also laid the groundwork for the activist tradition's ethos of *hyŏnjang*, that is, finding a way into *minjung* to convey their bodies, voices, and lifeworlds. The film's collaborative processes, ranging from the amateurish female voice-over (a tenant of the village) based on his discussion with the tenants about the scripts to screenings of the videos in their community, satisfied the participatory ideal of the committed documentary to transcend the boundaries between a filmmaker and her subjects, between film and social reality, and between production and reception. Finally, the voice-over emblematizes the activist documentary's role as an organizing agent of the community. For it states that the residents'

42 Activism

collective consciousness was cultivated as they realized that their struggle was in line with the resistance movements of other marginalized groups, including residents of other demolished towns. While acknowledging all the contributions of the work, I argue that *Sanggye-dong Olympics* was not intended to be a full-fledged documentary film and that Kim did not consider himself documentary filmmaker. As he has often remarked in interviews, "I did not know that it was a documentary film at that time. I just thought that I had to report as soon as possible. It was a propaganda film . . . for the purpose of arousing social opinion."[35] This confession relates to Kim's awareness that the work is not an end product of his documentary practice committed to and learning from the urban poor and other underrepresented subjects, but rather its starting point: "The production process of *Sanggye-dong Olympics* was the opportunity for me to question and answer how to practice film. I finally came up with the idea of 'needy documentary.' "[36]

The 1987 Great Struggle of Workers, a mass labor movement that exploded right after the June Democratic Struggle, encouraged collectives to assume workers (*nodongja*) and labor issues against capitalism as another major subject of the activist tradition. As Hagen Koo and Lee Won-bo have noted, the massive wave of labor conflicts from July to September 1987, marked by more than three thousand labor disputes that demanded workers' rights, abolition of military labor management and inhuman labor conditions, and guarantee of union formation and activities, enhanced the workers' collective class consciousness and promoted solidarity beyond individual firms.[37] Labor News Production (LNP: Nodongja nyusŭ jejaktan), formed by several former members of SVC, produced *Labor News No.1* (*Nodongja nyusŭ 1ho*) in March 1989. This seventy-three-minute video was motivated by labor activists' demand for "immediately filming the struggles that occur at different times and making it into a news format."[38] A considerable amount of its running time is devoted to on-the-spot records of the unions' rallies and workers' regional strikes across various workplaces. Aided by the didactic voice-over that specifies the location and date of each struggle, the collective's editing intercuts long shots of rallies and fights with extreme close-ups of individual participants, consolidating an alliance among the dispersed workers and reconstructing them as a collective body galvanized by labor activism (figure 1.1). What is crucial is the video's compilation format, comprising news bulletins (*sokpo*), education ("Knowledge Is Power": a discussion of two workers on the problems of labor-management relations), feature story ("Laborer's Eyes"), animation (which offers a caricatural satire on the state and capital), and short agitational visuals based on a mixture of still photos and labor songs. This hybrid of the disparate representational strategies can

Figure 1.1 *Labor News No. 1* (Labor News Production, 1989)

be viewed from multiple perspectives. LNP had several members from SFC, which included a translation of Guy Hennnebelle's article on the French radical documentary after May 1968 in *Theory of Film Movement*.[39] It could thus be construed that *Labor News No. 1* was partly inspired by the practices of the French *cinéma militant* during and after the May 1968 events to combine direct-action newsreels, analyses, lectures, agitprop, and didactic sketches related to workers' strikes. LNP's uses of various postproduction techniques for this work, which is evident in the appropriation of a TV news clip on violence during a strike through the interplay of slow motion and a majestic classic music track, attest not only to its pursuit of propagandistic, agitational, and pedagogical effects but also to its effort to elaborate on the aesthetics of montage in seeking nonfiction media's expressive possibilities, an effort distinct from the activist tradition's privileging of on-the-spot realism and its obsession with documentary authenticity. Another perspective is that *Labor News No. 1* can be read as an artifact of alternative media or "visual magazine," considering the labor activists' growing awareness of visual media as more effective than brochures and breaking-news pamphlets. As Bae In-jung, a former member of SFC and SVC who later formed LNP, recalled, "A key motivation of *Labor News* was the labor unions' desperate need of their independent media against the mass media that represented the interests of power and capital."[40]

44 Activism

LNP chose the 16 mm video camera not merely for accessibility, portability, and cheap production costs, but also for circulation of *Labor News* videos in VHS format through labor unions' in-house broadcasting networks.[41] In so doing, LNP pioneered the alternative distribution strategy adopted by other practitioners and collectives from the late 1980s. By using video for the tripartite network of production-distribution-exhibition, the collective could be compared to the US "video guerrillas" in the 1970s that employed the format not only to document a new type of on-the-scene reportage but also to create the grassroots- and community-oriented media system that opposed the commercialism of television industry.[42]

LNP was not alone in the film movement for making and circulating agitational and didactic nonfiction artifacts aimed to constitute workers as *minjung*. Jangsangotmae, a collective that left its significant trace on the history of film activism with the production and unauthorized screening of feature-length political dramas such as *O Dreamland* (*O! kkumŭi nara*, 1989, 90 min., a film about the Gwangju Uprising) and *The Night before the Strike* (*P'aŏp chŏnya*, 1990, 105 mon., a social realist feature film about the conflict between factory workers who attempt to form a union and the factory that hinders it),[43] made *The Workers Advancing from 87 to 89* (*87esŏ 89ro chŏnjinhanŭn nodongja*, Lee Eun and Lee Yong-bae, 1989, 42 min.) in 16 mm format, which chronicles the nationwide proliferation of the movements for forming labor unions across various workplaces and job groups, including the inauguration of the Korea Teachers and Education Workers Union. The National Film Institute (NCI: Minjok yŏnghwa yŏn'guso, 1988–1990) was an important collective of the film movement in the late 1980s and early 1990s, consisting of media activists as well as critics Lee Hyo-in and Lee Jung-ha. With their multidimensional activities, such as the studies on leftist film theories, journal publication, education, and film production, the collective pursued the idea of "national film" (*minjok yŏnghwa*), which would promote working-class consciousness as a precondition for revolutionary social change against capitalism and imperialism.[44] As the members of NFI declared in the inaugural issue of its journal *National Film* in 1989, "*Minjok yŏnghwa* has as its idea 'national liberation' (*minjok haebang*) which is also the working-class ideology of social reform, while also assuming as its subject *minjung* led by the working class."[45] What is notable in the activities of NFI was its awareness of the significance of *kirok yŏnghwa* as a strategic mode of its *minjok yŏnghwa* movement, in that it "could respond to the need for the news viewed from workers' perspective and be used for timely mass education."[46] It was based on this awareness that NFI practiced what it called the "planned report film" (*kihoek podo yŏnghwa*). Integrating preproduction,

The Development of the Activist Tradition   **45**

shooting, postproduction, and distribution with the help of videotape recording technology that had already been diffused in workplaces, *kihoek podo yŏnghwa* could be "a form able to convey the demands and will of *minjung* and be utilized to propagandize and agitate them most effectively."[47] Grounded in this activist infrastructure and ideology, NFI produced nine videos aimed to reveal the suppression and exploitation of the authoritarian state power and capital, to make recognized the problems of workers and the urban poor, and to report strikes and union formations underway between 1988 and 1989. What is most notable is *Kkangsuni* (*Kkangsuni, Syuŏp'ŭrodŏkch'ŭ nodongja*, Lee Sang-in and Lee Chang-won, 1989, 58 min.), about the struggles of female workers at the multinational medical supplies company Shure Products against its unnotified shutdown of the factory. Women's Visual Collective Bariteo (Yŏsŏng yŏngsang jiptan Paritŏ, 1988–1991), which consisted of film professionals, media activists, and the students of university film circles, submitted its critique on the patriarchal system of Korean society with *Every Little Grass Has Its Own Name* (*Chakŭn p'uredo irŭm issŭni*, Kim Soyoung, 1990), a thirty-eight-minute 16 mm docudrama made in alliance with Womenlink (Han'guk yŏsŏng minuhoe), which portrays female office workers' trouble in negotiating labor and housework and the necessity of forming their own union for gender equality.[48] The Documentary Film and Videomakers' Council (Tak'yumentŏri jakka hoeŭi), a temporary organization constituted in 1990 by the members from LNP, SVC, Bariteo, and others, produced two labor documentaries, *Battle Line* (*Chŏnyŏl*, 1991, 52 min.), which tells the story of the struggles of the Hyundai Heavy Industries Union from 1987 to 1991, and *For Our Song That Will Echo through Oakpo Bay* (*Okp'omane mearich'il uridŭrŭi noraerŭl wihayŏ*, 1991, 40 min.), a film that documents the strike of laborers at Daewoo Shipbuilding Corporation on Geojedo Island in 1991.

Despite their respective difference in subject, all these works are premised upon the correspondence between the images of the workers in struggle and the voice-over narration that interweaves explanation and persuasion. The voice-over, then, constructs the workers as collective subject with its agitational tone that has the effect of enlightening them with the awareness of unequal labor conditions and with the interpellation of them as *uri* (we). Like LNP's *Labor News*, the circulation of most of the works benefited from video technology as they were duplicated on VHS tape and distributed to unions and factories for educational screening and in-house broadcasting.[49] Again, this testifies to the medium-specific distinction between film and video that was shared by the participants of the film movement in the late 1980s: the former suited theatrical screening, whereas the latter was more efficient in

46 Activism

rapid filming and circulation for particular subjects and audiences despite its inferior visuality in comparison to the former. Given their combination of *sokpo* footage, news clips, and the interviews with union leaders, as well as their alternative modes of production, distribution, and exhibition, these nonfiction artifacts on the labors' struggles are in retrospect regarded as *kirok yŏngsang* derived from the activist film movements, rather than *tak'yument'ŏri* in the sense of a distinct genre grounded in its own institutional mode of film practice.

Among these propagandistic labor videos, *Kkangsuni* deserves particular attention due to the tension between its on-the-spot portrayal of workers and its larger didactic discourse. During preproduction, the filmmakers wanted to overcome the journalistic approach of other labor newsreels to the progress and consequence of struggles by paying attention to the "life and thought of the workers . . . as individuals."[50] This was reflected in the film's production process, which involved workers' participation in conceiving its storyboard, the filmmakers' shooting while living with them for two months, its voice-over that conveys the "first-person subjectivity of the youngest worker as its protagonist,"[51] and its realistic records of the workers' sit-ins (*nongsŏng*), cultural activities, testimonies, and poor living conditions in the factory. The filmmakers' desire to make a "microscopic story" about the "life of the female workers,"[52] however, is offset by the film's climax and ending, which mobilize the narrative of how they engaged the larger joint struggles of other workers and unions and how it came to awaken the protagonist's consciousness. Despite its verité-style strategy, distinct from other labor newsreels of the time, *Kkangsuni* does not totally deviate itself from their narrative scheme, which offers the promise of *minjung*'s enlightenment and liberation.

The 1990s: Institutionalization of *tongnip tak'yument'ŏri*

The year 1991 was a turning point in the evolution of the film movement into the independent documentary as an institutionalized mode of nonfiction film and video practice. Four activist nonfiction video works, including *Sanggye-dong Olympics* and *Battle Line*, were invited to the Asia Program of the second Yamagata International Documentary Film Festival (YIDFF) at a time when their public distribution and screening were still legally banned by the Record and Video Law (Ŭmban bidio bŏp).[53] The participants' experience of the YIDFF helped them to think of their work as beyond *kirok yŏngsang* or *sokbo*, namely, as documentary cinema. Markus Nornes's account of this experience validates this: "Fifteen aspiring filmmakers visited Yamagata where they had their first chance to see foreign documentaries. Before this, they could read about documentary history in the standard histories by Barnouw and Barsam, but the only films they had access to were government propaganda or network television."[54] Indeed, this account needs a slight correction, because the invitees, either activists or members of university cineclubs, had not regarded themselves as "filmmakers" before their participation in the YIDFF. This suggests that the YIDFF was arguably the first opportunity for the participants to develop their self-identity as *kamdok*. The influence of the YIDFF is also evident in two anecdotes on the presence of Shinsuke Owaga. On the occasion of the festival, Kim Dong-won came to know Ogawa, who had been keen interest in promoting regional alliances between Asian documentarians but was unable to attend it due to his cancer. Several months before Kim's visit to Ogawa's hospital, Byun Young-joo, a former member of Bariteo who would later produce the "comfort women" trilogy with her production company Docu-Factory Vista (Kirok yŏnghwa jejakso Poim), visited the Owaga Pro office and had a five-hour conversation with him, and joined Kim and other participants. The influence of Ogawa on Kim and Byun has been acknowledged both in English-language documentary studies and in a variety of local materials encompassing their writings and interviews. This is indeed more than their conviction that Ogawa's lesson would enhance the two activists' practice, which led to their formation of the collective Docu Purn (P'urŭn yŏngsang) after their return to Korea. As Nornes writes, "Purn's relationship to Ogawa was cemented by the tapes [of his films], which they watched carefully together and discussed. They were particularly shocked by the shooting style of the Sanrizuka Series."[55] Here it is suggested that the local idea of "committed documentary" or "socially engaged documentary" was concretized less with Kim's blurring of making and living among the residents in *Sanggye-dong Olympics* than with the transnational traffic of a particular mode of nonfiction film practice that aimed to promote interactions between filmmaker and subject, and between production and consumption. It can also be construed that Ogawa's emphasis upon the filmmaker's becoming part of her subject and upon the committed stance of her camera would enliven the Korean practitioners' politico-aesthetic aspirations to take part in *minjung* and to document the reality of *hyŏnjang*.

The practitioners' nascent self-awareness as *kamdok* and of their work as documentary cinema entailed reforming the communal production and alternative distribution in the 1980s film movement. Maintaining the distribution of its videos for community screening, Docu Purn devised and operated the "one-person production system" (*irin jejak shisŭt'em*), by which

48 Activism

a documentarist is in charge of preproduction, shooting, and postproduction. Similarly, SVC upgraded the communal production with a systematic division of labor, through which a documentarist takes the lead on a project and other members take different roles. This is also the case with Vista, represented by Byun's authorship. Those two modes of production, which were later popularized in the twenty-first century, allowed the collectives' members to make videos based on their long-term commitment to social places and actors, while also founding the system and workflow of independent documentary outside the mainstream film production in Chungmuro industry. They also set the tone for cultivating the members' status as directors expected to develop their own subject matter, style, and perspective.[56] Accordingly, the director's authorial signature and rhetorical voice were increasingly inscribed in the textual fabric of the films, unlike the 1980s activist videos, where end credits tended to present the name of a collective.[57]

This reform of the production system and the growth of documentary authorship were intertwined with the expansion of the social issues and subjects that the film production collectives engaged. Kim Dong-won's confession in the early 1990s suggests that this expansion was derived from the activists' concern with their direction in response to the sociopolitical changes surrounding the film movement: "I can't speak the language of the past any more. When the political suppression was severe, audiences kept their serious attitudes about our clumsy films made under tough conditions of production. However, now is the time we need changes."[58] In relation to this, Kim also used the term "post–Age of Resistance," which refers to the situation in which the explosive wave of mass protests seemingly subsided after the June Democratic Struggle, the collapse of the global socialist block as the Marxist background for the 1980s social movements, and the election of President Kim Young-sam in 1992. Kim's characterization of the mid-1990s as the "post–Age of Resistance," then, implies that the biggest concern of the film activists faced with that series of changes was "how to innovate their 'minjung-oriented spirit' as an object of film movement."[59]

Local critics have viewed the result of the concern as the diversification of subject matter. Maeng Soo-jin, for instance, summarizes as the tendencies of the 1990s nonfiction practice "the everyday" (ilsang), "progressiveness" (chinbo), and "the individual" (kaein).[60] Similarly, Park Nohchool notes that the post–Age of Resistance documentary "does not completely depart from the established themes in independent documentaries such as anti-statism and communalism," but rather "enlarges the boundary of subject matter and style to enrich the preexisting themes."[61] Added to this is that the expansion should be read in tandem with the post-1987 transition to the formation of civil society (*simin sahoe*), which led to the diffusion of various social movements. As Paul Y. Chang and Gi-wook Shin summarize, in maintaining their advocacy for democracy, the post-1987 new movements "addressed concerns that were previously marginalized in the larger movement for democracy" with the significant "discursive shift from *minjung* to *simin* (citizen)."[62] This societal change from the late 1980s indicates that the collectives turned their attention to the diversified issues connected to and fueled by civil society and religious organizations, such as human rights (*in'gwŏn*), women, education, and historical violence. At the same time, their practices also aimed to reload their ideological conviction in the pivotal role of *minjung* in the society's democratization and progress in their continual commitment to evictees, the urban poor, and workers.

Based in Docu Purn, Kim Dong-won deepened his engagement with the tenants in slums in alliance with the Catholic Association for the Urban Poor in *Haengdang-Dong People* (*Haengdang-dong saramdŭl*, 1994, 31 min.) and *Another World We Are Making: Haengdang-Dong People 2* (*Tto hanaŭi sesang: Haengdang-dong saramdŭl 2*, 1999, 42 min.). While continuing the female voice-over of a resident and the camera's approximate portrayal of the visceral battles against the police and hired mobs, the two films put more emphasis on the tenants' efforts to run their cooperative production and sharing economy. The narration's optimistic and didactic tone, then, reflects Kim's ideal of the community (*kongdongch'e*) of the urban poor "as an alternative to the capitalistic values of proprietary and competition."[63] As Kim describes in the production note of *Another World We Are Making*, "This philosophy of poverty is the basis of all social movements, and the only and most positive alternative for redeeming oneself and the world in crisis."[64] Besides his conviction of the value of *chinbo*, Kim's humanist trust in the power of *minjung* as the subject of democracy gained a historical perspective in *The Six-Day Fight in Myong-dong Cathedral* (*Myŏngsŏng, kŭ 6ilŭi kirok*, 1997, 74 min.). This history documentary, commissioned by the June 1987 Democratic Struggle Service Association, revisits the six-day occupation of Myong-dong Cathedral. It emblematizes Kim's maturity in directing and his *minjung*-oriented consciousness of history. Apart from his rich interweaving of interviews, archival footage, and photos, Kim employs reenactments to convey the subjective experience of a participant whose eyes were injured, and to reconstruct the heated internal debates of the participants regarding whether or not they had to continue their sit-in. While manifesting his resistance to a narrative of the protests as people's triumph,[65] Kim also brings together wide-ranging interviewees as participants who represent a diverse array of social subjects (priests, labor union activists, students, office workers, and the evictees who

50 Activism

temporarily occupied the cathedral). In so doing, Kim preserves his utopian belief in *minjung* as the driving force for a better society that the protests have left unrealized despite their termination of the military regime.

Another key figure of Docu Purn, Kim Tae-il, paved the way to establishing state and ideological violence as another subject of the activist tradition. His documentaries focus on the political victims of Cold War politics, such as unconverted, long-term prisoners (*pijŏnhyang changgisu, A Purple Handkerchief* [*Ŏmŏniŭi poratpin sonsugŏn*, 1995, 48 min.]), former North Korean partisans (*People Who Transcended Division* [*Pundanŭl nŏmŏsŏn saramdŭl*, 1995, 85 min.]), and the innocent citizens who were accused of being spies by the authorities (*Making the Spy* [*22ilganŭi kobaek*, 1998, 50 min.]). Kim has confessed that the faith of North Korean prisoners of war was clearly manifested in his first encounter with them in 1993, which encouraged him to make a series of documentaries based on his long-term interactions with them.[66] Driven by Docu Purn's solidarity with the civilian and religious associations for human rights that opposed the National Security Law (Kukka boan bŏp, enacted in 1948), including Sarangbang, Kim's documentaries express his aspirations to constitute the alternative to the official history of modern Korea with the bodies and testimonies of the subjects and their families that were excluded from it, and to highlight their capacity to act in the world. It is in this sense that he prefigured the growth of the documentaries about the truth-finding of the political incidents during the Cold War in the twenty-first century.

Hong Hyung-sook of the SVC made another key achievement of the 1990s independent documentary, *Doomealee: A New School Is Opening* (*Tumilli: Saeroun hakkyoga yŏllinda*, 1995, 70 min.). The film documents the efforts of villagers and students to resist the planned closure of Doomealee Elementary School, which was dictated by the Ministry of Education's merger and abolition of small-scale schools. SVC's engagement with the conflict reflected Hong's awareness that "if the 1980s were the age of grand discourses, now we need to turn our eyes and start a new conversation with nuanced and microscopic topics."[67] Based on this consciousness, Hong organically orchestrates the opposition between the villagers' struggles to protect the school as the optimal environment for educating their children and the educational authorities' bureaucratic, efficiency-oriented reactions to their demand. Eschewing the expository or didactic voice-over that undergirds the videos of the 1980s film movement, she adopts the observational mode of filmmaking and blends it with the voices of the villagers to represent the farmers' growing sense of communal solidarity and the children's idyllic life as inseparable from the school's nature-friendly environment. In so doing,

The Development of the Activist Tradition **51**

she elevates the ideal of the *minjung* community in the 1980s activist nonfiction artifacts to the quasi-anthropological study of its microcosm and thereby predates the politico-aesthetic approach of the social change documentaries in the twenty-first century. *Doomealee, the Very First Step (Shijaḱanŭn sunǵan: Tumilli tu pǒntchae iyagi*, 2000, 80 min.), a sequel to *A New School Is Opening*, validates SVC's long-term participation in the community as it compiles the memories of the teenagers who used to attend the school, which was eventually closed in 1995. Besides these two films, Hong demonstrated her directorial competence in *On-line: An Inside View of Korean Independent Film (Pyŏnbangesŏ chungshimŭro: Tongnibyŏnghwae taehan ťŭkpyŏrhan shisŏn*, 1997, 63 min.). Produced in tandem with the SVC's publication of the sourcebook *From Periphery to Center (Pyŏnbangesŏ chungsimŭro*, 1997) that brought together pamphlets, newspapce articles, and memoirs related to *yŏnghwa undong*, the film narrates the history of the activist videos and independent films from the 1980s to the mid-1990s. Here Hong employed two television sets side by side in order to perform a kind of horizontal montage of two—mutually supplementing or sometimes opposing—testimonies by the players on the scene, a strategy that partially invokes Jean-Luc Godard and Anne-Marie Miéville's *Numéro deux* (1975).

Byun Young-joo has recently confessed that her now-classical "comfort women" (*wianbu*) or "*Murmuring*" trilogy—*The Murmuring (Najŭn moksori*, 1995, 93 min.), *Habitual Sadness (Najŭn moksori 2*, 1997, 71 min.), and *My Own Breathing (Najŭn moksori 3: Sumgyŏl*, 1999, 96 min.)—"didn't started from the female victims of Japanese military sexual slavery but from [her] desire to make a documentary film for theatrical release." What stimulated this were her visits to the YIDFF in 1991 and the Berlin International Film Festival in 1994, where she was exposed to the films of Ogawa and Amos Gitai: "I wanted to make films like those I fell in love with."[68] This led Byun to borrow a 16 mm film camera and synchronous recording equipment from Ogawa Pro, to raise funds via the "one hundred feet of film purchase campaign" that solicited audiences' participation in the production of the first two films, to distribute them both in arthouse theaters and invited screenings at universities and social movement organizations, to enter *The Murmuring* in twenty international film festivals, and to export it to Japan in collaboration with Japanese civic groups.[69] With this integration of planning, distribution, exhibition, and publicity, which enhanced the collectives' alternative strategies of community-based screening and propagation in the 1980s, the trilogy pioneered the "coalition model" of social change documentaries that many activist films across various subjects adopted in the twenty-first century. In this model, a documentary film is viewed as having "the full range of

52 Activism

potential impacts on producers, participants, activist organizations, and decision makers" inasmuch as it is "part of a larger process that incorporates both production and distribution."[70] The trilogy's political impacts are also demonstrated by the fact that its three films, particularly *The Murmuring*, were in sync with the national public discourse on military sexual slavery in the early 1990s.[71] They were also allied with the rise of the civil society movement led by the Korean Council in support of the grandmothers who began to demand that the Japanese government officially apologize and make redress, which included their participation in the weekly protests that have been held every Wednesday since 1992 in front of the Japanese Embassy in Seoul. The trilogy's achievement, however, is not limited to publicizing wartime violence and its lingering trauma in the arenas of local and international politics. Byun's self-consciousness on her changing relationship to the grandmothers and her endeavor to incorporate it into her filming of their everyday lives and testimonies enabled the trilogy to be more than a faithful transnational adaptation of Ogawa's lessons. As she writes regarding the production process of the trilogy, "[Ogawa's] subjects are the people whose present lives are of dire importance. So is the present time of my subjects, but it results from their past experiences. . . . He was able to become a farmer himself, but I cannot become a comfort woman. . . . What kind of method do I have?"[72] This reflection allowed the trilogy to implicate in each film's structure the tension between the survivors' "will to proclaim" and their "will to deny."[73] In *The Murmuring*, Byun's camera negotiates between intimacy and distancing to capture the grandmothers' internal conflict between struggling to speak and remember and wanting to keep silent or forget, propelling viewers to mull over the deepness of the intertwined traumas that have long afflicted their bodies and psyches, from sexual assault to the postwar patriarchal suppression on their status after their return. For *Habitual Sadness*, the grandmothers' more friendly attitude toward Byun's team encouraged them to expose their communal lives and their contemplation of life and death in front of her camera. By privileging the camera's on-the-spot observation based on the shifting relationship between filmmaker and subject, and the power of talking heads in place of the expository voice-over or archival images, Byun's filmmaking cultivated the aesthetic and ethical terrains of the local committed documentary.

Two institutional factors, the establishment of the independent film (*tongnip yŏnghwa*) scene and the foundations of film festivals, fed into the three collectives' advancement of the activist tradition in the 1990s into independent documentary. The term "independent film" first appeared in the early 1990s as six film activism collectives dedicated to the production of videos and 8 mm / 16 mm films, including the NFI, organized the Korean

Independent Filmmakers Association (Han'guk tongnip yŏnghwa hyŏp'oe)[74] on January 31, 1990, based on the common spirit that their film practice was made in the "space outside political restriction and the economic subjugation to industrial capital."[75] It was the demise of the 1980s *yŏnghwa undong*, however, that drove the independent film scene's pursuit of the two values and the rise of the term as a slogan for alternative cinema. As Young-a Park aptly observes, "By the mid-1990s, the term . . . had gained currency since all the previous terms used for alternative films, such as *undong yŏnghwa* (activist films), *minjung yŏnghwa* (people's films), and *minjok yŏnghwa* (national films), suddenly seemed antiquated and irrelevant under the new civilian rule in 1994."[76] The economic growth of the Korean film industry from the early 1990 functioned as a challenge to those who had been committed to the 1980s *yŏnghwa undong*. Many members of the collectives, such as Jangsangotmae and the NFI, were recruited by the Chungmuro industry and the conglomerates (chaebol) that became interested in investing film and media, and had their debuts as directors and producers. While their entrance to the mainstream film industry "castrated the activist energy in tandem with the 'apolitical' character of the new generation,"[77] it also coincided with the dramatic growth of local film culture, which included Samsung's support of the two film festivals dedicated to independent films and documentaries, Samsung Short Film Festival (1994–1997) and Seoul Documentary Film and Video Festival (1996–2000).[78] As Kim Myung-joon, a former head of LNP, pinpointed, "The term 'independent film' reflected the identity confusion of many film activists as the time came to an end that they had declared themselves as the subjects of labor visual movement."[79]

Faced with the doubled influence of the industrial capital, namely, the growth of the cinematic public sphere and the assimilation of the dissident forces into the neoliberal autonomy of cultural production, the fights for freedom from state censorship (*kŏmyŏl*) became the only common denominator of independent filmmakers while also contributing to the institutional empowerment of their scene. Independent documentary was at the very heart of the fights. On June 15, 1996, Kim Dong-won was arrested by the police for the reason that Docu Purn's distribution of its videos into its supporters violated the Record and Video Law. Along with this incident, the collective consciousness of independent film professionals was ignited by the Constitutional Court's ruling on October 4, 1996 that the prescreening review (*sajŏn shimŭi*) specified by the provisions of the Motion Picture Promotion Law (Yŏnghwa chinhŭng bŏp) was unconstitutional. Their solidarity for struggle against the state censorship was reflected in the statement of filmmakers whose films were exhibited at the 3rd Samsung Seoul Short Film Festival on November

15, 1996: "We, the short and independent filmmakers participating in this festival, hereby make a strong declaration: we are against any kind of censorship or government intervention that infringes on our freedom to create. This is our right, because the censorship has already been declared unconstitutional by the Constitutional Court."[80] The struggle was intensified with the unauthorized screening of *Red Hunt* (*Redŭ hŏnt'ŭ*, Cho Sung-bong, 1997, 67 min.), a pioneering history documentary that unearths the hitherto untold stories of the victims of the April Third Incident on Jeju Island against the official history that described its cause as a regional communists' riot, at the Second Seoul Human Rights Film Festival in 1997, a festival organized by Sarangbang. Both the festival's head, activist Seo Joon-sik, and Kim Dong-won were arrested for violating the National Security Law and the Record and Video Law.[81] This fueled independent filmmakers' allied protests against censorship while also precipitating their attempt to liberate the Indie Forum (founded in 1996), a co-op festival in which selection and management were in the hands of their representative committee, from the prescreening review.[82] While the tension between the independent film scene and state censorship was not entirely alleviated in the twenty-first century, particularly during the neoconservative regime of President Park Geun-hye, which plotted and applied the "cultural blacklist," the filmmakers' struggles gradually achieved freedom of expression. It was in this context that independent documentary started to form an alternative cinematic public sphere beyond the circulation of small films and videos in non-normative screening spaces, such as communities, labor unions, and universities.

The proliferation of various film festivals since the mid-1990s, as Kim Soyoung perceptively summarizes, came with "the presence of cine-mania, [a] Korean version of cinephilia . . . the enactment of local self-government system . . . [and] the shift of the site of activism from the politico-economic to the cultural."[83] As demonstrated by the cases of the Human Rights Film Festival and the Indie Forum, a number of social organizations and activist groups, encompassing women, gays and lesbians, and labor activists, who reflected the diversification of the post-1987 civil movement, began to launch film festivals as a new public platform for exchanging their issues between the members of their community or with larger audiences. Thanks to these efforts, which also responded to the shift of social activism from the mass protests in the 1980s to the cultural realms of the 1990s, theme-specific film festivals, such as Seoul International Labor Film Festival (1997–2009),[84] Seoul International Women's Film Festival (since 1997), and Queer Films and Videos Festival (since 1998),[85] constituted the local "alternative public spheres/counterpublics where ideas, often-times repressed or ignored in larger contexts, are exchanged and explored."[86] The festivals also functioned as platforms for showcasing the films of Docu Purn and SVC and the labor videos of LNP (including *Labor News*) at a time when they were not commercially released in arthouse theaters.

The Busan International Film Festival (founded in 1996), which is distinguished from the theme-specific festivals by its regionalized programming strategy modeled after the Cannes, Venice, and Berlin festivals, was arguably the most influential to the documentary practitioners mentioned above. Existing works on BIFF in the realm of film festival studies have not given sufficient attention to its "Wide Angle" section devoted to showcasing short films, animation, and documentary films, despite their contribution to explaining the interplay of local politics, cultural policies, film professionals' aspirations, and the governmental drive to globalization.[87] Apart from the kinship between the festival's organizers and the practitioners of the Korean independent film scene,[88] it is worth noting that Wide Angle presented most of the 1990s nonfiction films and videos, including *The Murmuring, Doomealee,* and *A Purple Handkerchief* in its first edition in 1996, and *Red Hunt, Habitual Sadness, On-Line,* and *The Six-Day Fight in Myong-dong Cathedral* in its second in 1997. The exposure of these works to local cinephiles and general audiences, which included screenings, postscreening discussions, media coverage, and awards, legitimized them as documentary films characterized by an institutionalized network of production and exhibition. It also induced their makers to nurture their self-consciousness as more than activist, namely, as *kamdok*.[89] Hong Hyung-sook's recollection encapsulates this point: "Film magazines, arthouse theaters, cinematheques, and film festivals dramatically appeared all at once in the mid-1990s, which was probably the time for Korean documentary to start seeking its identity as cinema. At that time my film was screened at BIFF, and I had a strange experience of having been called as '*kamdok*.'"[90] Again, the impact of BIFF was no less than a shift in the self-identity of the key practitioners. As Nam Inyoung rightly points out, the audiences' increased access to practitioners' films via the festivals and other public platforms (including cable television networks) increased the need to reconcile the films' "internal consolidation" of the activists and community members directly concerned with the film's subject with their "external communicability" to larger audiences."[91] To be sure, this helps to explain the diminishing of didactic or propagandistic narration (characteristic of the activist artifacts in the 1980s) in the films of the late 1990s as symptomatic of their strategies to respond to a wider spectrum of spectators. More than this, I argue that the tension between the two demands was a prelude to the post-activist direction in the twenty-first century, in which both established practitioners

56 Activism

and many younger documentarians have negotiated between their engagement in social movements or issues and the technical, aesthetic, and formal experimentations with documentary modes other than the activist template.

The institutionalization of independent documentary in the 1990s, however, was not without political and ethical contradictions. In 1998, Japanese-Korean (Zainichi) documentarian Yang Yonghi argued that Hong Hyung-sook's *Reclaiming Our Names* (*Ponmyŏng sŏnŏn*, 1998, 70 min.), winner of the Woonpa Award for Best Documentary at the third BIFF, misappropriated nine minutes and forty seconds of footage that she had filmed and used for her own *The Swaying Spirit* (*Yureru kokoro*, 1996), a thirty-minute documentary that she made for Japan's NHK broadcasting network. The two films share the same subject matter, namely, Zainichi students' public declaration of their "Korean" names at Amagasaki High School in Osaka, Japan, and the psychic burdens and social discrimination that they faced as a result of the split between their two identities and names. Yang further claimed that although she helped Hong to produce *Reclaiming Our Names*, including her work as a guide for Hong's visits to the school and its students, Hong had edited the nine minutes and forty seconds of color footage just by converting it to black-and-white as if she had shot the segments by herself. The executive committee of BIFF did not accept Yang's claims, and the independent film scene was supportive of Hong's denial of plagiarism. It was not until 2020 that Yang's claims were confirmed by the apologies of two former members of SVC and a comparative screening of the two films at the Seoul Metropolitan Archives. The event, open to directors, producers, and critics, demonstrated that the school scenes are identical (except for color), and that the only identifiable credit for Yang's work on *Reclaiming Our Names* is "8 mm filming: Yang Yonghi," which does not explicitly acknowledge that the segments originally came from Yang's NHK documentary. Hong's alleged plagiarism stirred the local independent documentary scene to the extent that organizations, including the Association of Korean Independent Film and Video (KIFV), made formal apologies to Yang. Despite the independent film scene's move toward self-reflection, however, legal issues concerning the *Reclaiming Our Names* case remain unresolved: first, although BIFF made a belated official statement in July 2020 that apologizes to Yang and acknowledges Hong's ethical responsibility for the absence of proper acknowledgment of the segments' source and of the appropriate crediting to Yang, it declined her demand that BIFF withdraw the Woonpa Award given to Hong's film, for the reason that the legal prescription applied to it (ten years) has passed;[92] and second, though Hong also made a formal apology to Yang in a statement posted on her social media account in February 2020, she still insists that her use of the segments was not without Yang's permission because she had indicated to Yang her intent and Yang had given her the tapes based on their explicit agreement.[93]

There are two implications of the *Reclaiming Our Names* disputes in 1998 and 2020. First, more than raising the issue of filmmakers' ethics on an individual level, they lay bare the dark sides of the institutional agents that played a crucial role in the elevation of Korean activist nonfiction practices into independent documentary. As Sohye Kim rightly summarizes in her observation of the 1998 dispute, "Most South Korean film institutions supported Hong with the agenda of defending the insecure but important position of Korean independent film."[94] Faced with the first dispute, the jury members of the award concluded that the segments Yang filmed only functioned as "background" in Hong's film,[95] and the people involved in the independent film scene belatedly confirmed in their apologies to Yang that staff members of BIFF did not want the dispute to be problematized as a plagiarism case. Here it can be conjectured that just as BIFF did not want to jeopardize itself by acknowledging Hong's alleged plagiarism that would debase the authority of its award, so did the independent film scene, which was in the middle of establishing its own institutional sustainability, decide to take Hong's side because that acknowledgment would undermine not only her reputation but also its own reputation.[96] This doubled defense of both institutional agents against Yang's claim is also read as not having allowed Zainichi filmmakers such as Yang to be authorized players in Korean cinema, given that her North Korean nationality restricted her entrance to South Korea and her participation in the debate during the first dispute (she acquired her Korean citizenship in 2004).

Second, more significantly, Hong's disavowal of Yang's authorship through the denial of credit for the footage used for *Reclaiming Our Names* is suggested by the film's foregrounding of Hong's first-person voice-over, performed by actress Bang Eun-jin. The film reflected the transition of the identity of veteran nonfiction practitioners from activists to directors, and the use of the voice-over became gradually popular as a device that would guarantee the practitioners' self-consciousness about the filmmaking and the subjects filmed. In her brilliant paper presented at a forum organized by young documentary filmmakers who were concerned with the ethical issues raised by the second dispute between Hong and Yang, Kim Dong-ryung offers a lucid comparative analysis of the first-person voices in the two films in regard to the difference in each director's relationship to the Zainichi students. Whereas Yang's voice-over is deployed to invite viewers to observe the students' activities and emotions through her doubled subjective position, both as documentarian and Zainichi, Hong's narration does not fully penetrate her subjects

58 Activism

and therefore ends up with a self-indulging confirmation of herself as self-reflexive director. Based on this, Kim concludes that "a documentarian's ethics of production is inseparable from his or her aesthetic choices" and that Hong's film "betrays or at least is far from what its first-person narration tells [us it is]."[97]

In retrospect, the *Reclaiming Our Names* controversy implies that twenty-first-century Korean documentary cinema had to grapple with two tasks: first, as the platforms for films and videos became diversified in film festivals and commercial movie theaters, documentarians had to negotiate this institutional change, first, with their dual obligations to address the social subjects and activists directly concerned with particular sociopolitical issues and to communicate the issues to larger audiences marked by the expectation about what documentary films could be; and, second, while Hong's offense against Yang deserves ethical condemnation, her reliance on first-person narration in *Reclaiming Our Names* suggests that documentarians' self-consciousness propelled their experimentations with a diverse array of documentary modes other than the activist tradition's documentation of *hyŏnjang* that is assimilated into the discourse of persuading or agitating *minjung*.

The Year 1999: Into the Twenty-First Century

The last year of the 1990s witnessed two important activist documentaries. *Dandelion* (*Mindŭlle*, Kyung-soon and ChoiHa Dong-ha, 1999, 60 min.) features the Korean Association of Bereaved Families for Democracy (KABFD, Minjuhwa shilch'ŏn gajok undong hyŏbŭihoe), a human rights organization founded in 1986 by the family members of those who died in the national social movements in the 1970s and 1980s, including the mothers of martyrs (*yŏlsa*) Jeon Tae-il (a sewing worker and pioneering labor activist who self-immolated in 1970) and Lee Han-yeol (who was dead by the attack of a tear gas grenade on June 9, 1987, which ignited the June Democratic Struggle). Unlike the agitational or enlightening third-person narration that serves as a discursive nodal point of 1980s activist films and videos, the two directors privilege on-the-spot, verité-style records of members' struggles to solicit the Kim Dae-jung government's effort to enact the Special Act to Find the Truth on Suspicious Deaths; of their growing solidarity and collective consciousness through sit-ins in front of the National Assembly and other public spaces; and of the deep-seated sorrow and pain that they long preserved. A brief scene where a mother begins to cry, shot in a continuous take by a handheld camera and brief blurring, consolidates the two directors' sympathy with—and their respectful ethical distance from—her. This kind of scene, which testifies to the directors' intimate interaction with social actors, constitutes the bereaved families as more than victims, namely, as social movement activists, stimulating viewers' empathic identification with them as parents who lost their child, and linking their personal feelings and demands to larger social issues regarding state violence and human rights. The film won several awards at local and international film festivals and was later aired on TV, serving as a catalyst for passage of the Special Act on January 15, 2000.

Byun's *My Own Breathing*, by contrast, predated the "personal turn" of the early 2000s by positioning grandmother Lee Yong-soo as a surrogate interviewer with other former comfort women in the first part of the film, and by performing as interlocutor in her conversation with grandmother Kim Yun-shim and her deaf daughter in the second part. As Byun herself has remarked, these two modes stemmed from her authorial exploration of "what kind of documentary filmmaking method I have" given that "no matter how close my camera gets to the ladies, it cannot be their eyes."[98] The status of Lee Yong-soo, who sits side by side with other grandmothers and listens to their testimonies, exchanging her own experience, reflects Byun's perspective on the egalitarian relationship of the female subjects who were repressed and silenced themselves. As Hwang Miyojo rightly points out, Lee's embodiment of the position of the interviewer in place of Byun indicates that the comfort women "start to stand in front of the camera with their understanding of the power of film as a media of representation, as well as of the politics of representation."[99] The elongated conversation sequence in the second part (figure 1.2), then, inscribes Byun's ethical self-consciousness of her relationship with Kim and her daughter. During her interview with Kim, who kept her wartime experience of sexual slavery secret from her daughter (she was born with cerebral palsy because of that experience), it is revealed that the daughter already knew about it. The three phases of camera movement, first looking at the two in confusion, then zooming in on the daughter, and then zooming back to Kim's profile, render the conversation a reality mediated by Byun's ethical and embodied responses to this unexpected revelation: first, astonishment at the dissolution of the hierarchy of knowledge between the director and her subject, second, her temporary hesitancy to determine how much she will let mother and daughter speak, and, finally, her decision to make visible their bodies and their continued testimonies as that which elicits viewers' engagement and understanding.

The two films prefigured the dialectic of change and inheritance that would be demonstrated by the twenty-first-century activist documentaries that we will investigate in chapters 2 and 3. Both present three values of the

Figure 1.2 *My Own Breathing* (Byun Young-joo, 1999)

independent documentary that was formulated in the 1990s—namely, *chinbo* as an ideology that advocates human rights and equity, *ilsang* of the bereaved families and comfort women, and *kaein* as their identity inseparable from their collective social agency. While *Dandelion*'s alliance with KABFD pertains to the activist tradition's continual project of engaging social movements, Byun's self-reflexive inscription of herself as filmmaker-I and her embrace of grandmother Lee as an interlocutor in *My Own Breathing* attest to formal and representational strategies that were not familiar in the tradition but became popular in the twenty-first century in both activist and post-activist documentaries: strategies derived from directors' reflection on their relationship to social actors. The directors' self-consciousness has enabled many activist documentaries during the last two decades to update the tradition's aesthetics and politics.

2
Twenty-First-Century Activist Documentaries

Three Traditional Issues

Introduction

This chapter illuminates the succession and innovation of the activist tradition by discussing twenty-first-century social change documentaries that take as their subject three social problems that the early activists and their collectives engaged in dialogue with during the mass demonstrations in the 1980s and the new civil movements in the 1990s: state and ideological violence, labor issues, and disenfranchised subjects. The political regime change from the liberal governments of Presidents Kim Dae-jung and Roh Moo-hyun and the right-wing administrations of Presidents Lee Myung-bak and Park Geun-hye, as well as the economic and societal neoliberalization that was applied to both, has both maintained and transformed these three problems: social movements advocating for the human rights of political victims in Cold War politics and military dictatorship were refracted through the liberal governments' support for truth-finding (*jinsang gyumyŏng*) and reforming history and the neoconservative governments' maneuvers for stigmatizing progressive parties as pro-North (*chongbuk*) groups; the neoliberal restructuring of the labor market in the twenty-first century has enabled irregular workers (*pijŏnggyujik nodongja*) to resist job insecurity, mass dismissal, and industrial hazards; besides the social movements for the urban poor and the disabled, twenty-first-century Korean society has witnessed rights-claiming actions of new marginalized subjects, including small business owners as victims of urban gentrification and the activists for animal rights, who were not included in the democracy movement of the past. As I demonstrate below, the documentarians who addressed these three problems have advanced the activist tradition in two directions: first, while sometimes being directly aligned with the social movements and explicitly promoting social solidarity, many documentarians, including such veterans

Activism and Post-activism. Jihoon Kim, Oxford University Press. © Oxford University Press 2024.
DOI: 10.1093/oso/9780197760413.003.0003

62 Activism

as Kim Dong-won and Hong Hyung-sook, have tended to focus on each of the subjects as individual (*kaein*) rather than audiovisually constructing them as *minjung*. Second, the documentarians' growing self-consciousness of their identity as individual *kamdok*, of their relationship to the social actors, and of the documentary modes available to them has resulted in different ways of telling stories (including ethnography, experimental diary film, and observational documentary) than practiced by the enlightenment discourse of the 1980s activism, and of investigating the aspects of reality that were not noticed by the activist precursors, such as the mechanisms of the union and workplace themselves, the culture of the urban poor, the senses of disabilities, and animality.

State and Ideological Violence: *jinsang gyumyŏng* and *chongbuk*

A notable social movement that has continued since the beginning of the twenty-first century is one that investigates human rights violations during the Cold War period and authoritarian regimes. In 2000, the Kim Dae-jung government established the National Committee for Investigating the Truth about the Jeju April Third Incident (see chapter 5 for the incident) and Recovering the Honor of the Victims, inaugurating the Presidential Truth Commission on Suspicious Deaths (PTCSD: Ŭimunsa jinsang gyumyŏng wiwŏnhoe).[1] Although the PTCSD was active until June 30, 2004, it contributed to shaping the social atmosphere for collective efforts to find the truth of suspicious or innocent deaths caused by state and military power. Indeed, what was key to this was not only the political leaders who considered truth-finding and the reconciliation with Korea's ideologically contested past to be a stepping stone for human rights and justice. As Hun Joon Kim demonstrates regarding the National Committee for the April Third Incident, the "strong and persistent local activism, driven by local students and scholars, social movement activists, and journalists, was the single most important factor in the establishment of the commission."[2] *What Do People Live For* (*Saramŭn muŏsŭro sanŭnga*, Kyung-soon, 2004, 112 min.) testifies to the vibrancy of these actors as it follows the activities of the PTCSD. By tracking these activities across the Korean Peninsula, the film provides a glimpse of diverse social sectors—factories, universities, and troops—influenced by the state violence and ideological or political repression of the past. The interviews with the local activists, journalists, and historians who were involved in the activities serve to persuade viewers that finding the truth about the deaths and restoring the impaired reputation of the victims should be recognized as a crucial political issue of the present. This political climate of *jinsang gyumyŏng* in the twenty-first century has led to two trends of activist or social change documentaries that engage the social movements for advocating the rights and memory of the people affected by state and ideological violence.

The first trend is history documentary. Besides its advocacy for the social movements, it has also been motivated by its directors, who aspired to revisit cases of state-led violence and its victims or to construct a collective history of the ordinary people who survived or resisted the political and ideological turbulences of postliberation Korea. As the filmmaker who prefigured this tendency in the mid-1990s in Docu Purn, Kim Tae-il made *April 9* (*4wŏl 9il*, 2000, 125 min.), a film that constitutes a historical account of the People's Revolutionary Party Incident (Inmin hyŏngmyŏng dang sagŏn) in 1975, one of the most egregious cases of "juridical murder" (*sabŏp sarin*)[3] during Park Chung-hee's authoritarian regime, in which eight men were executed within thirty-six hours of indictment for violating the National Security Law and for plotting to overthrow the government. While documenting the sit-ins of the bereaved families of the victims designed to spur reinvestigating the case and reclaiming the men's honor, the film weaves testimonies of the families, accounts of progressive historians and activists, and a rich array of archival films and photos to provide an alternative historiography of the incident: the regime's fabrication of the incident as a spy case, the victims' pursuit of a better society, the families' devastated lives, and the National Security Law that still silences them, all function to counter the conservative view of stigmatizing the victims as communists.[4] *Forgotten Warriors* (*It'yŏjin yŏjŏnsa*, Kim Jin-yeol, 2004, 99 min.) portrays several grandmothers who were POWs, partisans during the Korean War who had been sentenced to imprisonment and who were still participating in social and labor movements (including their alliance with the nonconformist long-term prisoners), establishing them as both political activists and women who fought against the patriarchal norms of modern Korea. Guiding viewers through the grandmothers' past and present life, and contextualizing it chronologically with footage of the Korean War, Kim's voice-over expresses her changing relationship with one of the grandmothers, Park Soon-ja, including Park's initial discomfort with Kim's camera, and the director's sympathy with and admiration for their tenacious faith and desire for national unification.[5] If *April 9* represents a tendency of independent documentaries that engage history, namely, a historiography that rewrites a historical event that was distorted in its official version, or omitted altogether, Kim's emphasis on the rich layers of the personal testimonies by the female political subjects in *Forgotten Warriors* emblematizes

64 Activism

another tendency, one that aims to constitute microhistories of individual subjects, with their experiences, perspectives, and memories.

The second trend is investigative documentary. *The Gate of Truth* (*Chinshirŭi mun*, Kim Hee-chul, 2004, 105 min.) paved the way for that subgenre while also pioneering an approach that would flourish in the 2010s, one that treats various materials as objects of interrogation and recombination in ways that seek an alternative to the primacy of on-the-spot records as evidence of truth. The film reconstructs the mysterious case of a South Korean Army officer Kim Hoon, who was found dead inside an underground military outpost in the Joint Security Area in February 1998. The army concluded that Kim had committed suicide, but his father (a retired lieutenant general) and the civil society demanded the army to reinvestigate the case, suggesting that he might have been murdered because he had no obvious motive for suicide. Along with interviews with the attorney of Kim's bereaved family and the investigator from the PTCSD, the film recycles a variety of audiovisual materials, including CCTV footage of the scene, photo documentation, and video records of the forum in which forensic doctors examined and discussed the cause of Kim's death, which the director received from the family and the Korean Catholic Human Rights Committee. Without expository or persuasive commentary, the director's careful editing of the materials plays a key role in mobilizing the film's powerful rhetoric that exposes the Ministry of National Defense's infringement of human rights, its reluctance to reveal photographic evidence of the scene, its ignorance of the evidence that refutes the determination of suicide, the logical fallacy of the doctors who supported that conclusion at the forum, and the hypothesis that the US armed forces in Korea may have covered up the truth of the case. It is in this way that *Gate of Truth* prefigured the epistemological ground of post-activist documentaries, in that it asserts the kind of truth inaccessible with the camera's observation and recording of reality as *hyŏnjang*. Coupled with its narrative evocative of crime thrillers, the film's investigative collection and rearrangement of the materials expands the aesthetic and representational possibility of activist documentaries that engage with political incidents and their victims.[6]

Investigative documentaries of the 2010, too, have revisited cases of state and ideological violence, unveiling previously known truths and collecting the testimonies of victims and witnesses. *Red Tomb* (*Redŭ t'um*, Goo Ja-hwan, 2013, 92 min.) uncovers the hidden details of the National Guidance League Massacre (Podoyŏnmaeng haksal) in the summer of 1950, in which around ten thousand people were executed on suspicion of supporting communists during the early stages of the Korean War. By compiling a dense array of interviews with the families and neighbors of the massacre's victims, the film supports Kim Dong-choon's evaluation of the incident as emblematizing the "frantic anti-communism" of the Rhee Syngman government that drove it to execute "civilians and political prisoners suspected of opposing or posing a threat to the ROK."[7] *Land of Sorrow* (*Sŏsan'gaechŏktan*, 2018, 76 min.), directed by journalist documentarian Lee Jo-hoon, tells the story of the people who were kidnapped for forced labor in a camp in the coastal Seosan district to the southwest of Seoul during the Park Chung-hee regime. This correctional facility, in which about 1,770 inmates were made to work without payment on the district's land reclamation projects, was part of the Park government's disciplinary control of the Korean population through its social exclusion of vagabonds and the poor. Unlike other history documentaries that employ archival images to support the testimonies of social actors, the film uses footage from *Daehan News* to reveal and deconstruct the Park government's propagandistic campaign concerning the labor camps. The footage's persuasive debunking of the Park myth as the national hero of Korea's dramatic economic growth is strengthened by the testimonies of a dozen of former workers still living in the village about their poor living conditions and economic debts, and by the director's investigation of a US congressman's confidential report to demonstrate that the subsidies and salaries that should have been paid to the laborers were misused by the ruling Democratic Republican Party (Minju gonghwa dang) for its election campaign fund. Blending interviews and archival footage with dramatized reenactment sequences and drone-view images of the village, *Land of Sorrow*, with its high-quality cinematic representation, supports the petition by the survivors who demand the government reinvestigate the labor exploitation and the misuse of funds and apologize for them.

As Gi-wook Shin and Paik Nak-chung have demonstrated, anticommunism (*pan'gongjuŭi*) served as a ruling ideology that maintained the political hegemony of military governments during the Cold War.[8] In the words of Kim Dong-choon, modern Korea's governments relied on "war politics" (*chŏnjaeng jŏngch'i*), a politics of universalizing war in the public and private sectors with the result of establishing the segregation between "us" and the "enemy," and it still operates on the ideological, legal, and political levels despite democratization.[9] The authoritarian military regimes exerted their application of the National Security Law to suppress the democratization and labor movements and to stigmatize people and intellectuals devoted to them as dissidents. While the law has influenced the legal, political, and psychic dimensions of Korean society even in the transition to the postauthoritarian regime, twenty-first-century Korea has witnessed the shift from *pan'gong* to *chongbuk* or *chwap'a* (proleftist) ideology as a catchword that has proliferated

66 Activism

in the public sphere during both the liberal democracy regimes of Presidents Kim Dae-jung and Roh Moo-hyun and the neoconservative governments of Presidents Lee Myung-bak and Park Geun-hye. In this political and ideological context, twenty-first-century documentaries raise the awareness of human rights of the individual subjects whose faith and freedom are suppressed by *chongbuk* ideology.

Kim Dong-won's *Repatriation* (*Songhwan*, 2003, 149 min.) garnered critical accolades for linking his subjectivity to the political and ethical complexity of representing the subjects associated with *pan'gong* and *chongbuk* ideologies. The film was based on Kim's twelve-year recording of two POWs, Kim Seak-hyoung and Cho Chang-son, as unconverted long-term prisoners (*pijŏnhyang changgisu*) who were released in the spring of 1992. As Kim remarks in the middle of the film, editing the footage into a full-fledged documentary was motivated by his activist solidary with the humanitarian and unification movements for sending *pijŏnhyang changgisu* to North Korea, respecting their ideological beliefs and human rights and promoting North-South unification after the inter-Korean summit between Kim Jong-il and President Kim Dae-jung in 2000. Despite this activist context, however, Kim's voice-over resists the didactic tone of his previous films on evictees in the 1990s, instead presenting a multiplicity of self-reflexive attitudes: toward the film's production process and its thematic direction, toward the two POWs and other ex-prisoners who maintain their ideological convictions as integral to their dignity, and toward his knowledge of anticommunist ideology. As a result, the film does more than reveal the prisoners' politically and legally liminal position, and how their choices were affected by anticommunist state violence and torture linked to South Korea's shifting relationship to the North throughout the authoritarian regimes of the 1970s and 1980s. The film's rich and multifaceted portrayal of the psychic, political, and historical dimensions embodied by the prisoners is undoubtedly ascribed to its presentation of Kim's subjectivity, which acknowledges its production as a kind of learning processes. These processes include Kim's awareness of how his assumptions about North Korea were structured by South Korea's anticommunist pedagogy and media representations, his study of the ideological conversion system (*sasang chŏnhyang jedo*) that was applied to political prisoners (POWs and spies from North Korea) during the Cold War, his confession about the tediousness of gradually gaining reciprocal understanding in his filming of the two protagonists,[10] and his unfamiliar feelings when they praise North Korea's superior ideology and social system. Relying upon Bill Nichols's taxonomy of documentary modes, Hye Seung Chung and David Scott Diffrient classify *Repatriation* as a participatory documentary that "involve[s] the ethics and politics of encounter."[11] This approach, however, is not capable of pinpointing the ways in which Kim's political and ethical reflection in the film achieves a notable leap from the participatory mode that the traditional activism of Korean independent documentary developed in the 1990s. Instead, I agree with Markus Nornes's characterization of the film as an alternative to the traditional activist mode in that it is based on the "modality of documentary that anchors representations of the world in the subjective positionality of the filmmaker."[12] This modality is also indebted to Kim's maturing self-identity, from activist to filmmaker. A wide variety of materials (news clips, newspaper articles, footage from anticommunist Korean movies and dramas, photos of spy incidents during the Park regime) position Kim's personal reflection within Korea's larger historical, cultural, and political contexts, and Kim's digital visual effects convey his subjective understanding of their meanings, including the wave effect of the photos.

The most critically acclaimed and best-known activist documentaries that engage with the lingering effects of *chongbuk* ideology and its violation of human rights are Hong Hyung-sook's *The Border City* (*Kyŏnggye doshi*, 2002, 80 min.), *The Border City 2* (*Kyŏnggye doshi 2*, 2009, 104 min.), two films that portray Song Du-yul, a professor of philosophy and sociology at the University of Münster, Germany, who has been a political exile after his participation in antidictatorship activities in 1974, having visited North Korea eighteen times, following his political convictions and hoping to serve as a bridge between the two Koreas. The first *Border City* focuses on Song's life in Berlin, including his preparation for a return to South Korea promoted by an association of progressive scholars and civil society members who wanted to publicize his political thoughts in opposition to his stigmatization as a "pro–North Korean scholar." Hong's observational camera reveals how the requirement by the National Intelligence Service (NIS: Kukka jŏngbowŏn) that Song endorse the law-abiding covenant (*chunbŏp sŏyaksŏ*) has frustrated his return, and their conversations imply that his refusal to do so is linked to his freedom of thought, and to the violence of the National Security Law that represses it. While Hong's cinematography and Song's testimony establish him as a diasporic exile who shuffles between his dislocated life and his longing for home, her first-person voice-over signifies her perspective on the meanings of "border" that center around his liminal presence and the persistence of anticommunism in South Korea. This perspective is supplemented by Hong's multiple formal maneuvers: first, the evocative soundtrack by composer Yoon Isang, who did not return home after his antidictatorship activities; second, a rich collection of photos and footage associated with Song's activities in Germany and North Korea and the history of post–World War

68 Activism

II Germany, from division to the demolition of the Berlin Wall; and finally, cinematographic techniques and editing strategies that express Song's liminal status and Hong's personal reflections on the meanings of borders, including the slow-motion effects applied to the images that frame Berlin's landscapes and the remainders of the Wall. Hong's self-reflexive presence in the film's construction of reality is further stressed in her two attempts to associate Song's position with her personal experience. First, the film's candid camera scenes, in which officials from the NIS pressed staff on abiding by the National Security Law, allude to the official surveillance that has long monitored Song's activities in Berlin. Second, Hong's own return from Berlin after realizing her pregnancy during her location shooting supplements Song's masculine nostalgia for home, in tandem with the confession by his wife who compares Korea to the domestic space. It is thanks to all these expressive and self-reflexive devices that the film testifies to the evolution of Hong's work from nonfiction artifact to activist documentary film composed with cinematic craft and creativity.

The Border City 2, which tracks the political and ideological turmoil of Korean society after Song's return in 2003, likens Hong's self-reflexive presence to her political and ethical dilemmas. Hong's narration not only provides an anticommunist discursive network of the authorities and the press, which conclude Song is actually Kim Cheol-soo, an executive of Workers' Party of Korea (WPK, Chosŏn nodong dang), but also exposes her growing confusion about his identity as well as her fluctuation between trust and distrust ("whether or not Song is Kim Cheol-soo"). This personal dimension is extended into the film's poignant address to the public, as her voice-over articulates a vexing ideological question posed by Song's return to Korean society ("To South Korea, North Korea is a contradiction in itself: an other that is an enemy and at the same time is not"). It is also associated with Hong's ethical dilemma between her obligation to make Song's voice heard and her respect for his privacy, as the camera stares at Hong's face with his eyes closed in silence (figure 2.1), zooming in and out during her conversation with him after his interrogation by the Prosecution Service. By restricting Hong's self-reflexive presence to the ideological and ethical perspectives on the liminal subject, *The Border City 2* lays bare the enormous social influences that Song's presence had on South Korea, including the ideological conflict between the conservative and progressive parties, and the internal schism of the latter, which is encapsulated by a seven-minute, fixed-camera take in which Song, his attorneys, and his supporting group have a heated discussion on whether he should apologize at a press conference for having joined the WPK. Hong's narration after the conference, then, offers a keen summary of what made him

Figure 2.1 *The Border City 2* (Hong Hyung-sook, 2009)

convert his beliefs: "He surrendered in front of the history of division, of the National Security Law, of the ideology that forces him to choose left or right, of the power struggle between the progressive and the conservative, and of the madness of the press subject to vested rights."[13]

The neoconservative regime spanning the governments of Presidents Lee and Park proliferated the rhetoric of *chongbuk*, using it to stifle dissent and criticism. In particular, the NIS in the Park government insinuated *chongbuk* politics to "stigmatize and suppress progressive political forces."[14] In the political backlash after the liberal presidency of Roh Moo-hyun, activist documentaries in the 2010s engaged the impacts of *chongbuk* on individuals and social movement sectors with their two traditional tools, on-the-spot records and interviews. *Killing Alice* (*Aellisŭ chugigi*, Kim Sang-kyu, 2017, 81 min.) inherits Hong's attention to Professor Song's case as it tracks Shin Eun-mi, a Korean-American woman who gave public talks in South Korea in 2014 and 2015 based on her travels to North Korea. Documenting the events that the right-wing press labeled "*chongbuk* talk concerts," the film adopts the observational mode to portray how Shin's life in South Korea was under threat from *chongbuk* ideology, focusing on backlash among members of far-right organizations who called her a "pro-North spy." The use of social media images, news clips, and stop-motion effects help to attenuate and satirize the oppressive power of the red complex, while the free-floating, handheld camera gives proximate access to Shin's affective responses to the situation and the Park Geun-hye government's decision to deport her for praising North Korea. *Patriot Game 2: To Call a Deer a Horse* (*Aegukcha keim 2: Chirogwima*, Kyungsoon, 2019, 97 min.) revisits the Constitutional Court's 2014 order dissolving the Unified Progressive Party (UPP: T'onghap chinbo dang), a political verdict resulting from the NIS's prosecution of the UPP's left-nationalist lawmaker Lee Seok-ki for plotting an armed rebellion and violating the National Security Law based on a transcript of meetings held by Lee and his associates. In the words of Gi-wook Shin and Rennie J. Moon, in this political incident the Park administration "accused this small leftist formation of threatening national security via activities meant to support communist North Korea, including planned sabotage in the event of war."[15] Kyung-soon holds a series of roundtable conversations with five groups, lawyers, journalists, human rights activists, the convicted, and former UPP lawmakers, to construct multiple yet interrelated perspectives on the incident that testify to the neoconservative government's maneuvers to limit freedom of thought and expression. These perspectives encompass the journalists' account of how the press coverage of the incident was ideologically biased, the activists' views on how the UPP posed political dilemmas to the progressive bloc, and the lawyers' revelation of the problems in the juridical process of the case. More than a monotonous collection of interviews and testimonies, the conversation format becomes a refreshed representational strategy of the activist documentaries that take one of the traditional social issues—in this case, state and ideological violence—as their subject. For the format reveals not only the persistence of Cold War ideology even after the transition to a postauthoritarian society but also the internal complexity and contradictions of the political and social movement players who largely share ideals of democracy and progressive values.

Labor Issues: Beyond Documenting the Mass Struggle

In the late 1990s, the labor movements led by unions that belong to the Korean Confederation of Trade Unions (KCTU: Chŏn'guk minju nodong johap ch'ongyŏnmaeng, established in 1995) targeted the industrial restructuring and flexible labor relations that both the government and business circles aggressively implemented in the name of coping with the IMF crisis. Besides higher wages and better working conditions that the labor movement until the mid-1990s had demanded, labor struggles during the crisis aimed to stop the restructuring, which included the privatization (*minyŏnghwa*) of state-owned companies and services, outsourcing, and overseas relocation.[16] Since the early twenty-first century, labor activists have been faced with an increase in nonregular workers, which was caused by a highly stratified and deregulated labor market in the neoliberal economy. Unlike the relatively homogeneous group of workers that the mass labor movement in the late 1980s and 1990s had intended to enlighten and consolidate, Korean workers in the twenty-first century have been highly diversified in terms of labor time, salary, employment status, and so on, being divided into regular and nonregular workers. This division entailed a bifurcation of labor rights claims and movements, which Yoonkyung Lee has summarized: "The central concern for full-time workers is the right to work or employment security against massive layoffs and factory closings, whereas the key issues for non-regular workers and misclassified workers are the recognition of worker status and conversion into regular employment."[17] These two directions largely correspond to the two situations of labor movements in the twenty-first century. First, the growing awareness of the issues of irregular workers led to the formation of unions across different industries and occupations and the transition of workers' strategies, from militant strikes to sit-in protests during the governments of Presidents Kim Dae-jung and Roh Moo-hyun. Second, the neoliberal flexibilization of labor and the weakening of unions through pro-company unions, hired gangs, bullying, and lawsuits placed labor movements and the lives of workers in jeopardy under the institutional overlook of the neoconservative regime in the late 2000s. Even regular workers in Ssangyong Automobile, Hanjin Heavy Industry, and Cort-Cortech Guitar, to name just a few, staged prolonged protests against layoffs as these employers cut jobs and closed factories after the sale of firms to foreign capital. Engaging the two situations, documentarians and media activists have enriched the tradition of labor documentaries, resulting in two achievements: first, some collectives and filmmakers have updated their strategies of documenting workers' fights and distributing their films; and second, others have shifted the representational and thematic focus from large-scale unions' mass struggles to the issues of irregular workers (such as their precarious employment status and working conditions), the internal dynamics of labor unions, the details of work and workplaces, and the personality of the workers as *kaein*. The last theme is represented by a recent documentary *Sister J* (*Chaech'unŏnni*, 2020, 97 min.) directed by Lee Soo-jung, a former member of the NFI (see chapter 1). While documenting the thirteen-year struggle for reinstatement, from 2006 to 2019, by dismissed workers at

72 Activism

Cort-Cortech Guitar, the film focuses on the growth of Im Jae-choon (1962–2022) from an introverted ordinary worker to an activist who played a role on the theatrical stages in productions dramatizing the experiences of the workers, composed and sang folk songs about his experiences, and wrote a journal about his protests. Building on a participatory mode, Lee employs black-and-white cinematography and the standard aspect ratio (4:3) so that Im's thirteen-year fight is evocative of scenes from a silent film. Thus, these aesthetic devices are read as a way that a former member of the 1980s film movement negotiates the tastes of a wider audience while also refueling the activist tradition's support for the marginalized.

Labor News Production, which is still active, expanded its format for alternative nonfiction production at the turn of the twenty-first century from newsreels to short-length videos on current affairs (*chŏngse*), education (*kyoyuk*), and agitprop (*sŏndong*) programs. These three forms aimed to organize and educate members about labor union activities on the street or in workplaces, by means of community screenings and within-the-firm broadcasting networks.[18] Besides inheriting the strategies of militant cinema to promptly respond to the battlefields of everyday labor and struggles, maintaining the collective modes of production, and updating the alternative modes of distribution, these short videos originated from LNP's two demands for doing more than documenting and publicizing an on-the-spot record of labor struggles: first, increasing laborers' media literacy and their access to media technology, because these forms were used to train workers how to shoot and edit, so that they were able to have their media units record their struggle and edit their videos digitally; and second, diversification of distribution channels in response to the technical changes of platforms and infrastructures for alternative media practice and to social issues related to the precarious conditions of labor in the neoliberalized Korean society. concerning the first demand, LNP has produced numerous reportages, educational and propaganda films, and a four-part documentary, *A Hundred-Year Record of the History of Labor Movements in Korea* (*Nodongja yŏksa, paengnyŏnŭi kirok*, 2013, 237 min.). For the second demand, it has adopted networked digital platforms from jinbo.net, an alternative web hosting service founded in 1998 in reaction to the corporate monopoly over the internet and cybercensorship, to YouTube, with about fifty videos uploaded on its channel. Meeting these two demands, LNP's recent educational shorts are characterized by its wide-ranging embrace of digital imaging and postproduction. For instance, *I Am Kim Yong-kyun* (*Naega Kim Yonggyunida*, 2018, 11 min.) employs a wide variety of photos, infographics, and data visualizations to raise public awareness of high-risk workers. Kim Yong-kyun is a twenty-four-year-old worker and labor activist who was killed at a thermal power plant after being sucked onto a coal conveyor belt in December 2018. Responding to Kim's death, which aroused nationwide attention to the danger of subcontracted workers and contractors' lack of responsibility for increased deaths at their sites, the film digitally updates the tradition from the late 1980s of montage that LNP began to apply for agitational and consciousness-raising purposes. The film's title refers to the slogan on the banners held by protesters who showed solidarity with Kim at his funeral and at public demonstrations demanding legislation to alleviate the danger faced by such workers. The struggle led to passage of the Severe Workplace Disaster Punishment Law (Chungdae jaehae giŏp chŏbŏl bŏp) in January 2021.

These various attempts, however, did not mean that LNP abandoned full-fledged documentaries on labor movements. *On the Right Track: First Episode* (*Chŏllo wiŭi saramdŭl: Chŏk pŏntchae iyagi*, Lee Ji-young, 2001, 75 min.) constructs a powerful story about the seventeen-month struggle to establish a rail workers union when the government attempted to privatize Korail to promote deregulation of employment in the neoliberalized corporate economy. Unlike LNP's newsreels in the late 1980s and 1990s, the film refrains from a didactic or agitational voice-over and instead presents intimate conversations with those engaging in activities, such as interrupting meetings of the pro-company union (*ŏyong nojo*), fighting against the private gangsters hired by Korail, and making collective efforts to assist the election campaign of the candidate preferred by laborers. Lee's aspirations to "convey voices of *hyŏnjang* and present interviews as lived voices"[19] led to the film's stance opposing neoliberal capitalism, which is encapsulated in speeches by rail union representatives at the sites of the protests. Several montage sequences in the film, including the finale where protest footage is superimposed on images of a train running along a track, successfully create two key effects of political and social change documentary, that is, "amplifying movements" of the union and "creating coalitions"[20] between its leaders and members. With these effects, the film not only creates a powerful story about a rare triumph by laborers in struggle, but also offers a persuasive, antistate audiovisual discourse that counters the neoliberal flexibilization of labor markets. Apart from this film, LNP has also functioned to nurture filmmakers committed to activist engagement with labor issues and other social problems. After joining LNP in 1995, Tae Joon-sik transplanted to it the one-person production system in which he played the roles of director, cinematographer, and editor, making a series of labor documentaries such as *Days of Human* (*In'ganŭi shigan*, 2000, 116 min.), a record of the 450-day antirestructuring struggle by workers at Hyundai Heavy Industries, and *The War Waged by You and Me* (*Tangshin'gwa*

74 Activism

naŭi chŏnjaeng, 2010, 85 min.), which chronicles the seventy-seven-day strike by workers at Ssangyong Motors.

Kim Mi-rye, a member of Docu Purn, is one of the most remarkable filmmakers committed to documentaries about labor problems and struggles related to irregular workers. Her film *Nogada* (*Nogada*, 2005, 89 min.) investigates labor conditions experienced by daily construction workers. Starting with an intimate portrayal of her father, a construction worker who was still migrating from one site to another and waiting for an opportunity, the film contextualizes Kim's personal gaze at him within both historical and transnational perspectives rather than changing its mode to autobiographical or first-person documentary. As its title, a derivative from Japanese *dokata* (土方), explicitly indicates, the film rigorously develops a postcolonial diagnosis of the inequalities and contradictions experienced by temporary construction workers, which result from the subcontracting (*hachŏng*) relations that were transplanted from Japan during the Occupation period. This system, which applied to many industrial sectors in Korea after its liberation, including automobile and electronics industries, has been a key structural cause of labor conflicts and struggles. For its contradictory interdependence between an original contractor and its subcontractors has led to overdue wages (for instance, when a subcontractor evades responsibility for paying its workers when the original contractor goes bankrupt), devastating exploitation of labor conditions (for example, a subcontractor forces laborers to work overtime to meet the demand of its original contractor while not offering them welfare, health facilities, or job security in workplaces), and industrial accidents. With its verité-style proximity and vividness, Kim's camera attends to all these scenes of labor injustice and precarity in various construction sites, such as deteriorated restrooms and lockers, a worker being hospitalized due to an accident, and workers' occupation of the office of a subcontractor to protest their overdue wages. These scenes are sometimes connected to Kim's portrayal of her father, as the scenes of the workers' struggle against overdue wages are preceded by his oral testimony about how many times he received his pay late or not at all. More significantly, they are extended into Kim's visits to Osaka, through which she documents the rich history of how the unions representing construction workers have improved their labor conditions by gradually achieving unemployment allowances, senior employment, and mandatory safety education. In so doing, Kim builds a transnational solidarity between the precarious workers in both countries while also realizing political documentary's potential for "speaking for the marginalized, identifying problems, and making arguments for social change."[21]

Stayed Out Overnight (*Oebak*, 2009, 73 min.) shifts Kim's interest in the labor conditions for temporary workers to her long-term participatory documentation of the struggle against the massive layoffs of low-paid female retail and supermarket cashiers and sales assistants by E-land Group in 2007. The 510-day struggle, which involved a 21-day occupation of the company's branch store, raised nationwide awareness of the issues faced by female nonregular workers in the increased flexibility of the labor market, including the economic and gender restraints that doubly bind them.[22] As Jennifer Jihye Chun describes, "The physical space of the union occupation of the E-Land Homever store mirrored a battle zone. . . . Inside the store, union members were camped out on mats next to the row of locked-down cash registers at the front of the store."[23] This description finds its cinematic equivalent in the three-minute long take at the film's opening, in which the camera's horizontal tracking from right to left captures the row of the workers who are sleeping between the store's checkout stands at night. While chronicling the process of the occupation and its termination by the police, Kim's camera and voice-over commentary convey the women's growing class consciousness and their sense of communal solidarity.[24] At the same time, the film offers a broader perspective on the workers' struggle beyond the assumption that it manifests their liberation. Kim places the struggle within the growing media attention and the interventions of the company's general union and the progressive parties, including the Democratic Labor Party (Minju nodong dang) as the result of KCTU's attempt at political empowerment. The film's latter part, after the end of the occupation, pays attention to the workers' economic crisis and domestic conditions that determine their multiple identities, as precarious worker, mother, and housewife. These two focuses lay claim to Kim's feminist position on labor issues insofar as they reveal how the female workers were gradually alienated from the male-dominated labor movements while still being subject to their patriarchal family system.

Two documentaries in the late 2010s have advanced the representational and aesthetic templates of activist labor documentary while also expanding its thematic scope. *Flag, Blue Sky, Party* (*Kitpal, ch'anggong, p'at'i*, 2019, 168 min.), directed by Jang Yun-mi who made a personal documentary on her father as a longtime construction worker (see chapter 4), is perhaps one of the most remarkable achievements among recent Korean labor documentaries. Focusing on the efforts of KEC Branch Union as a member of Korean Metal Workers' Union (Kŭmsok nodong johap) to negotiate wages with a company that exploits a multiunion strategy to disallow its bargaining rights, the film relies on neither the participatory mode nor a dramatic narrative structure to reconstruct the beginning and end of the negotiations. Instead, Jang's self-effacing yet intimate camera activates an observational mode similar to Frederick Wiseman's. The camera guides viewers toward the union's diverse activities other than sit-ins and street protests, such as meetings, discussions, making and distributing pamphlets, and education, its members' conversations. The film's open-ended structure refrains from a linear and causal explanation of events and instead presents a specific kind of "mosaic," in which its sequences "do not merge into one impression . . . so much as supplement each other."[25] In this way, the film offers a careful examination of the union as a microcosm of challenges other labor unions face in the neoliberal economic system.

Underground (*Ŏndŏgŭraundŭ*, 2019, 88 min.), directed by Busan-based documentarian Kim Jung-geun, explores the work and environment of laborers at Busan Metro. As in his *The Island of Shadows* (*Kŭrimjadŭrŭi sŏm*, 2014, 98 min.), a documentary that brings together the testimonies of workers who devoted their lives both to Hanjin Heavy Industries and to their union activities, the film attests to Kim's interest in the individual and collective dimensions of workers. This time, however, his focus is as much on their working bodies than as on their testimonies. The viewer is able to see workers of various occupations at Busan Metro from dawn to night: a train driver, workers in the central control room, female cleaners at stations, mechanics inspecting carriages in the garage or maintaining their interior, and others who disassemble the carriages and repair wheels and other parts. All these diverse activities are recorded as the landscapes of work *as such*. Carefully framing the details of each workplace from fixed positions, Kim's camera is distinct from the typical cinematography of the traditional labor documentaries that captured the scene of the labor struggle with the instantaneity, immediacy, and mobility of the video camera to promote the laborers' emotional solidarity. However, Kim is also interested in figuring landscapes as "workplace" (chagŏpchang) rather than exploring them as aesthetic objects. This demonstrates that Kim sees Busan Metro as a large organism, its workers as cells that constitute and maintain it (that is, like the machine parts that make up a locomotive), in a way reminiscent of Wiseman's approach. The camera is thus an invisible observer, and individual shots form a window onto the world. Workers are portrayed in large maintenance depots, machines, and hallways, sometimes as small dots. Their bodies sometimes look precarious, seemingly overwhelmed by heavy machinery and parts. However, the bodies at work in the ensuing shots are still at the center of their frames. In this regard, *Underground* reveals Kim's humanist attitude toward labor and its subject. By paying attention to the process of work itself and the landscape of the work, *Underground* carefully renews the tradition of Korean labor documentaries while also bringing to the forefront the issue of nonregular workers, illustrated by the scenes that document the protests by cleaning workers and ticket cashiers who were fired, and by interviews with technical high school students who become aware of which jobs are regular and which are temporary after their field trip to Busan Metro.

Disenfranchised Subjects: Evictees, Disabilities, Animals

As urban sociologist Shin Hyun-Bang has demonstrated, the property-based urban redevelopment was maintained when Korea's traditional developmental state model befriended neoliberalization of economy and governance in response to the post-IMF crisis: "Continuity has been the essence of urban redevelopment practices in Korea under both the pre-crisis developmental state and post-crisis (neo-)liberalizing developmental state."[26] In the twenty-first century, large conglomerates and speculative capital (*t'ugi chabon*) in Seoul's urban landscape under the governmental patronage of deregulation have replaced dilapidated urban spaces—not simply traditional shantytowns but also old shops and housing areas—with new commercial and residential buildings, which in turn have caused a dramatic increase in rents and the enforced displacement of poor tenants and small business owners. This process, now known as "gentrification," has thus spawned a new type of evictee distinct from the urban poor living in shantytowns. Documentaries have turned their cameras to these new disenfranchised subjects. They partly seek to revivify Kim Dong-won's spirit of documenting the urban poor's condition of living in collaboration with the social movements supporting their rights of survival and housing. More significantly, however, they also take an observational, ethnographic, or experimental mode either in response to the subjects' new strategies of resistance and the new urban conditions surrounding them or in favor of interrogating the subjects' ways of living and culture. Accordingly, they mark a notable epistemological departure from Kim's humanitarian emphasis on the collective class consciousness of the evictees and their communal living.

192-399: A Story about the House Living Together (*192-399: Tŏburŏ sanŭn chim iyagi*, 2006, 126 min.), a film by Lee Hyun-jung (a member of the SVC), investigates a squatter group of homeless men living together in a small multiplex housing unit from October 2005 to February 2006, following its activities of offering free meals to other urban vagabonds and illegally usurping empty apartments and buildings under redevelopment. Although sometimes portraying the members' struggle to claim housing rights and their clash with

Seoul Metropolitan Government's officials, the film neither develops a dramatic or problem-solution narrative nor employs an expository voice-over, such as that used to highlight the formation of the evictees' class consciousness in *Haengdang-dong People* and to didactically establish them as communal subject *uri* (we) in *Another World We Are Making: Haengdang-Dong People 2*. Instead, Lee's camera activates the detached stance reminiscent of direct cinema, taking a closer look at members' everyday acts of living together and their group discussions in the house. This choice was what Lee intended, as she made clear in an interview: "In the early stage of this project, I thought that if I was making a documentary in the long term, my camera would observe the group from a distance rather than interacting with it."[27] Occupying this position of the seemingly uninvolved observer, spectators are invited to closely view the group's social microcosm, which includes the doubtful attitude of the activist who led the group, his growing conflict with other members who became suspicious of his urge for organized resistance, and the dissolution of the group. By leaving open the viewers' judgment on the internal conflicts and contradictions of the group in this way, the film provides a fresh perspective on the social movements of the urban poor while also challenging prior activist documentary's construction of their identity as unified *minjung*.

Sociologist Cho Uhn, too, contributes to the expansion and diversification of the viewpoint on the urban poor with her long-term ethnographic studies on a family of evictees from the mid-1980s to the late 2010s. In her fieldwork in the poor hillside village (*taltongne*) of Sadang-dong in Seoul in 1986, Cho focused on grandmother Jung Geum-sun and her family members (her son and three grandchildren) who were relocated to a public housing apartment complex in Nowon-gu (a northeastern county of Seoul), producing two documentaries, *Sadang-dong Plus 22* (*Sadang-dong tŏhagi 22*, 2009, 80 min.) and *Sadang-dong Plus 33* (*Sadang-dong tŏhagi 33*, 2020, 124 min.), and publishing a scholarly monograph *Sadandong Plus 25* (*Sadang-dong tŏhagi 25*, 2012). These multiple works based on the long-term research on a specific group of social actors over a long period remind one of Michael Apted's *7 Up* (1964) and *63 Up* (2019). Cho's filming of Jung's family from her own perspective, evolving from the observational mode of the first film to the self-reflexive exposure of her personal relationship to each of the members in the second film, accords with Jay Ruby's formulation of ethnographic film, which "should be produced by anthropologists as the result of a long-term, intensive field research project with the visible manifestation of culture in performative events that lend themselves to being transformed into filmable scenarios."[28] Seen from this perspective, Cho's ethnographic approach to Jung's family shares with Korean activist documentaries a penchant for the participatory mode that champions the filmmaker's intimate engagement with social actors. Notwithstanding this commonality, demonstrated by Cho's presence in the form of her voice-over commentary and her on-screen presence as interviewer, the two *Sadang-dong* films are politically and ethically distinct from Kim Dong-won's portrayal of the urban poor. Unlike *Sanggye-dong Olympics* and *Haengdang-dong People*, which aimed to be shown to the evictees and poor residents to cement their solidarity, Cho's films are distanced from the activist documentaries' aspiration to concretize the idea of *minjung* as a collective urban poor that shares a morality and a communal culture. Instead, Cho's camera investigates and lays claims to the "culture of poverty," the term that anthropologist Oscar Lewis coined to indicate a kind of specific subculture that perpetuates the behavior, worldview, and attitude of the underclass from one generation to the next.[29] Unlike Lewis's attention to alcoholism and domestic violence as characteristic of that subculture, Cho's anthropological gaze draws viewers' attention not merely to the attire, expression, and speaking tone of the family but also to the structural conditions of poverty that influence each member's effort to manage life, such as their lack of skills and knowledge, their unstable job opportunities, and their debts. These two directions of the two films resonate with the conclusion of Cho's monograph: "It is not that the culture of poverty makes Jung's family poor, but that their poverty, as well as the social structure of reproducing poverty, has become their condition of life."[30]

Commercial gentrification has become a notable social issue since the early 2010s. As Seon-young Lee and Yoonai Han write, it has been shaped by the economic, social, and spatial transformations whereby "neighborhoods serving local needs become hotspots for shopping, dining, and art, and the pioneers (who play a crucial role in the initial transformations), as well as residents, are displaced by franchised shops armed with big capital because of the extreme commercialization and rising rent."[31] Considered this way, commercial gentrification, despite its production of eviction, is an issue of urbanization that is specific to the neoliberal system and thus more or less distinct from the redevelopment of shantytowns and slums in Korea's developmental period: for it affects small business owners, youth, artists, and local community members who were not traditionally classified as the urban poor. This shifting demography of the people, whose heterogeneity does not fit into the relatively unified picture of *minjung*, has also entailed other types of resistance than the confrontational tactics of public demonstrations or sit-ins, including a variety of events designed to draw public and media attention, practices that express the spirit and slogan of protest in everyday life, and strategies for performing art activism.[32] A case in point that exemplifies this new trend is the antigentrification movement from 2009 to 2011 at Dooriban, a noodle restaurant next to the district of Hongik University in Seoul that was subject to demolition by GS Engineering & Construction. In alliance with the restaurant owner who fought against the unjust eviction, activists, filmmakers, artists, and musicians joined the protest, transforming the restaurant into the hub of support gigs, flea markets, talks, and film festivals.[33]

A couple of nonfiction films that portray the Dooriban protest accordingly reflect the aesthetics and sensibility of the new activist documentary distinct from those of the traditional independent documentaries on evictees. *Party 51* (*P'at'i51*, Jung Yong-taek, 2013, 101 min.) spotlights the musicians who gathered to help the owner of Dooriban, balancing the director's rhythmic editing, which punctuates their sonic and choreographic energies at a series of performances, with their communal efforts to organize the events of resistance, to strengthen their solidarity with the owner, and to show how their music was intertwined with a district that was increasingly affected by the force of neoliberal capital. A thirty-seven-minute film, *Generator of Dooriban* (*Turiban palchŏn'gi*, 2012), also documents the landscape and these protests, but with an experimental approach originated by its director Lee Won-woo, who has practiced avant-garde filmmaking since 2008. Employing a heterogeneous array of cameras and formats, Super 8 mm, 16 mm Bolex, and GoPro, Lee does away with expository or informative details of the resistance. They are instead used to inscribe in the images Lee's personal impression of what she witnessed at the site of resistance, which is manifested by the images' material and aesthetic dimensions. The rich grains and color spectrums of celluloid, while rendering figures opaque, convey Lee's affective responses to the coldness and heat that she experienced under the circumstance that gas and electricity supplies had been cut off at the restaurant. The camera's shaky motion and various shutter speeds, which create stop-motion effects, not only preserve the solidarity of the participants and the performative energies of the musicians but also validate Lee's creative adaptation of Jonas Mekas's diary films, in which the director's immediate perception of chaotic reality confronts "the assembled fragments of a time now lost."[34] By channeling her personal mode into documentation of social protests,[35] Lee's practice demonstrates two features of the twenty-first-century activist documentary: the technical, aesthetic, and epistemological diversity of nonfiction filmmaking beyond the confines of the activist tradition; and the possibility of multiple approaches to the same subject matter.

The growth of organizations of disabled people (*changaein*) since the late 1990s has contributed to the spread of the discourse on disability rights. While some organizations contributed to enacting the Antidiscrimination Law and amending disability employment legislation through nonviolent strategies, such as public education, publicity, and seminars, others, such as the Solidarity Committee of the Disabled to Obtain Mobility Rights (SDOMOR), disagreed with them and instead pursued radical direct actions.[36] Park Jongpil, who died in 2017, was a key figure in the activist documentaries and advocated the latter type of disability movements in the 1990s and 2000s. *Report on the Stripe of the Disabled* (*Pŏsŭrŭl t'aja: Changaein idonggwŏn t'ujaeng bogosŏ*, 2002, 58 min.) provides on-the-spot records of the public protests by the disabled activists of SDOMOR, a radical organization aimed to claim disabled people's mobility rights (*idonggwŏn*) to use public transportation as a response to an incident in 2001, in which a seventy-year-old wheelchair user and his wife fell down an elevator shaft at a subway station, which killed her and caused him severe injury. The street footage of the clash between the disabled and the police, shot on a shaky, handheld camera, impacts the viewer's affective and corporeal dimensions, therefore engendering what Jane Gaines has called "political mimesis," that is, the realist strategy of radical social change documentaries to make struggles visceral with sensationalized spectacle of bodies for the production of affects.[37] In addition to documenting the disabled's protests, such as occupying subway trains and buses and staging a sit-in in front of Seoul Metropolitan City Hall to arouse viewers' empathy and outrage, the film also provides scenes that serve efficiently for political pedagogy. Without any expository voice-over or interventional gaze, one scene of the film features a small disabled person in a wheelchair, showing how many people are required to help him to take the subway. As a critic rightly points out, "This scene demonstrates Park's cinematic maneuver in that it is intended to convey the shame and mental stress that the wheelchair disabled bear."[38] The film ends with intertitles that describe how the series of the protests led to the Seoul metropolitan government's promise to install elevators in every station of Seoul Metro by 2004. Despite his death, Park's activist advocacy filmmaking on behalf of the radical disability movement seems to have had lingering effects even in the early 2020s, in that disability groups still occupy rush-hour subway trains in response the government's failure to fully keep its promise.[39]

Documentaries on disability since the early twenty-first century, though, have paid more attention to disabled persons' desire, their peculiar modes of communication, and their efforts to accommodate themselves in the society and get through their physical limitations without necessarily being aligned with social movements for their rights. *Pansy and Ivy* (*P'aenjiwa tamjaengi*, Gye Woon-gyeong, 2000, 60 min.) paved the way in this direction as it intimately follows two sisters' quest for love, their process of getting married,

82 Activism

their frank conversation about love, sex, and health, with most of its observational camera positions settling at eye level. Framing the sisters' bodies and faces in close-up, the camera functions to render the agency of the sisters who speak and behave for themselves, challenging the conventions of humanitarian documentary that frames the disabled as social victims. As Eunjung Kim observes, the film's microscopic attention to the two women's effort to achieve marriage highlights the "disruptive potential of disabled bodies that exist outside the gendered imperative," which also defies the illusion that "disability can be erased in accordance with patriarchal cultural customs of fulfilling gender expectations and heterosexuality."[40] A similar observational strategy is also found in *Junha's Planet* (*Chunhaŭi haengsŏng*, Hong Hyungsook, 2018, 108 min.), a film that focuses on the tension between an autistic boy and his schoolmates in an alternative education institute. Hong's observational gaze inside the classroom achieves a Weisman-like investigation of the dynamic relationship between the individual and the community to which he tries to adjust himself, while also capturing the details of the institute that allude to his silence and his inexplicable states of mind. Without any recourse to human rights discourse, the two films' observational mode provides an alternative to what Pooja Rangan has called "immediations," a concept that refers to the tropes of participatory or expository humanitarian documentary, such as the voice-over that gives autists and the deaf or mute a humanized voice to explain what they mean and express, in order to emphasize "the mediated quality of their emphasis on immediacy."[41]

Planet of Snail (*Talp'aengiŭi pyŏl*, Yi Seung-jun, 2010, 85 min.), winner of the Best Feature-Length Documentary Prize at the Twenty-Fourth International Documentary Film Festival Amsterdam in 2011, is the best-crafted documentary on disability: "By rejecting some of the common tropes of human rights cinema (including the framing of physically 'handicapped' individuals as victims of an indifferent social system), Yi's unusual documentary encourages an alternative type of phenomenological engagement with subjects who communicate chiefly through touch."[42] Portraying a deafblind man Young-chan and his wife Soon-ho who has a spiral injury, Yi solves two ethical predicaments in documenting disability: first, viewers' voyeurism that in turn arouses their sense of guilt, and the second, objectifying the disabled as human beings who deserve pity. To this end, Yi carefully balances the observational mode with expressive techniques for embodying Young-chan's senses and viewpoints. The observational mode effectively draws viewers' close attention to Young-chan's domestic and public activities, his unfathomable states of mind, and his communicative acts. As Thomas Austin perceptively notes, documentaries that investigate the inner states of mind inevitably work with inherent limits to knowledge. In this type of film, "Viewers are prompted to feel with and for those on screen but, crucially, are also kept at a distance from them in ways that foreground the partial nature of the knowledge on offer."[43] While acknowledging his distance from Young-chan, Yi's employment of detached observation and camerawork that follows Young-chan's tactile perception of objects invites a phenomenological approach to what he feels despite his disability, a perception that Laura U. Marks could call "haptic visuality."[44] Two scenes stand out in this sense: the first is when Young-chan changes a fluorescent tube in his apartment; and the second is where he touches a tree in a forest. The aural ambience of the wind, if diminishing the illusion of reality and thus inscribing the director's maneuver, provides viewers with Young-chan's soundscape in ways that do not conceal its mediated quality of translating his inner sound into what humans with hearing could perceive. Eschewing the documentary trope of persuasive speech intended to give a voice to autistics and other disabled persons, a trope grounded in the Griersonian conventions of using a didactic and expository voice-over to construct a social viewpoint on a documentary subject,[45] the film occasionally employs Young-chan's first-person narration as a medium through which viewers are capable of identifying with his perception and consciousness. The narration rehearses his poems, illustrated by surreal images of natural landscape. With its multiple aesthetic devices liberated from the participatory mode, *Planet of Snail* offers a rich cinematic investigation of the disabled subject, which carefully navigates between his inhuman senses and realities and the humanized demand for translating them into the cinematic means employed for nonimpaired humans' appreciation and empathy.

Animals are a new type of disenfranchised subject in twenty-first-century South Korea. Existing environmental movement organizations, including Green Korea (Noksaek yŏnhap), new groups for protecting animals, such as Coexistence of Animal Rights on Earth (CARE, Tongmulgwŏn danch'e kĕŏ, established in 2002) and Korean Animal Rights Advocates (KARA, Tongmulgwŏn haengdong k'ara, founded in 2005), and well-known celebrities have contributed to disseminating the discourse on animal rights (*tongmulgwŏn*) in tandem with the increase in companion animals. In particular, KARA launched the Seoul Animal Film Festival in 2018, therefore demonstrating the burgeoning of theme-based film festivals associated with social movements in civil society. Woman documentary filmmaker Hwang Yoon has left her distinctive signature on the scene of Korean independent documentary in the twenty-first century through her engagement with animals. She has been in alliance with the movements for animal rights advocacy and was the first candidate for the proportional representation of the

Green Party (Noksaek tang) in 2015. Hwang's films, however, diverge both from the expository and enlightening rhetoric of mainstream television documentaries, by which nature and animals are objectified as what awaits human projection, and from environmental activist films' display of the spectacle of struggles. Instead, Hwang takes a posthumanist attitude toward animals, one that problematizes the anthropocentric binaries between humans and animal/nature/environment. As she asserts in her directorial statement, "The history of human civilization is one that has labeled animals as 'others' by distinguishing we humans from them."[46] Along with her predilection for using the terms "human animals" and "nonhuman animals,"[47] this reminds one of Cary Wolfe's Derridean posthumanism, in which questions on animals and their relationship to humanity "form the basis for deconstructing the various ways in which we have presumed to master or appropriate the finitude we share with nonhuman animals."[48] Hwang's debut feature-length documentary, *Farewell* (*Chakpyŏl*, 2001, 84 min.), guides viewers toward animals in a zoo, and its zookeepers and veterinarians who take care of them. Eliding the voice-over of TV documentaries that has an effect of reinforcing the anthropocentric perspective on wild animals, Hwang's camera takes an observational approach that frames faces of animals in close-ups and their postures and activities in cages in long shots. Hwang's reflection on the imprisoned lives of animals indirectly emerges in this type of aesthetic choice, when the long shots, sometimes in long takes or attenuated with slow motion, exhibit the bare bodies of tigers, elephants, jaguars, monkeys, bears, and so on, and when the close-ups propel viewers to ponder their affects, which express their vulnerability and mortality, but which evade humans' logocentric articulation. By laying bare portraits of the animals in such a way that undermines viewers' expectations of them as a part of the spectacle of the zoo, *Farewell* performs a critical cinematic pedagogy through which to interrogate the ways in which mainstream media exploit animal imagery. Hwang has made this point clear as her activist agenda for educating the public about animal rights: "Mass media thoroughly distorts and capitalizes on the miserable life of the animals by depicting them as though they live in the garden of the romantic dream. I wanted to divorce myself from the media's stereotypical image of the zoo and to make new images of it."[49]

One Day on the Road (*Ŏnŭnal kŭ kiresŏ*, 2006, 97 min.) brings Hwang's interest in animal rights to roadkill, that is, wild animals hit by cars (figure 2.2). Following activists who counted about six thousand victims on about six hundred roads in one year, the film asks viewers to expand their eyes so that they see an aspect of the road other than a product of human civilization: a road as occupied not only by vehicles but also by animals moving at varying paces,

Figure 2.2 *One Day on the Road* (Hwang Yoon, 2006)

including a frog, a snake, and a turtle slowly moving alongside the shoulder of a highway. This ecological picture, marked by the coexistence of humans and wild animals, is underlined in the film's ending, which juxtaposes the magnified face of a wildcat with the images of a road at night taken from a car rushing along on it. While the animals' mortality in *Farewell* is suggested by the camera's framing of their vulnerable bodies left alone inside cages, the dead bodies of a bird, a rabbit, and a wildcat are explicitly present on the roads either through Hwang's handheld camera wavering between long shots and close-ups or through a series of snapshots taken by the activists' cameras. Apart from the presence of death as eccentric event, Hwang's close attention to the dead bodies on the road, which required the risk of filming near rushing cars, attests to the rhetorical power of documentary's "endangered gaze" that "constitutes itself as an intersubjective and ethical trade-off." The filmmaker looking at death, in the words of Vivian Sobchack, "pays for the transgression of breaking a visual taboo by visibly risking his or her own life to represent the proximate death of another."[50] Unlike the distanced observation of the nonhuman residents in the zoo in *Farewell*, Hwang takes an anthropomorphic approach to the animals on the road, calling them "occupants on the ground." To this end, she inserts via intertitles the imagined monologues of an elk that tried to cross the road and was killed, and of a wildcat that was severely injured during a foray to find something to eat, embellished by lyrical, nondiegetic music. This imaginary embodiment of the animals' perception amplifies Hwang's humanitarian advocacy for *tongmulgwŏn* by conveying

86 Activism

what they need to survive and what they might feel about the ecological crisis caused by the increased construction of the highways. For Hwang, this device derives from her "quest for a new form," as she wanted to "represent [animals] in subjective and poetic ways rather than the realistic representation popular in so-called nature documentary."[51] Despite its nonrealistic devices, the film does not abandon Hwang's environmentalist pedagogical project to form an alternative public sphere in which the developmentalist, human-oriented colonization of the land can be problematized and discussed, by connecting the roadkill to the larger ecological issue triggered by the government's indiscriminate construction of highways. Therein lies the film's success, demonstrated by both its theatrical release and its community screening more than one hundred times, hosted by various civic organizations, including Green Korea.

Hwang's environmentalist exploration of animals was later extended into *An Omnivorous Family's Dilemma* (*Chapshik kajogŭi tillema*, 2014, 105 min.), in which she experiments with the first-person narration and her own on-screen presence to investigate the life and plight of pigs and the processes of meat production on industrial pig farms. Apart from circulation through local and international film festival circuits, the film was incorporated in the social activism of KARA in raising the consciousness about *tongmulgwŏn* and in the campaign against factory animal farms.[52] The anthropomorphic perspective of animals in *One Day on the Road* is also employed to imaginatively reconstruct how the pigs feel, but this does not necessarily result in reinforcing an ultimately human-centered viewpoint on the life of animals and their industrial exploitation. Instead, the film's narration combines Hwang's scrutiny of the pigs with her acknowledgment of the impossibility of fully approaching them, which is also reflected in the film's switching between her various positionalities—as documentarian, mother, wife, and vegetarian. This exposure of the multiple identities in favor of reflecting on the public issues of animal rights and environmental sustainability from Hwang's personal perspective demonstrates her foray into the local trend of personal documentary that I discuss in chapter 4.

Hwang's latest film, *Sura: A Love Song* (*Sura*, 2022, 102 min.), depicts the biodiversity of Sura Mud Flat in Saemangeum, an estuarine tidal flat on the coast of the Yellow Sea that was dammed by the Saemangeum Reclamation Project (originally launched in 1991 and completed in 2006), transforming it into land and a lake. Hwang's seven-year elegiac record of marine organisms and migratory birds in the flat resulted not only from her commitment to animal rights but also from her alliance with the grassroots resistance against the state-led development of the area, which started in response to the project and has continued, trying to stop the construction of a new airport that would undermine its vibrant ecosystem. This resistance, which can be called environmental activism, is indeed a notable twenty-first-century social movement advocated by some documentaries and alternative media practices that I shall discuss in the next chapter.

3
New Social Movements and Alternative Media Practices

The Multitude in the Plaza

The 2016–2017 Candlelight Protests were a decisive moment not only in the history of South Korean social movements but also in the activist strain of documentary cinema. Many documentarians and activists turned their cameras to the participants in the rallies while joining the media team of People's Action for Immediate Resignation of President Park Geun-hye (Pak Kŭnhye jŏnggwŏn t'oejin pisang gungmin haengdong), and their videos were circulated via social media and later incorporated in a documentary released by Cinemadal for community screenings: *Candlelight in the Wave* (*Gwangjang*, 2017, 111 min.), an omnibus film that consists of ten shorts. While inheriting the traditional activism's aspirations to use documentary as an axis of collaboration, an organizing agent, and a vehicle representing and speaking for social change, the film emblematizes the political and social contexts of the twenty-first-century activist documentary in terms of what collective subjectivity it addresses and what kind of social movements social change activist documentaries are allied with.

The large-scale street protests can be seen as validating that "civil society has remained a central actor in advancing democratic representation in the nation,"[1] given that social movement organizations, including People's Action, coordinated citizens' massive power to pressure the National Assembly so that the corrupt and incompetent president was legally impeached in March 2017 and a new government (President Moon Jae-in's) was instated via a special election in May 2017. However, what is more significant than the sustained role of the organizations is that this type of protest movement signaled a shift of collective subjects in the twenty-first century from *minjung* to the multitude (*tajung*), which Michael Hardt and Antonio Negri consider distinguished from other notions of social subjects. The multitude is, according to Hardt and Negri, reducible to neither the people (characterized by a single identity) nor the masses (which form an indistinct, uniform mélange)

Activism and Post-activism. Jihoon Kim, Oxford University Press. © Oxford University Press 2024.
DOI: 10.1093/oso/9780197760413.003.0004

inasmuch as it permits "a social multiplicity to manage to communicate and act in common while remaining internally different."[2] For this reason, the social movements led by the multitude, even massive-scale rallies, are premised upon differences in class, occupation, culture, gender, and sexual orientation in comparison to the traditional mass protests mobilized by a central organizing agent (composed of politicians and social activists groups) that endows the masses with a shared identity and purpose. The 2016–2017 Candlelight Protests attest to the dialectic of differences and the common element that lies at the heart of the concept of the multitude. They involved a multiplicity of subgroups and citizens who experienced the political, social, economic, and cultural inequalities caused by, among other factors, the government's anachronistic conservative policies reminiscent of the prior dictatorship; economic polarization; environmental crises in different provinces, and gender discrimination.[3] Protesters brought their different demands, slogans, and placards to Gwanghwamun Plaza, but with a shared awareness of the Park government's wrongdoings as their common problem. Thus, the participating subjects of the protests cannot be seen as *minjung* characterized by its shared class identity, but as the multitude divided into individuals distinct in class, gender, age, and occupation but nonetheless sharing a common affective enthusiasm for democracy and social change. As Yi Jin-kyung observes, "Many issues—MV Sewol, the blacklisting of artists, the agreement with the Japanese government on comfort women among them—were simultaneously at the forefront of people's minds,"[4] besides the collective sense of resistance to the Park government's political corruption and irresponsibility.

With its omnibus format that preserves the thematic and stylistic diversity of the short films in a horizontal manner, *Candlelight in the Wave* offers a collective yet heterogeneous portrait of the multitude as fluid and decentralized subjects who occupied the public sphere for a common purpose that nonetheless originated from their different motivations and perspectives. It includes Hwang-yoon's *Chicken in the Plaza* (*Kwangjangŭi tak*, 12 min.), about animal rights in factory farms, Kim Jung-geun's *Cleaning* (*Chŏngso*, 8 min.), about a female cleaning worker at a Busan Railway Station (as well as a participant in the rallies) who gives her account of her working conditions and insecure job status, and Hong Hyung-sook's *The Blue Whale Flies* (*P'urŭn korae nalta*, 5 min.), about a group of children who are learning the lessons of the Sewol Ferry Disaster and its impact on the protests with writing and symbol-making activities at an alternative education institute.[5] While the films included in *Candlelight in the Wave* share the participatory mode and images of the masses at the plaza, including the Sewol Ferry Disaster's bereaved families, as their anchoring points in building a larger story, the variety of social subjects

90 Activism

they portray suggests that the protests were premised upon an array of social movements in the twenty-first century that originated in the social, cultural and economic differences in *tajung*.

Two films in *Candlelight in the Wave* are particularly noticeable in the context of the two social movements that gained momentum in the 2010s: KangYu Garam's *Candlelight Feminists* (*Shiguk p'emi*, 9 min., later extended into a forty-minute film) and Park Moon-chil's *Blue Butterfly* (*P'aran nabi*, 9 min.).[6] The former brings together the voices of several young women activists from different feminists groups who joined the protests. The latter focuses on the story of a middle-aged woman in Seongju county, who took part in the regional struggles against the Park government's plan to deploy a radar system and Terminal High Altitude Area Defense (THAAD) launchers , a controversial US-operated technology to intercept ballistic missiles. While highlighting the social actors as among the numerous self-mobilizing subjects, the two documentaries also allow viewers to be aware that their motivations for joining the protests cannot be contained either within the master narrative of the 1980s mass demonstrations for democracy or within the interests of the liberal and conservative political parties. In *Candlelight Feminists*, the young feminists say that it was crucial for them to warn of and fight against the antifeminist rhetoric (that is, the corrupt President Park and her puppet-master Choi Soon-sil are female) shared by some people in progressive parties when they shouted slogans in the plaza. The woman in Seongju county in *Blue Butterfly* confesses that it was due to the Park government's manipulation of public opinion, through which Seongju residents were stigmatized as communists who were being influenced by outside forces, that she decided to be an activist for the anti-THADD campaign despite her original political conservativeness. Viewed together, both shorts valorize two implications that Sun-chul Kim observes in the protests. First, new rights-claiming voices and social movements in both liberal and conservative administrations in the twenty-first century, such as the feminist wave and the regional struggles against the installment of military or electric infrastructure, set the tone for the eruption of the massive rallies. Second, for this reason, the protests call into question such binaries as "left versus right" and "progressive and conservative" that are taken for granted in assuming that the protests are a continuation of the *minjung* movement in the 1980s: "It is far from surprising that labor, feminist, queer, and environmental activists, conventionally considered to be progressive, do not portray conservatives as their opponents. Rather, their fight is set against a broader system of oppression, irresponsibility, exclusion, and discrimination, characteristics shared by both the liberal and conservative political establishments."[7]

Establishing the two shorts by Kang Yu and Park as entry points, this chapter maps out an array of documentaries that engage the feminist and LGBTQ movements and environmental activism as two noticeable social movements that attest to the coalition of *tajung*. These two movements do more than testify to the internal differences between their subjects that are constitutive of *tajung*. In addition, during the last decade they have raised social issues that invite the engagement of activists and documentarians. Attending to the bond between the movements and social change documentaries, I demonstrate that, as in chapter 2, while some films employ the templates of cinéma-vérité to convey the voices and bodies of the subjects and to promote the public awareness of their problems and memories, there are others marked by the director's self-conscious approach to documentary language and the diversity of documentary modes that transcend the aesthetic constraints of the activist tradition.

This chapter's two additional sections are intended to explain innovations in the activist tradition of Korean documentary cinema in the context of twenty-first-century Korea, including the Candlelight Protests and the Sewol Ferry Disaster, which functioned as their common nodal point. The first section concerns the trend of alternative journalism documentaries, popular documentaries in which an investigative journalist or journalist-turned-documentarian probes social issues and reveals their causes. While their rhetorical devices, such as the strong presence of the journalist or documentarian, calls to mind Michael Moore's controversial political documentaries, the films derived from a particular local context in the late 2000s and early 2010s, namely, the two right-wing governments' suppression of the press (*ŏllon*). The alternative news agencies that have led the way in the trend toward alternative journalism documentaries, then, signal not only the malfunction of the press as a traditional public sphere but also the emergence of new media activist groups that share with the existing independent documentarians the counterpublic sphere and a set of common purposes: revealing the wrongdoings and injustice of state power and capital, and making public the pains and demands of the marginalized. The last section introduces two alternative strategies of activist documentary production in the twenty-first century: migratory-grassroots media activism and issue-based omnibus documentary filmmaking. Updating the tradition of collective filmmaking in the activist practices of the 1980s and 1990s, the horizontal format of these two strategies also incorporates the dialectic of difference and the common in the social movements led by *tajung*. While migratory-grassroots activism has engaged different regional issues in various places across South Korea, omnibus filmmaking has been based on the collective awareness of activists

92 Activism

and documentarians of a problem or social event that is common to and reverberates across the differences in *tajung*.

Feminist and Queer Documentaries: Against Hate and Discrimination

After Byun Young-joo's comfort women trilogy, the feminist wave of Korean documentary cinema began to surface at the turn of the twenty-first century, bifurcating into two directions. The first direction was a series of semiautobiographical documentaries made by female filmmakers that recount the history of their parents, siblings, and themselves from a personal perspective. Besides this trend, which I will discuss more deeply in chapter 4, there were a number of notable participatory, activist-oriented documentaries committed to the female disenfranchised subjects and advocating for their acts of resistance. These two directions of the period, in retrospect, were founded upon the birth and development of what Kim Soyoung called *yŏsŏngjang* (the women's sphere). By this, she means the rise of a new feminist-oriented sphere in civic society as an alternative to the bourgeois and androcentric assumption of the public sphere. It emerged, according to Kim, thanks to the increase in feminist publications and activities in both online and offline spaces, including Seoul International Women's Film Festival (SIWFF) dedicated to projecting women's issues on the screen and promoting solidarity among spectators, and the public ceremonies to commemorate the female victims of state-driven and corporate capitalism, such as irregular laborers and sex workers. "Two concepts of *yŏsŏngjang*, related to death, friendship and resistance, betray the accidental coming together of the female public sphere," Kim writes: "The public ritual for sex workers in the streets marks a new chapter in the women's movement in South Korea."[8] The establishment of *yŏsŏngjang* also stemmed from the more conspicuous diversification of local women's movements following the late 1990s. Apart from existing women's movement organizations, such as Womanlink, the Korean Council for Justice and Remembrance, and the Sexual Violence Counseling Center (Sŏngp'ongnyŏk sandamso), the feminist drive for social change in the 2000s encompassed campus feminists critical of the patriarchal values engrained in the educational and economic systems of the society, activists who resisted sexual violence and male domination within the progressive social movement organizations, and labor unions that fought against discrimination against female workers. This diversification of the movements, in the words of Song-Woo Hur, was predicated upon the awareness that "women are not a united group but composed of unique individuals and different social groups with multiple identities."[9] In retrospect, the issues raised by these various players have resonated with those of the feminist documentaries since the mid-2010s. But the films made before that period focus on three types of disenfranchised female subjects: former comfort women, female workers, and sex workers, all of which are associated with the movements for women's rights.

As Cho Jin-hee points out, it is paradoxical that "the labor documentaries until the late 1990s, including the newsreels of Labor News Production, had rarely been interested in female workers given that . . . their struggle were intense."[10] It was in this context that the feminist-oriented labor documentaries were produced in the post-IMF climate to make female workers visible, have their economic and gender discriminations known and discussed, and have their histories told. More than promoting a sense of solidarity between the working class as the building block for unified struggle against capitalists, the documentaries draw viewers' attention to gender hierarchy and marginalization within the class while also highlighting the menacing impact of the neoliberal restructuring on irregular workers' job security and right to live. *Parallel* (*P'yŏnghaengsŏn*, 2000, Lee Hye-ran and Seo Eun-joo, 70 min.), produced by the Workers' Video Production Enterprise HOPE (*Hŭimang*), features the three-year protest of 144 female dining hall workers at Hyundai Motors in Ulsan City against the company's mass layoffs in 1988. While there were a number of video-activist groups that documented the Hyundai Motors labor union's fight for workers' right to work and live, thereby revealing the company's brutal neoliberal restructuring, only a few of them focused on the middle-aged, temporary dining workers who had been excluded from the union's deals with the company for reinstatement of laid-off workers and who were eventually forced to leave the canteens.[11] In this struggle, the female activists were faced with the interference of a union whose leaders consisted of male workers, as one of them later recalled: "The union leaders considered [her] initial filming a 'routine shooting' of labor union events . . . [but later, the] leaders asked her team to reveal 'their true identity,' as they tried to confiscate her camera and equipment."[12] The tension that these activists experienced is reflected in the title of the film, as well as in its aesthetic and persuasive strategies. The title, *Parallel*, quoted from a dining hall worker's words, indicates the discrepancy not only between capital and labor but also between the female workers and male union leaders, who were unable to come to terms with each other. The absence of common ground between the two is punctuated by the film's alternating montage and handheld cinematography, through which the bodies and voices of the women, culminating in their fasting sit-in and in their loud arguments in the union's office, arouse viewers' emotional awareness of

94 Activism

the class and gender hierarchies (male/female, and regular/irregular worker) deeply rooted in the laborers' culture, in stark contrast with the union leaders' reluctance to understand the women's demands in front of the camera. Due to its clear political perspective on the marginalized status of female irregular workers in the male-dominated labor movement, screenings of the film at workers' communities were often faced with union boycotts. Despite this controversy, *Parallel* paved the way for a direction of feminist labor documentaries toward documenting and advocating for female irregular workers, as evidenced by *Stayed over Midnight* (see chapter 2).

The films of Kyung-soon expand the themes and perspectives of local feminist documentaries while also explicating public disputes on women's gender and sexuality in patriarchal society. Based on her location filming in Korea, Japan, and the Philippines, and blending her on-the-spot records with kinesthetic montage and animation sequences, *Red Maria* (*Redŭ maria*, 2011, 106 min.) constructs a mosaic of Asian female subjects distinct in nationality and occupation from one another, including female labor union activists as mothers fighting against Kiryung Electronics' layoffs, a Japanese middle-aged woman, Sato, who became an activist working for advocacy of irregular workers after she was laid off, a Filipina visiting housekeeper resisting the demolition of her shantytown, and the local members of the Sex Worker's Network (including prostitutes) working for the legitimation of their job in "sex labor" and against the Special Act on Prostitution (which began to be implemented in September 2004).

Kyung-soon's exploration of the relationship between work and women's bodies in the neoliberal economic system, and her bold criticism of the embeddedness of patriarchal biases in the public recognition of sex labor, are expanded into a transhistorical perspective in *Red Maria 2* (*Redŭ maria t'u*, 2015, 120 min.), in which her performative presence as investigator and interlocutor becomes more visible. Here the director's documentation of the bodies and testimonies of the Korean and Japanese SWASH (sex worker and sex health) activists, including their demand for human rights and legal recognition of sex workers against the two countries' social stigmatization of prostitution, is juxtaposed with her conversation with a group of Korean, Japanese-Korean, and Japanese scholars who offer a revisionist view on comfort women, one that suggests a nuanced understanding of their silence beyond the nationalist assumption of their subjectivity as sacred victims. The film's seemingly heterogeneous questioning of the past and present of comfort women and its juxtaposition of their issues with contemporary sex workers stirred heated debates, which focused on its depiction of Park Yuha, whose book *The Comfort Women of the Empire* (*Chegugŭi wianbu*, 2013) garnered polarized intellectual and civic responses. Distancing itself from the nationalist assumption of comfort women as innocent victims of Japanese imperial violence, the book aims to offer a nuanced understanding of the sexual, economic, military, and political factors that determined their different relationships with Japanese recruiters and customers,[13] but Park was sued by nine Korean comfort women for allegedly defaming them with the book's false and distorted content in 2013.[14] In an interview, Kyung-soon has said that she did not want the film to be seen as a comfort women documentary, and her interest in the historical issue of prostitution corresponded to Park's critique on the "discourse that discriminated or evaded prostitution and reinforced the image of comfort women as 'girls.'"[15] While concurring with the negative criticism that the film ignores the sheer difference of the conditions between sex labor under neoliberalism and that of comfort women forcefully mobilized for Japan's colonies, I would suggest that a key achievement of the two *Red Maria* films lies in Kyung-soon's rigorous assault on the patriarchal assumption of sex workers that even some feminist discourses have taken for granted, which departs from a humanitarian perspective on prostitutes as victims deprived of the rights to live, speak, and act.

The mid-2010s marked another crucial turning point of not merely local feminist movements but also of women's collective awareness of gender sensibility and misogyny as a driving force to bring about changes in every facet of Korean society. The participatory feminist activism via the hashtag declaration "#iamafeminist" on Twitter and other social media platforms in 2015, despite its ephemerality, "was able to disseminate its impact by continuing to connect with real-time gender issues and by initiating activism against misogyny both online and offline"[16] A murder case in 2016, that a woman in her twenties was randomly murdered by a man who had never met before in a public washroom, triggered "sticky note activism," which involved the posting of handwritten Post-it notes on the walls near Gangnam Station Exit No. 10 and the dissemination of their images via social media. As Jinsook Kim summarizes, this activism "played a crucial role in forming affective counterpublics" as it "facilitated the mobilization of women's affect, including grief, rage, fear, and guilt . . . and provided an alternative discourse of femicide."[17] Monitoring these notable events, Sohn Hee-jeong, a leading feminist critic, proposes the term "feminism reboot" to underline how the feminist movement since the mid-2010s departs from its predecessors in two ways. First, young women who had considered themselves autonomous subjects able to access social opportunities became aware of a web of political, economic, and gender inequalities that restrict their identity and desire under neoliberalism: "The glass ceiling (*yuri chŏnjang*), which postfeminism that incorporated neoliberalism

96 Activism

persuaded women to overcome by self-managing and a no-one-backs-you-up attitude, is now regarded as being intertwined with our life itself."[18] Second, the young women also witnessed the rise of "hate" (*hyŏmo*) as a dominant, pervasive affect of the neoliberal and neoconservative society since the early 2010s: "Women, sexual minorities, *chongbuk*, immigrant workers, disabled persons . . . those who exist outside the 'imaginary' dominant male subject become immediately the object of *hyŏmo*."[19] From this perspective, the surge of the new feminist wave since the mid-2010s started with two motivations: first, the collective awareness that a variety of feminist agendas relating to dating, marriage, childbirth, abortion, labor, and social positionings were perceived as crucial issues that pressed young female subjects in their private and public sectors; and second, growing alliances between dispersed female subjects who experienced discrimination (*ch'abyŏl*) and hate that had already permeated both virtual and social spaces in various forms of violence.

The activist documentaries that were produced during recent years respond to two strands of the "rebooted" feminist movements: first, fights against hate and misogyny, and second, young women's participatory acts for social change. Lee Sun-hee's *Face, the Other Side* (*Ŏlgul, kŭ majŭn p'yŏn*, 2018, 90 min.) tracks the activities of the Korean Cyber Sexual Violence Response Center (KCSVRC, Han'guk saibŏ sŏngp'ongnyŏk taeŭng sent'ŏ), a nonprofit organization founded in 2017 to interrogate online-based sexual violence and cyberporn cases, to help with their victims, and to advocate for laws against them. The documentary pays particular attention to the KCSVRC's efforts to counteract hidden-camera videos of women's public restrooms, child porn, and rape porn, including its investigation into the lucrative online-sharing network of those videos that operated based on the complicity between voyeuristic male consumers and the owners of online file-sharing websites.[20] The KCSVRC's activities are in dialogue with a series of collective feminist responses to the spread of hate, including that of online community Megalia, whose members made public online misogynists' use of pornographic and abusive graphic images and videos to humiliate women. As scholars averred regarding the emergence of Megalia, "The Korean web became a home for misogynistic discourses, neologisms, and styles of thinking that reflect and amplify the misogyny in the offline world. In addition to more direct forms of online misogyny, such as flaming, trolling, cyberbullying, and the circulation of revenge porn, which are directed at specific women, male users of online communities constantly produced and circulated discourses that mocked and reviled Korean women."[21] The film, too, offers a then-updated social portrait of how young feminists have taken the issue of digital sex crimes seriously, as the KCSVRC's activities turn out to be in alliance with a series of street sit-ins in 2018 by thousands of women protesters covered with masks, carrying banners with messages like "My life is not your porn," who condemned the authorities' improper responses to illegal filming.[22] Jeon Sung-yeon's *The Fearless and Vulnerable* (*Haeil ap'esŏ*, 2019, 85 min.) reflects the second tendency of the feminist movement in the "reboot" era, that is, politicization of everyday life, as it focuses on the members of a young political feminist group called Femidangdang; their activities, including campaigning in the upcoming presidential election and participation in the protests against the Antiabortion Law (Nakt'ae gŭmji bŏp);[23] and their efforts to link their individual lives to the group's communal meetings. Viewed together, *Face, the Other Side* and *The Fearless and Vulnerable* demonstrate that the verité-style representation of feminist documentary films is still a political tool for portraying consciousness-raising groups, built on "a pattern that is as satisfying for activists in the contemporary women's movement to watch as it is for women just wanting to learn more about women."[24]

Besides the consciousness-raising films directly allied with the recent surge of the feminism of the young, other feminist documentaries in the 2010s have diversified strategies and topics of women's documentary filmmaking by going beyond the confines of the discourse of sobriety, on one hand, and by expanding their interest into the ways in which women change their lifestyle, self-consciousness, and bodies, on the other. Jo Se-young's *Let's Dance* (*Cha ije taensŭt'aim*, 2013, 83 min.) paved the way for these films, emblematizing a renewed approach to the issues and experiences of abortion; the issue had long been taboo for the public and women themselves in the patriarchal system of Korean society, given feminist activists' long-standing and difficult struggles against the Antiabortion Law. Unlike other films aiming to support the campaign to win abortion rights for women, the film not only compiles interrelated stories of abortion across different generations but also rigorously employs a range of formal devices for reenactment, from slow-motion flashbacks (popular in television nonfiction programs) to a film-within-a-film that involves a surreal dream sequence wherein its protagonist, the alter ego of a young college girl majoring in film production who experienced an abortion during her film production, is drawn into a hospital decorated with grotesque colors and sets evocative of Tim Burton's expressionist movies, and witnesses her operation replayed with bloodshed, along with a male voice-over articulating the illegal abortion law. Coupled with a blurring effect through which the interviewees' faces are initially undisclosed, these nonrealistic devices achieve an entertaining yet poignant translation of the private into the public, or a transition from silence to self-confirmation. Without necessarily relying on the activist strategy of consciousness-raising, the film's performative

98 Activism

strategies efficiently convey the subjective dimension of the truths about the experience and memory of abortion while also undergirding abortion documentaries' confessional mode, in which "individual confessions become broadly compelling through their connections to a constellation of similar stories."[25]

For Vagina's Sake (*P'iŭi yŏndaegi*, Kim Bo-ram, 2017, 84 min.) demonstrates that educational needs that cover women's issue like health, childbirth, divorce, and so on, have been a driving force for women's documentary filmmaking. Inspired by a conversation with her Dutch friend, Kim commissions the film as a forum for women to get to know and discuss menstruation (*saengni*), still regarded as a taboo topic in late 2010s' Korean society. In so doing, Kim links her personal inquiry into the gender, bodily, legal, and cultural issues of menstruation to her encounters with various women across generations and national borders, and through online and offline spaces, weaving a tapestry of various accounts about their experiences. Her pedagogical approach to the issues, however, transcends the discourse of sobriety and instead achieves a dynamic mixture of information and entertainment as she rigorously uses vibrant infographics and animated images, including animated photos, expressive drawings of the vagina, and interviewees covered with pastel-tone moving drawings to visualize the history of the equivalent taboos in different cultures and to demonstrate the varying effects of female hygiene products, pads, tampons, and particularly menstrual cups that she and other foreign consumers advocate to use.[26] The deployment of these nonverité devices not only attests to Kim's documentary filmmaking as distinct from that of senior female documentarians, but also turns out to be efficient in conveying the knowledge and experiences of the monthly period in kinesthetic ways. By updating *Let's Dance* with the performative mode that underscores the subjective, embodied, and imaginary aspects of the factual, *For Vagina's Sake* adds a young woman filmmaker's new aesthetic and political prospect to the contemporary scenes of feminist documentary production. Simultaneously, the film does not totally abandon the activist tradition's commitment to the aspiration for social change, since its climax extends the knowledge and experiences in the grassroots and international movements fighting against sanitary pads manufacturers' attempt to increase the price of their products, and assisting underprivileged women in coping with their monthly period.

KangYu Garam, a member of the feminist culture event planning collective Girls, Play Girls (Yŏnghŭiya nolcha), has been the most prominent filmmaker to pursue feminist-oriented documentary production while varying its subjects. She has produced films that are different in their modes of production, but they commonly revolve around the construction of women's histories or feminist counterhistories. After completing her middle-length film *My Father's House* (*Morae*, 2011, 49 min.), a personal documentary that explores her father's and family's roles in relation to the history of Korea's rapid economic development and its real-estate boom, KangYu expanded her ethnographic filmmaking beyond her domestic space into social space in *Itaewon* (*It'aewŏn*, 2016, 95 min.), her first feature-length documentary that investigates the past and present of the Itaewon district in Seoul. The film brings together and preserves the bodies and testimonies of three elderly female residents—an owner of a country music pub exclusively open to American soldiers, and two former waitresses who worked at the district's camptown and now live as either unemployed or as a temporary restaurant assistant—as subjects who embody the memories of the district's postcolonial past. The three protagonists' accounts and bodies bear witness to the previously untold history of the women, including former waitresses and sex workers who bought into the American dream by getting married to US soldiers, who were stigmatized as *yanggongju* (a derisive term that refers to these women as willing whores) by the nationalist-patriarchal bias of modern Korea (see chapters 4 and 5). KangYu's gaze, then, extends into how history has been forgotten in the present of Itaewon as Seoul's global tourist district and a new commercial hotspot for shops and restaurants, when her camera observes the scenes of its annual global festival and the activities of young business owners who aspire to reform its environment for the sake of erasing its stigmatized images. The film's juxtaposition of the three women with the owners, then, is read as offering a critique on the process by which the memories of Itaewon have been written and simultaneously erased.

KangYu's feminist motivation achieves an activist expansion of her filmmaking with *Candlelight Feminists* and *Us, Day by Day* (*Urinŭn maeilmaeil*, 2019, 75 min.). The latter expands KangYu's engagement with the wave into an embodied history of its precursors, as it blends a confession of her own feminist trajectory with the chronicles of her friends, who were young feminists ranged against patriarchy and sexual violence in the late 1990s at college and in online spaces and who are still living feminist lives despite the differences in their current space and occupation: as an animal rights activist, as a women's health movement activist, as a feminist singer, and as a veteran anti-sexual assault activist. Again, the two films deepen KangYu's preoccupation with documenting and archiving the space and time of women: in these specific cases, female subjects as active agents who demand progressive social change. If *Candle Wave Feminists* highlights the solidarity of the young women activists who, despite their different affiliations (including Femidangdang,

Gangnam Station Exit No. 10, Flaming Feminist Action, etc.), used the plaza as political public sphere of the contemporary age, then *Us, Day by Day* adds to this solidarity a feminist historical perspective, in which the feminist movement since the mid-2010s is recognized not as unprecedented but as being rooted in the past struggles in and out of university campuses. In particular, *Us, Day by Day* as a feminist history documentary is read as advancing KangYu's ethnographic filmmaking method inasmuch as it foregrounds her horizontal relationship with the protagonists to the degree that the story of filmmaker and those of her subjects converge in the subjectivity of the "we" connected to the young feminists who are struggling on the streets against social misogyny and the Antiabortion Law. While it is hard to identify their stylistic and aesthetic consistency due to the variety of their nonfiction modes, the films of KangYu satisfy feminist documentary's auteurist project to represent stories that "hark back to the past," which are sometimes counterhistories that "contest common explanations of causality and change" (figure 3.1).[27]

In the mid-1990s, the Korean gay and lesbian movement began to surface in two directions to protest discrimination against sexual minorities (*song sosuja*) and to claim their equal rights in legal and institutional terms: first, the formation of grassroots LGBT groups, including Chingusai (Ch'in'gusai, meaning "between friends," a gay men's human rights group founded in 1994), which coalesced in an umbrella organization called Tonginhyeop (Korean Homosexual Human Rights Association) in 1995; and second, gay intellectuals' cultural activities to create queer visibility, which included

Figure 3.1 *Us, Day by Day* (KangYu Garam, 2019)

hosting the Seoul Queer Films and Videos Festival (founded in 1997).[28] However, it was not until the twenty-first century that the Korean documentary scene witnessed a full-fledged strain of LGBT-oriented nonfiction film practices. The production of LGBT documentaries was in sync with the growing visibility of *sŏngsosuja* in Korean media, culture, and society since the mid-2000s, and with the shifting dynamics of queer social movements during the last two decades. In tandem with the growth of public discourse on non-normative sexual orientations and media representations of them, the documentaries were produced and exhibited based on the local support of the Seoul International Pride Film Festival, the Seoul International Women's Film Festival, and other film festivals dedicated to independent documentaries, some of which enjoyed theatrical release.

More significantly, the documentaries were produced in the twenty-first-century context of the ongoing tension between the legal and institutional moves toward the rights-claiming of *sŏngsosuja* and the counterinsurgencies against their movements. For instance, local LGBT activism has advanced from periphery to center with its notable achievements for minority politics,[29] such as the 2004 recommendation of the National Human Rights Commission of Korea (Kukka in'gwŏn wiwŏnhoe) to delete from the Juvenile Protection Act (Chŏngsonyŏn boho bŏp) the clause that specified homosexuality as a harmful influence on youth, and the spread of queer culture festivals across Seoul and different cities since the mid-2000s. As Ju Hui Judy Han writes, however, "The underlying suggestion that youth must be protected from gender and sexual nonconformity persists to this day in sex education curricula and public decency clauses in a variety of educational, legal, and political contexts."[30] Apart from the legal and institutional barriers that thwart the rights and identities of sexual minorities, including the rights for gender change and same-sex marriage, the LGBT movements have struggled against the right-wing political climate of the Lee and Park governments, conservative Protestants' antihomosexuality campaigns, and the betrayal by liberal governments (Presidents Roh Moo-hyun [2003–2008] and Moon Jae-in [2017–2022]) of their promise of equality for sexual minority groups. A key issue that attests to those challenges to the LGBT movements is the social debate on the legislation of the Antidiscrimination Law (Ch'abyŏl kŭmji bŏp), which specifies prohibition of *ch'abyŏl* based on one's sexual orientation and identity. Though President Roh had introduced the bill as part of his presidential election campaign, it has not been legislated due to the ongoing antihomosexuality campaigns of right-wing, evangelical groups and the delays by political parties.[31] The growth of rights-claiming and the political-cultural backlashes against it have laid the foundation for the community-oriented

102 Activism

production of twenty-first-century LGBT documentaries, which was led by two notable media collectives aligned with sexual minorities.

PINKS: Solidarity for Sexually Minor Cultures and Human Rights (Yŏnbunhongch'ima), formed by filmmakers Kim Il-rhan, Lee Hyuk-sang, and others in 2004, has combined the activist documentary's aspiration to engage social injustice with feminist and queer politics, participating in the movements countering discrimination against sexual minorities and such public issues as the Yongsan Massacre (see chapters 6 and 7) and the Sewol Ferry Disaster. The group's commitment to the politics of coming out among sexual minorities is reflected in its filmography, as well as in its media activities.[32] Kim's *3xFTM* (2008, 115 min.) offers arguably the first cinematic representation of female-to-male transsexuals (FTMs) in support for the groups that demanded reform of the bill regarding gender change (*sŏngbyŏl chŏnhwan*) in 2006. Featuring the camera's intimate record of its three protagonists, the film relies on the power of their testimonies, which confess their desire to be a real man, their corporeal experience of performing themselves as male, and their profound dilemma in defining their self-identity within the gender/sex binary persistent in Korean society. The film's emphasis on the indeterminacy of sexuality that drives sexual minorities' ongoing self-interrogation in opposition to heteronormativity is encapsulated by one of its protagonists, who says, "I began to ask, What is the line between men and women?" despite the freedom to take his shirts off at the queer parade after going through breast removal surgery. The three protagonists' loquacity, as well as their comfortable gaze at the camera's lens,[33] not only suggests the extent to which their subjectivity and desire had remained socially invisible and unacknowledged, but also raises public awareness of a series of social restraints that surround them. Another protagonist was fired by his company for his graduation from girls' middle and high schools and felt embarrassed during the physical checkup for military service. These social and institutional discriminations correspond to transgender activist Ruin's study of Korea's Resident Registration (Chumin tŭngnok) system, whose controlling and management of citizens in the domains of public administration (including military conscription and marriage notice) reinforce heteronormative norms while also excluding nonbinary sexualities: "One trans male stated that if he were able to change his sex in the family register and change the first digit of the second half of his national id number to a 1 [signifying male, female for 2], he would no longer have to over-represent his masculinity and could pay proper attention to his femaleness."[34]

Lee Hyuk-sang's *The Miracle on Jongno Street* (*Chongnoŭi kijŏk*, 2010, 109 min.), produced in collaboration with Chingusai, tells the stories of four gays with whom he met and became friends in the subculture of Jongno, Seoul, which became prosperous in the 1990s with the openings of bars and cafes for gay sociality and cruising. They include Byung-kwon, a gay rights activist who has been part of the movement for homosexual workers, Young-soo, a chef who escapes from his loneliness and finds happiness after joining the gay choir G-voice (he died of meningitis during the film's production),[35] and independent filmmaker So Joon-mun, who confesses that his difficulty in communicating with the rest of his heterosexual staff in the course of shooting his debut feature-length film reactivated the traumatic memory of his military service, during which he was sent to a psychiatric clinic for his sexual identity.[36] Though its title brings to the forefront the street where gay intimacy and visibility grew, the film is less an ethnographic study of gay subculture than a tapestry of the intimate portraits that convey the everyday lives and voices of the subjects. Despite this intimacy, Lee ultimately develops the four subjects' personal stories as the vehicle for revealing structural contradictions surrounding the local queer culture and politics, such as the difficulty of producing queer films, queer subjects' inner conflict over coming out to their family, and the social prejudice and discrimination against them as the cause of HIV/AIDS. In order to raise public awareness of sexual minorities' social movements and private lives, PINKS distributed the two films in arthouse and independent cinemas. In the case of *3xFTM*, "It was originally planned as a film specific to film festivals and community screenings . . . but [the group] chose its theatrical release to publicize the issue of transgenders and to attempt at their cultural coming-out."[37] The collective's latest feature-length documentary, *Coming to You* (*Nŏege kanŭn kil*, Byun Gyu-ri, 2021, 93 min.) received increased public awareness as it was given the special documentary award at the 2021 Jeonju International Film Festival and had later about nineteen thousand theatrical attendances and a series of invited screenings in the US universities and organizations. Featuring two mothers of an FTM and a gay subject who are active members of the Parents and Families of LGBTAIQ People in Korea (PFLAG Korea, Sŏngsosuja pumo moim, founded in 2013), the film positions the mothers' efforts to take care of their own children and to participate in the group's activities within recent contexts in which sexual minority politics has been challenged: the postponement of the legislation of Ch'abyŏl kŭmji pŏp and same-sex marriage, right-wing Christianity groups' demonstrations against queer culture festivals, and the withdrawal of a transgender student who had gained admission to a women-only university in Seoul due to other students' massive opposition in 2020.[38]

Founded in 2001, WOM (UM), a women's film production collective comprising filmmakers Lee Hye-ran and Lee Young, among others, has

104 Activism

pursued films made by female filmmakers and addressed to female spectators, establishing as its mission "continuing the genealogy of [the first women's film production collective] Bariteo in the late 1980s by making a film movement that fits the change of times."[39] Besides Lee Hye-ran's *We Are Not Defeated*, a project aiming to historicize female workers' labor movements with their own testimonies, WOM's documentaries have primarily focused on the sexual and gender differences of minorities in women, such as teens, lesbians, and differently abled people, therefore contributing to challenging the essentialist idea of female identity and instead expanding the social and cultural agendas of feminist film practice. Lee Young's *Lesbian Censorship in School* (*Iban'gŏmyŏl*, 2005, 20 min.) and *Out: Smashing Homophobia Project* (*Iban'gŏmyŏl: Tu pŏntchae iyagi*, 2007, 110 min.) intimately illuminate the lives of teenage lesbians who were fighting against their school, which censored students' homosexuality (*iban*) as a more serious offense than drinking, smoking, and getting pregnant. For these two films, Lee Young experimented with the method of participants' on-cam self-recordings, through which its protagonist named Chun-jae had the liberty of recording her own confession or her conversation with other lesbian schoolmates while holding the camera wherever she was. As a result, her body is entirely off-screen or partially visible in the on-screen space: for instance, only her feet are visible when she is walking while letting the camera angle toward the ground. Given that Chun-jae's confession of her sexual identity and desire was based on Lee's respect for her privacy, leaving her face unveiled, the self-camera method intends to dismantle the hierarchy between filmmaker and subject and to place both on an equal footing. This collaborative experiment resonates with a specific kind of filmmaking that allows LGBT subjects to speak for themselves with their embodied speech and performative self-play—a technique that Thomas Waugh underlines as follows: "As we continue to emerge from our invisibility and silence, lesbian and gay filmmakers are often reluctant to impose that invisibility and silence on their subjects and seek means by which they may let their subjects speak rather than speak for them, let their subjects control their images rather than control them for them."[40] The strategy of letting subjects control their images is reflected not merely in the various angles and positions of the camera, which are extensive of Chun-jae's perception and consciousness, but also in her act of masquerading herself with dolls and pillows that serve as her stand-ins. In the second film, Chun-jae and her lesbian friends become more visible as they perform their self-images more actively. Though they still utilize darkness, dolls, hood, a paper mask, or partial self-images to negotiate between visibility and invisibility and between the private and the public, the film begins with the rap performance by the three teens that appeared in the first film, and moves on to Chun-jae's testimony about how to deal with her boyfriend, who does not exactly know her sexual orientation or want her to participate in Lee's filmmaking. Chun-jae indirectly responds to her boyfriend with her rap in the semi-music video sequence, in which she is shown as a girl with a video camera who films her classroom. The lyrics of the rap themselves express the heteronormative power of the educational system that forces lesbian subjects to confess ("Her voice gets louder, you lez lez lez. The classroom rings with it. Confess!"). The final music video sequence coupled with another rap, in which the three teens wearing school uniforms and masks stand on the rooftop of the school with self-confident posture, accentuates their growth as subjects who find themselves not only through their introspective journey but also through their solidarity with fellow minorities.

Troublers (*Puronhan tangshin*, 2017, 99 min.) brings Lee Young's aspiration to endow lesbian subjects with visibility to the larger contemporary battlefield of anti-LGBTQ hate fueled by right-wing Christianity, expanding the politics of sexual minorities historically and geopolitically, and inviting viewers to confront the intertwined ideological landscape of Korean society in a neoconservative regime. The film intersects its two narrative axes, each representing the previously unknown private lives of lesbians in Korea and Japan and the public spheres of society faced with the minorities' self-expression and their claim of human rights respectively. The first axis centers on Lee Muk (born in 1945) as a figure of Mr. Pants (*pajissi*) a slang term in modern Korea that refers to lesbians who change their gender role, as well as a lesbian couple in Japan who came out of the closet and lived together after the Tohoku earthquake in 2011. The bodily presence of Lee Muk, who appears to be a male senior, and her composed testimony about her troubled life, bear witness to the double strategies of minorities, disclosing and camouflaging their identity, who could not be socially visible or even legitimized under the patriarchal social norms of modern Korea. Lee Young, as a lesbian filmmaker, serves not only as an interlocutor who has an interpersonal, intergenerational relationship with Lee Muk, who embodies the previously untold histories of senior lesbians, but also as a distant observer of her everyday life in a rural community, including her conversation with several male neighbors curious about her sexuality.

The observational and dialogic tone of the first axis dramatically contrasts with the film's second axis, composed of Lee Young's on-the-spot records of the demonstrations by conservative Protestant churches and organizations against LGBTQ communities' social movement, which range from gatherings to prevent the legislation of Ch'abyŏl kŭmji bŏp and the Seoul Metropolitan Government's declaration of human rights to rallies opposing the Seoul Queer

Pride Parade.[41] Here viewers witness not only the naked face of conservative Christianity, that is, an irrational hatred of homosexuals via the demonization of AIDS and anal sex, but also the extent to which the opprobrium has been closely linked with an extreme right-wing anticommunist ideology that paints Others as *chongbuk* members. Lee Young applies her double cinematographic approach to the episodes of Lee Muk and the Japanese lesbian couple on this second axis. She sometimes actively intervenes in scenes of gatherings and rallies, inscribing in her camera visceral street protests against the queer parade and scuffles with queer activists who had a sit-in in the lobby of Seoul City Hall, resisting the Christianity organizers who blocked her filming. More significantly, however, Lee's stationary camera enables viewers to occupy the position of an invisible witness to the scenes of the Christians' protests as in the observational mode of documentary, while also guaranteeing the scenes' duration in which the viewers are keenly aware of the disturbing affects conveyed by the extremist speeches of their leaders and participants. This cinematographic strategy invites viewers to recognize the subjects of the violence, rather than manufacturing viewers' emotional response to it. When the stationary camera takes viewers to other rallies, including those against the bereaved families of the Sewol Ferry Disaster who demanded the Park Geun-hye government's thorough truth-finding measures, Lee's intention to juxtapose the lives of the lesbians with conservative Christians' intolerance becomes clear: to portray the pervasiveness of irrational prejudice in the neoconservative climate of society. Seen in this light, the film's narrative, which shuffles between the individuals and the square, reflects Lee Young's reference to the idea of intersectionality, through which she aims to depict how interlocking systems of power produce different modes of discrimination that affect those who are marginalized in society due to their gender, sexuality, and religion. As she remarks, "There exists an interconnectedness among multiple instances of hate directed at sexual minorities, the bereaved families, other minority groups, and women. I wanted to look into how oppressive and discriminating practices intersect in the space and time of all the groups."[42]

Environmental Activism: Daechuri, Gangjeong, Miryang, Seongju

South Korean environmental activism in various regional villages and cities in the twenty-first century has operated against the state power's economic developmentalism and its military-geopolitical reliance on the United States. It is possible to identify two directions of the activism during that period.

First, there have been villagers' struggles against the destruction of their conditions of living by the state-driven construction of infrastructure. A key local movement of this type is the citizens' fight against Korean Electric Power Cooperation (*Hanʼguk chŏllyŏk*) in Miryang (a city in Gyeongsangnam-do Province with a population of about 110,000) from 2008 to 2013 to stop the company's construction of 765 kV transmission towers. This type of regional struggle invited the participation of NGOs, specialists, and activists, demonstrating how they were linked to the larger civic environmental movement. The residents' fight in Miryang from the mid-2000s was triggered partly by their collective concern with the harmful effects of high voltage emanating from the already-installed transmission towers, and partly by the environmental organizations that opposed the Lee Myung-bak government's plan to construct the Shin-Kori 5 and 6 nuclear power plant reactors, for which the transmission towers were installed to transmit electricity that they would produce.[43] Despite their connection to environmental movements on the national level, however, it is significant to note that the struggles in Miryang were primarily driven by the local residents' right to survive (*saengjonʼgwŏn*) in their homeland than the ecocritical discourses led by the NGOs and activists. This suggests that the struggles must be read as the process by which the residents acquired their sense of resisting citizenship and community by combining their everyday living with a series of collective coalitions and direct actions.

Second, there also have been a series of regional struggles against military facilities and bases built by either the Ministry of National Defense or US Forces Korea (USFK). South Korean antibase movements have deep historical roots derived from the postwar Korean governments' pursuit of what Seungsook Moon has called "militarized modernity,"[44] and from the persistence of anti-American, antiimperialist sentiment in the collective consciousness of *minjung* since the Gwangju Uprising. Under these conditions, the public's negative perception of US bases surged in the early 2000s, as Koreans were enraged by the Yangju Highway incident in 2002, in which a US military convoy killed two fourteen-year-old Korean schoolgirls (Shim Mi-seon and Shin Hyo-soon) on its return from a training exercise, which led to candlelight protests commemorating the deaths. It was in those contexts that the antibase movement in Daechuri, Pyeongtaek, gained public attention, receiving support from civic groups, labor unions, and student activists on the national level. The movement countered the Ministry of National Defense's plan to acquire 199 acres of land from Daechuri village, based on the 2004 agreement between the South Korean and US governments to relocate Yongsan Garrison and to expropriate land surrounding Camp Humphreys for base expansion.[45] It was also linked to the protests from 2000 to 2002 against the unfair revision of the Status of Forces Agreement (SOFA) between the US and South Korean governments, through which the US military had the right to use Korean military bases. The anti-US sentiment demonstrated by the Daechuri movement prefigured the dissenting acts by residents in Gangjeong (a small coastal village on the southern side of Jeju Island) beginning in 2007 against the construction of a ROK naval base. Protesters were suspicious that the base was expected to accommodate facilities and weaponry of the US Navy. As in the case of the Daechuri resistance, Gangjeong village's antibase movement developed on the basis of the coalition between the residents' everyday resistance and the interventions and solidarity of environmental, religious, and antiwar activists concerned with the expansion of the military power and the destruction of the Gangjeong ocean that UNESCO had designated as biosphere reserve. As Lina Koleilat observes, while "resistance on the ground was mainly conducted by the villagers themselves" between 2007 and 2011, "The mayor reached out for support from religious groups and social activists throughout the Korean Peninsula to assist the villagers in their resistance."[46]

The intersection of geopolitical and environmental factors in the regional protests against military facilities was also applied to the regional activism against the Park Geun-hye government's THAAD deployment plan in 2016. It caused heated debates on the national level regarding whether or not the system would really work to defend South Korea from North Korea's ongoing missile threat. However, the struggles of the residents in Seongju county were targeted more at the government than at the right-wing proponents of the system who insisted that it would successfully protect against a missile strike. As Bridget Martin notes, "At the heart of the anti-THAAD movement [was] the recognition that the South Korean government has handled the THAAD deployment in an illegal and undemocratic way while yielding to US demands rather than protecting the safety of the South Korean people."[47] Indeed, the residents of the county, who had traditionally supported the right-wing party on which the Park government was based, felt that they were betrayed by the government, which made an agreement without any prior discussion with them. They also feared that THADD's electricity would severely deteriorate their health and produce. Thus, the residents' engagement with the anti-THADD movement was driven by their collective awareness of the THADD installation as a shattering blow to both their survival and their political trust. It was in this context that the residents established peace on the Korean Peninsula as the slogan of their resistance, in collaboration with religious and environmental activists who engaged in it. As in the struggles at Daechuri and Gangjeong villages, the anti-THADD protests enabled the residents to empower themselves as counterpublics against the post–Cold War geopolitical and military powers on the regional, grassroots level.

The activist documentaries about those environmental struggles are read as faithfully inheriting what Chris Berry has called the "socially engaged" mode of independent documentary film in East Asia, including Ogawa's *Sanrizuka* series made for and with the farmers resisting the government's seizure of their land for the construction of Narita Airport, as well as the traditional Korean activist nonfiction practices that aim to portray the collective subjectivization of urban evictees against the forces of state apparatus and corporate capitalism. The documentaries do more than produce an immediate record of the bodies of protesters revolutionized and mobilized against the police: they also intend to highlight the crisis of the community and the members' communal action dealing with it, serving to amplify movements and create coalitions, blurring the divisions between "production and consumption . . . [and] between subject and audience in the pursuit of [their] political and social goals."[48] More significantly, they produce a counterpublic sphere by articulating the views and opinions of the residents with respect to the regional issues that triggered their acts of resistance, rather than sticking to the myths of objective representation and balanced reporting. The residents' concerns with the impending destruction of their natural environment, their changing awareness of the government, and the arguments and perspectives of the activists who were allied with their struggles, all form the counterpublics' discourse on the issues. The discourse was neglected by mainstream news media, which tended either to downplay the residents' struggle as a NIMBY phenomenon or to exaggerate its spectacle of violence, which implies that their protests could have been instigated by external—"leftist" or "communist"—forces. Jung Il-gun, a member of Docu Purn, produced both *Daechuri War* (*Daechuri chŏnjaeng*, 2006, 44 min.) and *Memories of Daechuri* (*Daechurie salta*, 2009, 82 min.). The first film documents the police's violent suppression of the villagers' peace rallies, making available their testimony about the historical roots of the expansion of Camp Humphrey and their shared anti-US sentiment. Its sequel focuses on a group of "keepers," mostly young activists from different NGOs, who moved in Daechuri to oppose the expansion after the Ministry of National Defense restricted outsiders' entrance in 2005. Jung's intimate relationship to the keepers allows him to capture both their nonviolent demonstrations and their various activities to rehabilitate the deserted village, such as farming, house repairing, and the construction of the community memorial center. A series of static and handheld shots framing empty roads and houses in the film's ending expresses Jung's desire to preserve the

110 Activism

memories of the village despite the eviction of its members by geopolitical and military forces.

The documentaries allied with environmental activism in the 2010s achieve a higher degree of bond between aesthetics and politics than their predecessors, while also registering the spectacle of the antigovernment struggle, the community's communal solidarity and decision-making, and respect for the community members' right to survive. Cho Sung-bong, director of controversial history documentaries *Red Hunt* (see chapter 1) and *Red Hunt 2: State Crime* (*Redŭ hŏnt'ŭ 2: Kukka pŏmjoe*, 1999, 75 min.), engaged the Gangjeong village struggles with *Gureombi: The Wind Is Blowing* (*Gureombi: Parami punda*, 2013, 100 min.). The film's vivid portrayal of the scenes of peaceful resistance at the entrance of the village, at its rocky coast (Gureombi coast), and on its coastal sea bears witness to the activities of the vigils protecting the coast, and the arrestments and imprisonments of villagers and activists who nonviolently resisted construction of the naval base that would threaten villagers' livelihoods, the local ecosystem, and the peace of northeast Asia. Besides the camera's on-the-spot record of their clashes with the police, the film spends a considerable amount of time presenting images associated with the political, ecological, and religious grounds of the struggles to raise the awareness of the naval base issue for transnational advocacy. In contrast to the shaky handheld camera that approaches the scenes of the protests, Cho frames Catholic masses and a choreographer's performance on the Gureombi coast in long shots to highlight the mutual dialogue between people and nature. Montage sequences coupled with campaign songs, including aerial shots of the landscape from the upper side of a stream to the Gureombi coast in the film's opening, are inserted several times to audiovisually convey ideas about the coast: the source of pure water to residents of Jeju Island, the beauty of nature, the habitat of coral reefs and red-foot crabs, and the land that has millions of years history and relics. By highlighting those ideas, the nonverité sequences give aesthetic equivalents to the "peace and life" frame that both local and international activists developed "by juxtaposing the natural beauty and ecosystem of the island with the large, impending naval base."[49]

Ozi Film (Oji p'illŭm), a film production collective formed in 2011 by Park Bae-il and Moon Chang-hyun, has produced a series of documentary films that engage with the cultural and political issues of Busan and the regions in Gyeongsangnam-do Province, while also doing alternative media practices such as public documentary production education, internet podcasting, public access programming, and community-based distribution and screening. The group produced two films about the Miryang transmission tower struggles, *Legend of Miryang* (*Miryangjŏn*, Park Bae-il, 2013, 74 min.)

and *Miryang Arirang* (*Miryang arirang*, Park Bae-il, 2014, 102 min.), based on their long-term stay in the region from 2012 to 2015. The first film conveys voices and faces of several female senior residents, drawing out their memories of how their resistance began in 2005. The second film focuses on the women's struggles from 2013 to 2015, with their voices claiming how the construction of the tower has devastated their rural life and why their fight should go on. The two films commonly include several tropes that are frequently found in other environmental activist documentaries that aim to create political mimesis (visceral scenes of struggles that trigger public outrage) and to counter the mainstream media's distortion of the issue of the installation of social infrastructure (excerpts from news reports and from users' online comments that downplay the struggles as a NIMBY phenomenon). These tropes contribute to establishing Miryang grandmothers (*halmaedŭl, halmae* is a dialectal form of "grandmother") as counterpublics to the state power, giving powerful audiovisual evidence of how those who have been excluded from public discourse have cultivated their critical awareness of the state-driven nuclear power plants, articulated their voices, and developed collective solidarity. The two films also privilege the grandmothers' underrepresented stories, their communal lives of farming and eating together, and the natural details of the rural landscape both as their longtime base of living and as the site of their struggle. These three elements render the grandmothers resilient despite their frustration and sorrow over confrontation with the police. They, too, validate the two film's contribution from an ethnographic perspective, which demonstrates that "Miryang *halmaedŭl* are the visual embodiment of resistant culture under the neo-developmental state," and that the "production of [their] various meanings . . . is integrated with the rise and fall of the protestors' sit-in sites in fields and mountains as alternative spaces."[50]

A memorable scene in *Miryang Arirang* comprises two extreme low-angle shots taken from the bottom of a transmission tower, which calls to mind Joris Ivens's experimental documentaries about the machine-mediated modernity of the cities in the 1920s, such as *The Bridge* (1928). Coupled with the inserted testimony of a male senior farmer who confesses his anxiety over the tower, this poetic yet distancing cinematography marks Park's attempts to portray the landscapes of Miryang both as *hyŏnjang* of the struggles of its residents and as the site in which their memories and emotions are embedded. Park's auteurist signature, which pays as much attention to natural landscape as to the everyday lives and resistance of marginalized subjects, is more evident in *Sosŏngri* (*Sosŏngni*, 2017, 87 min.), a documentary about the grandmothers involved in the anti-THAAD struggles and the small rural village in which the facilities of THADD would be installed. Viewers are not able to see the scenes of the sit-ins by the grandmothers and the environmental activists who supported them throughout the film's first forty minutes. The voices of the grandmothers, often dissociated from their speaking bodies, are juxtaposed either with the observational records of their work at the farmland and their domestic spaces or with a series of panoramic long shots and drone shots that pictorially frame the village's river, mountains, and forests from day to night. More than expressing the significance of the natural environment in their idyllic rural life, the grandmothers' testimonies bear witness to the collective trauma of anticommunism and military forces during the Korean War, a trauma replayed by the news of the installation of THADD. Park's uses of several color filters in the scenes of the confrontation between the grandmothers and the right-wing pro-THADD groups and of nonrealistic sound effects coupled with several landscape images intend to present the grandmothers' anxiety in an uncanny manner. Along with all these devices that underline the affective and psychic dimensions of the resisting individuals, Park's stylistic cinematography is seen as a kind of "contemplative responses" to the environmental changes caused by military-geopolitical power, which aims to "create a space for acknowledging ambiguity and complexity"[51] rather than to provoke outrage and hope. In this sense, *Sosungri* represents a new experiment with environmental activism documentary, one that blends documenting residents' oral histories and their collective subjectivity in resistance with a focus on their surrounding landscape as object of investigation. The latter is linked to a group of films that are discussed in chapter 5.

Figure 3.2 *Sosungri* (Park Bae-il, 2017)

Expanding the Counterpublic Sphere: Alternative Journalism Documentary

The Korean documentary scene since the mid-2010s has witnessed the burgeoning of investigative nonfiction films produced and directed by journalists who established their independent news agency after having been dismissed by mainstream legacy news corporations. The investigative mode on which the films are built aims to interrogate and uncover hidden truths associated with the state or corporate power responsible for social injustice, and to expose them to the general public. At stake in contextualizing this relatively new breed of social change documentaries is the ways in which not only their formal and rhetorical strategies but also their institutional contexts, from their production to their distribution and consumption, relate to the activist tradition of Korean independent documentary, and to clarify why they can be seen as constructing their own alternative public sphere. In terms of the journalist-turned-filmmakers' background, most of them have worked for the investigative journalism team of their news service or produced well-known investigative journalism programs for Korea's national television corporations since the 1980s, such as *In Depth 60 Minutes* (*Ch'uchŏk 60pun*, KBS, since 1983) and *PD Note* (*PD suchŏp*, MBC, since 1990). The programs' purposes, production process, and rhetorical devices indeed were shared by many independent activist documentaries: their producers "operate[d] from a strong sense of right and wrong, prioritizing ethics over rules, working to expose wrongdoings, and providing a sense of conscience by spotlighting the interplay between the powerful and victims."[52] As Lee Seung-min points out, although there was little exchange between the two, investigative journalism and activist independent documentary offered their own alternative to the mainstream news media, *from its outside and from its inside respectively*: "Whilst independent documentary films emerged as a kind of alternative press against the mainstream news services that acted as a yes-man of the government, the investigative journalism programs played a role in unearthing social absurdity within the broadcasting system."[53]

It was during the right-wing regime of Presidents Lee Myung-bak and Park Geun-hye that investigative journalism left the mainstream media and started to build an alternative public sphere. The Lee government began to exercise tighter control of news content by appointing as chairmen of KBS, MBC, and YTN (Korea's first twenty-four-hour, state-affiliated news channel) persons who were friendly to its policy and ideology. This alleged management interference, which involved watering down news coverage of sensitive social issues and the discontinuance of *In Depth 60 Minutes* and *PD Note*, triggered

114 Activism

many journalists of the corporations to go on strikes. Countering the protests against the governmental control of the ownership and the limited freedom of press, the state-friendly appointees ordered dismissal of some resisting journalists, while also forcefully deploying others to the departments unrelated to their duties.[54] During this long-term struggle that endured until the transition to the liberal Moon Jae-in government, such journalists as Choi Seung-ho (former MBC PD who was dismissed for his involvement in the strike in 2012) and Lee Sang-ho (former investigative journalism reporter) formed their own independent news agencies, Newstapa (Nyusŭt'ap'a) and Gobalnews (Koballyusŭ), producing investigative reports and nonfiction artifacts that aimed to engage social issues uncovered or distorted by the mainstream press. It was thus no accident that *Seven Years: Journalism without Journalists* (*7nyŏn: Kŭdŭri ŏmnŭn ŏllon*, 2016, 121 min.) and *Criminal Conspiracy* (*Kongbŏmjadŭl*, 2017, 105 min.), two feature-length documentaries produced by Newstapa, take as their subject matter how the administrations of Lee and Park controlled public broadcasters, serving as a key catalyst for the resignation of the puppet chairman-appointees and their reform after Park's impeachment. The public attention of these films and Choi's *Spy Nation* (*Chabaek*, 2016, 90 min.)[55] brought into relief several previously unacknowledged correspondences between activist independent documentary and investigative TV journalism: reporting information and truth in opposition to the gatekeeping of mainstream news outlets, challenging power, advocating social change, fostering public awareness and moral outrage, developing long-term project based on preproduction and research, and featuring the role of the director as active participant in the event that he covers. Besides revealing the press control of the two right-wing governments, alternative journalism documentaries have expanded their thematic scope into other political issues. *The Reservoir Game* (*Chŏsuji keim*, Choi Jin-sung, 2017, 101 min.) investigates a slush fund belonging to President Lee, and *President's Seven Hours* (*Taet'ongnyŏngŭi 7shigan*, Lee Sang-ho, 2019, 79 min.) foregrounds Lee, who tries to resolve the mystery surrounding President Park's seven-hour absence after news of the sinking of the Sewol Ferry broke. The popularization of alternative journalism documentaries and their theatrical releases have benefited from the public's antipress sensibilities since the early 2010s: that is, disgust with the mainstream press and its reporters who, it is believed, cater to the interests of the neoconservative government and capitalist media enterprise moguls, including the *Chosun Daily*, the *Dong-a Daily*, and the *Joongang Daily*.[56]

Spy Nation, the most critically acclaimed work in this trend, demonstrates how alternative journalism documentary-making is able to craft a cinematic social problem film while also maintaining its journalistic protocols and standards. It features a spy case manufactured by the NIS under the Park Geun-hye regime, in which Yu Woo-sung, an ethnic Chinese who had fled to South Korea in 2004 and worked as a welfare official at Seoul Metropolitan Government, was arrested in 2013 on charges of spying for North Korea. Choi himself appears as an active investigative reporter striving to uncover the truth behind the case, interviewing his sister Yu Ga-ryeo, who later testified in court that there had been physical and psychological coercion during the NIS interrogation process, and chasing the NIS's agents involved in that allegations and prosecutors who had charged Mr. Yu with espionage. Choi's investigation does more than fact-check the prosecutors' theories to discover that the NIS allegedly fabricated Mr. Yu's incriminating documents, which eventually led to his being acquitted. Choi also unearths other cases of North Korean defectors who had falsely been stigmatized as spies by NIS's abusive and coercive techniques, while also revisiting the 1975 spy fabrication by the Korean Central Intelligence Agency (KCIA, Chungang jŏngbobu: the forerunner of the NIS in the Park Chung-hee regime), through which twenty-one Korean residents in Japan were indicted.[57] Choi's balanced approach to journalistic reporting and cinematic craft constructs an intellectually rich and emotionally moving discourse on the ideologically distorted portrait of Korean society, in which the anticommunist machinery of authoritarianism pervades its new conservative present in the name of *chongbuk*. What emblematizesthis point is the film's camera, which does not fear approaching big shots and asking for truthful testimony (as emblematized by the airport sequence where Choi meets with Kim Ki-choon, the former KCIA prosecutor in charge of the 1975 spy fabrication case who later became the chief secretary of President Park Geun-hye), and which stares at the agonized faces of the victims, including a former foreign student in Japan who is still living with the aftereffects of torture at KCIA.

Notwithstanding its ideological and formal commonalities with independent documentary filmmaking, investigative journalism's often "adversarial and populist"[58] rhetorics can be distinct from the voices of the activist documentary, which are able to vary the relationship between filmmaker and subject through "the body of the film: through editing; through subtle and strange juxtapositions; through music, lighting, mise-en-scène; through dialogue overheard and commentary delivered; through silence, as well as speech, [and] through images."[59] Instead of deliberately using those elements to construct an audiovisual discourse on reality and solicit the viewer's affective and emotional engagement with it, some investigative journalism documentaries produced thus far tend to foreground the reporter as the kernel of

116 Activism

their rhetoric, highlighting him as a kind of hero who debunks false truths, challenges power, supports victims, and provokes public outrage. Although these multiple registers of the filmmaker-in-text have been popular thanks to the politically controversial works of Michael Moore, the films' overreliance on the subjectivity of the reporter and their overemphasis on his particular perspective on a specific case may risk contradicting journalistic standards of truth commonly applied to both investigative journalists and politically responsible, independent documentarians.

A case in point is *The Truth Shall Not Sink with Sewol*, the first alternative journalism documentary of the 2010s based on the collaboration of Lee Sangho and independent documentarian Ahn Hae-ryong. In the middle of the film, which aims to unearth the Park government's incompetence in dealing with the Sewol Ferry Disaster, the viewer sees Lee announcing with a microphone to missing passengers' families that the mainstream news outlets distorted the truth of the situation of search and salvage, which reported that the joint task force of the government, militaries, and citizens "carried out search operations with the greatest resources ever." While Lee's personality as provocateur mirrors the moral resentment of the public at the corruption and deceit of both the government and the mainstream press, he pushes to the extreme his hypothesis that the government' authorities clandestinely impeded the installation of "Diving Bell" equipment where the ferry sank, and his condemnation of the mainstream media for framing Lee Jong-in, the head of Alpha Diving Corp. who had invented the equipment and proposed to use it for extended dives, as an opportunist who was obstructing the government's rescue efforts. In so doing, Lee does not offer fact-checking, substantial materials, or interviews with various persons as requirements of investigative journalism. The film's lack of in-depth analysis and verification, as well as its one-sided advocacy of Lee Jong-in's arguments, stirred another series of controversy over its aesthetic and discursive values.[60] What this controversy suggests, in my view, is that investigative journalists, in venturing into cinematic nonfiction work, need to bear in mind that "the more controversial your work, the higher the expectation will be for ethics and editorial standards."[61]

Despite this shortcoming demonstrated by *The Truth Shall Not Sink with Sewol*, the investigative journalism documentaries of the 2010s have undoubtedly entailed the productive intersection of alternative press and independent documentary in terms of their common purposes and functions. They also contributed to expanding the alternative public sphere of independent nonfiction media, in which previously underrepresented voices could be heard and previously uncovered issues or truths could be discussed. The ways that they have innovated the activist tradition of Korean documentary cinema are also evident in their financial and institutional dimensions and in their strategies for distribution and exhibition. As Jung Sooyoung writes, "In order to be free of any external pressures or interference, [the alternative media outlets] reject all advertisements and funding from government/interest groups, running exclusively on donations from supporter members. In other words, civil society and ordinary people are behind the rise of non-profit investigative journalism within South Korean society and the success of those economic models like Newstapa."[62] Besides its financial independence from those funding resources, Newstapa has also updated the "coalition model" that the Korean activist documentary has relied on since the 1990s.[63] In the case of *Spy Nation*, for example, Newstapa organized a campaign to raise funds for its theatrical screening via Daum's Story Funding website from June 13 to August 31, 2016, garnering almost $400,000 from 17,261 donors.[64] The film's distributor, Cinemadal, organized community screenings in various social organizations, including Korean communities in the United States, together with theatrical release. While many independent documentarians who seek financial support and increase the political impact of their films have used the same kind of strategies, Newstapa, like Robert Greenwald's Brave New Films, produced a series of video and text reports on the case of Yu Woo-sung, as well as *A Story of Confession* (*Chabaek iyagi*, 2013), a fifty-minute animated documentary focusing on the story of Yu Ga-ryeo, and made them available via its website and YouTube channel. Given this strategy of expanding the previous coalition model of political documentaries with streaming videos and social media tools that facilitate public discussion and screenings, I argue that *Spy Nation* can be seen as transmedia documentary, that is, one of "a set of nonfiction films that use the participatory culture of the web to enhance the possibilities for both a vibrant public sphere cultivated around important political issues and an activist culture invested in social and political change."[65]

Migratory-Grassroots Media Activism and Omnibus Documentaries

The growth of public access movements and the increase in local media activists gave rise to what I call "migratory-grassroots media activism" in the late 2000s. This was grounded in the nationwide network that media activists based in different parts of Korea organized in 2005 to promote their respective grassroots media movements, to share each movement's community issues, and to develop common strategies for public access, media democracy, and social change. In 2014, this type of media activism evolved into Act with

118 Activism

Media (Midiŏro haengdonghara), in which a group of social movement and media activists stayed in a community during a certain period of time and carried out an array of interrelated activities encompassing filmmaking, narrowcasting, music performance, screening, publication, and workshops. The first outcome of this project, *Act with Media in Samcheok* (*Midiŏro haengdonghara in Samch'ŏk*, 2014, 78 min.), demonstrates the ways in which this type of media activism updates the Korean activist documentary's tradition of collective news production. Composed of five videos and one radio narrowcast recording that were collectively made during five days, the piece focuses on the referendum of the residents in Samcheok in October 2014 regarding whether or not they would accept the government's nuclear power plant. The six projects included in the piece offer varying perspectives on the idea of grassroots democracy, including the oral testimonies of villagers about how they stopped the installation of the plant in 1998, the contested opinions on the government's plan that divided a community into two groups, grandmothers in a fishing village who work at the seashore and go inland to vote, and the confessions of their producers about how they felt about the issue and the residents. Since then, Act with Media has engaged in key environmental struggles in Miryang (2015), Gimcheon and Seongju (2017), and Jeju Island (2019), as well as in Yuseong Enterprise's union busting in Chungju (2016).[66] All the projects of Act with Media do more than inherit the purpose and strategies of traditional independent documentary. They have added up to a collection of short videos, recordings of narrowcasting and musical performances, and magazines simultaneously available for community and film festival screenings, as well as in PDFs and audio files on social media.[67]

While most videos are marked by the activists' participatory dialogues with villagers in action or by their observational or poetic record of the landscape that surrounds them, some videos are built upon aesthetic formats other than those of direct cinema or cinéma-vérité, such as low-fi music video and the documentation of performances by artists for the sake of expressing their solidarity with a struggle and its subjects. The diversity of the videos and media then interweaves their multiple subjects and formats into a unified issue that further yields collective action. In this way, Act with Media has illustrated an intriguing integration of migratory and grassroots or community-based media activism. The activists' visits to the communities for empowerment of their members and their use of the various media, including DIY videomaking, to implement the alternative modes of production and distribution resonate with the US video guerrillas in the 1970s. At the same time, Act with Media's encouragement of the residents' participation in its projects has also gestured toward the idea of community media, which encompass "a range of community-based activities intended to supplement, challenge, or change the operating principles, structures, financing, and cultural forms and practices associated with dominant media."[68]

The issue-based omnibus documentary has been another major trend of the twenty-first-century alternative activist nonfiction practices that is liberated from the format of long-form nonfiction films. This mode refers to a compilation of short films based on the engagement of multiple activists and filmmakers with the same social issue or theme. Thanks to its inclusive and participatory format, the omnibus film has been devoted to "generating dissent and attempting to mobilize the masses, based on filmmakers' contribution of short works to a larger whole that can encompass a range of directorial styles, narrative modes and genres."[69] The overall project, then, stitches together the discrete films into a larger theme associated with humans, communities, or social problems that solicit public awareness and solidarity, while maintaining differences in their subject and style. For these two reasons, it has some affinity with migratory-grassroots media activism in that it has involved filmmakers or activists' traveling to and staying in a given locale during a certain period of time. It is also distinct, however, because it has invited participation of the documentarians and collectives who already established themselves based on a one-person production system.

16 Takes of Korean Society (Pult'anŭn p'illŭmŭi yŏndaegi, 2006, 110 min.) pioneered this trend, as it compiled sixteen short films (five minutes in length) made by seventeen filmmakers and media activists. Led by Lee Mario as its executive producer, the project was conceived as a feature-length documentary in which different contributions would be consolidated into a larger portrait of a Korean society afflicted by its long-standing contradictions and its drive to neoliberalization. The contributions encompass wide-ranging subjects: the struggle of the workers at Giryeung Electronics, the antibase movement at Daechuri, peasants' fight against the Korea-US Free Trade Agreement and the WTO, female irregular workers, and conscientious objectors to mandatory military service. The result is a wide variety of approaches and issues, characterized by dynamic alternation between films' verité-style records of interviews and actions and the propagandistic or critical mixes of media images. Besides its preproduction that guaranteed both the stylistic and thematic discreteness of the films and their larger unity, *16 Takes of Korean Society* also demonstrated the strategies of alternative media for distribution and screenings. Along with community screenings, it was downloaded more than one thousand times on newscham.net (*Midiŏ ch'amsesang*) and later released on DVD. The solidarity of filmmakers and activists in facing a common issue has also been demonstrated in a group of omnibus documentaries produced about environmental activism in Gangjeong Village, including *Jam Docu Gangjeong* (*Chaem tak'yu Kangjŏng*, 2011, 8 films, 104 min.), which involved such veteran documentarians as Kim Tae-il, Hong Hyung-sook, and Kyungsoon, to name just a few, and *Gangjeong Interview Project* (*Kangjŏng int'ŏbyu p'ŭrojekt'ŭ*, 2012, 22 films, 80 min.), led by documentarian Mun Jeong-hyun (see chapters 4 and 6).

The omnibus documentaries since the mid-2010s have expanded their scope from regional struggles into two intertwined nationwide social events: the Sewol Ferry Disaster and the 2016–2017 Candlelight Protests. In response to the former, hundreds of documentarists and media activists, including Kim Il-rhan from PINKS and the late Park Jong-pil (see chapter 2), organized the 4.16 Solidarity Media Committee (4.16 yŏndae midiŏ wiwŏnhoe) and practiced their acts of filming from May 2014 to December 2018, producing and posting on YouTube sixty-six videos that document the efforts of private divers to rescue victims, the public protests and campaigns of their bereaved families for truth-finding and the legislation of a special act, public hearings on the ferry's sinking and the government's rescue process, interviews with the families for the purpose of interrogating their traumas and human rights issues, and ordinary citizens' activities of solidarity.[70] For its second year, the 4.16 Committee decided to produce omnibus documentaries based on preproduction and planning, which resulted in *Forgetting and Remembering* (*Manggakkwa kiŏk*, 2016, 7 shorts, 204 min.), *Forgetting and Remembering 2: Reflection* (*Manggakkwa kiŏk 2: Tora pom*, 2017, 6 shorts, 175 min.), and *We Remember: Trauma* (*Kongdongŭi kiŏk: T'ŭrauma*, 2018, 4 shorts, 138 min.). All three films were distributed via the transmedia strategy that involved crowdfunding, community screenings organized by Cinemadal, and showcases at film festivals, demonstrating political documentaries' shifting coalition model in which their social impacts are measured according to the synergy of filmmakers, movement organizations and activists, and audiences.[71] Just as public awareness of the Park Geun-hye government's irresponsible handling of the disaster fueled its collective drive to democratization,[72] so was the committee's integration of participatory documenting and omnibus documentary extended into media activities dealing with the 2016–2017 Candlelight Protests.

What is notable in the omnibus documentaries on the Sewol Ferry Disaster is the shifting temporality of activist practices in the service of engaging social movements. Indeed, the disaster has been a determining incident that sparked the cultural politics of making collective memories based on the participatory practices of the bereaved families and other social agents. For it has stimulated a variety of cultural and artistic forms that aim to mourn and commemorate the disasters' victims, to retrieve the traumas and memories of their families, and to make the memories available for knowledge and discourse that call for uncovering the truth and establishing social justice. Across diverse media, activities, and artistic projects, these forms have encompassed publication of a white book on the day of the disaster,[73] myriad literary or visual artifacts and musical, theatrical, and choreographic performances that attempt to document and memorialize the victims,[74] and an online platform (4.16 Memory Archives, www.416memory.org) for archiving photos, videos, and the documents produced by the families' committee and the investigation committees. It is in this context that Lee Seung-min labels the practices of the 4.16 Committee as "archive activism." While acknowledging documentary film in general as an archival artifact and the activist mode's long-standing penchant for long-term engagement with a subject, she seems to specify the committee's acts of documenting as both for the immediate present of the struggles for social justice and change and for the present haunted by its ineluctable link to the unresolved and traumatized past: "What is at stake is the meaning of documenting itself rather than the document's revelatory function. For the document at *hyŏnjang* is the medium of solidarity, of empathy, and of therapy through which to stage pain. In other words, what is immanent in the document is mourning and reflection. The document, then, functions as a repository for constructing and sharing social memory."[75]

Accordingly, the shots complied in the two *Forgetting and Remembering* films are geared toward producing different yet overlapping archival effects. Park Jong-pil's two films, *Salvage* (*Inyang*, in *Forgetting and Remembering*) and *Diver* (*Chamsusa*, in *Forgetting and Remembering 2*), offer viewers the opportunity to commemorate the activities and virtues of civilian diver Kim Kwan-hong, who was found dead in 2016, and to sympathize with his depression derived from his encounters with the dead, with on-the-spot records, footage of Kim's public speeches, and testimonies of his fellow divers and his wife. Tae Joon-sik's *Classroom* (*Kyoshil*, in *Forgetting and Remembering*) and Moon Sung-joon's *Touch of Memory* (*Kiŏgŭi son'gil*, in *Forgetting and Remembering 2*) portray the bereaved families as the agents of social justice and highlight the significance of their memorializing practices as they feature their activities to maintain the "4.16 Memory Classroom" (a classroom dedicated to preserving photos and memory objects of the victims at Danwon High School) and establish a memorial park at an recreation area of Ansan against the pressures of the school and the residents who did not welcome the park. By giving them political agency, the two films reflect the 4.16 Committee's ethical consideration of how to deal with the families. As an article published in the white paper of its activities asserts, "What is most serious in the press coverage of the disaster

122 Activism

is to confine the bereaved families within the 'frame of victim' (*p'ihaeja*) and duplicate their images as victims. By throwing a gaze of pity on the decreased and their families and rendering them the protagonist of a tragedy, this convention establishes them as a passive object of sympathy."[76] This ethical consideration, through which the families could be seen as positive agents beyond the public stereotype of them as victims or objects of mourning, was extended in a recent feature-length documentary *The Talent Show* (*Changgi jarang*, Lee Sohyun, 2022, 93 min.), in which members of the troupe Yellow Ribbon (*Noran ribon*, founded in 2015), mothers of victims and survivors, are portrayed as subjects dealing with a series of conflicts: whether or not they would join the troupe, which role they want to take in its plays, and how to negotiate their performance and practice with their everyday life. Meanwhile, a couple of films based on a montage of media images and footage of the testimony at public hearings held by the Investigation Committee, such as Kim Hwan Tae's *Five Enemies of Sewol* (*Sewŏl ojŏk*, in *Forgetting and Remembering 2*), create alternative discourses to the Park government's manipulation of the records associated with the disaster. By preserving the discreteness of all the perspectives, which are based on the filmmakers' intimate interactions with the families, the omnibus documentaries on the disaster are in line with the global trend of archiving as a key practice of digital video activism since the late 2000s, which has aimed to share common sentiments, to collect evidence, to build commemoration, and to strengthen social solidarity.[77]

Of all feature-length documentaries on the disaster, Joo Hyun-sook's *Yellow Ribbons* (*Tangshinŭi sawŏl*, 2019, 86 min.) deserves particular attention due to its consideration of the multitude and of archiving as the two notable features of recent activist practice. The film brings together portraits of six social actors, one father of a victim and five citizens who are not direct parties to the disaster. They are different in occupation, gender, and age, encompassing a college student majoring in archival studies, a middle school teacher, a cafe owner, a fisherman based on Jindo Island (near the site of the disaster), and a female activist: but they share the common experience of having witnessed it via media coverage. The film interweaves the portraits of the varying social subjects in two ways: first, the subjects' confessions about the shock and sorrow triggered by the disaster; and second, the camera's intimate filming of their everyday lives, in which they practice their acts of commemoration and of solidarity (*yŏndae*) with the families' protests: the college student pays a visit to the "4.16 Memory Classroom," hoping that her knowledge of archiving will contribute to a better society; the teacher shares her knowledge and feeling about the disaster with her students; and after having encountered some families who participated in a demonstration at his cafe, its owner volunteers to support their activities. All these activities resonate with what Lille Chouliaraki has called the "politics of pity" regarding the social bond between the scenes of distant suffering and the spectators who experience them via media. By this, she means the "symbolic mechanism of mediation that seeks to motivate the spectators' move from dispassionate observation to agency, to public conduct."[78] While fine-tuning the power of the interview and the camera's inscription of social reality as the two aesthetic templates of traditional activist documentary, *Yellow Ribbons* renders each social subject to be part of the multitude that is formed by "singularities that act in common."[79] In so doing, the film establishes itself as the archive of different yet interconnected stories about the trauma that the subjects experienced, and about how each of their activities for overcoming it leads to the larger initiative for solidarity. It is with these two effects that the film expands the thematic and representational boundaries of the traditional activist documentary. As this expansion is indebted to Joo's directorial decision and ethical consideration, the film, too, validates the ways in which the activist documentaries' diversification of styles and social issues in the twenty-first century has been grounded in directors' growing awareness of their self-identity as *kamdok* and their relationship to social actors, and in their different negotiations between creativity and actuality, or between aesthetics and politics.

#AfterMeToo

As the most recent outcome of the issue-based omnibus filmmaking, *#AfterMeToo* (*Aep'ŭt'ŏ mit'u*, 2021, 84 min.) brings together four shorts directed by women directors, including KangYu Garam and veteran documentarian Park So-hyun. The project aims to collect views on the lingering effects of the local Me Too (*mit'u*) movements triggered by female prosecutor Seo Ji-hyun, who claimed sexual harassment by a former senior Ministry of Justice official in a televised interview in January 2018.[80] The four episodes attend to distinct yet interrelated topics: the "School #MeToo" movement among teenagers to reveal male teachers' sexual harassment and misogyny, a middle-aged, working-class woman who attempts to articulate her experience of sexual violence in her childhood, the Me Too movement in the fields of art and theater, and the sexual self-determination of women who recall their uncomfortable sex with their partner. In so doing, they attest to the dialectic of difference and commonality that underlay the local Me Too movement as a resistance of *tajung*: namely, the subjects' difference in age, occupation, and class, on the one hand, but their common awareness of hate

124 Activism

and discrimination, and of the demands for articulating their experiences and making individual or collective action, on the other.

Each episode of this omnibus film, then, illustrates the formal and aesthetic diversity of the twenty-first-century activist documentary with its own distinctive style. The first film (directed by Park) on the "School #MeToo" movement is composed of coolly edited black-and-white snapshots that capture a female high school's spaces and the collective actions of its students, juxtaposed with their off-screen testimonies. The third film, directed by KangYu, features a performance artist who engaged in the anti-sexual harassment campaign in the theater world and translated that experience into her mime gestures. In the last film, the confessions of the anonymous women are interspersed with animated pictures expressive of their mixed feelings, such as guilty conscience and humiliation. At stake in these diverse approaches is more than the project's initiative to track down the rise and cooling down of the movements and to reflect on their sustainability: they are grounded in each director's interrogation of documentary form in regard to the mnemonic and ethical dimensions of the social actors who experienced psychic trauma or the suppression of the social sectors (schools and the art worlds, for instance) to which they belong. The anonymity of the interviewees in the first and last films demonstrates the two directors' respect for their privacy, but the reconstruction of their experiences with the still photos and illustrations succeeds in expressing the vivid yet complex memories of their pain, affects, and struggles. The documentarians' efforts to bridge form and issue, or aesthetics and politics, undoubtedly result from the growing self-consciousness of a documentary practitioner as individual *kamdok*, which is a hallmark of the twenty-first-century activist documentary. They also originate from the larger transformation of the Korean documentary cinema during that period—a sea change in form and aesthetic that we will investigate in Part II.

PART II
POST-ACTIVISM

4

The Personal Turn

Domestic Ethnography, the Essay Film, Reenactment

Personal Documentary (*sajŏk tak'yument'ŏri*)

Gina Kim's Video Diary (*Kim Jinaŭi pidio ilgi*, 2002, 157 min.) compiles video footage that Gina Kim recorded between 1995 and 2000, from the moment of her moving to the United States to her lonely and confined life in small apartments. Introduced as Kim's coming-of-age story, the film benefits from video technology with which she had been fascinated since her art school experience in Seoul and her study at the California Institute of the Arts: "I was intoxicated by the narcissistic feature of the medium. . . . I would hook up the video camera with the monitor and observe myself. It was like an I-watch-myself-film-myself kind of looking."[1] This fascination is reflected in the footage of her exhibitionist self-performances—dancing, brushing teeth, wearing Korean traditional garments (*hanbok*), cutting raw meat, observing her belly, and sitting aimlessly—in front of her camera. They are expressive of Kim's psychic and corporeal pains in struggling with isolation, silence, and anorexia. Her video camera is everywhere: it functions as a mirror in Kim's direct address and as an extension of her perception in the close-ups of objects; it observes her from the apartment's ceiling and walls, as well as from the tripod. These various camera positions resonate with video's status as border-crossing media. For the camera renders her apartment a technologically mediated space in which the boundaries between ritual and everyday life, between her physical self and her psyche, and between self-surveillance and theatrical staging are fundamentally blurred. Another border-crossing occurs in the intersection of videography and writing, as the footage is intercut with close-ups of the words and sentences from books and her dictionary, as well as with her memos written by hand and with a word-processor, for instance: "It was never food that I vomited and rejected. It was Mom's life. There is hope as long as I have life . . . and flesh." Both textual components ultimately establish Kim's psychic self and cultural identity as fluid, which also corresponds to the continual exchange between her ordinary life and her transgressive

---

Activism and Post-activism. Jihoon Kim, Oxford University Press. © Oxford University Press 2024.
DOI: 10.1093/oso/9780197760413.003.0005

128 Post-activism

performance, between her hatred of her hysteric mother and her longing, and between writing or speaking in Korean and in English (emblematized by her different costume plays with *hanbok* and a wedding dress). In this regard, Kim's video diary advances to the autoethnographic exploration of her diasporic identity fractured by the contestation of drifting and solitude, of freedom and alienation.

Kim's experimental video diary indeed echoed a special focus section in the inaugural edition of the Seoul Independent Documentary Film Festival (SIDOF) in 2001—one dedicated to "personal documentary" (*sajŏk tak'yumentʻŏri*). Two films included in the program are notable in terms of why its emergence in the early twenty-first century was problematic, compared to the activist tradition of the two previous decades. In *My Father* (*Naŭi abŏji*, 2001, 40 min.), Kim Hee-chul (see chapter 2) takes as its protagonist his father, who was a displaced person from North Korea and a "shoeshine boy" of the US soldiers during and after the Korean War, foregrounding his self who is in conflict with the father but who also comes to realize how much similar his habits and character are to those of the father. Made during her study at CalArts in 2001, Kim Lee-jin's *Kaleidoscope* (*Chumadŭng*, 2001, 52 min.) also focuses on her father, who was a juror working on Jeju Island. A key moment in the film is when the two together watch videotapes that Kim filmed during her last summer vacation at home. In contrast to the assumption that home movies are a truthful bearer of the good old days of a family, the father becomes embarrassed with his appearance in the footage, arguing that his image in the video is not true to what he thinks he was. Stop-motion effects used in the replay of the video clips, as well as Kim's deliberate nonlinear editing, reflect her self-reflexive consciousness not only of the epistemological gap between her father and his self-image but also of the generational gap between him and her. The two films' common features, such as the exposure of the director as subjective I, the use of the first-person voice-over, the compact digital video camera and digital visual effects as extension of the director's embodied perception and consciousness, and the discrepancy between the director and his or her family member, captured critical attention in light of how they informed the shifting topology of Korean independent documentary in the early 2000s. Kim Sunah read the two films as the "radical experiments with deconstructing the mode of political documentary in the 1980s and 1990s from its bottom," labeling them as "postclassical documentary" in contrast to the "classical" (activist) films and videos marked by the "disembodied voice, images subject to the voice, and the omniscient and neutral position of *kamdok* (director)."[2]

Personal documentary has diversified its form and subject matter, such that many younger-generation directors have increasingly produced feature-length and short films since the mid-2010s. Showcased in international and local film festivals such as SIDOF and the DMZ International Documentary Film Festival (DMZDocs), the films "'speak' from the articulated point of view of the filmmaker who readily acknowledges her subjective position"[3]—they can be a self-portrait or a portrait of another, they can be autobiographical or experimental, they are primarily based on lens-based records, digitally manipulated home movies, or animated figures, and they deal with well-known public issues or, as critic Lee Do-hoon observes from the 2019 SIDOF, "something unrepresentable: subjectivity, memory, sense, emotion, affect, desire, and unconsciousness."[4] While these diverse breeds of personal documentary undoubtedly mark notable aesthetic and epistemological departures from the activist tradition, a tension in anchoring the meanings of the term "personal" (sajŏk), which has often been understood as opposite to the public (kongjŏk) or political (chŏngch'ijŏk), has held sway in the discursive and institutional domains of twenty-first-century Korean documentary cinema. Young woman director Jeong Su-eun brought to the forefront the issue of the masculinist prejudice against sajŏk tak'yument'ŏri made by her fellow female documentarians in local film festivals in the 2010s. In her statement presented at a special forum by the 2017 DMZDocs, whose opening film was her One Warm Spring Day (Kŭ nal, 2016, 83 min.) about her paternal grandfather as a member of the South Korean Army and her maternal grandfather as a member of North Korean Army during the Korean War, Jeong writes:

> Personal documentary derives from the *private sphere*, which has traditionally been regarded as distinct from the *public sphere*, in which documentary has played its role. In this sense, it has been presupposed to be *apolitical and personal from the perspective of the social and public*. However, is it possible to totally define personal documentary as just a small, private, and individual story? . . . Who judges the supremacy of the public over the personal?[5]

Jeong's bold questions do more than reveal the gender bias implicit in the distinction between political and personal documentaries. More significantly, they also suggest that the concept of sajŏk tak'yument'ŏri has been an arena for contested ideas on the political legitimacy and authenticity of Korean independent documentary vis-à-vis its activist imperatives. If personal documentary is as political as personal, how do its representational strategies and subject matters relate to the public and political issues that the activist

130 Post-activism

documentaries have engaged with in dialogue with social movements? How does the former approach and tell the issues differently than the latter?

In order to answer these two questions, this chapter rehearses the twenty-year evolution of *sajŏk tak'yumentŏri* by teasing out the implications of the term *sajŏk* in light of the ambivalent relationship of post-activist practices to their activist predecessors. As a particular conceptual and general rubric, personal documentary refers to a variety of nonfiction films that take the director's first-person (*irinch'ing*) perspective as the focal point of exploring the director's inner self, his or her surrounding others, and/or a larger history and reality. For this reason, the proliferation of this practice has much to do with the emergence of the individual (*kaein*) as a vital agent in a given national documentary cinema in tandem with an array of sociopolitical, cultural, and technical conditions surrounding it. This is evident in Jim Lane's underlining of the "larger turn to the politics of selfhood"[6] as a precondition for US auto-biographical documentaries in the 1970s, and Kiki Tianqi Yu's association of the first-person documentary with the growing autonomy of individuals and the flourishing of self-expression in the first decade of twenty-first-century China.[7] The two studies also highlight the proliferation of lightweight film and video cameras since the late 1960s in the United States and of digital video since the mid-1990s in China as a common technical infrastructure for the inward gaze on the director's self and the outward gaze on his or her intimate social actors and surroundings. Lane's and Yu's approaches can also be found in Nam Inyoung's seminal 2004 study on the representational modes of Korean independent documentary from the 1980s to the early 2000s. As the contexts for the advent of *sajŏk tak'yumentŏri,* she singles out the rise of the new social movement, the growing interest in the stories of individuals other than the collective subject framed by the "grand narrative" of *minjung,* the rise of film festivals and auteurist film journalism as a major institutional factor for the shifting identity of practitioners from *hwaltongga* to *kamdok,* and the introduction of compact digital cameras.[8] These contexts imply that the meanings of *sajŏk* in *sajŏk tak'yumentŏri* point to the increasing emphasis upon *kaein* since the mid-1990s: that is, the individual in personal documentary refers to both the director who becomes conscious of his or her filmmaking process and his or her subjectivity in constructing reality and exploring truth, and the social actor whose everyday life and memory cannot be fully explored in the enlightening voice (which Nam calls the "grand narrative") of the early activist films and videos that aspires to unite marginalized subjects as *minjung*—a collective agency for social change.

Nam's study, however, does not go so far as to identify another crucial implication of the term *sajŏk* in *sajŏk tak'yumentŏri*: the personal as opposed to *kongjŏk* or *chŏngch'ijŏk*. What validates the significance of this connotation is the consistent production of a particular subgenre of personal documentary during the last two decades: a portrait of a director' own family, or what Michael Renov has called "domestic ethnography." Unlike *Gina Kim's Video Diary*, which pertains to autoethnography as a mode of nonfiction practice that takes the director's fluid and contradictory self as its subject, domestic ethnography employs family photos, home movies, various formal experimentations with the camera (including the director's self-exposure and his or her intimate approximation to family members), their oral testimonies, and the director's first-person commentary to form micronarratives of the family's everyday life and history. In the words of Lane, these micronarratives "are incorporated into a larger, more complex weaving that presents family or self less in a cause-and-effect logic and more as figures in tension with states of being referred to in the past and seen and heard in the present."[9] Lane's view indeed does more than indicate the extent to which the various aesthetic forms of self-inscription in the twenty-first-century Korean personal documentary depart from the aesthetic and discursive constraints of the activist tradition: it also underscores that a key driving force of personal documentary is the director's growing self-consciousness of his or her reality and subjectivity in the present as closely intertwined with the past. Suggesting this tension, too, Renov posits the domestic ethnographer as the subject that has "no fully outside position available,"[10] in that she, both as a family member and as a filmmaker, negotiates between her gaze into herself and an outward gaze toward other family members. Lane's and Renov's accounts help one to understand the emergence of domestic ethnography as part of the larger efforts to overcome the activist tradition's imperative to *hyŏnjang* as the place of a social problem in the immediate present, on the one hand, and its hierarchical relationship between a documentarian and her subjects, on the other. The latter aspect also explains the reason that personal documentary in the early 2000s was understood as in dialogue with the films of Kim Dong-won (*Repatriation*) and Hong Hyung-sook (*The Border City*), marked by their self-reflexive, first-person voice-over that ponders their unstable relationship to the subjects as the incarnation of postwar ideological violence. As Nam writes, "The filmmaking subject becomes less an invisible, authoritative person in control of images behind the camera than a counterpart of the horizontal conversation with its social actors who aspire to exhibit their voice and existence via the images."[11]

Building upon Lane's and Renov's insights into domestic ethnography as a mode that tests the epistemological liminalities of nonfiction practice and works on and across the unstable boundaries of the director faced with her

132 Post-activism

family members and their past, I argue that its consistency in the twenty-first-century documentary production has been rooted in the specific significance of the family (*kajok*) in modern and contemporary Korean society. The urgency of the family as a documentary subject is obvious given that the domestic ethnographies of the early years of this century coincided with the activist documentaries driven by the growing public demand for truth-finding on state and ideological violence (see chapter 2) and by the development of *yŏsŏngjang* (the women's sphere, see chapter 3). The personal documentaries of the period responded to the renewed understanding of the family not as a private community sharply demarcated from the public world but as a microcosm affected by the larger macroscopic, sociopolitical, and historical forces constitutive of Korean society. These forces include the persistence of traditional, Confucianism-based family values, including the patriarchal hierarchy of men and women, and of the Cold War ideology and trauma in a modernizing society characterized by the growth of women's rights and individualism. They help one to notice that in the twenty-first-century post-activist documentaries the concept of *sajŏk* in domestic ethnography has emerged as a political and aesthetic strategy that approaches history and reality by making untenable the established boundaries between the private and the public, by positing the family as the imbrication of the two, and by expanding the legitimacy of documentary reality into the everyday lifeworld of the director and his or her family members.

The gendered and generational tensions ingrained in the family enable directors of domestic ethnography to approach the past of their prior-generation family members with the dialectic of proximity and distance: the experiences of their parents or ancestors, for instance, have lingering effects on their present in the forms of continuing human interaction, stories, and memory objects (photos, journals, home movies), but the profound dimensions of the experiences, such as their untold truth, are also perceived as distant and even inaccessible. This dialectic has to do with a couple of recent studies on domestic ethnographies, which take as their framework Marianne Hirsch's concept of "postmemory."[12] For Hirsch, postmemory, which refers to the kind of memory that the "generation after" has of the personal and collective trauma of those who came before, is mediated by "imaginative investment, projection, and creation" from the "traumatic fragments of events that still . . . exceed comprehension."[13] In this regard, the variety of expressive materials and self-inscription devices in domestic ethnographies reflects directors' effort to grapple with the ambivalence of postmemory which cannot be fully understood but which influences their psyche and their relationship to the family. Accordingly, the films render the repercussions of patriarchy and Cold War trauma in the family complicated and difficult to resolve. A political achievement of the films, I argue, lies in their articulation of this complexity and difficulty as grounded in the awareness that the personal/private and the political/social/historical are fundamentally inseparable in the fabric of the family. For it serves as an alternative to the activist tradition's discourses of enlightenment, solidarity, and truth and reconciliation, all of which aim to achieve the immediate transfer of the personal problems of dispossessed individuals, including the victims of the Cold War violence, to the public arena for social movements.

The director's self-conscious experiments with nonactivist documentary expressions and his or her fluid yet questioning subjectivity as alternative strategies for exploring reality and history have recently propelled the growth of the essay film and video. Despite its protean, border-crossing, and transgressive aspects that defy any stable definition as a genre, an array of existing scholarly works on the essay film since the early 2010s have noted two integral features, that is, its activation of the filmmaker's thinking subjective agency and its mobilization of his or her personal and critical reflection.[14] As Renov neatly points out, these two features of the essay film contribute to renewing documentary cinema's exploration of the world through the filmmaker's perceptual and thinking apparatus while also overcoming its traditional binaries of subjectivity/objectivity and of the personal/the public. For the director "evidence[s] an attachment both to the documentary impulse and to the complex representation of [his or her] own subjectivity," demonstrating how the work "regards history and subjectivity as mutually defining categories."[15] In response to the growing awareness of this potential, the rubric "essay film" both as a specific mode of filmic practice and as a critical term has gained increasing popularity in Korea's documentary culture since the mid-2010s. This has occurred in accord with the global circulation of essayistic films and videos in the film festival circuit and art exhibitions, which was extended into the programming of local and international film festivals dedicated to documentary, and with the emergence of young filmmakers and artists who learned their traditions and canons from local and foreign universities. This chapter discusses the films of Kim Eung-su and Kelvin Kyung Kun Park in terms of how their multilayered and decentralized subjectivity is strategically used to mediate the personal and the public in favor of unfolding rich reflections on either pressing reality (the Sewol Ferry Disaster) or the history of industrial modernization.

In examining the ways that the variants of personal documentary articulate the filmmaker's subjective position in dialogue with her engagement with politics and history or her effort to redraw the boundaries between the personal

134 Post-activism

and the political, this chapter also discusses the uses of reenactment in several twenty-first-century Korean documentary films. This is primarily grounded in Nichols's view on the kinship of the "reflexive" and "performative" documentaries. The reflexive mode's penchant for exhibiting the filmmaker's subjectivity that constructs the represented scene of a nonfiction film, he argues, may also "draw our attention to the performative quality of the film," in which "realism finds itself deferred, dispersed, interrupted, and postponed."[16] For Nichols, this suspension of representation in the performative documentary aims to stress the embodied aspects of knowledge and memory in the sense that it "attempts to reorient us—affectively, subjectively—towards the historical, poetic world it brings into being."[17] The performative mode's affinity with the exposure of the filmmaker's subjectivity, as well as its effect of reorienting the historical world "subjectively and affectively," suggests why reenactment has increasingly been adopted as a notable device in the post-activist films of the twenty-first century, including domestic ethnographies, which turn their attention from *minjung* to *kaein*. My take on the films underlines that reenactment is expressive of directors' various efforts to approximate the psychic and mnemonic realities of traumatized social actors and to reconstruct the realities' encounter with history in ways distinct from their activist precursors.

Family, Patriarchy, the Cold War: Domestic Ethnography in the Early and Middle 2000s

As prominent cultural anthropologist Cho Han Haejoang ardently stresses, *kajok* and *kukmin* ("a member of the nation") are the "two main signifiers that have exerted the most power in the constitution of modern life in South Korea."[18] This means that just as Korea's modernization after the end of the Korean War has produced *kukmin* as its desired mass subject, so has it endeavored to nourish patriarchs (*kabujang*) who have identified the unity of the family with that of the nation. Korea's dramatic modernization since the 1970s, however, has also entailed that families have been the battlefield for the ongoing contestation of two forces that oppose each other: patriarchal norms and the division of gender roles, and women's increased opportunities for higher education and socioeconomic independence. Families in Korea and other East Asian countries, despite their modernization, are still affected by the traditional forces that have insisted upon "the powerful linkages between marriage and childbearing . . . highly asymmetric gender relations within marriage, [and] strong norms of intensive maternal investment in children."[19] Sociologist Chang Kyung-sup has coined the phrase "individualization without individualism" to explain the paradox characterized by the condensed drive to modernization, which dismantled traditional norms and societal systems, and the continuing allegiance to family values and relations. While the transition to industrialization, globalization, and neoliberalization from the late twentieth to the twenty-first century in South Korea has propelled the crisis of the traditional familial system and the individualization of its members, these two have not totally abandoned—or rather, paradoxically reinforced in some respects—existing family-centered values, such as age/generation-based hierarchy, gender division, the center of reproduction, and the emphasis on emotional ties.[20] It is in this paradoxical context that several domestic ethnographies made by the women documentarians in the early 2000s posit their family as the arena of these two competing yet coexisting forces that blur the boundaries between the personal and the political, articulating its generational and gendered crises from the directors' subjectivity that negotiates their individualist, feminist perspective with their inextricable emotional bond.

From another angle, the Korean family since the Cold War has been a community not only in which the tragedies of the Korean War (massacres, fratricides, families' separation) took place, but also in which its psychic and affective aftereffects, such as hate, antagonism, and fear, have significantly influenced its members and the relationship between them—for instance, a father who experienced the war and his offspring—throughout different generations in the forms of repressed memories and anticommunist fervor. Anthropologist Heonki Kwon argues for approaching the Korean War and its continuing resonance with postwar Korean society in terms of the "politics of kinship," which operates both as "an intimate social experience" and as "an element of powerful impersonal operations." He writes, "Postcolonial state building advanced the idea of political community as a family writ large rather than a society of individuals . . . in which an act to resist the particular mode of state building became equal in meaning to that of betraying the family and punishable accordingly."[21] Indeed, the fusion between *kukmin* and *kajok*, and between the public and the private, that underlies the "politics of kinship" is a dominant way that numerous museums, monuments, literary texts, and popular films have represented the tragedy and trauma of the Korean War. In their study on the displays in Seoul's National War Museum, Sheila Miyoshi Jager and Jiyul Kim demonstrate that they depict the tragedy of Korea as that of a single family that the Korean War divided into two.[22] Similarly, Hyangjin Lee contends that "the representation of nationhood in both South and North Korean films [about the Korean War] can be seen as an extension or variation of familyhood . . . amplified to a societal level."[23]

136 Post-activism

The domestic ethnographies produced in the first half of the 2000s are read as having sprung from directors' awareness of the family as where the social operations of the Korean War and patriarchy are experienced both in the mentality of its individual members and in the intimate relationship between them. The directors' personal self that is manifested in their voice and camerawork, then, explores the deeper origin of the familial trauma or conflict, wavering between the positions of observer, interrogator, and intervener, and negotiating between proximity (as a family member) and distance (as a filmmaker). The self's quest for the profound truth and reconciliation, however, often turns out to be a difficult task due to the gendered and generational gaps between himself/herself and his/her intimate others.

Three family portrait documentaries by women directors during the first half of the 2000s, *Family Project: House of a Father* (*Kajok p'ŭrojekt'ŭ: Abŏjiŭi chip*, Jo Yun-kyung, 2001, 44 min.), *Life Goes On* (*Ŏmma*, Ryu Mi-rye, 2004, 50 min.), and *Umma (Mother)* (*Ŏmmarŭl ch'ajasŏ*, Joung Ho-hyun, 2005, 82 min.), share the director's first-person narration, her on-screen presence, and a critical investigation of her own family. *Family Project* explores Jo's own middle-class nuclear family, centering around the past and present of her father. The testimonies of her mother and younger brother reveal that despite his successful career as newspaper journalist, would-be-politician, and professor, he has nonetheless been an authoritarian leader of the family. *Life Goes On* associates Ryu's own experience of raising her three-year-old daughter as a working mother with investigations into the lives of her own mother and her third-eldest sister in Russia. *Umma (Mother)* focuses on Joung's deep-rooted conflict with her mother, whom she had thought too hysteric and fanatic about Christianity. The three films signaled a trend of feminist first-person documentaries that recalls the surge of this mode in North America in the early 1980s after the dominance of activist-oriented nonfiction practices in the 1970s. Annette Kuhn has remarked that "there seems to have been something of a shift within feminist film practice away from collective and participatory ways of working and towards more individualistic approaches . . . which I have characterized as feminine writing."[24] It is worth additionally noting two other factors that contributed to the emergence of the films: first, Seoul International Women's Film Festival played an institutional and discursive role in supporting the films with its Asian Short Film Competition Award and Okrang Documentary Award, whose recipients were *Family Project*, *Life Goes On*, and *Mother (Umma)*; and second, except Ryu Mi-rye as a member of Docu Purn, the rest of the two directors studied filmmaking at the Art Institute of Chicago (Jo) or York University (Joung). It can thus be construed that they, as in the cases of Gina Kim and Kim Lee-jin who studied at CalArts, were exposed to and inspired by the diary films and autobiographical documentaries that attest to the post-verité tendency of the North American documentary.

As Nam Inyoung and Nam Lee write, the three films' strategies of foregrounding the director's subjectivity are used "to interrogate the most pressing feminist/gender issues of the time," including the pressure of the patriarchal familial system on mothers and daughters, and "to construct a new female self/subjectivity in the process of production."[25] The blurring of the boundaries between the self (documentarian) and others (family members) and between her identities as documentarian and as a family member is indebted to all the documentaries' performative aspect made by the directors' textual presence as filmmaker-I. The three films' common filmmaker-I aspires to accommodate two competing desires: to construct an organized story of the director's family and to render the filmed reality of the family as inseparable from her subjectivity. The negotiation of the two desires is reflected not merely in the films' first-person voice-over that shuffles between the director's chronological account of her family history and her unstable emotional attitude toward its members, but also in their handheld cinematography and punctual editing as prosthetic extensions of her subjectivity. As in the case of *Umma (Mother)*, cut-out animation sequences made of the family photos evoke Joung's psychic trauma caused by her mother's harsh words and hysterical attitude during her childhood. The three films' resistance to the clear-cut distinction between the subject and the others is also the case with the director's negotiation between her filming subjectivity and her identity as a family member. *Family Project* emblematizes the indistinguishability of the two subjectivities. During most of the film's running time, Jo assumes the status of a pseudoethnographer as her camera tends to maintain a certain degree of distance from her family members. The camera's position beside her mother sitting on a bench of a school's playground, for instance, suggests both Jo's intimate gaze and her distanced observation of the mother's inner state, including her decision to be free from her husband's patriarchal treatment and seek her independence. Jo's distanced position, however, is not consistently maintained throughout the film, as encapsulated by the scene in which she engages in her father's argument with her younger brother. Initially, Jo's camera observes the dispute from the farthest distance possible without intervening in it. As the father's emotion gets higher, her off-screen voice trying to calm him down can be heard while the camera maintains its position as outside observer. In this way, the reciprocity of Jo and her family members exemplifies the collapse of the boundary between a documentarian and her object of inquiry.

138 Post-activism

Apart from presenting their director's directorial signature and subject matter, the three films bridge the gap between personal and political by raising several feminist agendas regarding Korea's nuclear family system, such as patriarchy, maternity, and mother-daughter relationship. The films' feminist view on the family originates from the idea of their directors, as Jo remarks in an interview: "In Korean society, the history of an individual family has been regarded as something to be hidden, an object that has not deserved to be problematized or put on the table of public discourse. I thought that this attitude is the organized social power that prevents the internal suppression of the family from being overcome and rather reinforces it."[26] *Family Project* reveals the extent to which her father embodies the patriarchal gender ideology that embeds the socially structured binary opposition between men and women in the nuclear family. The ideology turns out to have profound influences on the father himself and other family members. Jo's camera does not hesitate to unveil the father's discrepancy between his public self (he delivers his public talk that argues for giving women more social roles) and his private self that has made his wife subservient to his will and wanted to decide the future of his children on his own. Jo's voice-over notes that she always clashed with him until she got married and left for the United States. Most significantly, Jo pays most of her attention to her mother, tracking the origin of her resentment and sorrow that she has accumulated throughout her life, giving up her professional career for marriage, sacrificing herself for her husband's social success, and taking care of her sick mother and mother-in-law. While unearthing what was repressed underneath the normalcy of the middle-class family, Jo also negotiates between her mother's concern that the film would be a negative portrait of the family, and her sympathetic gaze at the mother's pursuit of the freedom from her roles as mother, wife, and daughter-in-law, which is stressed by the slow-motion portrayal of her dancing in front of a mirror. Jo's interest in the social construction of maternity ideology is also found in *Life Goes On*. Here Ryu's effort to accommodate both her filmmaking and her fostering of her daughter drives her quest for deeper understanding of her mother and her elderly sister in Russia, positioning their different choices (her mother's having a relationship with a boyfriend after being liberated from her husband's family, and her sister's giving up her study due to her maternal duty) within what it means to become a mother in a society. *Umma (Mother)* manifests Joung's mother as an intimate Other whom she tries to understand but fears of resembling. Joung's gradual approximation to the origins of the mother's character, the mother's hardship during her marriage life, and her disconnection from her husband's family after his death, enable Joung to turn her camera back on herself, coupled with her confession that "this journey started with 'why my mom?' but it has returned with 'why me?'" Through this type of the inner gaze interlocked with the outward gaze on the mother affected by the pressure of patriarchy, the three feminist domestic ethnographies present their filmmaker-I as "a concrete individual in history rather than a universal voice, self, or perspective that assumes the position of *minjung* or enlightenment."[27]

The family portraits of male directors in the early and mid-2000s tend to focus on their family members more directly linked to Korea's postwar history, rewriting it from their first-person perspective. Kim Hee-chul's *My Father* investigates his father as a small hardware store owner, questioning where and how his machismo identity was formed and developed. Juxtaposing an array of family photos with Kim's intimate conversations with his mother and grandmother, the film demonstrates the impact of military modernity on the father's patriarchal personality and habits, such as his fetishistic attachment to the military uniform and the jeep, and his swear words to the wife and sons, supported by the testimony of the grandmother who supposes that they could originate from his military service with the US Army. It advances to reveal the influences that the father's character had on the rest of his family members, including Kim himself: the father's impolite treatment of the mother throughout their married life, and his insistence on sending his two sons to the Korea Military Academy. These influences extend Kim's personal ambivalent attitude toward the father—the coexistence of hate and sympathy—to the public dimension of the military-patriarchal complex that has long determined Korea's collective masculinity.

To Find Tiger Kim (*Paektusan horangirŭl ch'ajasŏ*, Ku Bon-hwan, 2006, 94 min.) takes as its subject the director's search for "Tiger Kim," whose tomb he annually visited with his grandparents: Tiger Kim was his grandmother's elderly brother and a former military officer who had about a dozen of medals for his service during the Yeosu-Suncheon Incident (*Yŏsun sagŏn*: a rebellion led by about two thousand left-leaning soldiers against the Syngman Rhee government's handling of the April Third Incident) in 1948 and the Korean War. In contrast to his grandfather's expectation that the film would pay tribute to Tiger Kim, for whom he worked during his military service, Ku's filming gestures toward demystifying Tiger Kim's legacy based on awareness that he was infamous for killing many innocent civilians during both incidents. Ku's questioning of the legacy develops from the knowledge that he gains from archival footage, TV documentaries, newspaper articles, and declassified US military documents. This process of demystification, however, entails Koo's unstable negotiation between the public and the personal as his journey shuffles between his visits to the bereaved families of the victims from

140 Post-activism

the rebellion and his witness of the grandfather dying of cancer. A family's complex history enmeshed with the class and ideological struggles of modern Korea is also the subject of *Grandmother's Flower* (*Halmae kkot*, Mun Jeong-hyun, 2007, 89 min.), which is inspired by the director's accidental discovery of the diaries of his late granduncle. Mun's journey leads him to discover the repercussions of Japanese colonialism and the Korean War in his hometown in South Jeolla Province as it was marred by the deep-seated conflicts of class, ideology, and religion since the feudal times: the village's north and middle sectors had been populated by noblemen and intellectuals and later embraced leftist ideology during the colonial age and the postliberation period, while commoners had lived in its southern sector, which was later influenced by Christianity and anticommunism. Mun serves as a personal historian who investigates and reveals the tragic story of his family caused by the conflicts, which centers around his grandmother and her family members: her elderly brother was killed for being a communist; her husband as former partisan died of overdrinking due to his trauma; and her younger brother gave up his return from Japan. This investigation, too, expands the film's scope beyond the personal history of the family as Mun encounters the now-tranquil landscape of his family's neighboring village, where a massacre of its residents by the Korean Army took place in the name of searching out commies, and travels to Japan for collecting the testimony of the grandmother's younger brother who embodies the Cold War trauma of leftist Korean immigrants in Japan. Besides a wide array of interviews with his family members and the residents in the town, Mun employs home movie clips, expressive cinematography, and several animated sequences marked by the contrast between black and red colors. The animated imagery as a device of reenactment is particularly effective in depicting the psychic and corporeal pains of the family members who were sacrificed by the red complex and the massacre and violence that it caused.

Each director's quest for writing his family history from his first-person viewpoint in these two films changes in the course of filmmaking, therefore inscribing and expressing his drifting subjectivity in dialogue with his familial others. In *To Find Tiger Kim*, Ku confesses that he wanted to film something dramatic in his meetings with the bereaved family members of those who were killed by Tiger Kim. As the members who were faced with Ku show him hospitality in contrast to his expectation that they would reprimand him and Tiger Kim, he further confesses his ambivalent reaction: he is relieved that they accepted his apology for Tiger Kim's wrongdoings, but is also disappointed at their tolerant reaction, which is not dramatic. More than demystifying the authenticity of documentary representation, this ambivalence testifies to Ku's split subjectivity, which negotiates between his ethical responsibility as a historian of his perpetrator family member and his self-consciousness as director. This split subjectivity is eventually linked to his change of the direction of his film from a story about Tiger Kim to a portrait of his grandfather, who was a producer of a Korean classic family melodrama, *Before Sunset* (*Hae ttŏrŏjigi chŏne*, Kang Dae-jin, 1960), when Ku decides to film his dying body every day and find the lost print of the film. Ku's final interview with his grandfather before his death further demonstrates Ku's complicated subjectivity, which is divided into a family member and a historian responsible for the wrongdoings of his ancestors. The grandfather disavows Ku's question whether or not he witnessed Tiger Kim's massacre, while also insisting on his respect for Tiger Kim ("Had he not been born, Korea wouldn't exist"). While Ku's historical consciousness is expressed via his alternation of the video footage of his grandfather and the newspaper articles and documents that demonstrate Tiger Kim's crimes, he also passes the camera to the grandfather after the unfinished interview. The grandfather's last point of view before his death is read as articulating the reciprocal understanding between him and Ku. The film's ending, as well as the unfinished interview, however, also informs the impossibility of Ku's giving total forgiveness to the grandfather, in that the footage of the Korean War in the end credits signifies his allegations about Tiger Kim's crimes. *Grandmother's Flower*, too, exhibits Mun's vacillating self, which negotiates between the identity of the historian marked by the sense of responsibility and that of a family member. Mun's quest for the family history is charged with his will to receive an apology from his mother's friend named Sook-ja, a descendant of the perpetrator who killed his grandmother's elderly brother. He asks his mother to visit Sook-ja and receive her apology for her ancestor's wrongdoings, but the film ends at the moment just before the mother's entrance to Sook-ja's apartment. This open ending reflects the difficulty of reconciliation in the intimate relationship between the descendants of the Cold War violence, as well as Mun's ethical considerations of how challenging it is for a social actor who is not a direct party to the past crime to be faced with its previously unknown truth.

Into the Larger History: Women Directors' Domestic Ethnographies since the Mid-2000s

In 2019, Ryu Mi-rye, director of *Life Goes On*, refuted the assumption of *sajŏk tak'yumentŏri* as "soft" in its subject matter and rhetoric: "I regret that it has been disparaged. It's never soft. It's so intense. . . . It's really hard and difficult to make

142 Post-activism

personal documentary because it wants to expand while capturing moments of the everyday."[28] In their attempts to overcome the bias that restricted the political value of independent documentary to the traditional stereotypical views on the discourse of sobriety and the grand discourse of politics and society, women directors of domestic ethnographies since the mid-2000s have stitched together the personal and the political to varying degreess, achieving notable formal and aesthetic innovations. Their films have been bifurcated into two categories. As the direct heirs to the domestic ethnographies of the early 2000s by women directors, the films of the first category include LeeKil Bo-ra's *Glittering Hands* (*Pantchaginŭn paksu sori*, 2013, 80 min.), a film that extends the personal story of her hearing-impaired parents into the larger issue of disability in the society, *Areum Married* (*Pakkang Arŭm kyŏrhonhada*, 2019, ParkGang Areum, 86 min.), a more popular autobiographical film that raises issues surrounding the domestic division of labor and the carrying out of studying and nurturing together in Parkgang's married life in France, and Han Tae-ee's *Welcome to X-World* (*Welk'ŏm t'u X-wŏltŭ*, 2019, 81 min.), which focuses on her bond with the mother who gradually attempts to leave her stepfather and seeks her second life, while also raising the problems of maternity in society, including mothers' career discontinuity (*kyŏngnyŏk tanjŏl*), their duty of child care, and their devotion to the husband's family. Recreating the director's intimate conversation with her mother, who strove to foster her family after her divorce, Kim Seung-hee's animated short *Tiger and Ox* (*Horangiwa so*, 2019, 8 min.) updates the feminist perspective on maternity in the early generation's domestic ethnographies with its expressive, rhythmic animation that evocatively illustrates single motherhood and the social stigmas attached to it.[29]

Several films in the second category of the domestic ethnographies since the mid-2000s reconstruct the turbulent microhistory of a director's family through the politico-ideological macrohistory of the Korean Peninsula and its neighborhood in the Cold War period. They are two films of Zainichi director Yang Yonghi, *Dear Pyongyang* (*Tiŏ P'yŏngyang*, 2005, 107 min.) and *Goodbye Pyongyang* (*Kutpai P'yŏngyang*, 2009, 82 min.), and Hong Jae-hee's *My Father's Emails* (*Abŏjiŭi imeil*, 2012, 90 min.). Jinhee Park considers the autobiographical mode of these films to be an aesthetic strategy that originates in the inextricability of the directorial self and her familiar others, of their private life and their surrounding social or ideological power: "The shared quality in both Hong's and Yang's films is their reflexive mode that examines their situated knowledge and position within macro Cold War history and micro family history by exercising 'epistemological doubt' upon accepted social ideologies."[30] Added to this is that this "epistemological doubt" stems from the directors' quest to be liberated from the "social ideologies" that bound

The Personal Turn   **143**

their personal selfhood and their family relationships. In this sense, their filmmaking as a learning process seems to be a precondition for the quest, as Yang confesses in her memoirs: "I wanted to be freed from such nouns as father's daughter, brothers' sister, woman, and Japanese-Korean. I turned my camera to my family because I wanted to be liberated from them after facing them head-on rather than to escape from them."[31]

In Yang's investigation into her own Zainichi family, *Dear Pyongyang* focuses on her father, who immigrated from Jeju Island to Japan and chose to be a pro–North Korean civil activist who supported the Zainichi community, inspired by the communist ideology of Kim Il-sung. The parents' ideological investment in communism and the pro-North Chongryon organization enabled them to send their three sons to North Korea in 1971 during the Repatriation Campaign, with which North Korea's propagandistic policy guaranteed the opportunity for better life to the Zainichi who had suffered social discrimination, poverty, and unemployment in Japan since the 1950s. Yang's filming of the lives of her brothers and their family members, as well as of her parents who visited North Korea to meet with them, nurtured her critical gaze on, and her sense of alienation from, its social and economic system, including its censorship of the lifestyle and culture from the West. As a result, *Dear Pyongyang* calls into question the meanings of what Yang's parents meant by North Korea as "homeland" (*choguk*) and what her brothers' homecoming (*kwiguk*) meant for them. In contrast to the praise of Yang's family as a model of the revolutionary and patriotic family, Yang's distance from her parents regarding the idea of North Korea is demonstrated by her awareness that her mother had long shipped a number of packages enveloping foods, toys, and daily supplies to support the brothers and their children along with money, on the one hand, and by his father who had not allowed her to criticize North Korea as *choguk*, on the other. Yang's ambivalent attitude toward her parents is expressed in the same type of shots, her first-person POV. For it testifies to a key trope of domestic ethnography as a specific mode of autobiographical nonfiction practice that acknowledges her involvement in the subjects being filmed. The film starts with a harmonious and cheerful conversation between Yang and her parents, with her hand holding a cup of beer to toast with them, wishing for their health on the occasion of a new year. This first-person POV linked to Yang's subjectivity as the filmmaker-in-the-text is repeated in the scene where her hand holds one of the medals that the North Korean government gave to her father (figure 4.1). Faced with a rich collection of medals as a token of the parents' long-standing fidelity to North Korea, Yang's personal gaze is followed by her narration that manifests her suspicion of its ideology: "What is my homeland? I have yet found an answer to it."

Figure 4.1 *Dear Pyongyang* (Yang Yonghi, 2005)

The fact that this question had long been mobilized by Yang's own unstable status of citizenship as the second generation of Zainichi is highlighted in the climactic five-minute-long take, in which her camera intimately closes up to her father who comfortably lies on the tatami floor. When she asks if it is okay for her to change her nationality to South Korea, her father says yes, in contrast to his previous taboo, while adding that he will not change his own nationality because of his unyielding loyalty to Kim Il-sung. Yang's subjective gaze at her father, which exemplifies domestic ethnography's activation of "a kind of intersubjective reciprocity in which the representations of self and other are simultaneously if unequally at stake,"[32] reconstructs the historical world of Zainichis' transnational migration to North Korea during the Cold War through the personal story of her family. The story, then, manifests both the ineffaceable difference of ideology between Yang and her father and their mutual effort to putting oneself in the other's shoes as the dialectic of distance and proximity that underlies domestic ethnography. Despite her ideological distance from her father, which makes it impossible for her to totally reconcile with him, Yang performs an interventional critique of her family's underlying patriarchy that took for granted the sacrificial devotion of her mother, as she asks him in hospital (for his cerebral infarction) to make a confession to her

The Personal Turn 145

mother for what she did for him and to show her his thankfulness in front of the camera.

While nodding to Park's insight that "the Cold War modulation within Yang's domestic relations is less about the ideological battles and more about recognition of *the Other within self*,"[33] I also argue that Yang's films do more than tell her "domestic" entanglement with her families in Japan and North Korea: that is, they also move Yang's "ethnographic" inquiry into the economic and societal reality of North Korea and the lives of its people. The latter aspect is particularly evident in *Goodbye Pyongyang*, a sequel of *Dear Pyongyang* that spotlights Yang Sun-hwa, a daughter of Yang's second oldest brother and her niece. In editing footage that she filmed from 1995 to 2004, Yang deliberately employs her home movie approach to Sun-hwa and other family members in North Korea in ways that reveal the impacts of its exclusive economic and cultural control on their material and psychic life. Yang's camera captures a refrigerator and other living items at Sun-hwa's house, with her voice noting that they were indebted to the financial support from her mother in Japan. It also depicts blackouts of the house, caused by the daily limit of electricity supply (two hours per day) in Pyongyang. Yang's account, which overlaps with an episode in *Dear Pyongyang*, tells the story of the brother, who liked classical music and coffee in Japan but passed away in North Korea after his thirty-year struggle with depression. While paying attention to these dark sides of the homeland of Yang's family marked by their transborder split, her liminal subjectivity inscribed in the film's camera and voice-over also offers a nuanced perspective on North Korea, which is not her singular nation-state linked to the sense of belonging but which is a home of reality where a new generation of her family has been growing. Yang's filming of Sun-hwa's going to school recalls her own childhood, so that her camera zooms in to Sun-hwa as she approaches the school building. Sun-hwa is also portrayed as representing young members of Yang's family who hope for their better life, as she sides with the only son of the youngest brother as a classics lover who skillfully plays the piano in the darkness of the blackout. The fact that Yang's camera could not follow Sun-hwa for lack of a filming permit inside the school makes Yang realize Sun-hwa's return to the reality of North Korea as well as her own ineluctable distance from its system.[34]

My Father's Emails reconstructs the life and memories of Hong Jae-hee's father right after his death. In a way that echoes Hirsch's formulation of postmemory, Hong juxtaposes testimonies of her family members, including her mother, older sister, and younger brother, with family photos, footage of newsreels, excerpts from emails that her father left to the family, and dramatized reenactment sequences. The film's earlier part chronicles the personal

146 Post-activism

narrative of the turbulent life of Hong's father through the official history of modern Korea after the end of Japanese Occupation. After his refugee to South Korea before the Korean War, Hong's father worked for the US Army during the postwar period, nurturing his anticommunist sentiment as a way that displaced persons could survive in South Korea; under the Park Chung-hee regime, he traveled to Vietnam on the occasion of the Vietnam War as an engineer and to Saudi Arabia during the oil crisis in the 1970s as a construction worker for his pursuit of profitable opportunities; the failures of these opportunities made him suffer from alcoholism and depression, so that he was estranged from his family members for long time, self-isolating in his room. The film's second part takes a closer look at the mental traumas of Hong's father, suggesting that they could be caused by the frictions from the military and developmentalist drive of modern Korea. Hong's uses of reenactment dramatize her exploration of these ideological origins, as the blurry images of the father, such as his sleeping after too much drinking and his domestic violence toward her mother, are intertwined with the mother's testimony that he used to repeat "the 38th parallel" (*samp'alsŏn*) and "6.25" (*yugio: the day of the Korean War's outbreak in 1950) when he got drunk, and that her brothers' involvement in the leftist Podoyŏnmaeng (see chapter 2) during the Korean War prohibited him from traveling overseas, which frustrated his utopian desire for emigration to foreign countries for a better life. This Cold War ideological trauma deeply engrained in the father's psyche is also supported by his emails, one of which expresses his discriminatory prejudice against people from Jeolla Province as "commies."

Hong's ambivalent attitude toward her father and his surrounding historical contexts attest to a typical approach of domestic ethnography to the director's intimate Other and her liminal position. On the one hand, she confesses her own antipathy toward her father since her university days, which made her inclined to the Marx-Lenin philosophy and the leftist-oriented student movement. She eventually left home after his accusation that she was a communist. On the other hand, Hong inscribes herself in her present age in several reenactment scenes. In one of them, Hong enters her father's former room, where he slept after heavy drinking as his children, including Hong in her childhood, watched from a distance. Her performative presence as the filmmaker-in-the text overlaps with a sentence from her father's email that expresses his deep-seated regret for doing so. This fantasmatic reenactment, then, not only undertakes Hong's effort to approximate the kernel of her father's trauma in the form of "conjoining facts and interpretations, of detecting the unresolved presence of one within the other,"[35] but also expresses Hong's belated awareness of her memory about it as postmemory. Her imaginary projection of herself onto the recreated scene of the past corresponds to postmemory as a "*structure* of inter- and transgenerational return of traumatic knowledge and embodied experience."[36] Hong's juxtaposition of the excerpts from her father's email with the scene, then, signals her deeper, if imperfect, understanding of his trauma and of its underlying historical origin. Ultimately, the film presents Hong's delicate yet impossible effort to understand and reconcile with her father as a deep-seated public issue of the Cold War trauma that has long haunted both his generation and their descendants.

Young female filmmakers' negotiation with the larger history of Korea in their domestic ethnography films is not limited to the Cold War but addresses the more recent socioeconomic moments of its industrialization and neoliberalization and its impacts on individuals. In Ma Min-ji's *Family in the Bubble* (*Pŏbŭl p'aemilli*, 2017, 78 min.), her inquiry into the origin of her family's economic crisis is linked to an urban, anthropological study of the economic and housing changes in Seoul. This inquiry involves Ma's recollection of home videos that her mother filmed, from the family's happy moment in the middle-class apartment in 1989 to the last video, which records its empty living room under seizure in 1997. These home movies as a typical material of domestic ethnography stand in contrast with Ma's first-person shots of the small villa of the family and their economic troubles, therefore producing "an experience of a 'then' of the production of the home mode documents and the 'now' of the production of the appropriation film itself."[37] These personal documents, too, also intersect with an array of newsreels and illustrations that situate the heyday and decline of Ma's family within the contexts of the real estate booms since the Park Chung-hee regime and how the apartment has become the incarnation of the middle-class dream in tandem with the urban development of Seoul and the growth of the construction industry since the 1980s.[38] This extensive use of the archival materials marks the film's notable departure from the feminist-driven domestic ethnographies of the early 2000s that employ family photos or home movies in a supplementary manner. For the film weaves a larger historical discourse on the dramatic development of the Gangnam District from the late 1970s to the late 1990s, during which the massive apartment construction "created a middle-class place and cultivated middle-class identities by congregating people with similar socioeconomic backgrounds in specific apartment complexes."[39] Simultaneously, Ma incorporates the influences of the economic changes on the family's trajectory in her precarious subjectivity. Besides the contrast between the images of her parents' small villa and the spectacular landscape imagery of the Gangnam District, the parents' persistent dream of the rise of real estate bubble is portrayed not only as Ma's object of understanding but also as what she wants to overcome. This is the reason that the film spends a considerable amount of its running time introducing Ma herself as a subject under the neoliberalized economy, one that makes individuals vigilant to economic crises and shifts, after the dissolution of the bubble through the post-IMF social restructuring. Though Ma began to live in a place distant from Gangnam because she was fed up with her parents' way of life, her tuition loan and unstable conditions of employment are viewed as interlinked with their debt that she has to cope with, a major crisis that is still forcing young subjects to undergo economic and social uncertainties.[40] Despite its refreshed account of the socioeconomic and urban history of Seoul since Korea's age of modernization, it is due to Ma's self-therapeutic motivation for understanding her parents and seeking her better life that the film converges on her present instability.

Optigraph (*Opt'igŭraep'ŭ*, 2017, 104 min.) by Lee Won-woo deserves particular attention in the strain of domestic ethnography since the late 2000 owing to its rigorous intersection of documentary and avant-garde cinema. The film presents Lee's pursuit of the life of her maternal grandfather, Chang Suk-yoon (1904–2003), who wanted her to write his autobiography. After his immigration to the United States, Chang worked as an agent of the Office of Strategic Services (which would later become the CIA) in several countries in Asia during World War II and was appointed as the head of the Bureau of National Police just before the outbreak of the Korean War. Investigating this intriguing figure who embodied the geopolitical and ideological conflicts across Asia in its colonial and postcolonial eras, Lee is not interested in reconstructing Chang's life and memoirs into a cause-and-effect narrative that would supplement or counter its official history. Employing and shuffling between analog and digital camera formats, including Super 8 mm and 16 mm cameras, Lee instead films her journeys to India, Myanmar, Chungking, and Washington, DC. Some of her footage exposes the celluloid filmstrips registering different light exposures that bear the trace of her personal impressions on what she observed and experienced. The footage's lucid material qualities, marked by the strips' small gauges and scratches, as well as the spontaneous and sometimes jerky camera movement, call to mind the predilection for Jonas Mekas's film diaries that Lee demonstrated in *Dooriban Generator* (see chapter 2). The footage's emphasis on the communal moments of Lee and her fellow filmmakers who accompanied her on her travels renders the records of the places no less Lee's travelogue than an organized investigative journey into Chang's trajectory. This thus validates Stella Bruzzi's observation that travelogues tend not to be "structured around an argument or indeed around a desire to impose narrative cohesion,"[41] while also marking

The Personal Turn 149

her memory of Chang as a kind of postmemory that demands the work of imaginative reconstruction.

In order to acknowledge and close her distance from Chang, Lee gradually turns her attention to the larger colonial and post–World War II historical contexts of his life. Lee's growing awareness of the intersection of the personal and the historical enables her to visit the National Archives and Records Administration (NARA) and investigate disparate documents and archival newsreels related to Chang's past. What she experiences there, however, is a series of gaps, omissions, and absences inherent in the archived materials. What supplements this lack inherent in the archive is Lee's attentive watching of several newsreels related to the Korean War, with their slow motion and freeze frames expressing her personal appreciation of its traumatic remainders, such as the faces of POWs and of orphan children who were begging on the street. Associating this observation with her filming of a Korean War memorial in Baltimore, Lee's internal monologue, "All memories become edited and all memories are directed," suggests that her personal mission to achieve the belated wish of her grandfather is extended to the loaded question as to how history is represented and constructed. The film's remaining parts after her archival research attenuate the intertwinement of the personal and the historical once again, as she complies celluloid footage that she filmed during several political rallies and funeral or memorial ceremonies, including the Candlelight Protests in 2008, the funeral of President Roh Moo-hyun in 2009, and the consolation ceremonies for the victims of the Yongsan Massacre (see chapters 6 and 7) and the Sewol Ferry Disaster, and in the course of her solidarity acts with workers fired by Ssangyong Motors and those who struggled against Samsung Semiconductor's neglect of the workers who died of leukemia. While the film does not offer a decisive judgment on Chang's career and instead leaves it open to the audience, Lee's political awareness entails a shift in her perspective on him, implied by excerpts from a TV documentary that spotlight the massacre of people who were allegedly involved in Podoyŏnmaeng, a historical crime from which he might not totally be exempt.

Jang Yun-mi's *Under Construction* (*Kongsaŭi hiroaerak*, 2018, 89 min.) is another precious accomplishment of domestic ethnographies in the late 2010s. The film portrays Jang's father, owner of a small construction company who is in preparation for his retirement after his lifetime devotion to construction work across the southern Korean Peninsula. Unlike other personal documentaries since early in the century, the director's presence in the reality being filmed is austere owing to Jang's avoidance of the use of the confessional voice-over as the enunciator of her filmmaker-I. Even without recourse to the archival footage of a public history, the film succeeds in constructing a vivid

150 Post-activism

ethnographic-aesthetic portrait of Jang's intimate Other, one guided by her subjectivity and creativity. Jang fuses her observational view on the details of his office and workplace (helmets, steel, machines, tools, and dirty work uniforms) with her poetic and self-reflexive gaze on the places associated with his memories of the construction works. Her off-screen conversation with her father evolves from the surface of his work ethic, composed of diligence and the pursuit of profit, to the deeper psychic dimension of his anxieties about taking a rest in the age of developmentalism and industrialization and about bodily aging faced with his retirement. The father's profound oscillation between the two states of mind is implied by the intermittent silence of his testimony and his request for a smoking break. The reciprocity of Jang and her father, then, moves on to her accumulation of the images and sounds associated with his memories of workplaces since Korea's rapid industrial modernization. Coupled with the father's voice dissociated from his body, the images include the shipyard on Geojedo Island whose cafeterias and dormitories he participated in constructing, the apartment complex where shipbuilding laborers live, and shipbuilding itself. Just as these images allude to the heyday and decline of the national shipbuilding industry, so does other audiovisual imagery express Jang's personal reflection on her father's times of work and his physical and mental state. As she asks him when he got angry while working, he talks about the dangerous expressway that he crossed 162 times, as well as the sleepiness and fatigue that he had to endure during his trips. This confession is associated with Jang's handheld close-up of his hands while driving, a series of blurry images with lights emanating from running cars, and their noise. Without any expository commentary or confessional voice-over about their journey to his prior workplaces, Jang's audiovisual expression lucidly inscribes her questioning and thinking self in the texture of the film, therefore providing a personally rich portrait of the individual who in turn embodies the larger history of industrialization.

The Essay Film

Before its sheer visibility in documentary filmmaking and discourse throughout the 2010s, two filmmakers paved the way for the essay film that rewrites history through their questioning directorial agency. Kim Hong-joon, a former member of SFC (see chapter 1), filmmaker, festival programmer, and professor, made *My Korean Cinema* (*Naŭi han'guk yŏnghwa*, 2003–2006, 123 min.) comprising nine short films. The project's essayistic aspects can be found in Kim's production process and his technological tools, as he remarked: "I was like a preacher proclaiming that the age has come that anyone could make a film only with a video camera, but I have not practiced it thus far. . . . My working method was that of *sup'il* (literary essay)."[42] This reminds one of Alexandre Astruc's prescient envisioning of the impact of new audiovisual technologies on the variation and popularization of personal film-making as writing: "Today the improvement of 16mm, tomorrow television will multiply the possibility of cinematic expression," he writes. "There will no longer be a dividing line between amateur cinema and professional cinema."[43] Based on his extremely low budget, a video camera, and the minimal equipment for reviewing and editing the VHS copies of films, Kim develops his personal reflection on the cultural, industrial, geopolitical, and gendered aspects of Korean cinema while rewriting its history through his knowledge, experience, and memory—as evidenced by the project's third episode, *Smoking Women* (*Tambae p'iunŭn yŏja(tŭl)*, 2003) and its ninth and final piece, *A Short Film about Joseon Cinema* (*Chosŏn yŏnghwarŭl marham*, 2006). This involves exposition of his multiple subjectivities (filmmaker, cinephile, and scholar) as a feature of the essay film: for instance, Kim as a filmmaker who began his career as an assistant director for Im Kwon-taek and as a cinephile who had grown up watching many Korean movies in *My Chungmuro* (*Mai Chungmuro*, 2003), the project's first episode that investigates Chungmuro as both the headquarter of Korean film industry and the complex of movie theaters from the 1960s to the 1990s.

In her *Koryu: Southern Women, Southern Korea* (*Kŏryu*, 2000, 75 min.),[44] produced by Vista, scholar and filmmaker Kim Soyoung extends her personal visit to her family's hometown (Kosung) into seemingly disparate yet intertwined microstories about an old woman in Kosung who learned Korean against the patriarchal norms of the society and two women who experienced dislocation in the modern and contemporary eras of Korea (a Chinese restaurant owner who immigrated to Kosung and speaks both Chinese and Korean, and a young Korean diaspora who lived in the United Kingdom and Germany). Signified by the film's title, staying and leaving, and life and death, Kim's digressive journey embodies the structure of the essay film. Accordingly, Kim's subjectivity straddles her feminist ethnographic inquiry into women's language through different generations, folk culture (inspired by her folklorist father, Kim Yol-gyu), and the liminal identity of diaspora woman, on the one hand, and her personal reflections on the origin of her family and how her MiniDV is capable of dissolving the boundaries between filmmaker and its surrounding world (which invokes Agnès Varda's self-reflexive play with her digital camera in *The Gleaners and I* [2000]),[45] on the other.

152   Post-activism

In twenty-first-century post-activist nonfiction practices, Kim Eung-su and Kelvin Kyung Kun Park are two most remarkable practitioners of the essay film. The two directors have sought to activate their questioning or reflexive self by employing various formal devices or modes of enunciation that express their personal view on the past and present of Korean society. More than reflectivity, subjectivity, and multiple formal devices, the films of Kim and Park demonstrate that the development of the essay film as a mode of expressing subjective agency and personal expression has been linked to the renewal of their participation in Korea's public events or its forgotten memories and histories. In this sense, they suit what Timothy Corrigan considers the cornerstone of the essay film, namely, the director's expression of her thinking self in relation to her public life as "multiple and changing domains of various registers and as a place of contestation through experience."[46]

As Lee Do-hoon summarizes, Kim Eung-su is "a representative essayist of our contemporary times in that he has sought historical truth through his own autonomous thought and his experiments with film form."[47] Since the mid-2000s, Kim has elaborated on various rhetorical strategies of the essay film encompassing travelogue film, docufiction, internal monologue, and image-sound disjunction. *The Past Is a Strange Country* (*Kwagŏnŭn natsŏn narada*, 2007, 90 min.), for instance, revisits the deaths of two university students (Kim Se-jin and Lee Jae-ho) who self-immolated during a demonstration against the New Military government in 1986. Instead of using archival footage of the intense student movement to commemorate the two as martyrs (*yŏlsa*, see chapter 6) of democratization, Kim expresses his painful negotiation between his aspiration to approximate the hidden truth of the incident and his ethical awareness of the impossibility of mourning their deaths through his postsynchronized interview with five witnesses of the incident, a Brechtian device meant to acknowledge his subjective voice that addresses viewers. *Without Father* (*Abŏji ŏmnŭn sam*, 2012, 80 min.) shuffles between the transnational life of the Japanese writer Yoko Kawashima Watkinson and Kim's travel with a Japanese woman named Masako. Kim distributes his three selves (the first fictional self that investigates Watkinson, the second who accompanies Masako, and Kim himself, who surveys and reflects on the two stories, their corresponding two selves, and the film's making) in the forms of internal monologue and letter, exhibiting himself as the enunciator who has multiple incarnations and expressive means to address the viewer differently. In this sense, the film attests to what Laura Rascaroli identifies as a key structure of the essay film: namely, the "structure of a constant interpellation" in which "each spectator, as an individual . . . is called upon to engage in a dialogical relationship with the enunciator, to become active, intellectually and emotionally, and interact with the text."[48] *The City in the Water* (*Mul sogŭi toshi*, 2014, 80 min.) develops Kim's meditative quest for a trace of a village submerged by the construction of Chungju Dam in 1985 through a variety of landscape images encompassing both static and moving cameras, oral interviews with former village residents, excerpts of past radio broadcasts, and old still photographs of the village. In all these cases, Kim plays with an essayistic mode of filmmaking that channels his destabilized yet self-reflexive and exploratory self into public subject matters, such as the memory of democratization, diasporic identity and the national, and the impact of the state-led infrastructural change on rural communities.

Kim's essayistic efforts to mediate the personal and the public are also demonstrated in his two films on the Sewol Ferry Disaster. *Oh! Love* (*Oh! Sarang*, 2017, 75 min.) and *Surreal* (*Ch'ohyŏnshil*, 2017, 69 min.) express Kim's reflexive approach to—and his ethical distance from—the traumatized psyche of either an ordinary man who recalls the disaster, or a father whose son survived it. Featuring a middle-aged, small-scale computer store owner named J. who accidentally sees a man wearing the yellow ribbon (which has been the civic symbol of commemorating the disaster and its victims) on a bus trip, *Oh! Love* reframes the objects and landscape images that Kim filmed at the places relating to the disaster within a personal perspective. Kim presents J. as a kind of in-between character who transcends the rigid boundary of fact and fiction. J. derives from the owner's real-life experience of having recalled the disaster, while his internal monologue expresses Kim's reflection on the disaster as an event that has impoverished any political, legal, and scientific solutions: that is, J. is a hybrid of the personal and the public, partly because he comes from Kim's authorial subjectivity, and partly because he represents an individual of the public who encountered the disaster and sympathized with the tragedy (after J.'s encounter with the man who wore the ribbon, he takes his teenage son to the park in pursuit of a sense of condolence). The objects and images, which include a bundle of yellow ribbons tied on the trees of a park and on the barricades at the pier where the ferry sank, banners and flag cards to commemorate the disaster and its victims at the pier and Gwanghwamun Plaza, people who indifferently pass along or attentively stare at the banners and cards, the strong wind that blows over the landscape of the sea, high waves and dark clouds, and the damaged structure of the ferry itself, which was salvaged in 2017, then, are viewed from Kim's perspective on the world haunted by the aftermath of the disaster. Several classical music tracks, including Richard Wagner's *Liebestod* (Love-death), amplify Kim's philosophical and religious quest for the profound meaning of love faced with death.

154   Post-activism

Kim's transformation of a real-life social actor into an essayistic character is also the case with *Surreal*, a film about a real-life father who accompanies his son on a freshman orientation trip. Given that the son attended the very school that many victims did, these two characters reflect fathers who lost their sons in the disaster, or fathers in the broadest sense who see their grown-up sons leaving their care. Kim's camera focuses on the face of the father who pays attention to his son, as well as on that of the son from the father's perspective. The camera's doubled gaze, that is, both the father's and Kim's, is in parallel to the intertitles that Kim employs to make visible the father's internal monologue about his love and his sense of letting his son go. Coupled with the alternation of added classical music and silence, the form of intertitles refers not only to the father's inner words but also to Kim's deliberate effort to make them heard in a different way than spoken words, as he remarks: "I had the difficulty of dealing with words inside silence, or making the inaudible words audible. That's the reason that I used letters instead of a voice."[49] The sense of alienation created by the silence and intertitles, then, reflects Kim's ethical distancing from the traumatized psyche of the families who lost their children, as well as his search for approximating their inner landscape.

While Kim's films have navigated through different subgenres of the essay film, Kelvin Kyung Kun Park, who studied at UCLA and CalArts and was influenced by Chris Marker and Allan Sekula, have elaborated upon heterogeneous images, sonic discordance, and expressive camerawork to realize "the idea of essay film as a cinema centered on disjunction."[50] In his *Cheonggyecheon Medley* (*Chŏnggyechŏn medŭlli*, 2010, 79 min.) and *A Dream of Iron* (*Ch'rŭi kkum*, 2014, 98 min.), these formal devices create multiple interstices, from which Park's reflection on the now-obsolete or monumental factories and machines wavers between the history of Korea's rapid industrial modernization and his obsessive return to dreams and mythic times revolving around the sublime images of metals. *Cheonggyecheon Medley* stemmed from Park's involvement in an artists' collective that aimed to document the people and small-scale factories of the metalworking network around Cheonggyecheon, a 10.9-kilometer-long stream in downtown Seoul. The stream was restored as a key project of Seoul's then mayor Lee Myung-bak (who later became president) from 2003 to 2006 to convert Seoul into a global metropolis represented by a new central hub, where its renewed tradition would be dynamically surrounded by high-rise buildings and new marketplaces. The areas around it, however, are also the arena where existing small-scale merchants and factory owners have struggled against the state- and corporate-driven gentrification.[51] In documenting the vestige of the modern production system, Park thought that "portraying people of Cheonggyecheon as the working class or in terms of gentrification was not able to convey the emotions that I felt from the area's numerous factories and machines."[52] Bringing to the forefront Park's letter to his dead grandfather who ran small-scale, run-down metal workshops, *Cheonggyecheon Medley* emblematizes the essay film as a subjective mode of filmmaking to negotiate between the personal and the public through a rich shuffling of heterogeneous expressive elements—observational shots, rhythmic and intellectual editing styles, visual effects, and archival imagery—designed both to document the now-obsolete steel manufacturing factories in the central alleys of Seoul and to find a clue to his own nightmare triggered by the recurring images of iron.

The film's opening sequence establishes Parks subjectivity as a site of instability, and as a nexus through which the history and material reality of the factory town is mediated. Coupled with a dizzying yet fascinating array of images on which parts of the iron manufacturing machine, springs, and hands of a worker are superimposed, Park's voice-over describes steel's distorted surfaces (figure 4.2). Park's subjectivity signified as "I" here introduces an unapproachable origin of his recurring obsession with images of iron. It then guides viewers toward a series of handheld shots that follow steelworkers through the alleys of Cheonggyecheon and observe their molding of liquid steel into

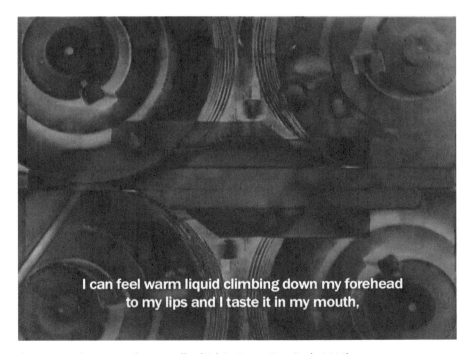

Figure 4.2 *Cheonggyecheon Medley* (Kelvin Kyung Kun Park, 2010)

156 Post-activism

stable machine parts, and toward archival imagery of the steel industry during the Japanese Occupation. Park's letter to his grandfather connects his traumatized anxiety over metals to the colonial reference to the steel industry as a driving force of Korea's industrial modernity. This validates Laura Rascaroli's view on the epistolary form as germane to the essay film in the sense that the letter is a form "that radically mixes and merges private notations and commentary on public matters, the record of both everyday life and momentous events."[53] This connection, too, reminds one of Nicolas Abraham's theory of "transgenerational haunting," which resonates with Hirsch's concept of postmemory. For it means that repressed secrets are passed from one generation to the next in the forms of recurrent story, image, or phantom. For Abraham, at stake in transgenerational haunting is that the phantom is the "invention of the living," in that "what haunts are not the dead, but the gaps left within us by the secrets of others."[54] In *Cheonggyecheon Medley*, Park extends the gap between himself and his grandfather into other gaps activated by the essay film, such as the aesthetic gap between sounds and images, and the epistemological gap between himself as ethnographer and the workers in Cheonggyecheon. The evocative soundtrack of Paolo Vivacqua aestheticizes Park's affective and corporeal impressions on the materiality of metals, machines, and the remainders of industrial modernity, stressing that his scrutiny of the archival imagery of colonial and postcolonial Korea derives from his invention of the ghost of the grandfather. This poetic mode, emblematized by the sound effects and the film's fragmentary editing, also inscribes Park's subjectivity in his ethnographic observation of the workers and his interview with them, therefore expressing his self-reflexive distance from them. Despite acknowledging the incongruities of the personal and the collective this way, however, the film's configuration of iron as a kind of free-floating signifier mobilized by Park's shifting subjectivity reveals the unconscious or allegorical dimension of industrial modernity that eschews the chronological historiography of steelmaking in Korea, an expository and objectivist narrative scheme that underlies mainstream historical documentaries. Park's expression of the impact of the modernity as traumatic and impressive is grounded in his concern with how to mediate the personal and the public, as he remarks: "The dream image draws its clues from the collective mental system rather than the individual experience. What seems to be a personal nightmare is actually the image of the trauma of the collective unconsciousness."[55]

A Dream of Iron varies Park's penchant for the poetic engagement with the sociohistorical world, employing multiple intellectual or emotional reflections, inventive editing styles, and ingenious cinematography to update his investigation into the impact of Korea's industrial modernity on both personal and collective levels. Here Park's epistolary form leads to a letter to his fictional ex-girlfriend Seung-hee—who became a shaman to find a god after breaking up with him—establishing his self as pursuing gods and rituals in "seemingly conflicting history and chaotic appearance where there exists something sublime." What makes Park distinct from other local documentary filmmakers in pursuit of an account of industrial modernity in Korea is not just his distancing from a chronological, cause-and-effect, or problem-solving narrative scheme in favor of his poetic, impressionist approach to its historical documents and landscapes: he, too, aspires to create a refreshed association between Korea's heavy industries of steel manufacturing and shipbuilding and its religious or mythic elements in the name of gods, unraveling the sublime as a node to bind the two. To this end, Park's camera scans the surface of petroglyphs in Ulsan that illustrate whales, shamans, animals, and fishermen, while also accumulating the details of the steel factory complex in Pohang Steel and of the shipbuilding complex in Hyundai Heavy Industries and labeling them as "modernity's new gods." Park's linking of the mythic with the modern in the name of the gods, in a way similar to *Cheongyecheon Medley*, derives from his ethnographic and historical interests, each introduced by his observation of the Buddhist rituals of a temple and by archival footage of the dramatic economic and infrastructural changes under the rule of Park Chung-hee, respectively. Just as Park's composition of these seemingly disparate elements attests to the fragmentary and digressive structure of the essay film, so does his rhythmic assemblage of gigantic images, including a five-minute take of a suspended portion of a ship under construction, marked by the transition from recorded sound to silence, reflect Park's subjective perception of them as incarnating the sublime linked to the primordial origin of industrial modernity. Park himself makes a case for this connection, as he has said: "Perhaps the overwhelming feeling that the cave dwellers would have experienced when seeing whales may be the same as my feeling when I see these ships and witness their sheer scale. There is a feeling of the sublime."[56]

Here one might surmise that the essay film has recently been led by such male filmmakers as Kim and Park in contrast to the leading role of young women filmmakers in the growth and variation of domestic ethnographies. Some recent essay films indeed attest to their underlying masculine perspective. Park's recent *Army* (*Kundae*, 2018, 90 min.) riskily straddles aesthetically glamorizing the bodies in military training as a process of how an individual young man named Woo-chul is reshaped into a part of the collective, and addressing the contested public issue of Korea's mandatory military service through his private memory and his subjective eyes on Woo-chul's inner state of mind. However, a couple of recent films have testified to the feminist creativity of young women directors invested in the essay film, refuting the binary assumption. Jang Yun-mi's thirty-six-minute film *Anxiety of Concrete* (*K'onk'ǔrit'ǔǔi puran*, 2017), for instance, provides a rigorous disjunction of sounds and images as an aesthetic strategy of activating her thinking self, while also experimenting with a kind of female writing that blends fiction and fact. The film juxtaposes slow and rhythmic panning shots of Sky Apartment located in a poor hillside village in Seoul (which was built in 1967 and demolished in 2016), and close-ups of dilapidated details. Her voice-over tells a story about the life of a patriarchal working-class family in a small apartment from the perspective of the young daughter, who has just lost her milk teeth. Preserving the respective autonomy of the two tracks, and disallowing any hierarchy of one over the other, Jang opens up multiple interpretative avenues for their relationship in the light of whether or not Sky Apartment is where the family lived, and how much her own subjective experience is reflected in the family's story. In those senses, the film's horizontal assemblage of image and sound successfully leads to the essay film as "an in-between form that moves freely from fiction to nonfiction,"[57] while also achieving both a materialist study of urban redevelopment and a quasi-literary narrative of the economic and mental conditions of the working class.

Kim Bo-ram's *Baek-gu* (*Kaeǔi yŏksa*, 2017, 83 min.) extends the autobiographical records of her experiences and surroundings, a wandering dog and a supermarket under demolition in a hillside village in Seoul, her relocation to another part of Seoul, her conversations with new senior neighbors in the town, her fifteenth change of residence, her remembrance of childhood, and her reflection on her economic precarity, into a diffusive storytelling that constructs the essayistic subjectivity's modes of drift and constant revision. Kim's question about the "history of the dog" named Baek-gu (which the film's original Korean title means) is ultimately left answered, but this failure turns out to be in exchange for her effort to collect rich details of our everyday reality, which is emblematized by her voice-over at the film's end: "What was ousted and excluded. What disappeared when we did not concern. What I miss, but I cannot find once again . . . The time being erased of what disappears." In this sense, Kim's observational camera that redeems the details, and her ambulatory, nonchronological, and associative modes of reassembling her audiovisual records push the potential of small, seemingly apolitical, stories to an extreme as an antidote to the masculine prejudice against personal documentary. In this way, *Baek-gu* achieves a qualitative leap from the self-portrait of a filmmaker to the thinking self's reflection on the complexity of time and space that underlies everydayness.

Reenactment: Approximation to History Affectively

Reenactment, or the recreation of prior events with various degrees of authenticity, was fairly common in documentary filmmaking of the pre–World War II era when there was no cinematic record of a historical event that a documentary filmmaker wanted to represent. Having been marginalized due to the development of the lightweight recording apparatus that became standard in nonfiction filmmaking in the 1960s, reenactment from the late 1980s gained a new momentum as a device that "could not reveal the truth of events but the ideologies and consciousness that [could] construct competing truths."[58] Since the early twenty-first century, it has been regarded as spanning "diverse history-related genres" linked by "their combined use of different medial forms."[59] This description reflects the wide spectrum of reenactment-based screen art and entertainment in recent years, from a staple of commercial documentary films to experimental documentaries and to documentary installations in contemporary art. A key force that drives the various uses of reenactment is its capacity to articulate traumatic experiences of violence and suffering, including their spectral and mnemonic dimensions, in affective ways that overcome their unrepresentability. For Vanessa Agnew, the popularity of reenactment in contemporary art and media is indicative of history's "affective turn," that is, "of historical representation characterized by the collapsing of temporalities and an emphasis on affect, individual experience and daily life rather than historical events, structures and processes."[60] Agnew's consideration of reenactment as affective is significant not only because its collapsing of temporalities and its privileging of experience over structure envisage different modes of storytelling than the cause-and-effect narrative of official history, but also because its emphasis upon the corporeal and psychic aspects of the experience provides an alternative to the Freudian model of trauma studies, on which the assumption of trauma's unrepresentability is grounded. In parallel to the interest in reenactment as a remarkable device of rendering history and memory affective, documentary scholars, such as Joram ten Brink and Deidre Boyle, have discussed the increasingly vital role of reenactment in documentary filmmaking in terms of its capacity to address death, catastrophe, and trauma, and to retrieve the affective and embodied aspects of memories.[61] In so doing, they are concerned with a kind of reenactment that allows for the uncanny repetition and working through of the memories of victims or survivors in a fantasmatic form through which imaginatively reconstructed or broken memories of a past event meet a present staging of it.

160 Post-activism

Post-activist Korean documentaries engaging with the memories and experiences of an individual in this century have increasingly employed various strategies of reenactment, regardless of whether they aim to supplement or counter the official history of modern and contemporary Korea. In either case, the strategies' attempts to repeat memories and experiences are read as what Bruzzi has called "approximation," a double act of bearing witness to and acknowledging absence from the past. For Bruzzi, approximation promotes a more fluid relationship between reality and imagination, between testimony and the indexical record, and between evidence and its absence, founded on "the moment of transition from one state (of innocence, of not knowing) to another (of knowledge and experience)."[62] Approximation's transitional relationship between the seemingly competing elements of documentary, as well as its transformative power, lies at the very heart of several documentaries in the 2010s that aspire to retrieve the subjective and affective dimensions of the past that *kaein* experienced and preserved, and to use them in varying negotiations with history: to rewrite it, to expose its gaps, or to extend it into the present.

Manshin: Ten Thousand Spirits (*Manshin*, 2013, 104 min.) documents the life and work of one of the most representative female shamans (*mudang*), Kim Keum-hwa, who has been celebrated as a Master of Important Intangible Heritage since the 1980s. Artist and filmmaker Park Chan-kyong adopts the strategy of realist dramatization in that the film's three major episodes starring three actresses, Kim Sae-ron (the role of Kim Geun-hwa in childhood during the Japanese Occupation), Ryu Hyun-kyung (Kim during the Korean War), and Moon So-ri (during the Park Chung-hee regime), are "the least distinguishable from . . . the conventional representation of past events in fiction."[63] Park's reconstruction of Kim's experiences and memories in her different pasts, however, also activates his stylized approaches: a dry female voice-over offers viewer an expository account of Kim's rituals and their underlying meanings while sometimes occupying her subjective position in narrating her fear of, and fascination with, being possessed by shamanistic gods and summoning up the spirits of the dead. The subjective aspect of Park's reenactment comes into being most saliently in camerawork that encompasses the stylized uses of a Steadicam, a crane, and a drone camera that embody the perspective of the gods and spirits, and Kim's POV shots expressive of her perceptual and mental ecstasy. While these subjective cameras and gazes defy the objectivist assumption of conventional ethnographic filmmaking, Park does not abandon his anthropological inquiry into Kim's ritual (*gut*) performances as religious ceremony and folk culture and into the shaman's liminal status as a medium in this world and the next world, as demonstrated by her oral testimonies, footage of her activities in the present, and interviews with folklorists. Ultimately, the three reenactment scenes start with the subjective and embodied restaging of Kim's supernatural initiation and then advance to position her personal experiences within the larger postcolonial history of modern and contemporary Korea. The Ryu Hyun-kyung episode, which consists of her witnessing of the dead bodies and her looking for refuge in Incheon, is linked to archival footage of the Battle of Incheon and news clips of the 2002 Yeonpyeong Incident (a confrontation at sea between North Korean and South Korean patrol boats along a disputed maritime boundary in the Yellow Sea), as well as to the video record of Kim's performance in 1998 to console the ghosts of the unnamed dead during the Korean War in front of the thousands of tombs. Similarly, the Moon so-ri episode during the Park Chung-hee regime in 1972 dramatizes not only her surreal experience of predicting the death of her neighbor but also the regime's ideological atmosphere marked by fear of North Korean spies and the drive to modernization that stigmatized traditional shamanism as superstition. Park's project to reconfigure the history of Korea through Kim's experiences and memories culminates in the film's last episode, which retraces her increased appearances on television after her induction as National Intangible Heritage and her public performances since the 1980s. Besides using footage of Kim's TV images to demonstrate how shamanism became mystified and spectacularized, Park superimposes onto an image of the sea from one of her recent *guts* an extremely heterogeneous array of archival images associated with dynamic historical events of Korea since the 1980s: the Gwangju Uprising, the shamanistic ceremony of *minjung* culture, the 2002 World Cup, the Sewol Ferry Disaster, and the 2008 Candlelight Protests. As Jecheol Park notes, this hypermediated form of intermedial montage "enable[s] Kim's shamanic practices to address a multiplicity of sufferings and losses and to express a multiplicity of hopes and wishes."[64]

Staging an individual's subjective experience and memory connected to the spiritual and the spectral, *The Pregnant Tree and the Goblin* (*Imshinhan namuwa tokkaebi*, Kim Dong-ryung and Park Kyoung-tae, 2019, 115 min.) differs from *Manshin* in its strategy of reenactment and its relationship to history. The film focuses on recreating the fantasies of former sex worker Park Insun in a former US military camptown (*kijich'on*) whom the directors first met and began filming in 2002, and who is also one of the three protagonists of their previous documentary *Tour of Duty* (2012, see chapter 5). As codirector Park Kyoung-tae clarifies, the film's use of reenactment dates back to the directors' pursuit for an alternative to the verité-style documentary associated with the social movement for supporting military sex workers as victims of the state's exploitation and violence: "There was a demand for informing the structural contradiction of *kijich'on*, but Insun was not the kind of person who could show and tell it. For she did not know language well and was always drunk."[65] This impossibility led the directors to develop the mode of docufiction as both an alternative nonfiction storytelling of a traumatized subject and a self-reflexive critique of the ways in which different accounts and stories about the subject and her haunted space (in this case, the remnants of the camptown) are constructed and forgotten. First, based on Park Insun's fantasies as well as her drawings, which render them with grotesque and surreal imagery, the directors create a female ghost named Lotus (*kkotpuni*) and three death messengers (*chŏsŭng saja*). While Lotus represents the spirits of the unnamed sex workers who wander about the camptown's deserted lands, alleys, and bars due to their experience of unwanted pregnancies, abortions, and sexual and military violence, the three death messengers, originated from her drawings and spoken words, are reflective of Park's encounter with death and her overcoming of it. Second, the directors also devise two additional characters, a feminist scholar associated with the legal dispute with the government for its compensation for former military sex workers, and artist-curator who assists her. The scholar's video interview with Park turns out to be useless as legal evidence because of her inability to articulate her memories consistently. This suggests the gap between the discursive condition of a legal testimony, which ought to verify Park's victimized status, and Park's memories and experiences, which are effaced in the official history of the US camptowns and their workers and which remain unspeakable by the language of the law. The artist-curator, meanwhile, serves as a character who investigates the larger history of the town named Bbaetbul and the deaths from the Chosun Dynasty to the Park Chung-hee regime that regulated the camptowns and their workers, in the hope of organizing an exhibition showcasing Park's drawings and the remainders of the town (photos of female workers during its heyday, and the now-deserted bar where the photos are found). These multiple—legal, anthropological, historical, and artistic—perspectives on Bbaetbul are overlaid with the discussion of the three death messengers about different stories surrounding *kijich'on* in the light of how some of them are stereotypical and how others remain untold.

In this way, the directors' docufiction reenactment creates a distanciation effect that invites viewers to investigate "how the stories about *kijich'on* are made, who makes the stories, and how they disappear."[66] It is with this effect that the film establishes Park as an individual whose memories and stories point to gaps in the historiography on military sex workers, in comparison to *Manshin* that portrays Kim Geum-hwa as an incarnation of the postcolonial history of Korea. More than betraying the documentary expectation of factuality and argumentation, the film's fantasmatic reenactment successfully dramatizes the liminality of the US camptowns that Grace Kyungwon Hong observes: "The camptown is a kind of ghost space, both here and there and neither. And it does indeed produce ghosts of all kinds. This ghostly state of in-betweenness, characterized by both life and death but belonging fully to neither, represents the complex juridical condition of these camptown residents."[67]

Comfort (*Podŭrapke*, Park Moon-chil, 2020, 73 min.) combines two types of reenactment, animated images and the casting of social actors, founded upon two interrelated ideas of performativity. The film pays homage to a former comfort woman Kim Soon-ak (born 1928), who became an activist in the 2000s and donated her property to found the Museum of Military Sexual Slavery by Japan in Daegu before her death in 2010. The film employs animated sequences, video footage of Kim, and a series of testimonies by activists and caretakers who have known her. The animated sequences do more than reconstruct Kim's turbulent trajectories of life, which encompass her sexual slavery in China by fraud, her work in the brothel during the US military government, her operation of the prostitution industry at *kijich'on*, her experience as a housekeeper, and her uncomfortable relationships with two sons, one of whom had a violent character due to people's bullying him for his mixed-blood appearance. The animated images' expressive elements, such as simplified and symbolic lines, caricature-style icons, and the multiplication of grotesque figures, convey Kim's subjective feelings of traumatic experiences whose evidentiary record is not available: for instance, when Kim's testimony describes the physical and mental pains of having served thirty to forty Japanese soldiers per day. This nonobjective aspect of the animated images corresponds to what Nichols has called the "evocative" quality of performative documentaries, which are "more iconic than indexical," which "do not explain or summarize so much as imply or intimate," and which stress "the referential turn toward . . . an experiential domain, expressively substantiated."[68] It, too, validates the "evocative" use of animation in animated documentaries to visualize "ideas, feelings, and sensibilities . . . in often in an abstract or symbolic style," which allows viewers "to imagine the world from someone else's perspective."[69] While this evocative, iconic reenactment of Kim's emotions and feelings supplements what it might be difficult for the official history of comfort women to represent, Park also films several young girls based in Daegu watching Kim's video interviews and reciting her memoirs in the museum (figure 4.3).

This type of casting social actors can also be found in Kim Dong-won's *My Friend Jung Il-woo* (*Nae ch'in'gu Chŏng Iru*, 2017, 84 min.), which pays tribute

Figure 4.3 *Comfort* (Park Moon-chil, 2020)

to the priest Jung Il-woo (aka John Vincent Daly, 1935–2014) who devoted himself to social movements for workers and the urban poor. For the film, Jung's fellow activists and Kim offer four voice-over narrations. They perform different yet overlapping memories of Jung, bringing Jung's spirit and legacy into the shared world of the present. Park's strategy of casting social actors is on the same page as Kim's, because the social actors are initially positioned as spectators who watch Kim's presence on the image projected behind them. As they recite Kim's memories in their own voices, this performative act of repetition attests to what Jennifer Allen sees as the role of spectators in theatrical reenactments: "As the script shifts from actors to spectators, interpretation is no longer about authenticity but reception: the question is not 'Is this reenactment true to the past?' but 'Is this reenactment true to our present?'"[70] The generational gap between Kim and the ladies goes beyond documentary authenticity, and their awareness of Kim's memories through their performative acts is capable of linking the memories to their shared present marked by the feminist social movement since the mid-2010s: for the ladies confess their prior experiences of sexual harassment in their workplace and how Kim's life story and spirit, embodied by their recitation, have empowered them. In this sense, the strategy of recitation demonstrates a key underlying motivation for the uses of reenactment in the post-activist documentaries: to connect the personal to the political.

New Subjectivities

The domestic ethnographies, essay films, and reenactment-driven documentaries all attest to the "dramatic, even explosive, appearance of new subjectivities"[71] as the hallmark of the post-activist practices of the twenty-first century. This chapter has accounted for that appearance of subjectivities, which point to *kaein* both as the director's self and as an individual social actor, in terms of the filmmakers' various self-reflexive efforts to experiment with documentary forms and aesthetics, to reconfigure *sajŏk* as entwined with the political and historical, and to redefine the public through the mediation of individuals' perception, memory, and consciousness. All these efforts, I argue, valorize Alisa Lebow's insight that what is political in the first-person mode of nonfiction films is not reducible to the "political themes it treats": rather, it "entail[s] a radical critique of subjectivity while also . . . enacting the political by . . . 'inventing new ways of making sense of the sensible.'"[72]

In sync with the directors' new ways of making sensible the corporeal and affective dimensions of an individual's subjective experience, what makes those variations of the "personal turn" notable is their common idea of documentary temporality: that is, all the exhibitions of the subjectivities in the films that I have examined in this chapter are built upon the filmmakers' varying formal and aesthetic attempts to deal with memory and history, and their awareness that a documentary film's engagement with reality in the passing present is inseparable from and always overlaps with the rich yet often inaccessible layers of the past. The filmmakers' venture into the first-person mode in the forms of voice-over, uses of archival footage, and fragmentary or associative editing, and so on, is then read as making their work distinct from the classical activist films and videos that aimed to document unjust reality of the recent past and to make that record into audiovisual discourses of sociopolitical report, enlightenment, and persuasion in the present tense of *hyŏnjang*. The directors' distinct epistemological approach to documentary time, then, necessarily has led to their renewed attention to the places and landscapes of reality along with the task of how to represent them. These two are indeed suggested in many of the films examined in this chapter and probed in more detail in the next.

5
The Audiovisual Turn

From *hyŏnjang* to Memoryscape

Places and Landscapes

As discussed in the introduction, Im Heung-soon's *Factory Complex* employs shots that present various places and landscapes associated with the history and contemporary lives of Korean female workers. He treats the images as autonomous objects aligned with the bodies and voices of the workers, rather than as the sites of labor struggles underway. The autonomy of the images lyrically or metaphorically framing places and landscapes in *Factory Complex* can also be found in *Scenery* (*P'unggyŏng*, 2013, 96 min.) by Korean-Chinese filmmaker Zhang Lu, a documentary that investigates the dreams of fourteen Southeast Asian migrant workers. The workers' oral testimonies, presented in the form of their direct address to Zhang's camera, function as a key medium of bearing witness to the initial utopian desire that brought them to Korea. However, the images of their workplaces (construction sites, factories, restaurants, etc.) as well as the urban places (alleys, subway stations, etc.) surrounding their towns exist independently of the interviews, all of their emptiness evoking the frustration of their dreams, their sense of alienation from Korean society, and their diasporic anxiety about precarious life. The power of this emptiness to contain these affective registers supplementing the workers' testimonies becomes more obvious as the camera maintains its gaze on an alley in the town of migrant workers even after a male social actor has left the frame; that is, after the camera has exhausted its primary function of recording his speech.

The Color of Pain (*Bora*, Lee Kang-hyun, 2010, 136 min.) (figure 5.1) and *Watchtower* (*Mangdae*, Moon Seung-wook, 2014, 64 min.) refresh Korean documentary cinema's concern with labor and urban redevelopment (*chaegaebal*) that its activist precursors engaged. *The Color of Pain* investigates the conditions of labor and the mental and physical subjectivity of laborers in contemporary Korea, focusing on the national healthcare system in place at various workplaces (steel factory, piano manufacturing factory, mannequin

Activism and Post-activism. Jihoon Kim, Oxford University Press. © Oxford University Press 2024.
DOI: 10.1093/oso/9780197760413.003.0006

Figure 5.1 *The Color of Pain* (Lee Kang-hyun, 2010)

manufacturing factory, etc.), a farm, and a quarry. While this film addresses these workplaces, particularly the factory, as a traditional subject matter engaged by traditional Korean independent documentary films, it does not represent the workplaces as the simple background of laborers' mass protest, strike, or sabotage. Instead, Lee's camera collects wide-ranging material details of the workplaces, including fires, flares, and flickering lights produced by a steel factory in the film's opening sequence, welding workers surrounded by machines in another steel factory, and processes of excavating and manufacturing stones in the quarry. In so doing, it captures the traces of the visible and sonic conditions of the various labors without any expository voice-over, therefore amplifying viewers' sensory experiences of them.

Watchtower vividly captures dilapidated landscapes of Yaksa-dong, a small town in Chuncheon (capital city of Gangwon Province) that was marked as a sector of urban redevelopment, focusing on a watchtower constructed during the Japanese Occupation, and on its old houses and surrounding alleys. While engaging this type of a community in the crisis, the film's mode of practice is sharply distinct from those of the traditional activist-oriented Korean independent documentaries, including Kim Dong-won's seminal *Sanggye-dong Olympics*, predicated on participatory engagement with the demolition of an old town, the forced dislocation and relocation of its residents, and the struggle of the residents against the redevelopment. For many shots in the film, Moon uses various cinematographic techniques and temporal rhythms to frame the scenic landscapes of Yaksa-dong. The dilapidated objects of the watchtower,

168 Post-activism

including a corridor, windows covered with dust, and walls in faded colors, are inscribed in the camera as the traces of its long history, encompassing its use for observing fire on the town during the Japanese Occupation and for prison surveillance after the liberation. By dealing with the watchtowers, alleys, and old houses of Yaksa-dong as autonomous segments charged with their visual richness stressed by added lyrical music, *Watchtower* introduces to the viewer a situation in which the town's decaying present becomes permeated with its buried past.

The four films, as well as their common tendency to treat a place or landscape as a space pervaded by the time and history of its human residents and to isolate its images as autonomous entities, emblematize a notable tendency of Korean documentary cinema since the 2010s. To be sure, this tendency to emphasize the visible and sonic qualities of images with expressive camerawork and montage, avoiding voice-over narration or cause-and-effect narrative, pertains to what Bill Nichols has characterized as the "poetic" mode of documentary practices,[1] which dates back to European modernist filmmaking's productive intersections of documentary and avant-garde cinema in the 1920s and 1930s.[2] From another angle, the emphasis on form and aesthetics in the Korean documentary films that take the place or landscape as their primary object for investigating its present and its underlying history or memory is in line with the recent global popularity of the various crossovers of documentary and experimental cinema, which have been identified by such terms as "experimental documentary" (Lucas Hildebrand) and "avant-doc" (Scott MacDonald).[3]

In these contexts, this chapter characterize this tendency of recent Korean documentary filmmaking as the "audiovisual turn" in two senses. First, this term teases out these films' aesthetic and technical procedures of amplifying the visual and auditory qualities of the image portraying a place or landscape, as well as these procedures' effects of providing a fresh look at the present of the place or landscape, or drawing the viewer's attention to its connection to a forgotten history or the memory of the people who occupy it. Second, more significantly, these documentaries' emphasis on the audiovisual qualities of a place or landscape by framing it as an autonomous entity and creating the disparity of image and voice marks remarkable aesthetic and epistemological breaks from the activist tradition, which was governed by the cinéma-vérité ethos of privileging the director's engagement with *hyŏnjang* of social events (strikes or antidemolition protests) and their subjects with a participatory, handheld camera, and a cause-and-effect narrative developing the progress and consequence of the events. In the verité-style activist documentaries, social spaces, such as the factory or the urban town under impending redevelopment, are marginalized as the social and geographical background against which those political actions take place and develop. Recent nonfiction films discussed in this chapter, on the contrary, use aesthetic devices in ways foreign to their precursors, bringing to the forefront a place or landscape as the very locus of both present reality and past memory or history.

More than the aesthetic break of the recent documentaries from the activist tradition, the second sense of the "audiovisual turn" signals their epistemological distinction, namely, the shift in understanding natural or built environments from *hyŏnjang* to "memoryscape"—a term that is used in memory studies as a synonym for the spaces and locales significant to people's mnemonic relationship to the past. While existing studies on the term focus on concrete physical and territorial spaces occupied by museums, statues, squares, and artifacts that narrate or commemorate a particular event of the past,[4] I identify three types of memoryscape that the recent documentaries render, based on their directors' understanding of private spaces, urban places, and memorials and spaces of memory activism, as the "the product[s] . . . of the relations between people and the site in question itself."[5] Of particular importance is the last type of memoryscape because it is linked to an array of local activist movements for truth-finding of a traumatic political event in the Cold War, mourning its victims, and advocating their rights. As I demonstrate in my reading of *Jeju Prayer* (*Pinyŏm*, Im Heung-soon, 2012, 93 min.) and *Tour of Duty* (*Kŏmiŭi ttang*, Kim Dong-ryung and Park Kyoung-tae, 2013, 150 min.), filmmakers who have led the "audiovisual turn" renew Korean documentary cinema's longstanding activist commitment to local politics by shedding new light on the sites of social protests and state violence and by innovating the ways of reclaiming the memories of their victims or bereaved families. Their directorial agency also marks the ontological shift of the sites from *hyŏnjang* as the space of struggles happening *in the present tense* to memoryscape, in which remainders of *past events*, if seemingly invisible, are viewed as cohabiting with *the present*.

With its analyses of the two films, this chapter also introduces two films of Oh Minwook, a documentarian based in Busan, the harbor city known as a cinematic city due to its hosting of BIFF since 1996 and its institutional and material support for filming on location, as a notable local case of the "audiovisual turn." Besides these relatively well-known examples, Busan has been a major city where the practice of Korean independent documentary filmmaking has been developed since the 1990s, and it is in this context that activists and directors have explored various dimensions that compose the city's present and history. As such, the Busan-based documentarians of the twenty-first century, including Kim Jung-geun (see chapter 2) and Park Bae-il

170 Post-activism

(chapter 3), have been grappling with people's ways of living through their investigation of the places of Busan. Based in a collective Takju Cooperative (T'akchu johap) together with documentarian Kim Ji-gon, Oh has made remarkable achievements in the cinematic investigation of the modern history and ruined landscape of Busan with his experimental documentaries charged with formal and aesthetic rigor.

Three Memoryscapes, the Audiovisual Turn, and Its Time-Images

The domestic ethnographies discussed in chapter 4 resonate with the audiovisual turn's attention to the places or landscapes as fundamental to understanding reality and history. For they treat the private space of a director or his or her family members as integral to understanding the experiences, memories, and sentiments of the social subjects who once inhabited or still inhabit it. The films' rendition of the domestic or residential space as a type of memoryscape is also demonstrated in *A Long Farewell* (*Chibŭi shigandŭl*, Raya, 2018, 73 min.), *Land and Housing* (*Pongmyŏngjugong*, Kim Kiseong, 2020, 83 min.), and *Queer Room* (*K'wiŏŭi pang*, Kwon Aram, 2018, 29 min.).[6] Distinct from the essay film or domestic ethnography, the three documentaries isolate houses or rooms as autonomous aesthetic objects that speak for themselves as they overlap with the testimonies of their inhabitants. *A Long Farewell* compiles the stories of thirteen residents at Dunchon Jugong Apartments in Seoul who are faced with relocation as they are scheduled to be demolished based on the rebuilding (*chaegŏnch'uk*) plan developed in 1998 (the demolition and relocation were completed in 2018). While the residents' stories offer different memories of their lives in the apartments and their varying relationships to it, such as the sense of belonging, comfort, and growth, their voices are heard without the speakers being present on-screen. In this course, the camera presents a wide-ranging collection of details inside and outside the apartments (facades, passageways, and gardens, and each unit's windows, curtains, doors, sunlight, shadow, photos, and appliances), establishing the complex itself as the film's protagonist (the film's Korean original title means "the times of houses"), and figuring each detail as an object that explicates the memory and sentiment of each resident. Rehearsing the aesthetic isolation of the built and natural elements that compose a dilapidated housing complex, and the archival collection of the stories of its residents, *Land and Housing*, a documentary that investigates Jugong Apartment (built in the 1980s) in Bongmyeong-dong, Cheongju, in 2019, adds an ecocritical overtone to the rebuilding process. Here, viewers witness a group of young students who are not residents of the complex but who regularly visit its surrounding gardens to explore their still vibrant ecosystem, and a series of rhythmic, quasi-elegiac landscape shots in which trees are cut down one by one by heavy vehicles. The camera's isolation of domestic space with its residents' voices disentangled from their bodies in *A Long Farewell* is also the case with *Queer Room*, a twenty-nine-minute film that compiles testimonies of five young residents in four alternative share houses open to sexual minorities. While the interviewees use domestic space to generate shared queer identities, to consolidate a couple's partnership, or to raise the importance of privacy, comfort, and control at home for their sexual orientation and desire (one participant says, "I don't have to hide my identity and anything from these people I live with"),[7] all these subjects turn out to be implicated in the spaces and objects of the houses, including the rainbow slogans and stickers posted on an interior wall, and a shelf that displays books on feminism and gender studies. Viewed together, the three films' isolation of the living space and their sound-image disjunction demonstrate the audiovisual turn, which engages the social issues of the activist tradition, urban redevelopment, and queer politics, with experimental cinematic strategies akin to those of the "avant-doc."

There has also been a thread of documentaries since the late 2000s that, take as their protagonist an urban space or architectural construct derived from Korea's modernization and later subject to redevelopment or rehabilitation in service of investigating its details and its political and social histories. These films' attention to that space as memoryscape addresses the renovation of the historical buildings or areas into facilities for other contemporary purposes in the twenty-first century in Seoul and other major cities, a process also called "urban regeneration" (*toshi jaesaeng*). But they also coincide with the proliferation of museums, monuments, and cultural districts that construct the public memory of their foundation, their operation, and their larger history.[8] These urban transformations have contributed to reconstructing Seoul as a city occupied by the "locales without [the] suggestion of continuity . . . where the antiquity of the culture rests indeed on the display of the flag, a memorial, replicas of heritage, streetlamps, and such."[9]

Kimu: The Strange Dance (*Kiihan ch'um: Kimu*, Park Dong-hyun, 2009, 62 min.) explores the former headquarters building of the Defense Security Command (Kukkun gimu saryŏngbu), which was later rebuilt into the National Museum of Modern and Contemporary Art Seoul. The film features interviews with professors of architecture as well as a chronology of national events (in the form of intertitles overlaid with images) relating to the building

172 Post-activism

from the late nineteenth century to the early twenty-first century in order to contextualize it within the cultural and military history of colonial, modern, and contemporary Korea and to offer contested perspectives on urban redevelopment that include both the preservation of traditions and renovation for future uses. This historiographic project, however, is intercut with the film's experimental cinematography to frame the building's appearances, to summon up spectrality in its vacant interior spaces, and to capture old houses and alleys in its neighboring towns subject to redevelopment, and with evocative sound effects. Filmmaker and artist Seo Hyun-suk has produced documentaries and installations that explore a monumental building or space and its underlying history of modernist architecture and urban planning in Seoul. *The Lost Voyage* (*Irŏbŏrin hanghae*, codirected with An Chang-mo, 2012–2017, 50 min.), whose first version was showcased in the Korean Pavilion of the Venice Biennale in 2014, deals with Sewoon Arcade (Seun sangga), a complex combining small-scale electronics retailers and residences that was built in 1966 by the visionary architect Kim Swoo-geun and became later an object of Seoul Metropolitan Government's *toshi jaesaeng* project in the early 2010s. While foregrounding testimonies of the architects, urban planners, and city officials involved in the master plans of Seoul's rapid modernization, the film interweaves disparate materials and expressive strategies to provide multiple perspectives on Seoul's past and present, which include negotiation between the architectural avant-garde modernism and the state's developmentalist policy, the larger political and social contexts of the plans, and a dialogue between the plans' ideals and the voices of the contemporary residents. As a result, it employs a vast array of archival footage and photos from the Park regime and world histories of the 1960s and 1970s, intersecting them with lyric and evocative landscape images of the arcade, with a series of direct-address interviews with small business owners of the arcade and intellectuals who explain its heterotopic aspects, and with their performative recitations of excerpts from the texts on architecture and modernism.

Im Cheol-min's *Glow Job* (*Yagwang*, 2018, 81 min.) views a now-dilapidated movie theater named Bada Theater (Pada gŭkchang) in Seoul's center in the light of the memories of queer intimacy. His ethnographic inquiry into the places for queer subculture in Seoul is built on two experimental approaches: the discrepancy of sound and image and the long-take cinematography of a stationery camera. The theater's empty auditorium, its vacant screen, and its entrance are presented in a series of fixed shots. Offering viewers sufficient time for contemplation, this vignette invokes both the cultural status of the theater as a cruising spot for gays in Seoul, and other similar movie theaters (Pagoda Theater, Seongdong Theater, and Keukdong Theater) that have already disappeared.[10] The intersection of darkness and light that fills the empty auditorium introduces the allegorical temporality of the past as both the heyday of moviegoing and that of the gay subculture in Seoul. The overlapping of the past and present in the empty spaces of Bada Theater is repeated in another series of fixed shots in extended duration that portray other now-vacant cruising spots (a restaurant, corridors in its building, and its toilets) in Seoul. Im's experimental documentary, however, does more than embellish the decay of the cruising spots in the past with nostalgia. The void of Bada Theater is filled with a dense flow of surreal sounds, including that of the seagulls, which go beyond its chronological past by evoking the power of cinema to project collective dreams. The sound effect of the gay meeting application Grinder is also heard in the course of the shots framing the restaurant, corridors, and toilets. This sound-image disjunction suggests the replacement of physical intimacy in the cruising spots by virtual intimacy in the dating app, blending the past of queer subculture with its present. Im's conceit for reconstructing the vanished sites of vernacular queer intimacy is also evident in the film's climactic sequence, in which a film-within-a-film titled *Nagwon* (the name of a neighborhood in the Jongro district for gay cruising) is presented in the form of 3D images of an imaginary paradise (the Korean term *nagwon* also denotes "paradise"). As Ungsan Kim observes, this sequence copes with the "disappearance of the physical evidence of vernacular queer history by technically suspending the flow of time and crystallizing the very cruising site in the form of a digital archive."[11] All in all, *Glow Job* illustrates Im's effort to channel his experimentations with cinematography and audiovisual montage into the queer memoryscapes in the past and their imaginary reconstruction in the present.

The last type of memoryscape, namely, memorials and spaces of memory activism, perhaps offers documentarians the most significant context of their experimental investigation into places and landscapes. As discussed in the introduction regarding the inauguration of the Truth and Reconciliation Commission in 2005, their proliferation in twenty-first-century Korean society and culture is indebted to the liberal political atmosphere of the Kim Dae-jung and Roh Moo-hyun governments, in which activists, intellectuals, and artists were able to illuminate countermemories of the Korean War, the Gwangju Uprising, and the April Third Incident (Sasam sagŏn) in 1948, a political event that began with an attack by a few hundred communist guerrillas on the local police in Jeju Island, which eventually led to counterinsurgency operations by the police and the US Army, who were responsible for a bloody mass massacre of eighty thousand civilians (nearly one-third of the island's entire population), including many who were falsely accused

174 Post-activism

of being communists or rioters.[12] These are historic events that the military dictatorship's monolithic, ideologically codified narrative had long described as a communist riot or invasion (the Korean War). The political atmosphere coupled with memory activism has had a significant impact on the reconstruction of the public memories on these events, which has propelled investigating their unknown realities, including massacres and atrocities committed by South Korean and/or US armies, provoking the mourning of bereaved families, revealing their untold stories, and making efforts to restore the honor of victims. The demands for truth-finding, previously repressed testimonies, and destigmatization have been applied to the victims of postcolonial Cold War politics, such as the military sex workers in the US camptowns (*kijich'on*). Constructed in several cities (Paju, Dongducheon, and Uijeongbu) near the DMZ during the US military rule from 1945 to 1948, the camptowns, populated with clubs, bars, and brothels that only US soldiers and foreign tourists were allowed to enter, thrived from the 1960s to the 1980s, regulated by the Korean government that registered the workers and mandated their regular examinations for sexually transmitted diseases.[13] As a number of seminal studies on the camptowns demonstrate, despite their role in the economic development of postwar Korea and the geopolitical settlement of the US military power in the Korean Peninsula, the sex workers were subject both to social stigmatization evidenced by their derogatory names, *yanggalbo* (Western whore) and *yanggongju* (Western princess), and to sexual harassment and exploitation by US soldiers as their customers or partners.[14] In the twenty-first century, when the camptowns began to be shut down and were subjugated to urban redevelopment and regeneration, human rights and feminist activists as well as researchers have conducted archival research and oral interviews to construct the countermemories of former sex workers in terms of their survival under—and their resistance to—the dominant ideologies, patriarchal norms, and misogynist crimes,[15] and, in so doing, to assist lawsuits against the government's forced treatment for the diseases.[16]

What followed these changes has been a remarkable increase in the memorials, monuments, and museums associated with political and ideological violence in the turbulent moments of twenty-century Korea, evidenced by Jeju April Third Peace Park constructed in 2008 and the DMZ Museum in 2009, and by the repurposing of the places of massacres into historic sites (*sajŏkchi*).[17] As Suhi Choi observes, they "bring countermemories that previously were kept in vernacular sites (civilians' and soldiers' bodies and minds) into official sites (the official commemorations)."[18] Here it becomes evident that the investigative history documentaries in chapter 2 and the domestic ethnographies about the family members involved in the Korean War in chapter 4 coincide with the production of these social and cultural memoryscapes insofar as they probe either the historic sites of state violence or its repercussive impact on the individual or collective dimensions of the present. More than attending to the public sites and memorials, however, the films validate the intertwining of spatiality and temporality that underlies documentarians' interest in the everyday spaces and natural landscapes surrounding their own family members, as well as survivors, victims' families, and villagers. With this awareness of the places as memoryscape, the directors' intervention in the official history of the political events aims to counter its linear temporality, therefore reconfiguring the present of the subjects as permeated by their previously untold, repressed, or traumatized memories of the past.

Local critics have paid attention to the ways in which Korean documentary films since the 2010s have increasingly investigated various places and landscapes. Building upon the place studies of Henri Lefebvre, Yi-Fu Tuan, Edward W. Soja, and Doreen Massey, all of whom understand landscapes and places as socially, ideologically, and materially produced and thus central to the phenomenological and psychic formation of human subjectivity and memory, Lee Do-hoon proposes the term "spatial turn" (*kongganjŏk sŏnhoe*) to indicate this tendency. Classifying several types of space, such as urban space, rural space, and the space of state or capitalist violence, he argues that in these documentaries places and landscapes are understood as the "network of intertwined social powers, wills, ideas, and practices rather than as the physical space where events take place."[19] Lee Seung-min coins the term "space documentary" (*konggan tak'yumentŏri*) to underline the gradual increase in Korean documentary's attention to the places and landscapes that began in the early 2000s and flourished in the 2010s. For her, space documentary "represents social place or landscape not as a space of progressive present tense that is interlocked with an event, but as one after it occurred."[20] Lee Seung-min further singles out several aesthetic features of space documentary: it is not subordinated to the narrative causality of conventional documentary, delaying or suspending the temporal progression of documentary narrative; it is often characterized by deliberate close-ups and self-conscious long takes, and auditory effects that propel the viewer to feel the sensory dimensions of the place or landscape and thereby guide her toward its past.

To be sure, both "spatial turn" and "space documentary" point out the ways in which the emergence of these documentaries has responded to spaces produced by Korea's modernization as remainders of what it was. These spaces encompass shantytowns or old districts subject to the processes of urban redevelopment that have continued from Korea's rapid urbanization in the 1980s to its embrace of a neoliberal economy in this century. They are also natural or artificial landscapes traumatized by the ideological and political conflicts of Korea's postcolonial, authoritarian, and postauthoritarian eras, with some being monumental spaces that have incarnated the modern and contemporary history of Korea but now remain deserted, yet haunted as what Pierre Nora has called "sites of memory" (*lieux de mémorie*), where "a sense of historical continuity persists."[21] Despite this valuable contribution, however, these local discourses suffer from a couple of flaws. Lee Do-hoon's "spatial turn" concerns only *what* these films represent, bypassing which technical, aesthetic, and ontological characteristics of these films contribute to producing the places or landscapes as specific cinematic spaces. In this sense, this term risks encompassing too many documentary films that portray places or landscapes, given that all the films that might be grouped under the term do not necessarily employ the experimental approaches that I consider to depart from activist documentary's aesthetic and narrative assumptions. Lee Seung-min's "space documentary" surely identifies these approaches, but it ultimately does not result in a sound theorization of the images that they produce. For it replaces the temporal dimension of the audiovisual qualities of the cinematic space by the term "space," which might render the films in question as merely taking social places or natural landscapes as their subject matter. To clearly tease out the documentaries that demonstrate the technical and aesthetic procedures of the audiovisual turn, and to theorize the ontology of their images that invite viewers to experience the place or landscape as the fundamental juncture of its present and its memory or history, I employ Gilles Deleuze's concept of the "time-image."

In his two *Cinema* books, Deleuze provides three concepts that illustrate the aesthetic and ontological underpinnings of the time-image in postwar modern cinema, particularly its reconfiguration of cinematic places and landscapes. The first is what Deleuze has called the "pure optical and sound situation"[22] as a precondition of the time-image. Unlike the classical cinema, in which the image of the place or landscape is subject to an indirect representation of habitual linear time marked by the clear distinction between past and future, the pure optical and sound situation allows the place or landscape to be an autonomous entity disconnected from the protocols of narrative causality and spatial coherence. By allowing viewers to appreciate the visual and sonic qualities of the place or landscape, the rise of this situation reveals "connections of a new type, which bring the emancipated senses into direct relation with time and thought."[23] The pure optical and sound situation of the time-image closely relates to what Deleuze calls "any-space-whatever," a pure empty or disconnected space extracted from the geographical location of a place or landscape. Deleuze considers any-space-whatever to be a singular, fragmented space dissociated from the spatial continuity of shots, a space of "virtual conjunction, grasped as pure locus of the possible."[24] Here the "possible" refers to the space's sensory and affective qualities implicated in its surface, which suggest the power of a virtual past invisible (that is, not yet actualized) but immanent in the space. The any-space-whatevers in modern cinema in *Cinema 2*, such as "deserted but inhabited, disused warehouses, waste ground, [and] cities in the course of demolition or reconstruction,"[25] crucially allow one to envision the documentary time-image that expresses and investigates places or landscapes charged with their sensory and affective qualities, and with their virtual past. The third is the disjunction of the audible and the visible. Deleuze observes that with the advent of modern cinema the sound of film—be it dialogue, voice-over, or added music—became freed from its dependence on the visual image and acquires autonomy. In modern cinema's experimentations with the voice, it is detached from its corresponding body and surrounds the visual image that presents an empty place or disconnected landscape (which accords with any-space-whatever). The visual image, then, renders the place or landscape legible, so that viewers are invited to read it beneath its surface: here a visible trace of a past event or memory in the present is absent, but this absence is supplemented by a voice that embodies the event or memory immanent in the virtual past. In this way, Deleuze argues that the sound-image disjunction in modern cinema reconfigures the place or landscape as "*archaeological, stratigraphic, [and] tectonic,*"[26] as it takes viewers back "to *the deserted layers of our time which bury our own phantoms.*"[27]

Several existing works in cinema and media studies have demonstrated the effectiveness of applying these three Deleuzian concepts associated with the time-image to the experimental documentary practices of portraying and examining a place or landscape that break with the objective or conventional documentary cinema to unearth layers of time other than its chronological present. Elizabeth Cowie's fascinating account of documentary time is informed by Deleuze's view: "The pastness of the documentary image is not its time in the present but in the now of its subsequent encounter [with] the memory of place and of the material experience of sights [and] sounds."[28] Cowie further distinguishes two ways of experiencing place and landscape in documentary in terms of the Deleuzian pair of the movement-image and the time-image. While a documentary based on the movement-image posits a place or landscape as audiovisual evidence that is visible, there is another type of documentary film that, according to Cowie, shows it "as immanent, and as 'time-image' in a freeing of depicted time from the temporal causality of cinematic representation as a chronological succession from then to now."[29] The second type of documentary film, then, presents the time-image of the place or landscape with production of the pure optical and sound situation that renders the place or landscape as any-space-whatever. In his Deleuzian take on Claude Lanzmann's *Shoah* (1985), D. N. Rodowick identifies how the film's evocative juxtaposition of incommensurable image and sound establishes the Holocaust as both a historical event and an unimaginable or unrepresentable one beyond the confines of discourse and visibility. While the landscape of Auschwitz remains silent to what it witnessed, its visual images bear the trace of the concentration camp as they are asymmetrically related to the oral testimonies of the survivors, who cannot entirely tell what they experienced in the camp. As Rodowick writes, "By its persistence in the present, the landscape gives visible testimony to what cannot be represented in the voice. In turn, the voice excavates a past entombed in the landscape and hidden from sight."[30]

Through Deleuze's concept of the time-image, one can better understand how the emphasis on the audiovisual qualities of the images framing a place or landscape in the experimental documentary can have the heterogeneous yet powerful effect of claiming its reality as the fundamental imbrication of the present and the past. The concept also helps one to grasp not only how memoryscapes are taken as a documentary's object of scrutiny in relation to the suppressed mourning of survivors who experienced pain and loss, but also how the documentary constructs the place and landscape as cinematic memoryscape. Bearing in mind these two effects of the concept, I examine *Jeju Prayer* and *Tour of Duty* in terms of their configuration of the time-images that activate the political work of memory and history in the natural or artificial landscapes haunted by the forgotten or hitherto untold testimonies of the traumatic past. Demonstrating the audiovisual turn, these two documentaries deserve particular significance partly because their memoryscapes deal with memory activism for the victims and survivors of the geopolitical and ideological suppression in the Cold War era, and partly because they are positioned within the two post-activist contexts, namely, the transition from activist to *kamdok* and the attention to the pain and grief of marginalized people as *kaein* rather than a collective subject for social change.

Places and Landscapes Haunted by the Past: *Jeju Prayer* and *Tour of Duty*

Im Heung-soon's debut theatrical documentary *Jeju Prayer*, which was showcased in the Jeonju International Film Festival and DMZ International Documentary Film Festival in 2012, exemplifies a kind of experimental documentary that reconfigures a geographical place and its landscape in the present as a space haunted by repressed histories and traumatic memories of the past. Apart from its inheritance of Korean documentary's interest in traumatic political events, the film has received local critics' positive acclaim because it "pays more attention to the present landscape of Jeju Island than to the figures and testimonies of survivors and families."[31]

The film primarily documents two sides of the island: its bright side as the tourist attraction marked by the natural beauty of Hallasan mountain, the many trails (*ollegil*) that open onto the mountain and are loved by hikers and trekkers, and the seashore that surrounds the island; and its dark side as the site of the April Third Incident.[32] Illuminating this dark side of the traumatic event, which which the dominant anticommunist ideology of South Korean state politics has still largely influenced people to view as a communist insurgency, *Jeju Prayer* features interviews of the survivors who must live on while tarrying with the ghosts of the dead (their parents, spouse, children, or siblings) and bearing the memory of the massacre, including Kang Sang-hee (a grandmother of the film's producer Kim Min-kyong) who lost her husband during the incident. By relying on interviews of the survivors, the film certainly inherits Byun Young-joo's still-influential "comfort women" trilogy (see chapter 1). Updating this tradition, *Jeju Prayer* connects the evocative power of oral history to the rituals of shamanism for commemorating the dead and their topoi. Accordingly, the geographic places of the island are reinvented as the site of "necropolitics"[33] in the postliberation Korean Peninsula, alluding to its ideological struggles and ruptures.

Although embracing the survivors' oral testimonies as its material for recuperating their memories and the spirits of the dead that still await mourning, *Jeju Prayer* distinguishes itself from Byun's trilogy. Her three films comprise the subjects' testimonies about memories of their wartime physical and sexual assaults, observational shots of their everyday surroundings and activities, and the camera's intimate registration of their weak, ill, and old bodies that suggestively—without using any archival footage or reenactment—bear witness to the colonial and national violence inflicted on them, and the decades of physical and psychic hardship as its posttraumatic effect. In employing and interweaving these three components, *Jeju Prayer* also dedicates considerable running time to portraying not just ordinary settings and objects of the survivors' houses and their workplace (such as mandarin farms), but also various natural landscapes of the island. The details of these shots include trees in the wind, empty farms occupied by scarecrows and fleeting wind, the stone ground of a former shrine in the forest in the rain, a windy, rocky seashore with flying seagulls, mandarins fallen on the farm grounds, a deserted vacant

180 Post-activism

lot with weeds and flowers, and the details of Hallasan mountain covered with snow. All the places and natural landscapes are seen to create an optical and sound situation in the Deleuzian sense. Without any directorial voice-over that would explain what these places or landscapes mean, the visual images function as autonomous entities that are not spatially contiguous with the survivors' bodies. This autonomy is amplified in the images' sonic dimension, as the soundtrack comprises either natural sound effects that create the sense of silence and absence, or nondiegetic contemporary classic music whose co-existence of lyrical melody and uncanny cacophony suggests the uncanny presence of the spirits of the victims in the present. Even though featuring Kang Sang-hee, Im's camera attends to a series of exorcism rituals intended to mourn and commemorate her dead husband, and to an array of natural and domestic objects in and outside her house along with the sound effects of dogs barking and the wind.

All these emphases on the audiovisual qualities of the images do not present the landscapes, farms, and domestic places in Jeju Island as a setting against which the survivors' testimonies or actions take place. Nor are they incorporated into the larger historical narrative mobilized for a cause-and-effect account of the incident. Rather, Im's creation of the pure optical and sound situation conjures the time-images that invite viewers to contemplate the landscapes and places and thereby to encounter twofold intersections of the past and the present. On one hand, Im's poetic and scenic treatment of the island in relation to its repressed or forgotten history curiously depends on, as critic Yoo Un-seong rightly observes, "de-historicizing landscape inasmuch as Im chooses to vividly reveal the cold beauty of its nature as such, indifferent to any human matter."[34] On the other hand, this aestheticized portrayal of the landscape does more than highlight the contrast between the absence of the visible trace of the massacre and the persistence of its victims' spirits and of its survivors' memories, both of which are supplemented by the oral testimonies that exist autonomously from the film's visual layers. Im consistently introduces deliberate dissonances between the survivors' voices and what the camera shows. For instance, the spoken memory of survivor Han Shin-hwa narrates how she escaped from the massacre with tremendous ordeals, including an injury that has restricted her ability to use her hand. The camera, then, does not show her speaking body and instead presents static shots of the mandarin farm. Shin-hwa's voice is here detached from her body and supplements the landscape of the farm from off-screen space, while the visual images of the landscape allude to both the absence of the visible trace of her confession and the persistence of her life as a mandarin farmer who has to tarry with her trauma. This sequence initially demonstrates what Frances

Guerin and Roger Hallas see as the temporal and spatial dislocation of voice and image in the documentary that retrieves the traumatic memory of victims or survivors: "Words, particularly those of oral testimony, are still connected to the body of the sufferer while the material image implies a separation (spatial, temporal, or both) from that which it captures."[35] But more significantly, the disjunction of the image and the voice in this sequence, in Deleuze's words, forms "two dissymmetric, non-totalizable sides . . . that of an outside more distant than any exterior, and that of an inside deeper than any interior."[36] In this sense, the verbal testimony recuperates in ways that break the scenic beauty and silence of the places and landscapes framed by Im's poetic cinematography. It is in this gap between the visual and the audible that the past speaks. The way that the natural and everyday memoryscapes speak the past, then, resonates with a stack of stones devoid of the names of victims in the April Third Peace Park, with their enduring materiality provoking visitors "to imagine the ongoing constitution of memories that continues to take place between the present and the past."[37]

Jeju Prayer also employs strategies other than the pure optical-sound situation and the sound-image disjunction to emphasize the contrast between the beauty of the present island and the invisible presence of its past history, or between the persistence of the past and the absence of its visible trace in the present. A notable one is to include episodic scenes that trigger viewers to associate the political and cultural landscapes of the island in the present with the trauma of the past incident in multiple ways. From a cultural perspective, the images of the beautiful landscapes elicit not simply the silence of nature that does not explicitly speak of the incident, but also the ways in which the images can be viewed from tourists' perspective. The gap between the trauma of the past and the state-sponsored promotion of the island as a global tourist destination is evident in the vignette introducing Cheonjiyeon Falls (Chŏnjiyŏn p'okp'o) as one of the most famous tourist spots in the island: a couple of shots show student tourists enjoying its landscape in contrast to the intertitle informing about "the place where many citizens were killed." From a political perspective, it turns out that ideological and geopolitical conflicts still affect the present of the island as they did in the past. The film's Gangjeong Beach sequence testifies to this point. Here the viewer is able to observe the scenic landscapes of the beach, which are followed by its resident's off-screen testimony commenting on how many people were killed there, and a series of handheld verité-style shots immediately engaging and documenting the protest of the residents who had been fighting against the Jeju Naval Base at the beach. Im's inclusion of the sequence demonstrates how his aesthetic exploration of the places of the island inherits Korean documentary

182 Post-activism

cinema's activist aspiration to intervene in social movements and thereby to create collective awareness of their corresponding social problems. For the struggle of Gangjeong village against the construction of the naval base was supported by the alliances of both local environmental activists and an array of independent documentary directors, who produced *Gureombi: The Wind Is Blowing* and such omnibus documentaries as *Jam Docu Gangjeong* and *Gangjeong Interview Project* (see chapter 3).

Tour of Duty portrays the current lives and past memories of three former military sex workers, Park Myoyeon, Park Insun, and An Sungja, who experienced physical and psychic suffering at the hands of US GIs with whom they had a relationship, and from the Korean government that controlled their bodies and town. Based in the cities known as *kijich'on*, the film's codirectors in the first decade of the century had produced each of their verité-style documentary films based on their longtime commitment to the old women in collaboration with the nongovernmental organizations that helped with their rehabilitation. Park Kyoung-tae's first encounter with Park Insun was extended into his first feature-length documentary, *Me and the Owl* (*Nawa puŏngi*, 2003, 84 min.), and Kim Dong-ryung later produced *American Alley* (*Amerik'an aelli*, 2008, 90 min.), a socially conscious documentary film that portrays women from Russia and Philippines working as entertainers in the GI clubs of the camptowns. Despite their participatory engagement with the camptowns and their disenfranchised female subjects, the codirectors challenge and expand the boundaries of traditional Korean independent documentary. As film critic Clarence Tsui, who saw the film at the Yamagata Documentary Film Festival in 2013, observed, "Moving away from the cinema verité-style which marked their previous individual outings about [the] towns . . . [Kim and Park] have opted for a poetic touch which could bring their subjects' scarred psyches to the fore in a visceral way that trumps the straightforward newsreel-and-interview approach."[38]

What Tsui calls the "poetic touch" indeed refers to the film's various formal and aesthetic devices that Kim and Park rigorously employ. While the story of Park Myoyeon is narrated in the form of the directors' interview with her, those of Park Insun and An involve their off-screen internal monologues, whose modes of enunciation shuffle between letters, dreams, and fantasies. Besides these different voices that do not rely solely on the camera's factual evidence of the three women's bodies and testimonies, An's memory is performatively staged as she roams around and inside the ruin of "Monkey House," a state-run detainment center that segregated, treated, and rehabilitated sex workers with venereal diseases. These different modes and voices tangentially employed across this film function to preserve the three former sex workers' fragile bodies, to redeem their voices, and to treat and investigate the places or landscapes of the camptowns as ruins that they still live in and wander across. The camptowns had their economic and subcultural heyday during the Cold War, but they now remain decayed and deserted, subject to the local governments' urban redevelopment. In this context, these socially constructed spaces in which the three protagonists still persist can be seen as the ruin whose dilapidated and deserted appearance in the present bears the underside of its utopian or repressed past, as they are existentially linked to the women's memories of the sexual, racial, and ideological oppression or exploitation imposed on them, and to their unaccomplished dream of emigrating to the United States for a better life. As Jeehey Kim perceptively notes regarding the film, "The process of ruin creates a spatial and temporal palimpsest in postcolonial Korean society where the gendered system of the nation-state continued to exploit female bodies. *kijich'on* serves as a palimpsest of colonial traces and memories overwritten by the US imperial desire for military expansion into East Asia under the guise of the Cold War."[39]

It is through the film's creation of the Deleuzian optical and sound situations that it reconfigures the three women's surrounding places and landscapes (that is, the ruins) as the "spatial and temporal palimpsest" associated with their present lives, and with their memories that are buried and wait to be unearthed. These situations correspond to the varying strategies of isolating and highlighting the visual and auditory qualities of the places and landscapes in the camptowns in relation to the corporeal and psychic subjectivity of the former sex workers. Park Myoyeon's memory of her pains and ordeals is staged in the small, old snack bar she has managed for her living. As the directors interview her, their camera attends both to her voice and body and to the details of her surroundings in the snack bar, such as its kitchen sink, empty walls and tables, and seasoning cases. The directors' editing of these static shots is so fragmentary that viewers have the opportunity to contemplate the snack bar as the old yet significant space connected to Myoyeon's past and present. The camera's static framing amplifies the autonomy of these objects and their decayed appearances as its accompanied sound effect creates an atmosphere of stillness. This atmosphere is deliberately broken as she tells how she had aborted twenty-six babies and eventually had a hysterectomy at age twenty-nine, after confessing, "It's so painful for me to recall the past now. . . . I had to endure and keep everything inside." Here the camera shows her face yet often goes back to the everyday objects while the voice of her painful memory is heard off-screen. Through this dissonance between the visible and the audible, those contemplative shots of the snack bar reveal that it is both the personal and the social space in which her repressed memory

184 Post-activism

of sexual exploitation imposed by the (post)colonial and national control of the disenfranchised women has been accumulated and condensed. The connection between the snack bar as ruin, her painful memory of abortions, and her sense of guilt for aborting the babies is extended into the film's portrayal of Myoyeon's body as corporeal ruin, when the camera indifferently sees her injecting herself as an everyday act.

The triangle of Myoyeon, her surrounding place as ruin, and her body as ruin can be found in Park Insun from different angles, who makes her living by rummaging garbage cans while roaming around different natural and artificial surroundings of *kijich'on*. Here Insun's collecting of cans, and her hobby of painting grotesque images (such as a spider with a woman's head) that relate to the painful memory of her American husband and her two daughters who left her, on the pages of outdated calendars or the garbage cans, invoke Walter Benjamin's allusion to ruin, as well as his characterization of the ragpicker as the allegorical figure who seeks the fragments of the past in the remainder of the present.[40] But the film achieves a more profound construction of Insun's surroundings as ruin as the camera does more than follow her wandering and painting: that is, even after Insun has left the frame, the camera sometimes lingers on her house populated with salvaged trivialities, and on the camptown's derelict buildings, shanties, empty dance halls, vacant alleys, all of which contrast with the images of government banners promising the redevelopment of the town. This optical situation that makes the images of space autonomous and empty and thus open to viewers' contemplation culminates in Insun's final scene, in which she wanders along the iron fence demarcating the now-deserted former base of the US Army and performs shamanistic acts of cursing her traumatic memory of failed marriage and wishing for her health, such as feeding birds and throwing candies made in the United States. Even after Insun has left the frame, the camera still captures the natural landscape of the forest in a few static shots. These visual images, which last too long even as the film stops depicting Insun's acts, configure the forest itself as an any-space-whatever through which viewers can recognize its actual present as haunted by the remainder of Insun's trauma. This indiscernibility of Insun's memory and her present is then highlighted through the sounds of birds and crickets followed by a cry of an unknown woman (who can be seen as Insun) and a nondiegetic shamanistic sound of percussions. Consequently, the film's strategies of creating the pure optical and sound situations and rendering the places and landscapes of *kijich'on* as disconnected, autonomous anyspace-whatevers construct the ruin as time-images in the actual present that are always imbued with their virtual past.

Along with the film's poetically observational camera, its disjunctive montage of the visual and the auditory forms the time-images of *kijich'on* and its surrounding landscapes. The film opens with a static long take of a forest around the ruin of the former US military base, coupled with the deliberately tuned sound of wind and water. This static-frame observation continues in a couple of ensuing shots, whose focus narrows down to the details of the base's ruin, including stone columns as the remnants of the buildings that populated the base, and overgrown bushes and weeds that suggest how long the base has been abandoned (figure 5.2). Here the soundtrack of barking dogs and chirping crickets, based on the synchronous recording of the sound from the base's artificial and natural ruins, is gradually overlapped with another stream of sound that begins to be heard from a distance, a series of verbal commands by US soldiers who must have been trained on the base, including the soldiers' repetitions of commands while running. The volume of the latter soundtrack grows louder as the directors capture several tombstones (it is unknown whom they belong to, purportedly deceased military sex workers) deserted in the forest and focus on an unknown yellow building in a fixed camera position, until it fades out in the last couple of shots where viewers encounter the building's dimly lit interior. By intermixing the natural auditory elements of the ruins of the base and its surrounding forest with the imaginary sound of the US soldiers, in combination with the accumulative editing of their autonomous visual details, the directors create an optical and sound situation

Figure 5.2 *Tour of Duty* (Kim Dong-ryung and Park Kyoung-tae, 2013)
Image courtesy: Kim Dong-ryung and Park Kyoung-tae.

that does not establish the film's geographical space and time. Emphasized by this montage that marks the shots of the static frame as fragmentary time-images, this audiovisual quality of the shots in the opening sequence dissociates the landscapes of the forest and the ruin from a chronological ordering, instead reconfiguring the landscapes as the liminal zone between sex workers' memory and the postwar history of the US-Korea military alliance, and between the factual evidence of the past and the nonfactual imagination or retrieval of it. The discordance of the visual and the auditory, which allows dissolving the boundaries between the memories of the women and their present and thereby constructing the places and landscapes of *kijich'on* as legible spaces covered with their past, is manifested again in the bridge between the story of Myoyeon and that of Insun, in which the tranquil scenery of snow-covered nighttime alleys is overlaid with a director's off-screen commentary that creates a fissure between body and voice: "As people die with deep pains . . . they become little memory particles, roaming around the place they used to live. They cause depression in the living. People call them ghosts, phantoms, or goblins." Here the disembodied voice-over dissociated from the synchronous soundscape of the visual informs viewers that the three women are specters that embody their repressed memory and trauma, while also prompting viewers to read the ruins of *kijich'on* as haunted spaces in which their multiple voices are entangled.

Oh Minwook's Local Experimental Documentary

Lucas Hilderbrand argues that even though the concept of experimental documentary is ambiguous and open, works that pertain to it share an "interest in form and mediation" and an "engagement with the realities of history, politics and culture." Through these two attributes, experimental documentaries employ innovative media-specific elements even when dealing with history, politics, and culture. Accordingly, they rely on "visuality (cinematography that does not strive toward commercial production values, layered images, non-plot driven digital effects) and temporality (fragmented narrative structures, contrapuntal sounds, pensive silences)."[41] Through these two elements, experimental documentary filmmakers seek alternatives to the documentary's objectivist assumptions by examining both "their own subjectivities" and "variability of truth,"[42] while also extending their exploration of form and media into their interest in history, politics, and culture.

As I shall discuss in detail in chapter 7, young documentarians in the twenty-first century have rigorously deployed digital cinematography and postproduction techniques to explore the form and medium of cinema and the filmmaker's consciousness and subjectivity, and to engage and convey realities beyond the objectivist assumption of documentary evidence and truth. Among the filmmakers, Jung Jae-hoon is particularly noticeable due to his digital experimental documentaries that take as their subject an old town under *chaegaebal* and a factory. In his debut feature-length film *Hosugil* (*Hosugil*, 2009, 72 min.), about the details of a small town in Eungam 2-dong, Seoul, Jung employs a low-fi digital camera equipped with a zoom lens to capture not merely the neighbors, animals, and objects in the landscape but also their affects, including boredom and anxiety, coupled with vivid sound effects stimulating viewers' sensory response to impending demolition (*ch'ŏlgŏ*). This is extended into the second half of Jung's next film *Turbulence at Dodol Hill* (*Todori ŏndŏge nan'giryu*, 2017, 212 min.), which comprises extremely degraded shots that he took while working at a shipyard in Ulsan for three months with his phone camera. As this sequence passes from the exterior structures of the shipyard to its interior workplace, the images lose many details of their referents, including a molding machine and a welder in flames, to the extent they look nearly to melt down. These senses of visual obscurity and chaos are strengthened by the growling noise of machines. Here it becomes obvious that the visual degradation of the images stemmed not merely from the phone camera's lack of technical fidelity but also from the intense sensory stimuli imposed by the machines and tools in the shipyard. This sensory overload and chaos must have been attributed to Jung's embodied investigation of the inhuman power of his workplaces. In this sense, his low-fi cellphone filmmaking mediates the aesthetic dimension of the nonhuman, industrial world while also conveying Jung's subjective sensory experience of labor.

Oh Minwook has explored the layers of time implicated in places and landscapes in Busan with his foray into experimental documentary. His debut feature-length documentary, *Ash: Re* (*Chae*, 2013, 65 min.), exemplifies the ways in which the grammar of structural film characterized by the repetition and variation of specific formal and representational elements in the tradition of experimental cinema is extended into an investigation into places in Busan. They include Busan Citizens Park, which was returned to the city after the Japanese colonial period and the post–Korean War presence of USFK (US Forces in Korea), a redevelopment site, and its surrounding ruins, such as an empty building and the remains of a collapsed apartment. Oh configures all these spaces as objects of audiovisual experience, modulating the differences in the sound effects and the framing and duration of their corresponding images. His way of dealing with the space as an autonomous aesthetic object

188   Post-activism

separated from its spatial contiguity and chronological ordering taps into what Deleuze refers to as the transition from the "movement-image" to the "time-image."

A Roar of the Prairie (*Pŏmjŏn*, 2015, 75 min.) is a documentary that captures the slow disappearance of Bumjeon-dong in Busan (now integrated into Bujeon-dong) for two years, from 2013 to 2015. The film starts with intertitles that explain the official history of Bumjeon-dong, which was a racetrack during the Japanese colonial period and a USFK base known as "Camp Hialeah" after the Korean War, along with a camptown that was busy enough to be called a "red light alley." As in *Ash: Re*, however, Oh's interest is far from that of making an audiovisual discourse that would support this official history. The spaces of ruins and the abandoned objects that pertain to a series of images in *Ash: Re* become all the more dominant in *A Roar of the Prairie*. Oh's static camera documents and accumulates corners of empty narrow alleys, houses with faded walls, wet wood chips, rubbish left on the streets, debris of reinforced concrete left on a site of demolition, doors and rooms viewed between or through collapsed walls, and the interiors of a devastated building once used as a gymnasium. The sound effects synchronized with those images bifurcate into two channels. First, there is a sound recorded in the fields of filming at a time when the town underwent destruction and disappearance. And second, there is a stream of disjunctive sound effects whose visual sources remain unidentified, such as ambient sounds of rain, firewood, wind, ticktacks, and mechanical noise. This dense soundtrack that evokes off-screen space dissociates the viewer's perception from the chronological present and guides her toward the past layers of the town that remain invisible but nonetheless persist in the present. There is one impressive sequence in which this audiovisual power is amplified. After roaming around the empty and decayed alleys of the town on a rainy day, Oh's camera frames a tree with a silhouette of branches. Subsequently, a siren that sounds like a warning of airstrike or curfew is inserted along with the sound effects of the whistle and horn, and the silhouette that looks like a branch turns out to be the barbed wire through Oh's use of double exposure over time. An ensuing shot is a close-up of a waving Korean flag, which is in sync with the voice of a resident who says that South Korea was freed from its crisis thanks to the US military. It is in the next long shot that what is seen in the previous two shots is revealed. The barbed wire is an area on the left side of the alley (the ruins of the US military unit), and the Korean flag on its right side was hung by the resident, who is still living in the village despite its redevelopment. In this way, the past of Beomjeon-dong coexists with its present. The voice of the resident, which continues through the still-heard siren, rehearses the history of the village, occupied by the Japanese and by North Korean partisans during the Korean War.

Compared to *Ash: Re*, a notable way that Oh deepens his approach to experimental documentary in *A Roar of the Prairie* is to record and preserve the bodies and voices of the inhabitants who remained in Beomjeon-dong. His experimental approach to these social actors and their testimonies differs from that of conventional ethnographic films. The residents as interviewees do not fill the whole screen space. They only live their daily life embodying the past of Beomjeon-dong, as revealed by the appearance of senior women running a shabby supermarket or small laundry. Sometimes their postures are fixed, with their gaze staring at the camera like a model in a long-exposure photo, as evidenced by Oh's interview with an old woman running a junk shop. Her figure overlaps with the shots following the back of an unidentified old man with crutches who cruises around the alleys every night. The fixed and moving subjects alike are surrounded by the decaying alleys, buildings, and objects. If the image of the old woman signals the presence of death that is evoked by the stillness of photographic imagery, the handheld shots capturing the old man with crutches are the images of a ghost who dissolves the boundary between life and death while witnessing the decay of the town. The dissolution of the boundary between life and death, and between the past and the present, is extended into that between reality and fiction, and between human and nonhuman. In the midst of the testimony of the supermarket owner, what is inserted is an image taken with a camera from a subjective perspective. Oh's camera takes the supermarket owner's point of view this way, through which her testimony is disentangled from her talking head and linked to the imaginary of her past that is invisible in the present. In the sense, this technique demonstrates Oh's attempt at a kind of "psychogeographical landscaping" in the sense that the landscape of the town is "subjectively read beyond the objective record," as he renders the landscape to be "living space or historical place."[43] The camera embodying the subjective point of view is also connected to the shot of abrupt camera movement that shows a stray cat. The movement, then, appears to embody the viewpoint of the cat as an inhuman actor that has lived and witnessed the time of disappearance.

Oh's experimental strategy of disconnecting the habitual links between sound and image, and between testimony and body, evolves into a rich audiovisual experience of the ruins and objects that remain in Beomjeon-dong, and of the past that permeates its residents. The experience is ultimately linked to the opening ceremony of Busan Citizens Park and the construction of a highrise apartment that was underway in Beomjeon-dong. By preserving the past as the ruin that cracks the progressive temporality of Busan's economic and

190 Post-activism

cultural development, and by reconstructing the experience of the past in an uncanny and rich manner, *A Roar of the Prairie* resonates with Oh's following account of its production process: "When the past that we tried to erase turned into a past that we want to commemorate, and when Beomjeon-dong arrives at a distant future that will become another present after time goes far away, the past that its future residents want to hide and erase could be the green meadows (the Park) and skyscraper (the high-rise building)."[44]

Pains and Ruins

In the context of the activist tradition that has engaged state and ideological violence as well as its victims, what are the larger implications of the "audiovisual turn," through which documentary time-images render sites and spaces as memoryscapes? First, the films built on the turn depart from the activist tradition's chronological and cause-and-effect storytelling that leads to either the collective resistance of the survivors or bereaved families as dissident subjects or the revelation of previously uncovered truth. And second, the films' time-images are not assimilated into what the activist impulse to advocate social movements (including memory activism) privileges, such as the discourses on fact-finding, restoring of honor, human rights, and juridical justice. The films' rendition of the memoryscapes as the nonchronological, complex juncture of past and present, as well as their attention to natural environments, domestic spaces, and workplaces, offers an alternative to the authorized museums and monuments in regard to the politics of traumatic memories and mourning, given that the latter "strive for coherency, linearity, and durability" and that they are "either distanced or isolated from everyday space."[45]

Jeju Prayer and *Tour of Duty* are based on the directors' intimate engagement with either the survivors of the April Third Incident or the former military sex workers of *kijich'on*. In this sense, their common amplification of the sensory qualities of the places and landscapes is seen to update the political and ethical aspirations of Korean independent documentary. With such technical devices as long takes, expressive or static camera framing, and sound-image disjunctions, the places and landscapes in both films are perceived as the nonhuman agent that has long witnessed and preserved the collective memory of the victims and survivors and their individual traumas, however illegible or invisible their trace might be. For the directors, the vivid audiovisual qualities of these places and landscapes are the means to inscribe the sensory and affective dimensions of their painful memories that could otherwise remain unspeakable or unrepresentable. Regarding the paradoxically beautiful images of *Tour of Duty* that are coupled with the uncanny sound effects, Park Kyoung-tae has remarked that they "allow spectators to embody the trauma of the people of *kijich'on* [rather] than to learn its history."[46] Similarly, Im has once said that his consistent poetic approach to the empty landscapes or houses in his films is grounded in his awareness that "our society lacks a space for expressing and addressing psychological wounds."[47]

In the recent Korean documentaries that testify to the audiovisual turn, the invention of time-images with Deleuzian formal and aesthetic devices for isolating and amplifying their audiovisual components demonstrates that the films' directors have actively responded to the increased production of both dilapidated spaces and monumental sites in the twenty-first century, to the point of transforming the natural and built environments into cinematic memoryscapes. The directors' documentary responses have consequently led to reconfiguring these places and landscapes as ruin in Walter Benjamin's sense, or as allegory from which a keen observer of the present could read modernity's buried past and its unfulfilled future.[48] For this reason, the ruin's state of decay makes visible not merely the imagined present of a past, but also the present's inevitable destruction in the face of time's devastating irreversibility. By expressing the temporal ambivalence of the ruin, its time-images, then, attest to Korean documentary's renewal of participation in reality and history. This renewal, stimulated by the growing significance of public memory during the last two decades, indeed is also the case with another documentary component: namely, archival photos and footage whose investigation and reuse guarantee another Benjaminian undertaking of post-activist practices.

6
The Archival Turn

Memory Wars and Materialist Historiography

Kim-gun: The Archive and the Memory War (*kiŏk chŏnjaeng*)

In *Kim-gun* (*Kimgun*, 2018, 85 min.), a documentary that searches for the identity and trace of a then anonymous member of the citizen militia ("Kim" is one of the most popular Korean last names, and "Gun" is a Korean title equivalent to "Mr." that is used for young men) during the Gwangju Uprising, a series of photographs preserved and made public by the May 18 Democratization Movement Archive are raised as the materials for supplementing the accounts and recollections of the people who engaged the traumatic political event. They also become the film's objects of investigation, as well as the arena for the memory war surrounding the acute ideological conflicts that have centered around how to historicize the event and evaluate its meanings. In 2015, far-right politics columnist Ji Man-won proclaimed that North Korea had secretly sent six hundred troops to Gwangju to instigate the "riot" (*p'oktong*) against the New Military's martial law. In so doing, he showed the faces of 128 citizens who were captured in the photos and have survived the government troops' violence, as the evidence of NK "special forces" who were active in Gwangju. To supplement this fabricated conspiracy theory deep-rooted in the anticommunist, extreme-right ideology, Ji further said that he had used an image analysis system based on a facial recognition software application that could allegedly match the physiognomic traits of the faces in the photos taken in Gwangju with those of the surviving citizens. In response to this political scandal that has recently been refueled in the public sphere,[1] director Kang Sang-woo developed his first feature-length film by closely examining the photos that Ji had used for his theory, focusing on some that register the young citizen known at that time as "Kim-gun," the very person that Ji had stigmatized as the "No. 1 NK special force" (the "No. 1" means that Kim-gun is now a top-tier figure of the North Korean government) based on the image analysis system.

Activism and Post-activism. Jihoon Kim, Oxford University Press. © Oxford University Press 2024.
DOI: 10.1093/oso/9780197760413.003.0007

Kang's approach to the photos is twofold. First, a stand-in for the director shows surviving militia members the photos of Kim-gun, using a laptop and a cell phone that magnify his face. The interviews with the survivors do more than establish the photos as evidence of Kim-gun's presence in the uprising: the photos trigger the members' own memories about who they think he was, what each of them did during the protest, and what traumatic experiences he underwent. The film's investigative form of narrative, reminiscent of Errol Morris's *The Thin Red Line* (1988), which Linda Williams has underlined as exemplary of the postmodern documentary that signifies the partial or multiple versions of truth,[2] does not lead to an objective evidence of who Kim-gun really was (although a few citizen-survivors say that he had been a ragpicker before the uprising). It becomes evident, however, that Kang is as much interested in collecting those different voices and memories of the survivors as pursuing Kim-gun's identity and destiny. Second, Kang deals with the photos as archival documents whose meanings and memories are not fixed and stable but rather subject to the ongoing processes of political decontextualization and recontextualization. By juxtaposing the photos of the traumatic past with interviews in the present, Kang consolidates them into a collective archive of polyphonic yet interconnected voices of the surviving citizens, a counterarchive against Ji's fake digital forensic database. This is evident in the contrast between two images: the first image, a photograph showing a mass of citizens gathered at the center plaza of Gwangju on a day of the uprising, is marked with an array of red dots that Ji highlighted as the existence of "NK Special Forces." This contrasts with Kang's digital manipulation of the photographic fragments taken by journalist photographer Lee Chang-seong between May 22 and 23, through which the fragments are rearranged into a new scrolling sequence that lays claim to the voluntary engagement of nameless citizens in the protests against the military dictatorship (figure 6.1). This technique sheds new light on the individual photo that might otherwise remain fragmented, therefore grafting all of them onto a new meaningful association that reflects Kang's own view on who ultimately led the protest: "[The film offers] a new perspective on [the movement] by focusing in close-up on the countless 'Kim-guns' who were there on the ground during the carnage."[3] Again, this resonates with the film's conceptual approach to the archive of the past: both the archive itself and the meaning of its documents, if questioned and dispersed, should be something to be reconfigured and recreated from the perspective of the present.

The mystery of who Kim-gun was that the film did not solve was eventually resolved in the real world in May 2022 as a Gwangju-based citizen named Cha Bok-hwan called the May 18 Foundation and confirmed that, having

Figure 6.1 *Kim-gun* (Kang Sang-woo, 2018)

watched the film, he was Kim-gun. More significant than this social impact is that Kang's use of the photos of the uprising can indeed be contextualized within a notable tendency of recent Korean documentary filmmaking since the early 2010s, one that is characterized by the growing use of found footage as existing moving images gleaned from various media resources. Broadly, the term "found footage" has been associated not simply with a variety of historical materials available for the director's interrogation of the past but also with a particular mode of filmmaking in documentary and experimental cinema, one that is distinct from the camera's direct registration of the event or subject that existed in front of it. In the history of documentary filmmaking the compilation film appeared first in the latter part of World War I,[4] and the films of Dziga Vertov and Esfir Shub, as well as those of the 1920s and 1930s European avant-garde school, developed disjunctive editing to highlight the metaphoric qualities of newsreels and other existing materials or create a dialectical tension between them.[5] The penchant for collage in these historical traditions later led to the emergence of the compilation film as a notable subgenre of the North American avant-garde cinema in the 1950s and 1960s. The films of Bruce Conner and Arthur Lipsett juxtapose disparate audiovisual materials to endow them with new historical meanings in ways that render history fragmentary and multifaceted rather than linear, chronological, and unified.[6] While such filmmakers as Emile de Antonio, Péter Forgács, Craig Baldwin, Thom Andersen, and Adam Curtis, to name just a few, have practiced compilation filmmaking from the late 1960s to the present by excavating fragments of archival footage and turning them into new associations for reconstructing histories in dialogue with the urgency of the present, the modes of filmmaking that extensively use found footage have largely remained marginal in documentary cinema. As Bill Nichols notes, "Found footage, already understood as a rapidly accumulating resource, simply did not have the immediacy of freshly recorded material, be it staged, reenacted, or caught on the fly."[7]

Nichols's account of the marginalized status of found footage has a peculiar underpinning in the larger context of the activist tradition since the 1980s. The emphasis upon the camera's bond to *hyŏnjang* has been established as a leading tenet of the Korean activist film and video and independent documentary in the 1980s and 1990s that aimed to legitimatize itself as an alternative medium for intervention in social movements. As discussed in Part I, the participatory mode of documentary practice, characterized by the interaction between filmmaker and subject as a token of the documentary's authenticity and its commitment to social change and politics, has remained a major aesthetic paradigm of Korean activist documentaries in the twenty-first century. In this context, deploying archival images extensively in Korean documentary cinema had not until the early 2010s been visible as a notable aesthetic tendency to conceive the whole fabric of an individual work, much less as a subgenre. That is, in most Korean independent documentary films before that period, archival images were mainly used to supplement verbal statements or arguments delivered by the director's voice-over or through interviews with social actors. First, the history documentaries of Kim Tae-il, Cho Sung-bong, and Kim Jin-yeul (see chapters 1 and 2) employ archival footage of *Daehannews* (Taehan nyusŭ, the weekly film newsreel produced from 1945 to 1994 by the NFPA) and TV documentaries or reports in favor of illustrating the testimonies of the victims of state and ideological violence. Or the footage was used as an audiovisual support for the counterdiscourse of historians, activists, and the narrator that explained what had been excluded or distorted by the official history of the violence. Even when the domestic ethnographies in the twenty-first century (see chapter 4) featured home movies and photos to trace back the private history of the filmmaker and to explore his or her relationship to societal change, they frequently merely supplement the filmmaker's personal account or reflection rather than investigate archival materials as specific evidentiary objects and transform them in order to reinterpret their original codes and messages. While all these documentaries' aspirations to revisit and rewrite history from personal or counterpublic perspectives undoubtedly led to documentarians' growing awareness of the significance of the archival documents as an integral material for their research on a past event and their encounter with its subjects, it

196   Post-activism

has been a relatively new tendency in the 2010s that the documents are more extensively appropriated and reworked to the point that they are situated as a major fabric of a documentary film. Seen from this brief recapitulation of how archival materials were used, this tendency raises the question whether or not—or, to what extent—it diverged from the formal, aesthetic, and political assumptions of the activist tradition since the 1980s.

In answering this question, this chapter examines the ways in which several Korean documentary films in the 2010s use various archival footage concerned with the distant or recent histories of Korea. In so doing, I characterize the films' increasing attention to the existing image as the "archival turn" in two senses. First, the term suggests that the extensive uses of found footage allow filmmakers to develop modes of documentary filmmaking—such as compilation documentary and essay film, which are driven by formal experimentations with documentary image and montage—other than the participatory mode distinguished by the supremacy of the camera's immediate, on-the-spot witness of reality and the director's immediate contact with social reality or its actors. Second, and more significantly, the term also indicates that the films' appropriation, investigation, and rearrangement of found footage is grounded in the two interrelated ideas of the archive—the concept of the archive as the official institutions concerned with collecting, preserving, and organizing the documents or objects of the past, and the documents or objects themselves; and that of the archive in which the meanings of its documents or objects are open to reinterpretation and reinvention in dialogue with the present or other documents and objects of the past. The latter concept of the archive suggests that photographs and film or video footage as indexical documents are more than objective evidence of the past: that is, they demonstrate their inherent excess, ambiguity, and disruption, all of which resist the imperative to the ordered and clear-cut signification of the past as the underlying principle of the former concept of the archive.

The filmmakers who appropriate, reassess, and even manipulate found footage are accordingly motivated by the desire to unveil and deconstruct its intended meanings and aesthetic effects, as well as by the idea of endowing it with a new historical perspective in relation to their engagement with the politics of the present. These two motivations are linked to the two larger contexts of the post-activist documentaries in the 2010s, which in turn attest to the filmmakers' negotiation between the personal and the public: on the one hand, the filmmakers' uses of archival materials for documentary modes other than that of the activist tradition have been undoubtedly grounded in their self-consciousness as *kamdok*; on the other hand, the filmmakers' attempts to reread the materials have been justified by their impulse to engage a series of contemporaneous social events that have triggered collective memories of a past, including "memory wars" that have been occurring throughout the twenty-first century. As I demonstrate in the following, these two motivations of the "archival turn" in recent Korean documentary can be assessed in dialogue with Walter Benjamin's idea of historiography and its closed correspondence with found footage filmmaking.

Found Footage, the Archival Turn, and Benjaminian Historiography

What I call the "archival turn" in recent Korean documentaries means that they consider the form and meaning of found footage to be structured by the archive as the discursive, technical, and institutional apparatus that determines the storage and signification of past documents and other materials. A brief outlining of the influential concepts of the archive suggests that the directors' engagement with found footage is quintessentially political. For Michel Foucault, the archive has to do with the ways in which political powers of knowledge are operated in the forms of the discursive-technical-institutional complex, inasmuch as it refers not simply to heterogeneous records and materials of the past per se but also to the system of governing how to access and remember them and how to make them sayable and visible. That is, what Foucault conceives as the archive is a "system of enunciability" in which documents or historical materials are "grouped together in distinct figures, composed in accordance with multiple relations, and maintained or blurred in accordance with specific regularities."[8] Foucault's idea is echoed by Jacques Derrida, who writes, "There is no political power without control of the archive. Effective democratisation can always be measured by . . . the participation in and access to the archive, its constitution, and its interpretation."[9] Seen from Foucault's and Derrida's insights, not only the institutions for producing and storing documents in different forms and media (such as museums, libraries, and broadcast services) but also the documents themselves are the crucial site of politics, in the sense that the latter is marked by a set of particular codifications and conventions that determine the meaning of past events and subjects that they convey.

Engaging the archive and its materials as the site of politics, the "archival turn" in recent Korean independent documentaries also echoes what art critic Hal Foster calls the "archival impulse." Foster coins this term as a catchword for indicating the characteristics of archival art in contemporary art scenes that questions the traditional concept of the archive (encapsulated by Foucault's and Derrida's accounts) and instead considers the archive itself as the object of reinvention by recreating the documents' meanings and even the past itself. For Foster, the "archival impulse" is marked by the practice's employment of historical information (including found image, text, or object) in ways that foreground its materials as "found yet constructed, factual and fictive, public yet private."[10] In doing so, Foster continues, archival art "assumes anomic fragmentation as a condition not only to represent but to work through [and] proposes new orders of affective association."[11] Although Foster does not explicitly address the uses of found footage in documentary filmmaking as alternatives to assuming it is factual and stable evidence of the past, Stella Bruzzi's observation suggests that appropriating and reassessing the footage with juxtaposition and manipulation are closely aligned with archival art's penchant for "anomic fragmentation" and "new orders of affective associations": "The fundamental issue of documentary film is the way in which we are invited to access the 'document' or 'record' through representation or interpretation, to the extent that a piece of archive material becomes a mutable rather than a fixed point of reference."[12]

Foster's understanding of archival material as "found yet constructed" in the context of archival art, too, is closely aligned with found footage filmmaking and its Benjaminian undertakings. Found footage film echoes the Benjaminian notion of montage because of its affinity for the heterogeneity of borrowed images, which are later reorganized into a new statement or narrative through juxtaposition with other images or materials.[13] Assuming montage as a predominant method of found footage films, too, resonates with Benjamin's concept of the "dialectical image"—a specific form of the encounter between past and present, now and then. This image, for Benjamin, is dialectical not simply in the sense that it belongs to "a particular time" of the past but in the sense that it attains "legibility only at a particular time"[14] of the present. As the theorists of found footage films note, Benjamin's dialectical images take on a double existence: they are "both in a state of stasis, as they are pre-ascribed, and in flux, as they are forever being recontextualized."[15] In this vein, Catherine Russell considers found footage films to produce a "counternarrative of the memory trace" insofar as their appropriated material "belongs to a contingent order of time."[16] Found footage filmmaking's production of the counternarrative corresponds to Benjamin's association of the dialectical image with what he calls "materialist historiography," a broader methodology of historiography as antithetical to the notion of history as the progression of linear time."[17] As Russell further summarizes, the film or video archive could be used as material for activating this Benjaminian historiography marked by the contingent encounter between present and past, insofar as it "has become one of our most valuable resources for a language that can

The Archival Turn   199

speak to the impasse of what [Benjamin] calls historicism, or mystified forms of historiography."[18]

Benjamin's demand for "materialist historiography," as well as his assumption that it appropriates fragments of the past "in a moment of danger,"[19] supports not merely found footage filmmaking in general but also the two concepts of the archive that the "archival turn" in recent Korean documentaries presupposes. Their filmmakers consider either archival images or the institutions concerned with producing and collecting the images as allegories of how the knowledge and memory of past events is visually and discursively constructed. Rather than using archival records to reinforce the linear progression of history, the documentaries also transform the records into dialectical images in which their legibility and meanings are acquired in their encounter with the present issues in which the filmmakers engage. These two concepts correspond to the political, epistemological, and technical contexts of the "archival turn" that are evidenced by *Kim-gun*.

First, *Kim-gun* attests to the battle over commemorating the Gwangju Uprising as a major "memory war." Kang Sang-woo perceives the battle as a present "moment of danger" that demands a Benjaminian consciousness of forging his film as a constellation of past materials. As I discussed in the introduction and chapter 2, memorials and national memory of the political events in the postliberation Korea, including the Korean War, the political incidents in Park Chung-hee's dictatorship, and the mass protests and political sacrifices during the 1980s, have constantly been in flux in tandem with changing presidential administrations as well as in response to the social movements of the parties concerned with the events in the twenty-first century. The contestations suggest that the traumatic or ideological effects of these events are still lingering in the individual and collective unconsciousness of contemporary Korean society, and that the memories of the events have been recalled and refueled when the society has witnessed social and political incidents similar to the prior events. An anecdotal case in point is, as Hyun Ok Park demonstrates, that the bereaved families of the Sewol Ferry Disaster, with their multidimensional activism for investigating its cause and legislating a special law, have enunciated it as "the second Gwangju [Massacre]."[20] In this context, the filmmakers' efforts to transform archival materials relating to the events into dialectical images are read as expressing their awareness of these two implications of the "memory wars" in twenty-first-century Korean society. In *Kim-gun*, Kang's intervention in Ji Man-won's use of the photos for his ongoing political campaign intended to deny the democratic undertaking of the Gwangju Uprising and instead to stigmatize it as a "communist riot" demonstrates that archival documents associated with the near and distant

200 Post-activism

histories of postcolonial or authoritarian violence and suppression have increasingly been used in response to the urgency of the moments in which the ideological and psychic cacophonies of that violence and suppression reverberate in the present's political arenas.

Second, Kang's use of the photos of the Uprising in *Kim-gun* validates a significant epistemological shift both in the status of archival materials used to construct history and memory and in the documentary approach to those materials as a form of historiography that is characterized by the renewed encounter between past and present. Marianne Hirsch's concept of "postmemory," a kind of inherited memory shared by the generation that follows the subjects of a personal or collective trauma through constructed narratives or memory objects,[21] fits into that kind of documentary historiography that Benjamin could consider "materialist." For it indicates not simply a temporal distance between the traumatic past and the present, or between the generation that experienced that past and the one that did not, but also possibilities for other strategies of approaching the past from the perspective of the present, interrogating an official historical meaning of its record and embracing the record's evidentiary obscurity as a point of departure for making different associations and interpretations. Indeed, Kang's background as a director of the generation who did not actually experience the uprising enabled him to feel "unfamiliar with the raw feelings of anger and guilty" and to perceive the 86 generation's making of the event a point of national heritage as "forced."[22] This distance, however, allowed him to use the photos of the uprising as building material for the film's investigative narrative, geared toward not only seeking the identity of the then anonymous "Kim-gun" but also capturing the previously unarticulated memories of the interviewees who participated in the protests. The dialectic of distance and renewed memory-making evident in *Kim-gun* falls within other postmemory-generation filmmakers and artists who deal with the Korean War and other ideological or political conflicts "not merely to recover the historical 'truth' of the Korean War, but also to examine the very historical and cultural conditions in which the remnants of historical materials are consistently explored, understood, and even obliterated."[23]

Finally, Kang's use of digital manipulation and viewing interfaces to magnify and juxtapose the photos of the uprising suggests that video and digital technologies make archival records accessible and reassessible while also offering directors a technical means of creating "dialectical" images marked by a renewed encounter between past and present. This has been demonstrated in the dramatically increased availability of newsreels and documentary footage on the colonial and postcolonial histories of Korea that were produced by the NFPA (now known as KTV), United States Information Service–Korea (USIS), and national broadcasting services (KBS and Munhwa Broadcasting Cooperation, for instance), via YouTube and the digital archives of those corporate or state institutions. Besides the proliferation of these archives and platforms, Kang's use of the photos from the May 18 Democratization Movement Archive is placed within the digitization and archiving of photos, newsreels, documents, and oral testimonies by many governmental agencies and memorial museums in the twenty-first century in response to the growing demands for public memory-making and fact-finding. For the filmmakers who have evidenced the "archival turn" of Korean documentary, this technical and institutional availability of archival materials is extended into nonlinear, contingent, and random ways of digital editing, which echoes Russell's insight into the correspondence between digitization and Benjamin's thought on the archive: "Techniques of copying, downloading, fragmenting, collecting, and recombining have democratized the archival function, in which the arts of appropriation are responding not only to materials borrowed from the past but to the history of [the present] and the future."[24]

These three underlying contexts of the Benjaminian "archival turn" are also the case with three recent documentary modes activated by the extensive uses of archival materials: first, compilation documentary, evidenced by the two feature-length documentaries by Kim Kyung-man, *An Escalator in World Order* (*Miguk'ŭi baramgwa bul*, 2011, 118 min.), *People Passing By* (*Chinaganŭn saramdŭl*, 2014, 86 min.); second, the essay film that includes *Yongsan* (*Yongsan*, Mun Jeong-hyun, 2010, 73 min.); finally, investigative documentary, demonstrated by not only *Kim-gun* but also *Nonfiction Diary* (*Nonp'iksyŏn taiŏri*, Jung Yoon-suk, 2013, 93 min.). My discussion of these three modes focuses on the ways in which found footage as the material of the past leads to the development of the post-activist forms built on the Benjaminian idea of historiography as a way of engaging the "moments of danger" in contemporary Korean society. The moments are then perceived as the repetition of contested or traumatic pasts in new guises. *An Escalator in World Order* is a compilation documentary that investigates the historical origin of pro-US ideology in the early twenty-first century. *Yongsan* is an essay film that highlights the director's subjectivity as the locus of memoires triggered by current issues of urban redevelopment and state violence; and finally, *Nonfiction Diary* is a metahistorical investigative documentary that takes the archival records of traumatic events as the raw material for constructing an alternative, multilayered history of capitalism's negative impacts on Korean society in the early 1990s and onward.

Kim Kyung-man's Compilation Documentaries

Kim Kyung-man is arguably the only Korean practitioner who has self-consciously pursued the method of compilation film, excavating and shedding new light on a vast array of archival images that document the political and cultural pasts of Korea since the twentieth century. The images that comprise *An Escalator in World Order* are mostly gleaned from *Daehannews*, as well as from *Liberty News*, produced by the USIS, from Korea's liberation era to the 1980s. Based on his careful study of US-Korea footage from official government archives, Kim creates new associations that draw viewers' attention to the larger history of Korea's military, political, economic, and cultural reliance on the United States in the twentieth and twenty-first centuries. Concerning his approach to this vast array of images in creating these associations, Kim once remarked as follows: "In the newsreel shots should be treated not as a given historical document but as a material."[25] Here the "historical document" suggests leaving intact the message and signification originally intended by the newsreels, while the "material" means to examine the newsreels from a temporal distance and disclose their underlying codes and ideological underpinnings.

Kim's idea of dealing with the newsreels' archival footage as "material" clearly indicates his subjectivity as collector. Benjamin highlights the collector as a key figure who detaches the outdated object from its use value and places it within a new order from a present perspective. A found footage filmmaker can be regarded as the Benjaminian collector insofar as her strategies of extraction and recombination draw the viewer's attention not simply to her found footage as "[her] object" but also "its entire past":[26] that is, the larger history of its production and reception. While Russell notes that the found image "always points . . . to an original production context,"[27] Jaimie Baron writes that it also implicates "a previous intended context use of reception."[28] In *An Escalator in World Order*, Kim exploits graphic parallels between archival newsreel images that are distant in time and place to unearth their common propagandistic context of production as well as their common intended use of reception. For instance, the scenes of bombing runs in the Korean War are extended into similar images of military training, combat, and weapons after the event: *Liberty News* footage of US intercontinental ballistic missiles, excerpts from *Daehannews* footage that reports on the deployment of US tactical weapons in Korea as well as Korean-US joint military exercises, and the Korean military troops dispatched to the Vietnam War. These images do not merely testify to their propagandistic use in persuading Korean audiences of the past to identify with the US-oriented order of the Cold War, but also reveal

The Archival Turn   **203**

their own visual codes that served to reinforce the proliferation of pro-US ideology. When brought together, the images turn out to share two common kinds of gazes: the camera's gaze toward the weapons (exemplified by full shots that highlight the awe-inspiring appearance of missiles or cannons) and the gaze from the weapons (such as the aerial views from missiles or bombers). The former gaze establishes a fetishistic identification with the weapons that symbolize the imperialistic power of the United States, which is supported by a male narrator's authoritative voice-over that refers to an intercontinental ballistic missile as the "torch of liberty." Similarly, the latter gaze from the weapons, which highlights an accelerated, transcendental view from above, recalls Paul Virilio's influential account of the complicity between the technologies of vision and the machinery of warfare.[29] Kim's graphic matches of the temporally distant newsreels so as to reveal their common context of production and reception are also applied to his collection of images relating to Korea-US summits. By accumulating and matching the gestures and activities of Korean presidents who visited the United States for the summit (Rhee Syngman, Park Chung-hee, Chun Doo-hwan, and Kim Dae-jung), such as shaking hands with US presidents, making a speech at the press conference, and attending welcoming receptions or cultural performances, Kim stresses that these images were recursively used to reinforce Korea's pro-US ideology when they were incorporated into official newsreels. In this way, the images also lay claim to an ideological scheme shared by different Korean presidents; that is, they have repeatedly asked for the support of the US government for Korea's entry ticket to the world order, from the Cold War period to the neoliberal age, regardless of whether the governments were military dictatorship or liberal democracy. The visual and ideological similarities between the images associated with the Korea-US summits, then, deliver to the present viewer revelations about the nature of the images, as they form a new constellation of modern Korea's different pasts that breaks apart the official narrative about the linear progress of its history.

Inspired by canonical found footage films or poetic compilation documentaries, *An Escalator in World Order* employs ironic disjunction between the voice of the propaganda film and what its image shows to draw viewers' attention to the logic of signification embedded in the newsreels produced by the NFPA as the apparatus of the official archive. For instance, Kim deconstructs *Daehannews'* coverage of the Miss Universe Festival held in Seoul in 1980 as an event celebrating Korea's rapid economic development at the domestic and international levels by juxtaposing the event's images with those of another historical event whose news was censored by the authorities. The newsreel's female voice-over tells the viewer that the festival's participants waved and

204   Post-activism

used the word "wonderful" at their street parade, while what the viewer sees is footage of street demonstrations for democracy and the riot police's violent suppression of them with tear gas, which includes videos of the Gwangju Uprising. This ironic discrepancy suggests that the impetus behind avant-garde filmmaking's preoccupation with the official archival image lies in what Sven Spieker refers to as the image's double aspect, a coexistence of order and chaos. Spieker writes that the bureaucratic systems of classification that make possible the instrumentalized operation of the archive are inherently open to the "condition under which the unexpected, the sudden, the contingent can be sudden, unexpected, contingent."[30] Spieker's view on the productive disorder that inherently lies in the bureaucratic archive suggests that although its objects and documents are arranged under the principle of classification and are subject to a rigid system of signification, they can reveal their underlying codes and unexpected meanings once they are removed from their original context and displaced into new forms of association. By creating that new association between the two contrasting images and coupling it with an ironic sound-image disjunction, Kim follows what Foster has called the "archival impulse," which considers the newsreel's bureaucratic archive less as permanent and stable than as "found yet constructed."

Considering its larger structure, *An Escalator in World Order* is indeed not a compilation film that solely consists of existing footage: rather, it is based on Kim's creative intersection of compilation film and observational documentary. In the film's beginning, Kim alternates archival images of the past with those of the twenty-first century that he shot with a digital camera: for instance, the images of the recovery of Seoul by the allies on September 28, 1950, are extended into those of the public ceremony that celebrated the sixtieth -anniversary of the recovery (figure 6.2). Additionally, Kim's self-shot footage of a national prayer service held by the Korean Christian Association (whose ideology has been influenced by American Christianity since Korea's liberation) overlaps with the images of a public demonstration in the late 1940s that protested the withdrawal of US armed forces from Korea. After combining the long series of images gleaned from Korean and US newsreels, Kim concludes his film with another series of self-shot footage to highlight the extent to which the history of the political-economic-religious complex between the United States and Korea since the latter's liberation deeply extended into multiple aspects of Korean society in the early twenty-first century. The footage includes observational shots of an English village, a state-sponsored theme park in which children learn English in immersive ways, and the large rally of the Korean Christian Association in 2010, in which George W. Bush was invited not simply as former president of the United States, but also as

Figure 6.2 *An Escalator in World Order* (Kim Kyung-man, 2011)

an elder of the Presbyterian Church USA. Kim's selection of images does more than attenuate the pro-US ideology that has persisted throughout the tumultuous history of modern Korea, as a rescuer of South Korea from North Korea's communist threat, as a prototype of its economic and cultural modernization, and as the root of its conservative evangelist Christianity. It springs from Kim's oblique critique of the diplomatic and educational policies of the Lee Myung-bak government during which the film was produced. In terms of diplomacy, the government tried to "strengthen and improve the US alliance based on a long tradition of friendly relations, common values and mutual benefit,"[31] and the inclusion of Bush's speech suggests that he was the president with whom Lee had a summit meeting in 2008 to establish that alliance. This diplomatic policy also entailed the English Village promoted by the Ministry of Education as a major project grounded in the "language ideology that Koreans need to improve in English to participate in the global economy."[32]

Seen from these diplomatic and pedagogical contexts, Kim's creative juxtaposition of governmental newsreels and culture films with his self-shot footage of Korean society during Lee's government offers a fresh look at the Benjaminian notion of the "dialectical image." While the concept legitimizes

206 Post-activism

the great variety of found footage filmmaking as a broader method of Benjaminian historiography that is antithetical to the notion of history as the progression of linear time, what is interesting in *An Escalator in World Order* is its attempt to establish as its overall structure a mutual dialogue between the past and the present in ways that supplement each other. That is, past archival images gleaned from disparate sources bear witness to the prehistory of Korea's dependence on the United States in the neoliberal, neoconservative age, while the seemingly observational record of the present is haunted by the persistence of past images that were highly instructive and disciplinary for mass propaganda but are now seen as outdated. The mutual dialogue between the new associations of the footage and the director's on-the-spot engagement with the persistence of pro-US ideology demonstrates that *An Escalator in World Order* updates activism's traditional commitment to social issues and historical reality.

Kim's establishment of the Benjaminian dialectical image as a larger structure of his documentary is varied in *People Passing By*, which emphasizes his activist orientation. The film accumulates shorts that capture diverse people of contemporary Korean society for its first twenty-seven minutes. After horizontal tracking shots following containers and factories in Incheon Port, the fixed-camera shots that frame the backs of workers going to work at GM Korea (GM Daewoo) headquarter set the film's tone and focus. In these shots, a man who distributes flyers to the workers is highlighted as much as their appearance from behind passing through the main entrance of the factory. An ensuing shot exhibits subjects that allude to the circumstances of the man (and the flyers he distributes): a banner of all the laid-off workers asking to negotiate with the company's president, some of them who holding sit-in for their reinstatement, and other workers wearing mourning clothes to urge the government's investigation into the mass dismissals at Ssangyong Motors (see chapter 2). Following *An Escalator in World Order*, Kim's compilation documentary does not mark a total departure from traditional Korean independent documentaries but rather renews their political commitment, given that labor issues and struggles have been a key concern of the activist tradition since the late 1980s. Kim captures the subjects of the participatory labor documentaries, but does not establish them as the working class of the struggle or rely on the cause-and-effect narrative scheme to explain its development and consequence. Instead, his impressionist cinematography, attenuated by majestic slow-motion effects, emphasizes the gestures of alienated workers and the atmosphere of the workplace surrounding them. The images of the workers extend to another series of images after the film's first sequence. It unfolds selections from newsreels from 1945 to 1966 produced by the USIS or the NFPA, which encompass documents of the people who are swept away in the chaotic ideological clash during the three-year postliberation period before the establishment of the Republic of Korea in 1948, refugees who fled from the Hangang River to Busan during the Korean War from 1950 to 1953, and various workers who were mobilized for the state-led economic development plan promoted under the Park Chung-hee regime. All these images reveal diverse aspects of the people, while also drawing viewers' attention to the faces of the individuals who strove for survival in the modern history of Korea. Kim's accumulative and associative montage create linkages between the various people and works mobilized in different sites, such as forest management, land reclamation, beautification work in the streets, housework in rural areas, breakwater construction, railway burial work, labor in tunnels, glass processing, textile factories, bicycle-manufacturing factories, and so on. The figures of the workers are organically and gradually connected in the same visual rhythm, to the point that similar gestures in these works are orchestrated and united into the whole national body mobilized for the state-led economic development plan. Again, this demonstrates that Kim Kyung-man deepens his project of dialectical, materialist historiography with the poetic mode in *People Passing By*. Several classic music tracks, such as Frederic Chopin's Piano Sonata no. 2 and Gustav Mahler's Symphonies nos. 1 and 6, are harmonized with the visual elements to convey the sentiment of the people that encompass Korea's past and present. In this sense, Kim's compilation method serves as the Benjaminian redemptive criticism that illuminates the forgotten images of the people from the present perspective, in that the workers during Park's developmental era are extensively linked to contemporary workers in struggle in front of GM Korea.

Essay Film: *Yongsan*, the Yongsan Massacre, and Protest Suicides

As its title indicates, *Yongsan* is a documentary on the Yongsan Massacre (Yongsan ch'amsa) on Tuesday, January 20, 2009, in which five protesters who had resisted Lee Myung-bak government's plan for the redevelopment of Yongsan district, and one policeman, were killed by a fire that broke out in a lookout on the rooftop of Namildang building during a raid of Special Weapons and Tactics officers and riot police from the Seoul Metropolitan Police Agency on the long-term sit-in resistance of evictees' groups. Depicting the struggles of the survivors and bereaved families protesting the authorities' violent suppression and commemorating the victims of the incident, Mun

208 Post-activism

Jeong-hyun, director of *Grandmother's Flower* (see chapter 4), associates the incident with the larger traumatic history of state violence during the era of military dictatorship in the 1970s and 1980s, and particularly with the deaths of the students who fought for democratization and those of the workers who struggled against unfair labor practices. This reflection does not simply recount the public history of the authoritarian violence and the deaths caused by it, including student protesters' self-immolation in 1991, but also activates Mun's personal childhood memory of Lee Han-yeol, who had lived in Mun's neighborhood and was seriously hurt by a tear gas grenade during a large-scale university student demonstration on June 9, 1987, which ignited the June Democratic Struggle.

Yongsan can be seen as a work that marks the post-activist turn of Korean independent documentary in terms of its theme and form as well as its positioning of the director. The film takes as its subject the issue of urban redevelopment, a key issue of the activist tradition exemplified by Kim Dong-won's *Sanggye-dong Olympics* and *Haengdang-dong People*. However, it does not offer a linear chronological narrative that would constitute a coherent discourse on the cause and effect of the Massacre, nor a persuasive message advocating the rights of the victims and other evictees involved in the sit-ins in the redevelopment area. Unlike the verité-driven Korean independent documentaries rooted in their director's immediate involvement in current social events and investigation of their realities, *Yongsan* deals with the massacre in a way that blends past and present, as a crisis of individual and collective traumas. In this sense, the film foregrounds Mun's own subjectivity as an agent that does not merely document the struggles against the massacre but also investigates its relation to the history of state violence and his own memory of the deaths caused by the violence from various angles. This reflection on the historical and recent events through Mun's own subjectivity places *Yongsan* within what Timothy Corrigan has considered as a tendency of essayistic filmmaking that investigates the truth and ethics of social events through the director's personal view. In Corrigan's words, such an essay film renders its filmmaker's subjectivity as consciously mobile within the "reports not only about facts, realities, people, and places discovered and revealed but also about the possibility of agency itself within a state of current affairs that is no longer transparent nor easily accessible."[33]

In *Yongsan*, Mun's camera shuffles between the families of the dead and the members of citizen organizations who protest the authorities' violent suppression, and the everyday people who sympathize with the dead but ignore the tragedy itself. Instead of revealing the truth of the fire or making a conclusive argument that the state's urban redevelopment policy should be held responsible for the tragedy, Mun's voice-over explicitly exposes his ambivalent self-position, wavering between the people who fight for the dead and those who do not confront the issue. In this sense, the voice-over consents to the essay film's authorial voice that "approaches the subject matter not in order to present a factual report (the field of traditional documentary), but to offer an in-depth, personal, and thought-provoking reflection."[34] This unstable authorial voice also validates the affinity between the mode of the essay film and the trope of the first-person documentary in that it constructs Mun's subjectivity as "a site of instability—flux, drift, perpetual revision—rather than coherence" by undertaking a "double and mutually defining inscription—of history and the self."[35] Again, his unstable subjectivity attests to the film's essayistic mode, which comments on a public event from his personal perspective, or, to mediate the public and the personal in dialogue with the massacre as a "moment of danger" not only for disenfranchised subjects but also for activists and documentarians who were committed to them. On the one hand, Mun's narration serves to position the victims of the massacre within the context of deaths in the larger history of state violence, therefore demonstrating his *minjung*-oriented historical consciousness. On the other hand, however, Mun's self-confessional voice-over also acknowledges the ethical plight posed by his absence from *hyŏnjang* of the state violence at a time when the massacre occurred. In dealing with the political crisis of the society in the neoliberal urban redevelopment and his own personal crisis that it caused, Mun's authorial voice situates itself an agent that continually drifts between his reflection on the present and his recollection of the deaths of the past.

The archival footage collected and manipulated by Mun serves as a key element that mobilizes the mode of the essay film and constructs his subjectivity as a "site of instability." In the film's beginning, Mun's voice confesses that he was not on the site of the massacre, exposing his own sense of responsibility as a documentarian who is expected to engage in an on-site struggle in everyday politics. This confession is accompanied by video footage of the day that he later collected and reassembled. By slowing down the footage with the help of video technology, Mun draws the viewer's attention to the gazes of the onlookers who were watching the fire flaming from inside the watchtower so that the viewer is able to notice the sympathy and powerlessness that the onlookers and Mun share. In this regard, Mun's manipulation of the footage of the massacre ethically reflects on his present self, who was not able to immediately access it. The video-based slow motion, too, functions as a fulcrum for blending Mun's consciousness of the present tragedy with his personal memories of the student democratization movements in the 1980s and early 1990s, as it is extended into other video footage that depicts student rallies

210 Post-activism

in universities and the funeral ceremonies of the students who were killed or burnt themselves to death and who were declared "patriotic martyr" (*aeguk yŏlsa*). Here it becomes obvious that the video-based slow motion plays a pivotal role in constructing Mun's subjectivity as a kind of palimpsest of the past and the present and rendering the juxtaposition between the two sets of video footage as a Benjaminian dialectical image of the recurrent state violence and its victims. This juxtaposition created by Mun echoes Corrigan's Benjaminian view of the essay film as a work that recovers or rescues the meaning of events from a "'homogenous empty time' through a freeze-frame of insight described as 'the now of a particular recognisability.'"[36]

This point is also apparent in the film's ensuing progression, in which Mun's camera depicts not simply the protests against the massacre but also the family members of the patriotic martyrs who still commemorate their death and fight for democracy and a better social life, including the mother of Lee Han-yeol, who lived in Mun's neighbourhood during his childhood. Mun's engagement with the remainders of the violent past in the present enables him to revisit the footage of the past and put its meanings under constant reconstruction as the archival video images of the Gwangju Uprising and the funeral of Lee in 1987 are slowed down again. The film's ending, in which all the images of the past and present are reverse played at fast pace, stresses once again that the capacities of video technology, including collecting and reediting past footage, shifting between images of different times, and slowing down or halting images, are effective in establishing the subjectivity of the essay film as a "site of instability" and in positing essayistic filmmaking itself as engendering the "archival impulse." Included in this reverse-play vignette are images linked to the self-immolations from the age of the mass protests against dictatorship in the 1980s and early 1990s to workers' protest suicides against neoliberal new market policies and mass dismissal in the twenty-first century. In this sense, Mun's remix of the footage gleaned from public archives and his personal video collection and his replay of it via reverse motion do more than give expression to his self-reflexive subjectivity. They also attest to the way that the massacre functioned as a present moment of danger that propelled Mun to revisit the pasts of social movements from a renewed perspective. The images of the deaths and funerals are used for his materialist historiography beyond the official history of martyrdom in the democratization movement, in that they allude to the "gradual change of protest suicide from an aggressive political weapon meant to spur mass protest towards a more defensive act by workers who use death to communicate frustration, weariness and despair as they protest injustice."[37] In this context, the images are extensively associated with the street protests of the victims' families and the activists who were supporting fact-finding on the massacre and punishment of the police officers responsible for it. It is in this way that Mun's visit to the past images stems from his urgent but careful intervention in the "memory war" on the massacre, which calls for remembering the victims' claim to survive. As Hieyoon Kim rightly observes, the film's ending "creates a new spaces where multiple temporalities and plural pasts can join together to reclaim [the protesters'] right not to be forgotten or overwritten."[38]

Nonfiction Diary and the Crises of "Compressed Modernity"

Nonfiction Diary investigates the progress and consequences of the crimes committed by the Jijon Clan (Chijonp'a), a group of five serial killers motivated by the goal of "killing the rich," in terms of how the crimes could be associated with the political and economic contexts of the 1990s. The clan murdered five innocent civilians after torturing or raping them and ate their corpses. As they were arrested in 1994, their murder spree became one of the most infamous and scandalous serial killing incidents in the history of modern Korea. The film's director, Jung Yoon-suk, attempts to approach the underlying motivations of the clan's crimes and its members' unique madness. Although it does not engage with current events, *Nonfiction Diary* continues the participatory mode of Korean independent documentary in two respects. First, Jung plays the part of the investigator who interviews a variety of people, including police detectives who arrested the murderers and investigated their crimes, a human right lawyer, a prison guard who explains the crimes' political and economic contexts, and a pastor and nun who were responsible for trying to reform the murderers until their execution. Second, the film supplements the interviews with a vast array of photographs (including those of the clan members and of their on-the-spot reenactments of their crimes) and footage drawn from television news and video archives in a way similar to other traditional Korean independent documentaries committed to investigating the truth about past events caused by political and ideological conflicts since the twentieth century or documenting the events' traumatic effects on the present (see chapter 2).

However, *Nonfiction Diary* also departs from the traditional Korean independent documentaries that explore historical events and construct a coherent narrative of their cause and effect. Although the film's overall structure develops from the time of the clan's crimes to the execution of the death penalty, the historical events that it investigates are multiple, thus obscuring its

212 Post-activism

linear construction of knowledge. In his investigation of the murders, Jung shifts his focus to the clan's attempt to take revenge on society, which for them meant using extreme violence to attack the increasing class division caused by the inherent imbalance of a capitalist society. For Jung, the clan's motivation for the horrific crimes is symptomatic of the structural crises that the rapid capitalist modernization of Korean society necessarily fostered in the early 1990s after liberation from the military-authoritative regime and an accelerated drive to catch up with globalization. This awareness enables Jung to connect the clan's murders with other seemingly unrelated traumatic incidents that occurred during the same period as that of the murders and signaled the structural catastrophe of the capitalism-driven society: the collapse of the Seongsu Bridge (Sŏngsu daegyo) in Seoul in 1994 (which claimed thirty-two victims) and that of the Sampoong Department Store (Samp'oong baekhwajŏm) in 1995 (which claimed 502 lives). By associating these three traumatic events, Jung tells viewers how they are consolidated into a large picture of moral corruption and staggering incompetence that was of product of what sociologist Chang Kyung-sup has called "compressed modernity." The terms refers to Korea's rapid economic, political, and social shifts to modernization and globalization after the end of military dictatorship in the late 1980s in an extremely condensed manner. Extending Ulrich Beck's idea of "risk society," Chang argues that a key aspect of Korea's compressed modernity has been the emergence of social crises, including the IMF crisis in 1997, which were indicative of the instabilities and contradictions inherent in the extremely condensed developments of Korean society's economic, political, and infrastructural systems: "As South Koreans have undertaken production, construction, exchange and consumption activities on unprecedentedly massive scales within the shortest time imaginable, they have concomitantly confronted various risks associated with such economic activities in a similarly massive and fast manner."[39] As the human rights lawyer argues in his interview, the collapses in 1994 and 1995 could be homogeneous with the clan's crimes, in that they were all caused by neoliberalizing society's negligence of safety management and economic polarization.

In juxtaposing the three incidents, Jung also positions them within the larger tumultuous political context of the time in 1992 when President Kim Young-sam formed the new civilian government (*munmin jŏngbu*), whose slogan spoke of its intent to construct a *sin Han'guk* (New Korea) through *segyehwa* (globalization). Jung's interweaving of all the traumatic events against the backdrop of this political transition was driven by his Benjaminian historical consciousness, which led to an insight into the past, "now of a particular recognisability," or at a present moment of crisis. Jung's following remark testifies to this consciousness: "After the fall of the military dictatorship in 1988, Korea underwent a period of very rapid neoliberal economic development. The events dealt with in the film are drawn from this period. . . . There is a connection between these events. And . . . the social problems recognized by the Jijon Clan are still in effect today."[40] Viewing the film from the present moment, what evidences the recurrences of the problems in the 1990s are the devastating economic polarization of twenty-first-century Korean society and the Sewol Ferry disaster.

Jung's approach of collecting the archival static and moving images associated with the different events is meant to make them into a Benjaminian constellation: a new assemblage of images from different pasts, whose meanings are made anew when they are grouped in a new linkage from the present perspective. Benjamin writes, "Image is that wherein what has been comes together in a flash with the now to form a constellation. . . . For where the relation of the present to the past is a purely temporal, continuous one, the relation of what-has-been to the now is dialectical."[41] To create the constellation of the seemingly unrelated traumatic events in the manner of Benjaminian historiography, Jung conceives *Nonfiction Diary* as a mixture of investigative and compilation documentaries. While synchronizing archival images of the different past events with interviewees' testimonies, Jung also juxtaposes the images so that they are decoded under the principle of montage through which "the past is transformed from a fixed space of forgetting to a dynamic time of historical imagination."[42] Here it is worth noting that Jung's historical imagination is realized via his consideration of images as allegories of the past that serve as a counternarrative of history in that they imply "a certain randomness [and] a seriality without necessity."[43] This is manifested in the film's opening sequence, in which the video and televisual images as evidence of the three incidents and their political and economic contexts (the transition from the military dictatorship to *munmin jŏngbu*, and Korea's industrial and economic modernization) pass in a rapid montage via the split-screen technique. Jung's collage of all the images coupled with the split screen highlights the images' disparate aspects, thereby reflecting the idea that our history is no longer represented via the transparent, linear, and cause-and-effect narrative but is rendered fragmentary and unstable. In this context, the collage style reveals the status of archival images as the detritus of mass media and the allegory of postmodern historical consciousness,[44] while also challenging them as a counternarrative of crimes that is marked by appropriation, nonlinearity, and fragmentation.

Developing the collage-like assemblage in the opening sequence in the rest of the film, Jung also uses archival images to construct what Michael Zyrd has called the "metahistorical form commenting on the cultural discourses and narrative patterns behind history."[45] In a way similar to Kim Kyung-man's accumulation and graphic matches of archival images, Jung's nonlinear accumulation and juxtaposition often unveil the history beneath and behind television and other audiovisual records of the three traumatic incidents, and even their ironic undersides. For instance, there are clips of a television debate program in which a group of panelists, among them psychiatrists and sociologists, discuss how to prevent such horrific crimes as the Jijon Clan's. The panelists ascribe these sorts of crimes to various causes, including the crisis of the national police system and the loss of the society's collective morality. When footage of the debate is linked to time-lapse photos (which are extracted from Jung's self-shot observational footage of the rural landscape in which the crimes took place) in which the murderers' innocent answers in the court are juxtaposed in intertitles, it turns out that none of the panelists could provide a compelling answer about the truth of the crimes. In this way, Jung's assemblage of the clips reveals the impasse of the debate program as an apparatus for constructing public opinion and its underlying ideologies. An ensuing series of images precipitates this ironic effect: footage from *Daehannews* in which Confucian citizen organizations promote the restoration of human dignity and morality to prevent antihuman crimes. Both the enlightenment discourse in the TV debate and the Confucian discourse in the newsreel provide an account of the crimes and the solution to them when these two visual documents were created, but none of them turn out to be efficient when they are juxtaposed with Jung's self-shot rural landscape of the present in which the profound psychic dimension of the crime is unfathomable. This ironic effect created by the contrast between the present and the past testifies to what Baron has called the "intentional disparity," a disparity "based on our perception of a previous intention ascribed to and (seemingly inscribed within) the archival document."[46] In fact, the sense of "intentional disparity" has been noticed in a foreign film critic's comment on the film: "Jung is interested in the tension between the way this era looked and sounded in the media, and how people remember it."[47] By highlighting the tension between the archival images' metahistorical dimensions and the ways in which the images are understood in the present, Jung deals with the images as "found yet constructed"—and ultimately as new material for a new constellation of history.

Memory Wars Continue

The Age of Beasts (*Modŏn k'oria: Chimsŭng*, 2021, 48 min.) is an episode from *Modern Korea* (2019–present), a KBS-produced documentary series that revisits key events of modern Korean history through footage of its diverse programs—news reports, talk shows, dramas, and public service and information features—from its voluminous digital archives.[48] The series, which included fifteen episodes as of April 2023, has demonstrated a productive platform intersection of recent Korean documentary cinema, as the series was not only aired on television but also invited to the Jeonju International Film Festival in 2020 and the International Film Festival Rotterdam in 2021. More significantly, it also signaled the reach of the "archival turn" beyond independent cinema, namely, into national TV documentary, whose expository and authoritative conventions have tended to subjugate archival photos, films, and videos to supplement the accounts and arguments of "voice of God" narration. Among its episodes, *The Age of Beasts* gains particular recognition due to the authorship of Jeong Jae-eun, who left a remarkable signature of Korean women's cinema with her debut feature film *Take Care of My Cat* (*Koyangirŭl put'ak'ae*, 2001, 112 min.) and has made a series of documentaries about urban or residential spaces, public buildings, and architecture (*Talking Architect* [*Malhanŭn kŏnch'ukka*, 2011, 95 min.], *Talking Architecture: City Hall* [*Malhanŭn kŏnch'uk: Sit'i hor*, 2012, 107 min.], and *Ecology in Concrete* [*Ap'at'ŭ saengt'aegye*, 2017], 80 min.).

As a compilation documentary based on Jeong's riveting montage of clips from KBS television programs, *The Age of Beasts* confronts viewers with the societal and cultural misogyny of the postdictatorship period from the late 1980 to 1994, as well as the improvement in women's status and growth of women's social movements against sexual violence and for its victims. The former discursive thread is interwoven with news reports on human trafficking (*inshin maemae*) and a stack of diverse TV melodramas that depict rapes, abductions, and female characters' pains and nightmares. The tales of sound and fury marked by the excess of patriarchal violence and female resistance run parallel to the second discursive thread, composed of other TV dramas, including a moot-court fiction, based on the two advancements in women's rights in the early 1990s. The first is passage of the Special Act on Sexual Violence (Sŏng p'ongnyŏk t'ŭkpyŏl pŏp) in 1993, triggered by social disputes over a 1991 case where a woman killed the man who raped her 21 years ago, and a 1992 case where a 21-year-old female college student murdered her stepfather with her boyfriend due to his longtime sexual assaults. The second is the establishment of the concept of sexual harassment (*song hŭirong*), provoked by a press conference held by a female research assistant in Seoul National University who disclosed her professor's sexual misconducts and his retaliation (she was excluded from rehiring).[49] Viewed together, the two discursive threads constitute a materialist constellation of hatred and discrimination, as well as of women's struggles against them and solidarity with their victims, in service of the urgency of the contemporary feminist wave (see chapter 3). The vast array of archival materials, if heterogeneous or anomic, is given new meaning inasmuch as they recall the MeToo movements across various social and cultural sectors since 2018, and women's ongoing fights both in online and offline spaces against spycams, cyberporn, and online sex crimes—including the Nth room (Npŏn bang) case in 2020, in which more than seventy victims, including underage girls, were forced to upload videos depicting their involuntary acts of sexual slavery and exploitation in chatrooms on the encrypted communication app Telegram.[50] Jeong's remark on archival documentary suggests that her excavation and rearrangement of the materials is grounded in the awareness that the feminist movement against sexual misogyny and gender inequity must involve a "memory war" to create a renewed constellation of its past and present: "Making archive documentary is to operate the application of disk defragmentation. If the hard disk is running slowly, you need to defragment the disk to remove the empty area inside the storage device."[51]

The "archival turn" made by all the directors discussed in this chapter allows them to activate investigative documentary, compilation documentary, essay film, and metahistorical documentary that challenges the prevalence of the camera's encounter with reality as the evidentiary and political authenticity of nonfiction practice. While marking a notable break from the participatory mode of activist or committed documentary, the filmmakers' concern with found footage and the formal experimentations mobilized by its various uses attest to the filmmakers' sustained engagement with the realities of history and politics, which is seen as renewing the activist tradition's aspiration for social change. As Lucas Hilderbrand convincingly points out, contemporary filmmakers and artists who devote themselves to formal experimentations with the visuality and temporality of documentary records aim to "create [an] alternative portrait of history and negotiate the complex reconciliation of their own experiences and ideologies with capital-H history."[52] Seen in this light, the filmmakers' aspiration to use found footage for their formal innovations demonstrates their underlying Benjaminian "portrait of history" in which the archive as the record of the past is "under construction" in its dialectical relationship to the present. The filmmakers' portraits, then, suggest that their post-activist archival modes are based on two assumptions: that archival documents lie at the heart of the ongoing political and mnemonic battles (as evidenced in *Kim-gun* and *Yongsan*); and that they can serve as the building block for renewing our understanding of the past in dialogue with the pressing problems of society (as demonstrated by the films of Kim Kyung-man, Jung Yoon-suk, and Jeong Jae-eun).

In Hong Jin-hwon's *melting icecream (Melt'ing aisŭk'ŭrim*, 2021, 70 min.), the archival turn's material historiography goes so far as to associate the material and technical dimensions of photographic and video documents with another type of memory war—not the ideological war centering around a significant political event, as in the case of *Kim-gun*, but the war regarding which historical records deserve to be preserved and historicized and which other records are excluded. The documentary focuses on the processes of restoring water-damaged films of such collectives as the Institute of Social Photography (Sahoe sajin yŏn'guhoe) and National Photography Institute (Minjok sajin yŏn'guso) committed to documenting sites of student protests and labor movements in the spirit of *minjung* art in the late 1980s and early 1990s, featuring interviews with the collectives' members. The testimonies about the motivation and principles of their photographic practice lay claim not only to the activist tradition of Korean documentary cinema but also to the larger wave of *mjnjung* art movement, as they rehearse their obsession with *hyŏnjang* as an alternative to the mainstream press, which neglected the struggles, as well as their effort to foreground the power of the people in fights as the collective agency for social change. In this regard, the film's documentation of the restoration processes is read as allegorizing the project of the twenty-first-century liberal democracy governments (whose leading members, the 86 generation, pertained to the movement sphere [*undonggwŏn*]) to glamorize the democratization movement and to monumentalize its heroes.

Apart from the members' confession about how the collective utopian energy against the dictatorship and for democracy became compromised with the turn to the *munmin jŏngbu* in the early 1990s, Hong's challenge to this now-official historiography summons up another series of documents, a collection of videos which were uploaded on alternative and progressive internet press site newscham.net (*Midiŏ ch'amsesang*) but which became later inaccessible. The videos, often opaque, degraded, and pixelated on the verge of being abstracted, are perceived as what media theorist and artist Hito Steyerl famously called the "poor image," a kind of itinerant image subject to copying, pasting, ripping, and degeneration in the digitally networked system of image production and circulation. More than marking a stark contrast with the celluloid films that are treated as the objects of restoration, the videos compel viewers to notice what they still preserve: intense street fights and desperate sit-ins of workers across various workplaces and occupations, including temporary female workers at Korail and E-land Homever (see chapter 2), immigrant workers, and a male worker shouting about the abolition of irregular jobs from a ledge (figure 6.3), who desperately struggled against the Irregular Workers Protection Act (Pijŏnggyujik poho bŏp), which was legislated in

Figure 6.3 *melting icecream* (Hong Jin-hwon, 2021)
Image courtesy: Hong Jin-hwon.

2006 during the Roh Moo-hyun's liberal democracy government despite the labor society's concern that it would facilitate companies' mass dismissals. That is, the videos may lack the transparency and accuracy of their visual trace that viewers expect from the image of indexical truth claims, but, coupled with the workers' shouts and cries that intermittently penetrate the scenes of restoration, point to what happened and who was in front of the anonymous video cameras. In this regard, the videos incorporate Hong's compelling post-activist consciousness of the entanglement of precarious subjects in the neoliberal system with the precarity of the images that lay claim to their desparate voices and gestures. For his compiling of the videos derives from the fact that they are far from restoration and preservation applied to those of *minjung* in the celluloid films, in the sense that they are not treated as the material for a capital-H history—in this case, the history of the democratization movement. This accords with Steyerl's insight into the political underpinnings of poor images: first, they are excluded and forgotten from the capitalist audiovisual economy of image consumption that privileges high resolution and clarity; and second, for this reason, they include the traces of contradiction and conflict that are caused by the economy. As she writes, "Poor are poor because they are not assigned any value within the class society of images—their status as illicit or degraded grants them exemption from its criteria."[53] Seen in this light, Hong's achievement lies in retrieving the materiality of those videos, evidenced by their surface traces of degradation and dissolution, in order to forge a new historical awareness that although *minjung* might be missing, the disenfranchised subjects and their economic precarity in the postauthoritarian society should be remembered in the present tense. This type of awareness, which is premised upon Hong's consideration of the digital in contrast to the photochemical, is what lays the groundwork for other directors and artists in the next chapter, who have used it to expand the politico-aesthetic boundaries of Korean documentary cinema.

7

The Digital Turn

Seeking Truth Differently

Twenty-First-Century Digital Documentaries beyond *hyŏnjang* Realism

With the gradual proliferation of 6 mm personal camcorders and affordable software applications such as Adobe's Premier, digital technologies began to offer an alternative to celluloid-based or analog video cameras in the local independent film scene of the early twenty-first century. Many documentarians and media activists embraced their multifarious capabilities, including the portability of the digital video (DV) camera, its prompt access to reality, extended recording time, and nonlinear editing as reigniting their practices. This was predicated upon the belief that these capabilities would galvanize the verité tradition's participatory ethos and its *hyŏnjang* aesthetics, just as the lightweight film cameras and analog videocams had functioned as the media for the activist nonfiction practice of the late 1980s. This belief was also linked to another utopian promise that digital filmmaking's relatively low-cost and do-it-yourself possibilities would help nurture and spread the "one-person production system" that started to develop in the 1990s in such established collectives as Docu Purn and Seoul Visual Collective, which would further bridge the gap between the professional director and the independent amateur filmmaker. It was thanks to these two overlapping threads of awareness that there was no notable resistance to the technological transition from the analog to the digital in the production of activist and social change documentaries in the twenty-first century.

This does not necessarily mean, however, that documentarians' adoption of digital technologies has exclusively resulted in either the participatory aesthetic of speaking for the marginalized or the realistic aesthetic of recording real-life details. For the turn to the digital coincided with Korean documentary cinema's post-activist drive, which made more dispersed its modes of production, distribution, and consumption in the twenty-first century. Documentary filmmaker Choi Jin-sung wrote that "the most fascinating

Activism and Post-activism. Jihoon Kim, Oxford University Press. © Oxford University Press 2024.
DOI: 10.1093/oso/9780197760413.003.0008

aspect of digital technologies would be their capability to change the form of independent documentary and to expand its ways of expression."[1] This was in dialogue with the "postdocumentary" discourse that emerged in the independent documentary culture of the early 2000s, a discourse based on the awareness that "a filmmaker's personality was manifested in his or her style," and that "other rhetorical devices unavailable from existing classical documentary films more intervene in his or her film."[2] These two threads of awareness suggest that the uses of digital technologies have gestured toward filmmakers' pursuit of alternatives to the epistemological ground of the activist mode, or of other strategies for documenting reality and making truth claims than its authenticity grounded in the belief that a documentary image is produced based on the camera's causal contact with real history and people. A case in point that demonstrates this pursuit is the personal documentaries in the early twenty-first century that I have explored in chapter 4, in that they were driven by the filmmakers' self-reflexive presence and intervention in profilmic reality in the attempt to question and redraw the boundaries between their subjectivity and their outside world, fact and artifice, and public discourse and private record or scrutiny. That is, the filmmakers' DV camera as well as the visual effects applied to editing functioned as the mediator that rendered the boundaries permeable, and as the prosthetic extension of their unstable self.

This chapter maps out three forms of twenty-first-century Korean digital nonfiction film, "postdocumentary diversion," "virtual reality (VR) documentary," and "subjunctive documentary," that attest to the expansion of Korean documentary cinema's "ways of expression." They are premised on what Michael Renov has called "documentary disavowal," a term pointing out an epistemological challenge to the modernist conception of the documentary as a practice driven by an instrumental rationality. By questioning the absolutist, single-minded notion of objective truth, Renov argues, the act of disavowal finds its technical grounds in the postfilmic media technologies, including digital video and its corresponding software applications. For the technologies introduce material instability and mutability as complying with the "hinge ideas of ambivalence, of vacillation, undecidability, split belief."[3] While concurring with Renov's insight, I argue that a more significant contribution of the three forms of Korean digital documentary is widening the horizon of documentary practices and thereby multiplying their production of reality and truth in ways that are irreducible to the traditional activist mode. The films of "postdocumentary diversion" unearth or playfully satirize the profound ideological contestations of the postauthoritarian Korean society with their rigorous employment of digital visual effects to manipulate existing media images or create animated sequences. VR documentaries augment the performative documentary's emphasis on the subjective and embodied aspects of truth with their capacities to allow the viewer to be immersed in simulated reality, to have an empathic relationship with its social actors, and to question the boundaries between truth and fiction. And finally, subjunctive documentaries, which involve computer-generated imagery and digital non-linear editing to scientifically reconstruct reality beyond the camera's record, aim to investigate and unveil truths of the Yongsan Massacre and the Sewol Ferry Disaster that have had profound impacts on contemporary Korean society.

Postdocumentary Diversions

A post-activist mode of documentary fueled by digital imaging and postpro-duction processes in the early 2000s undermined documentary's imperative to sobriety and veracity for the sake of playfulness, artifice, and satire. This mode corresponds to what John Corner has called "documentary as diversion," that is, new forms of factual production that privilege a performative, playful element. By this element, Corner means nonrealistic styles, reenact-ment, anecdotal knowledge, and the director's self-conscious display of socia-bility in reality TV shows, all of which question documentary's authenticity and seriousness. A more profound implication of documentary-as-diversion is signaling a rhetorical and functional shift of documentary practice: that is, the elements of documentary-as-diversion constitute a "postdocumentary" context, as it is exempt from—or, often aims to deconstruct—three classic functions of traditional documentary, first, "providing publicity for dominant version of citizenship," second, "journalistic inquiry and exposition," and fi-nally, "radical interrogation and alternative perspective."[4]

Patriot Game (*Aegukcha keim,* Kyung Soon and ChoiHa Dong-ha, 2001, 90 min.) and *Fuckumentary* (*Ppŏkk'yumentŏri: Pakt'ong jilligyo,* Choi Jin-sung, 2001, 95 min.), two films that playfully debunk how the Park Chung Hee regime's authoritarian ideologies of patriotism, anticommunism, and developmentalism persisted in Korean society and its collective unconscious-ness, could be considered films that emblematize documentary-as-diversion. The two films criticize the Park Chung-hee syndrome, a phenomenon in which Park as the former authoritarian reader became rejuvenated as a na-tional hero at a time when South Korean society struggled to overcome the post-IMF economic downfall.[5] The critical discourse at that time praised *Patriot Game* as freeing itself from Korean documentary's obsession with realism and the director's consciousness of authenticity. The co-filmmakers of *Patriot Game* consistently demystify the testimonies of right-wing nationalist intellectuals (Cho Gab-je and Father Park Hong) and the seniors brainwashed by Park Chung-hee's ideologies. In so doing, they employ intertitles (an interview with Park Hong is coupled with such intertitles as "Marxist-Leninists" and "National Liberationists [*chusap'a*]") and the archival footage of the Park era mixed with satirical punk songs (for instance, a punk version of the campaign song for Saemaul undong [New Village Movement], Park's political initiative launched in 1970 to modernize the economy and lifestyle of rural villages).[6] All these playful and performative devices demonstrate that the film's radical interrogation of the origin of the New Right historiography in the early twenty-first century is made with other representational and aesthetic strategies than the enlightening and expository rhetorical devices of the activist documentary that would confirm a documentarian's political authority to report previously unknown facts and truths. The film's hybrid of live action and graphic or typographic images and its aesthetics of music video and parody are indebted to low-cost digital visual effects that independent filmmakers started to play with early in the century. As Choi Jin-sung clarifies, "The film's pastiche-like synthesis of images, its mixture of multiple genres, its blending of fiction and nonfiction, and its use of various parodies, all testify to an achievement that the digital brought to Korean independent documentary, while also signaling a new mode of documentary."[7]

Indeed, Choi offers a rigorous digital synthesis of live action and graphic images in his own *Fuckumentary*, another satirical attack on the doctrines of Park Chung-hee. In investigating the social conflict around the Kim Dae-jung government's plan to establish the Park Chung-hee Memorial Hall in 1999,[8] Choi extensively uses digital postproduction tools to manipulate both images of right-wing speakers who highly admire Park's political and economic legacies, and the newsreels associated with his era. Choi's playful critique of Park's dictatorship, which right-wing intellectuals hailed as the foundation of "Korean-style democracy," is intensively configured in a music video sequence that also radically transforms the archival materials of Park's regime against the backdrop of industrial metal music. Here, Park's iconic photo, his figure in military uniform as the leader of the May 16 military coup d'état in 1961, is duplicated in various sizes and juxtaposed with the bleached and grainy footage of the marching of soldiers on the ceremony of an Armed Forces Day, with his key doctrines printed in red—"Anti-communist Policy" (*pan'gong gukshi*), "Military Culture" (*kunsa munhwa*), and "Developmental Dictatorship" (*kaebal tokchae*). Park's iron rule attenuated by this vignette is followed by a split screen in which his face is divided in two. On its left

224 Post-activism

side, there are newsreels of the Park regime that show his key doctrines, soldiers, construction workers, and the people mobilized for an anticommunist, antispy rally; its right side is filled with images of the victims of the Park regime's achievements and the people's resistance to it, such as female workers in a factory, students in an anti-Yusin demonstration, and crying mouths that symbolize the regime's suppression of the freedom of speech. Viewed together, the conflict between these two series of the images that is made by Choi's spatial montage leads to a playful and poignant critique of the Park Chung-hee syndrome. For it vividly demonstrates that "the Yusin regime was militarist, constructionist, mobilizational, anticommunist, organicist, and biopolitical—in short, fascist in a broad sense."[9] With its capability to challenge the traditional activist documentary's aspirations to realism and sobriety, Choi's digital editing enables local critics to characterize *Fuckumentary* as a film that represents postdocumentary: "Through its appropriation and combination of different genres and its employment of digital manipulation for transforming images, postdocumentary creates various meanings and undermines the formal authority of traditional documentary."[10]

The postdocumentary diversions enabled by digital editing appeared once again in a couple of critically acclaimed nonfiction films in the late 2010s. The two films, then, mark a contemporary version of the post-activist tendency in that they attend to Korean society's ideological issues as a key political subject of traditional activist documentary while also conspicuously being liberated from its aesthetic and representational idioms. *Bamseom Pirates Seoul Inferno* (*Pamsŏmhaejŏktan soul bulbada*, 2017, 120 min.) is a documentary about the college punk duo Bamseom Pirates and their struggles with government censorship, including the arrest of their producer and manager, Park jung-geun, for violating the National Security Law with his controversial tweets that were seen as praising North Korea. For the film, Jung Yoon-suk employs hybrid visual languages of live action records, computer graphics, and typographic imagery to create several music video sequences associated with their songs and performances. As Jung explains in an interview, the use of these languages is intended to visually translate the auditory and lyrical components of the band's songs in stylistic ways that intersect with his handheld camera capturing their visceral performances: "In terms of the film's graphic design, I did all CG work using only the basic templates in Final Cut X in the same way as the band did with the PowerPoint slides for their performance. Likewise, its typography was designed by recombining with fonts provided by default in the software's editing tools, except the North Korean font that I downloaded."[11] Accordingly, the MV sequences share the extravaganza look characterized by their dense layers. The visual track of the song

Figure 7.1 *Bamseom Pirates Seoul Inferno* (Jung Yoon-suk, 2017)

"Commands from North Korean Communists" (*Pukkoeŭi chiryŏng*), for instance, comprises fragments of a 1970s propaganda film sponsored by Korean Anti-communism Association, as well as North Korean typographic images of its lyrical components (figure 7.1). The archival imagery is surrounded by its kaleidoscopically distorted counterparts, thus resonating with the band's indescribably loud music that falls somewhere between grindcore punk and black metal. The visual density and distortion stresses the song's sarcastic appropriation of North Korea, which corresponds to the song's lyrical lines, such as "Commands from North Korean communists," "Hail Kim Jung-il," and "We love the Communist Party," all of which playfully critique the National Security Law and anticommunism. This entertaining quasi propaganda, however, ultimately leads to the band's vanguard assault on the social and economic issues of contemporary Korea, as the same North Korean typographic images present such commands as "Increase the welfare budget," "Guarantee three labor rights," and "Cut tuition." Here it becomes evident that Jung's hybrid visual languages of the moving image translate the political performativity of the band into the aesthetic performativity of sound and image.

How to Stop Being Korean (*Han'guginŭl kwandunŭn pŏp*, Ahn Kearn-hyung, 2018, 120 min.) investigates the historical roots of contemporary Korean far-right nationalism represented by the Taegeukgi (Korean flag) Rallies, a phenomenon that became particularly noticeable after President Park Geun-hye's impeachment in 2017. The film's first part is seen as a fake documentary narrated by the "Voice of Opportunity," an imaginary radio of the Committee of the Peninsular Opportunist Association. Based on the adaptation of Choi

226 Post-activism

In-hoon's novel *The Voice of the Governor General* (*Chŏngdogŭi sori*, 196768, 1976), a text that explores the ways in which the official ethno-nationalism of the Park Chung-hee regime reproduces the imperialist ideology of the Japanese colonial period, Ahn's script for the "Voice of Opportunity" takes the form of a transcript of a male and a female narrator, who inform their audience that the power of the Japanese governor, which had laid the foundation of opportunism (*kihoejuŭi*), has been persistent in the Korean Peninsula even after the Japanese exited it after the August 1945 surrender. When the voices' didactic and propagandistic messages are juxtaposed with Ahn's footage of the Taegeukgi Rallies, their seemingly anachronistic tone turns out to resonate with the ideological unconscious of the participants in the rallies, that is, the attachment to the ethno-nationalism of the Park regime that they believed would be rejuvenated by Park Geun-hye's presidency. This is supported by the film's second part, which consist of a rich archival accumulation of texts, newspaper articles, and photos that reveal the history of opportunism from the Japanese Occupation era (excerpts from pro-Japanese [*ch'inil*] lyrics, poems, and novels) to the Rhee Syngman government and to the Park regime (newspaper articles and photos that feature people's worship of their greatness). By intersecting the heyday of opportunism with its distorted or ruined present, the multiple devices employed for *How to Stop Being Korean*—the script, the voices, and the constructed archive—do more than operate the postdocumentary diversion that blurs truth and fiction, and historical discourse and its parody: they encapsulate fake documentaries' formal richness in the sense that they are used to "do and undo the documentary form, the film's subject (theme, topic, storyline, characters), and the moral and social orders."[12] What is notable in Ahn's project to reveal the "moral and social orders" of opportunism is his use of digital stop-motion technique to capture and express the Taegeukgi Rallies, so that the movements of the Korean flags and participants are blurred like crooked waves. According to Ahn, this obscure yet poignant visuality of the footage results from his deliberate juxtaposition of the slowed frames of the same photographic object with the frames at a standard rate, as well as his deliberate rearrangement of the frames in nonchronological order.[13] These two procedures render the resulting images of the rallies marked by the tension between photographic stillness and cinematic motion. In this way, they reveal the participants' psychic and ideological dimension, which would remain unnoticed if the footage had been shot at the standard rate. The tension of stillness and movement, then, also lays claim to the overlapping of the past (the time of Park's ethno-nationalism) with the present (that of the Taegeukgi Rallies) as Ahn's historical consciousness, which underlies his wide-ranging research on the archival materials related to opportunism.

VR Documentary

Virtual reality has increasingly been adapted to various subgenres of film during the last several years. Many university laboratories specializing in media art, as well as film production and financing companies including Barunson E&A (the production company of Bong Joon-ho's *Parasite* [2019]), have been experimenting with VR films across fiction, documentary, and animation for entertainment and educational uses, fueled by the production- and development-supporting programs of the Korea Creative Content Agency, and by the major film festivals' launching of the special section showcasing them, including the Busan International Film Festival's VR Cinema, which started in 2017.[14] The Korean film industry's growing recognition of VR as a promising technology for innovating cinematic storytelling and experience has centered upon the rhetoric of immersion, through which the participant feels as if submerged into the image space surrounding her. As Yoo Young-gun of CGV (the leading multiplex cinema chain in Korea) states, "Visual elements are not enough to accomplish what VR is up to, which is to expand to a form of storytelling with its immersive characteristics maximized."[15] Immersion has indeed been raised as a key trope that has driven many practitioners across the globe to venture into VR nonfiction artifacts, which are expected to offer experiences of reality and history that are unavailable from the standardized cinematic apparatus based on the viewer's stationary frontal position, the frame and two dimensionality of the image, and the distance between the viewer and the screen. For instance, Chris Milk, an interactive media artist who has played a vital role in stretching virtual reality into a new canvas for storytelling, argues in his TED talk that "VR feels like truth—you feel present in the world you are inside and present with the people you are inside of it with," while also establishing it as the "ultimate empathy machine."[16] Also, Nonny de la Peña has introduced the concept of "immersive journalism" as producing a news form in which people can gain first-person experiences of the events or situation described in news stories, one that allows "the participant . . . to actually enter a virtually recreated scenario representing the news story."[17] The trope of immersion, however, is achieved only through VR's optical illusion or its activation of the user's sensory responses. As I have argued elsewhere, the experiences of immersion and SoP (sense of presence) in VR are ineluctably premised on the negotiation of two visions that seemingly contradict each other: first, a disembodied vision that transports viewers to a simulated world, and second, an embodied vision guaranteed by the freedom to control kinesthetic movement and direction of gaze.[18]

The idea of immersion as a negotiated aesthetic experience is relevant to explaining the controversy surrounding the first episode (2020, 52 min.) of *Meeting You* (*Nŏrŭl mannatta*), a series of human documentaries produced by and aired on Munhwa Broadcasting Corporation (MBC). It features MBC's project to recreate Nayeon, who died of a mysterious illness aged seven in 2017, for her mother Jang Ji-sung in collaboration with six VR studios.[19] After being exposed to the interviews with her that are interspersed with observational vignettes of the family, viewers shuffle between Jang in her VR accoutrements surrounded by green screens in the studio and what she sees in her headset, including the digitally composited scenes of her meeting with Nayeon's avatar: the virtual daughter invites Jang to touch her, and they sit together at a table set with a birthday cake. The film's alternation between Jang's perspective (inside the VR environment) and the behind-the-scene processes (its outside) indeed bespeaks the ambivalent aspect of VR in regard to its quest for creating an immersive and embodied mode of storytelling. The realistic rendering of Nayeon's avatar, the sensors responsive to Jang's interaction with it, and the avatar's response to her inputs, including changes in facial expression, all contribute to empowering Jang's emotional and affective immersion in the world where she affectively experiences the temporary resurrection of Nayeon. The behind-the-scene elements, such as the green screens, the headset, and the graphic 360-degree space that encloses Jang, however, all testify to the otherworldliness of the VR environment distinct from her phenomenal reality, coupled with the scripted aspects of her exchanges with the avatar. As Violet Kim rightly observes, these production details of *Meeting You* "suggest less an independently realistic VR creation . . . than one whose significance is based on the narrative history of the family, and subject to the manipulation of the documentary producers."[20] This ambivalence in the VR environment, marked by the coexistence of Jang's embodied vision and the environment's disembodied viewpoint preconstructed and administered by the production team lies at the heart of the mixed responses to *Meeting You*: "While some people praise the 'creative' use of the new technology, others criticize it for being 'emotionally manipulative.'"[21]

Despite the two extreme reactions that it stirred, the VR project featured in *Meeting You* helps one to identify a particular mode of documentary practice to which VR is more convincingly applied, namely, nonfiction artifacts based on the reenactment of historical events or mnemonic realities. In the current applications of 360-degree spherical video to documentaries, the subjects of reenactment encompass, like theatrical and television documentaries, experimental film and video, and media installations, "the place of memory, testimony, and narrative construction in historical knowledge . . . the imaginary and fantasmatic aspects of character and performance in documentary film and media, and the role of documentary in the construction of social fantasy; the therapeutic value of reenactment; [and] the uses of embodiment in various kinds of learning and pedagogy."[22] Bill Nichols's formulation of reenactment as a set of fantasmatic styles that foreground the embodied restaging of memory and knowledge alludes to the reason that many VR documentaries have increasingly adopted and reworked it: "Reenactments, like other poetic and rhetorical tropes, bring desire itself into being and with it *the fantasmatic domain* wherein *the temporality of lived experience . . . find[s] embodiment*."[23] Here, the "fantasmatic domain" is what VR's disembodied vision convincingly offers with its capacity to transport the user. The viewer's embodied vision is linked to the "lived experience" of the social actor associated with the memory or account of an event depicted in the virtual space. Considering these two effects, the reenactment-based VR documentaries are seen as remediating the performative mode of documentary that "underscores *the complexity of our knowledge of the world by emphasizing its subjective and affective dimensions*."[24] The VR documentaries of Gina Kim and Kwon Hayoun attest to the successful remediation of the performative mode, as they deliberately negotiate VR's embodied vision and disembodied perspective to offer viewers the opportunity to have an affective experience of the traumatic event or memory in the past that is distinct from the camera's inscription of profilmic reality, to encounter the constructedness of its virtually restaged world, and to reflect on their ethical position faced with the event or memory.

Gina Kim's *Bloodless* (*Tongduch'ŏn*, 2017, 17 min.) deals with the traumatic and repressed memories of the military sex workers that served the US Army in *kijich'on*, followed by another VR documentary, *Tearless* (*Soyosan*, 2021, 12 min.), that transports viewers to a "Monkey House" (see chapter 5) virtually recreated based on their memories. It imaginatively reconstructs the last living moments of a real-life sex worker named Yoon Keum-yi, who was brutally murdered by a US soldier at the Dongducheon *kijich'on* in 1992. In reconstructing the last hours of Yoon's life, Kim deliberately negotiates between VR's embodied perspective for its viewer and its 360-degree field of vision to avoid exploiting the footage that would reproduce the original violence. In so doing, she associates the viewer's experience of SoP (Sense of Presence) in the past with different subjective viewpoints that evoke the fantasmatic elements of the reenactment. Kim's statement is clearly indicative of these two purposes to eschew what Brian Winston has called the "tradition of the victim" in Griersonian documentary on social problems.[25]

230 Post-activism

> With VR, *the viewer is no longer a passive spectator, who can take voyeuristic pleasure from a spectacle in front of them (and at a distance)*. Upon realizing the potential of the VR, I came up with a way to tell the same violent story, *without showing and exploiting the image of her.* After studying the neighborhood where she lived and worked, *obsessively walking in loops around the brothels, mimicking her itinerary on the night of her murder, I determined to have her ghost guide us: to the perfectly preserved dilapidated streets, the club that she met the soldier, and finally the small room she was mutilated and died.*[26]

The film's two-part structure demonstrates how VR's spherical vision and spatial structure are effectively used to remediate the performative mode of documentary that renders history and memory as the intertwining of subjective and factual components. Its first part, comprised of thirteen spherical shots filmed on location, follows the trajectory of Yoon by transporting viewers into the contemporary streets of Dongducheon as the site of the former camptown. The 360-degree video is used to create the omnidirectional, seamless images of the streets' details, the nearly empty roads and stores from day to night. The viewers' SoP in the streets is heightened thanks to the video space's separation from their phenomenal reality, but it is unclear what character they can identify with, because the scenes of the streets are presented without any directions about where to look. Instead, the film's intertitles, which present the historical demography of a million prostitutes over ninety-eight US camptowns since the end of the Korean War, encourage viewers to use their freedom to control the direction of viewing to explore and embody the persistence of the past, whose trace is no longer visible in the streets of the present. The viewers' embodied vision is then channeled into the sound of clicking heels that can be heard from a distance in accordance with the falling of darkness, and with the gradual transition from the panoramic to the compressed view. In the course of these changes, a woman in an attractive outfit and heavy makeup appears and passes by, with the sound of the heels getting louder and then diminishing. As the space is further compressed into narrow alleyways, viewers' gaze is cut by her sudden appearance right in front of them. The viewers' confrontation with her bodily presence is so close as to almost cover their field of vision. While the vivid sensory and visual stimuli imposed on the viewers are intended to maximize experience of immersion and presence, on one hand, the woman's appearance and disappearance and the transition of the shots do not fail to indicate VR's disembodied vision, a vision whose viewpoint is fluid and indeterminate and which is out of the viewers' control. Since viewers' embodied gaze must be identified with the vision for their immersive experience, the first part of *Bloodless* activates multiple viewpoints that they occupy during navigational exploration of the streets: from the viewpoint of an external explorer to that of a customer who is looking for a sex worker, and to that of the perpetrator who will kill the victim. By allowing the viewer to be aware of these multiple points of identification as well as the transition between them, the first part heightens the sense of immersion and presence while also creating a critical distance from it. It is through this ambivalent experience that *Bloodless* offers viewers an avenue for making an empathic relationship with the victim and for posing an ethical question on the potential correspondence between their viewpoint and that of the perpetrator.

The film's second and last part, a three-minute single-take scene, constructs a panoramic view of the victim's small, dirty room as her workplace, giving viewers an impression that they float in space. This static view continues until blood slowly flows out from beneath the blanket and gradually diffuses on the floor. Here, the 360-degree scene does more than create the experience of SoP in the scene of violence. It also enables viewers to contemplatively observe the fantasmatic reenactment of the scene, triggering their inability to react to violence and their sympathetic relationship with the victim. The fantasmatic aspect of this scene is further strengthened in the sense that the victim's body remains invisible in the room: it appears only on the mirror on the left side of the room two minutes after the beginning of the scene. It is possible, then, to conjecture that the victim, who appeared in the first part, witnesses her own death in her spectral presence, occupying the same viewpoint as the viewer. It is in this way that the scene's fantasmatic elements and its 360-degree space invite the viewer to have an intersubjective, embodied relationship with the victim as ghost, or, to temporarily become a ghost. As Kim remarks regarding *Bloodless*, "In this work viewers are able to have an uncanny experience in which they become a strange, indeterminable entity—neither victim nor voyeur."[27] This device of the viewer's becoming-ghost, in my view, strives to avoid the risk of "improper distance," namely, users' tendency to "[prioritize] their own experience of transportation and exploration . . . over engagement with the testimony of the other"[28] in their experience of humanitarian VR projects that endow them with a proximate encounter with the other in pain and suffering. By propelling the viewer to recognize the moral demand and risk implicit in VR, this last chilling moment of *Bloodless* demonstrates how it can creatively be deployed to remediate the performative mode of documentary that posits reality and history as permeated by imagination and subjective experience.

Kwon Hayoun's *489 Years* (*489nyŏn*, 2016, 11 min.) refers to the length of time that it would putatively take to clear the DMZ of its more than one million mines. This VR animated film is in line with a trend in twenty-first-century

232 Post-activism

art exemplified by postwar generation artists who "endeavor to engage spectators kinesthetically and affectively by means of emphatic 'seeing' . . . in order to compensate for the impossibility of experiencing the 'real' trauma of [the] DMZ."[29] The film draws on the voice-over of a former South Korean soldier named Mr. Kim recounting his duty and experience on patrol in the DMZ at night, while also utilizing the 3D computer-generated imagery that reconstructs his memory. The computer-generated images built in the videogame-like virtual environment in a sense offer viewer a vivid, realistic representation of what the former solider might have witnessed and experienced in regard to the border zone that people are aware of yet tend to imagine due to its underlying political, military, and ideological contexts: namely, a kind of forbidden zone onto which South Koreans' collective imagination on North Korea as their ambivalent Other, on its military tension, and on its nearly untouched natural ecosystem have been projected. In order to depict the DMZ as the liminal space in which an array of dichotomies are blurred and mutually permeated, such as the opposition between military violence and fascination with nature, and the geopolitical reality of North-South division and the soldier's personal experience in the zone, the artist deploys the first-person-shooting perspective guided by the virtual camera to invite the viewer to identify with and embody Mr. Kim's perception and memory, through which the viewer is placed in the midst of his transformative nocturnal journey. The result is at once informative and uncanny, a performative reenactment of traumatic reality overlaid with fear and ethereal dream.

These ambivalent aesthetic and emotional aspects in *489 Years* reflect the artist's conceptual and technical approaches to VR's immersive spatial design and 3D CGI (computer-generated imagery). While the artist considers VR's navigable space and its first-person perspective to create the viewer's SoP in the reenacted mental and natural landscape of DMZ, she also thinks of VR's 3D animation as the means to express the subjective dimension of Mr. Kim's memory and to trigger the viewer's distanced reflection on his testimony. This idea is reinforced by the fusion of both realistic and hyperrealistic impressions that its CGI creates. As Kwon remarks, "In virtual reality, there is no frame, we are completely immersed in it so in a way is more difficult than cinema. . . . using animation [VR] allows me to keep a distance and to assume the subjectivity of artist . . . after all, the truth is not fixed. Truth is so subjective and is always in the process of being transformed."[30]

While this statement validates Kwon's idea of VR as a mediated empathy machine, there is a key moment of *489 Years* in which viewers' sensory experience dynamically shifts from their immersive navigation of the animated DMZ space to a distanced reflection on their empathy with Mr. Kim. It starts with Kim's recounting of his night patrol through the DMZ, during which he found an unmarked minefield. Amplified by the sound effects of heartbeats and background noises of the forest, his nervousness and fear grow stronger as the virtual camera is synchronized with Kim's movements, including his lying on the ground, with which the viewers' embodied vision is performatively identified. When Mr. Kim says that at the end of the twenty-minute emergency he could turn his attention to the beauty of surrounding nature, the virtual camera leaves his POV and flies above the forest, thus providing a aerial view of the whole landscape of the DMZ. The view is transcendental and disembodied because it does not originate from the viewers' change of direction. It is nevertheless linked to Mr. Kim's imagination of what impressed him most during his service in the DMZ. The camera then pans across the whole landscape of the barbed-wire fences that mark the DMZ, whose panoramic view turns out to be Mr. Kim's fantasmatic recreation. For the film ends with a series of fire explosions on the fences. This fantasy-like ending suggests that the factuality of Mr. Kim's testimony is inseparable from the subjective reconstruction of his experience and memory, onto which his impression of mines and flowers and his hope for peace and unification are projected. In short, the climactic and final scenes of *489 Years* derive from VR's creative interplay of the embodied and disembodied visions, of empathic witness and distanced observation, and of the factual account and the fantasmatic work inasmuch as it is employed for documentary's take on the traumatic experiences of the political, ideological, and military borders.

Infographics, CGI, and Subjunctive Documentary on the Sewol Ferry Disaster

CGI flourished in documentary production during the latter half of 2010s. Although this trend does not result in an animated nonfiction film that consists of graphic images in its entirety, simulations and infographics have increasingly been used in recent documentaries that reconstruct past events and unravel information, knowledge, and argument on previously unearthed facts or truths. The films that have led this trend are grounded in the mode of alternative investigative journalism (see chapter 3), in that they were derived from Project Bu (P'ŭrojekt'ŭ pu), an initiative that popular liberal journalist Kim Eo-jun established in 2015 to produce documentaries aimed at offering alternative information and views on key political and social issues of contemporary Korea in opposition to mainstream right-wing news media. Based on Kim's collaboration with veteran documentary filmmaker Kim Ji-yeong, the

234 Post-activism

project has made *The Intention* (*Kŭnal, pada*, 2018, 110 min.) and *Ghost Ship* (*Yuryŏngsŏn*, 2020, 49 min.), two films on the hidden truth of the sinking of the Sewol Ferry. Both extensively present infographics and CGI, juxtaposing them with a voice-over narration and interviews with professionals or other social actors. In so doing, they not only gained commercial successes in the theatrical exhibition of local documentary films but also provoked debates in the public sphere regarding their hypotheses and conclusions about the truth and fact of the disaster.[31]

What has remained under scrutiny is that the digitally animated expressions play a crucial role in supporting a certain rhetorical mode of documentary that structures the two films. I am interested in examining what kind of mode those expressions serve to develop, what sort of epistemological value this mode is built on, and what kind of truth the films claim, while also evaluating their achievements and limitations. Both are built upon what Mark J. P. Wolf has called the "subjunctive mode." By this, Wolf means a subgenre of documentary "concerned with what *could be, would be, or might have been*,"[32] one that conveys not simply information on an actual object or event but also speculation and hypothesis about it. In the era of computer imaging, this type of documentary tends to employ simulated images to indicate and reconstruct such an object or event, which the photographic camera or human vision unable to observe, or which only mathematical constructs, such as fractal objects, rotating hypercubes, and other geometric forms, can illustrate. As a primary case of subjunctive documentary, Wolf points to films that illustrate scientific discovery, theory, and hypothesis, but his further remark allows us to associate it with documentary usages other than the visualization of scientific research, medical experiments, product design and testing, and architectural simulation: namely, "objects and situations that are thought to have existed or that could exist in the material world."[33] In other words, the subjunctive mode can be applied to any past event whose photographic evidence might be absent or unavailable, an event that awaits further investigation and speculation.

In this regard, the subjunctive mode's activation of reconstructing the event recall Linda Williams's insight into two contradictory ways in which films of "New Documentary" have undermined an essence of truth through a set of textual strategies—including reenactment—designed to present contingent and relative truths of a past that is often unrepresentable, traumatic, and violent: "On the one hand the postmodern deluge of images seems to suggest that there can be no *a priori* truth of the referent to which the image refers; on the other hand, in this same deluge, it is still the moving image that has the power to move audiences to a new appreciation of previously unknown truth."[34] In the subjunctive documentary aimed at reconstructing that kind of past event or object, digitally animated or graphic imagery is effectively used to question an official version of its truth and instead to present alternative or "previously unknown" truths due to its double aesthetic figurations that have been applied to contemporary science documentary. On the one hand, that kind of graphic expression includes numbers, maps, graphs, tables that "enable often complex natural and social phenomena to be introduced and explained in easily digested ways,"[35] as well as geometric reconstructions of events where there exists no photographic record. Along with this symbolic exposition of information and facts that has traditionally been used in science documentary, its contemporary counterparts often employ photorealistic CGI that aesthetically fulfills the viewer's quest for authenticity with its visual resemblance to the referent in reality "in the service of dramatic reconstruction"[36] of historical events, on the other. The two documentaries on the Sewol Ferry Disaster develop their subjunctive investigation and reconstruction of the recent past events whose truth has remained unknown, contingent and contested, by blending these two representational strategies of digitally animated visualization that shuffle between mimesis and abstraction.

The Intention and *Ghost Ship* apply a kind of conspiracy theory to the mystery of the sinking of the ferry. Drawing on numerous sources of data, including those from the ship (named *Doola Ace*) that witnessed the ferry's sinking first and the radar logs of ships submitted by the Korean Coast Guard, *The Intention* casts doubt on the Park Geun-hye government's explanation that the disaster was caused by the ferry's cargo overload and the crew's inexperienced steering. The data from the ferry's automatic identification system (AIS), which register information on a ship's registration number, nationality, latitude, longitude, speed, direction, and angle, are given particular importance in the film's investigative approach to the cause of the incident, given that the government submitted them during the trial of its crew as key evidence of their mistaken handling of the ferry's wheel. By decoding and analyzing the data with a computer, the film's production team strives to prove that some of them do not match the government's explanation of the ferry's speed and route before it sank. The ferry's abnormal operation around 7:00 a.m. on April 16, 2014, is also demonstrated as the team cross-checks the data from that time, which indicate a dramatic increase in the frequency of transmission and a sudden increase in speed. This is juxtaposed with testimonies of survivors who felt trembling of the left front of the ferry, footage of the cameras installed in its cargo hold, and videos that several student victims in the cabins filmed with their mobile phones. Finally, the film compares the information on the ferry's location of sinking from the Jindo VTS (Vessel Traffic

236 Post-activism

Service) Center with what the captain of the *Doola Ace* recorded, showing that these two accounts do not match. Based on those findings, supported by interviews with maritime professionals and physicists, the film ultimately puts forward its hypothetical claims that the ferry's AIS data were manipulated and that the real cause of the sharp turn to the left that survivors felt before the sinking was because its left anchor hit the sea bottom. *Ghost Ship*, a sequel to *The Intention*, pushes the claim about the government's data manipulation further, supporting it with computational analysis of the AIS data and comments from experts. This time, the production team discovered that the Sewol Ferry's AIS data, revealed by the Park government, might originate not from its real operations but from somewhere in Shenzhen, a southern city in China. Based on this discovery, the film develops further claims: that an unknown hacker in the city was commissioned (allegedly by the government) to manipulate the data and transplant them to the VTS centers around the accident site; and that the hacker had to fabricate data from thousands of ships near it in order to make them believable—in the words of the team, "to move the trajectory of one ship, someone had to move those of thousands of ships." This suggests that there were certain ships that exist in the data but have never existed in reality. Herein lies the film's title, *Ghost Ship*.

The two documentaries on the disaster extensively employ CGI, maps, and other animated imagery to develop subjunctive reconstructions of what might have happened on the day of the disaster and thereafter, speculation on the cause of the sinking, and the government's manipulation of data. They commonly start with the infographic method, through which the AIS data as pure numbers are translated into lines, curves, and dots on a map of the sea. These abstract figures help viewers to intuitively recognize the information that a photographic record could not convey and instead only the AIS data indicate, by illustrating the latitude, longitude, direction, and speed of the ferry. The data also function as significant signs in themselves when *The Intention* presents which numbers of them are abnormal and when *Ghost Ship* compares two AIS data sets, the first set stored at the VTS centers and the second sent to other ships. This visualization, which aims to demonstrate the government's fabrication of the AIS data, is then extended into the two films' exploitation of what José van Dijck has called the "pictorial effect" in CGI-based scientific documentary. By this, she means the use of digital animations to "areas that conventionally resist visualization, such as the very abstract, remote, or inaccessible." By satisfying the demand for photographic verisimilitude, the digital animations allow "visual substantiation of conditional, hypothetical, or even speculative scientific claims stating 'this could have happened in the past' or 'this is what could happen, if . . .'"[37] In *The*

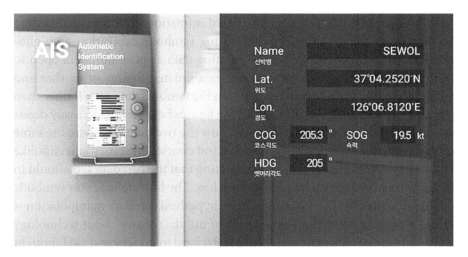

Figure 7.2 *The Intention* (Kim Ji-yeong, 2018)

Intention, the production team deliberately employs computer-generated images of the ferry based on the software's three-dimensional modeling and rendering, blending visual constructedness with resemblance (figure 7.2). The simulations of the ferry's turning to the left and of the passengers' falling to the deck are presented with an array of lines against the backdrop of the black-and-blue background, so that they appear less to be the photographic record of the real voyage than the hypothetical visualizations of how it might have occurred. This type of pictorial effect is strengthened as the computer-generated images are juxtaposed with the 2D simulation of the ferry's trajectory made by a laboratory of the Korean Maritime and Ocean University, which focuses on illustrating the gravitational impact on its left side at the time of the sinking. Simultaneously, those purely mathematical constructs of the ship turn out to have a powerful realistic effect, inasmuch as their rendered details sufficiently represent some aspect of the real vessel in the physical world, and they are seamlessly interwoven with footage from cargo cams (which document quaking of the vehicles aboard), CCTV records of the ferry's interior, and victims' videos that bear witness to its sharp tilting. Here it becomes evident that the simulations of the ferry do more than document a probable reconstruction of the event: thanks to their photographic realism, the simulations function as what Annabelle Honess Roe has called "mimetic substitution," a representational strategy of animated documentary to illustrate something (in the case of *The Intention*, the ferry on the day of the disaster) "that would be very hard, or impossible, to show with the conventional live-action alternative."[38]

Ghost Ship varies the techniques of digital animation while also maintaining the propensity for data visualization, fusing symbolic exposition with photorealistic dramatization. Besides presenting data as pure numbers open to computational analysis, the film also uses animated figures of mother and child to illustrate the relationship between the two AIS data sets. Rather than pursuing photographic verisimilitude, the figures help viewers to easily digest complex knowledge of the AIS, namely, how the two data sets share the same information on a ship's location, velocity, and course. The fancy and childlike rendering is also the case with demonstrating that the two data sets should in principle be stored only in the ship's black box. The film's reliance on symbolic graphics for the didactic exposition of its hypothesis on data manipulation is indeed what director Kim Ji-yeong had in mind: "A story about technology could scare viewers because they could feel it hard to understand. So I thought that fancy and childlike characters could make it easier to approach."[39] Those familiar figures side with the film's opening, which presents the dramatic reconstruction of how the hacker in Shenzhen manipulated the data. Here the sequence was rendered with the Unreal Engine, a game engine developed for the first-person shooting game *Unreal* in 1988. Given this technical asset, this type of imaging uses Machinima as the real-time computer graphics engine to produce cinematic 3D animation sequences. The engine is capable of not only rendering 3D characters and sets equipped with photographic resemblance but also operating its virtual camera, whose viewpoints "refer to the established domain of film cameras."[40] The film's opening Machinima sequence fulfills the demand for a dramatic reconstruction of an event in virtual space as it tells a story about the hacker's fabrication of AIS data, creation of a Swedish "ghost ship" that has only a communication number, and the hacker's encounter with unidentified clients who ask him to manipulate the AIS data related to the ferry. While foregrounding the artifice of the characters and sets due to their low level of photorealism, the variety of shot sizes and viewpoints applied to this sequence helps to create the cinematic impression of reality, which in turn amplifies the film's subjunctive claim on how and why the Park government tried to conceal certain information on the incident.

What kind of achievements do the two subjunctive documentaries make vis-à-vis Korean documentary cinema, a field in which many films are still predicated upon the camera's activist registration of social realities and actors to guarantee political commitment? First, digital imaging's capacities to make both abstract visualizations and pictorially realistic effects expand documentary cinema's construction of facts and truths beyond the camera's reach and visibility, so that it is able not simply to present evidence of reality but also to unveil its hidden or unknown dimensions and to develop speculative claims on its probable truths. Second, the two films' foregrounding of data as their key material reveals scientific empiricism as their common epistemological ground, inasmuch as they focus on investigating and analyzing the data to undergird their claims of truths and facts. Here, infographics and CGI are used as the scientific instrument for discovery and revelation, two functions that were built into the camera, and by extension, the cinematographic apparatus in the nineteenth century. Considering this tradition, Brian Winston has argued that direct cinema's adoption of the camera to collect and unearth reality established the epistemological assumption that "documentary becomes scientific inscription—evidence."[41] Seen in this context, the various visualizations of data in the two films signal that digital imaging is now given as much scientific weight as the camera, and that the former is particularly efficient to providing evidence and truth claims of realities that are invisible or elusive to the latter. This is particularly evident in that the infographics and CGI are predicated upon the scientific empiricism of data visualization, according to which seeing is believing and thinking. As data visualization pioneer Edward Tufte argues, data visualization with mapped pictures, lines, curves, and diagrams serves to demonstrate "how empirical observations turn into explanations and evidence" inasmuch as it is derived from the "universal principles of analytical thinking."[42]

Simultaneously, however, the two films' reliance on infographics and CGI results in several limitations to their subjunctive mode. First, their repetitive display of the AIS data, often coupled with dynamic motion, aims to capture the viewer's attention, presenting the information as visually arresting and pleasurable (i.e., spectacular images). The spectacle of data, then, brings a kind of fetishism to the two films' scientific empiricism, mythologizing their subjunctive reconstructions and speculations of past events, obscuring flaws in their truth claims, and sealing off possibilities for counterarguments. The numbers of the data as spectacle also obscure the fundamental impossibility of representing the computational dimensions of the digital, its codes, algorithms, and processing, an impossibility that renowned media theorists such as Alexander R. Galloway and Wendy Hui Kyong Chun have underlined.[43] That is, the numbers tell nothing about, and show nothing of, the details of the system, but the two films' spectacular display of them results in reinforcing the belief that they are the key evidence of the data manipulation. The AIS data are displayed on the director's computer, on the diagrams, and on the maps of the ocean, while also being translated into the photorealistic reconstruction of what might have happened to the ferry and how a Swedish ghost ship could have been fabricated to conceal the data manipulation. In this way, the two films

240 Post-activism

attempt to present the AIS data as evidence of their speculative claims, but they bypass any other possibilities than the conspiracy theory for the data's mismatch with the real trajectory and location of the ferry. Consequently, the two films present the AIS data as not just factual evidence but also objects of seeing as such, leaving unproblematic their common epistemological assumption that seeing is believing.

Second, the two films' spectacular treatment of data with infographics and CGI ultimately reinforces the authority of the experts who persuade viewers to believe in a conspiracy theory in the name of scientific truth and veracity. Discussing the rhetoric of the visual spectacle of data in animated documentaries, Leon Gurevitch argues that "experts often act as qualifying forces, leading the viewer through the significance of a set of data or explaining the implications of a simulation and the data that underpin it."[44] The presence of the various experts that lend their authority to the two films' claims is so obvious that any visual forms, such as the footage of cargo cams and the victims' videos in *The Intention*, serve only to support their commentaries and testimonies. It is also in this way that infographics and animated simulations are rhetorically used, inasmuch as they act as "a visual language that does not simply function to explain the apparent facts of a situation, but also to persuade the viewer that they are party to visual information created by, and normally consumed by, the expert."[45] The two films' association between their subjunctive mode and the authority of the experts is most obvious in the appearance of Kim Eo-jun throughout. Regarding his starring role in *The Intention*, Kim Ji-yeong has remarked: "How boring it could be if it told a story about data from beginning to end! If the film's narrative centers on Kim Eo-jun, who is stating surprising facts throughout the world, it will help general audiences to understand difficult information more easily."[46] While partially facilitating this informative effect, Kim's authoritative voice in the two films ultimately forces their scientific empiricism (which underlies the uses of the multiplied visual forms and experts) to serve his conspiracy theories. Herein lie the two films' deadlock: their conspiracy theory obscures deep-seated structural problems posed by the political and social events that the two films revisit, that is, the crisis of the governmental security that deals with national disasters, and the trauma of the bereaved families of the victims. It is here that *Two Doors* (*Tu kaeŭi mun*, Kim Il-rhan and Hong Ji-yoo, 2011, 99 min.), a controversial film that investigates and reconstructs what happened on the day of the Yongsan Massacre, is read as achieving a politically meaningful leap using the subjunctive mode, as it eschews the fetishistic belief in scientific empiricism and pursues a different approach to digital documentary production.

The Digital Turn **241**

The Battle of the Apparatuses: *Two Doors*

Two Doors, produced by the collective PINKS (see chapter 3), is one of the best-known and most controversial documentaries that spotlight the Yongsan Massacre. The film's controversial aspects can be found in the tragedy's political and legal dimensions, which encompass who caused the fire between the police and the protesters, and who was responsible for the deaths of both dissident citizens and a young policeman. Interestingly enough, the film also stirred debates among veteran independent documentarians about its strategic and representational deviations from the activist works in the late 1980s and 1990s that aimed to speak with and for the urban poor who had been forced to leave their town by the government's pursuit of urban redevelopment and beautification. Kim Dong-won, who laid the foundation for the activist documentaries' political commitment to the evictees' right to survive, said in his conversation with Hong Hyung-sook: "From the standpoint of the traditional documentary that privileges the power of recording, *Two Doors* might seem like a film made without effort."[47] Here Kim contrasts the film's extensive appropriation and assemblage of existing materials relating to the incident with a filmmaker's *hyŏnjang* recording of the struggles of the evictees based on living among them or becoming part of their lives, with its raw images conveying affective forces demanding social change. Kim's skepticism about the film's lack of on-the-spot scenes indeed relates to its different focus on the issue of urban redevelopment, unlike the traditional activist films that privileged the evictees' perspective and addressed their community. Unlike Kim's films and other activist documentaries that established socially disenfranchised people, as both their subject and their primary audience, *Two Doors* does not include interviews with evictees involved in the demonstration or the bereaved families of the victims, which would be used to defend their position against state power and the right-wing press that stigmatized them as "rioters" (*p'okto*). The subjunctive mode of documentary that the film's codirectors adopt, then, indirectly responds to those two strains of criticism while also marking its rhetorical and aesthetic departures from the strata of activist documentary.

The film's subjunctive mode reconstructs the incident in two series. The first series retrieves the progression of the incident according to a timeline that spans the Seoul Metropolitan Police Agency's orders to the SWAT team on January 19, 2009, the team's arrival in Yongsan at 3:30 a.m. on January 20, the entrance of its agents into Namildang at 6:20, the agents' attempt to enter the lookout at 6:50, the first fire inside the lookout at 7:06, and the critical second fire at 7:20. This timeline is interspersed with the second series, which reconstructs

242 Post-activism

the trial of the seven evictees who were charged with starting the fire that killed the squad, without any member of the SWAT team being indicted for killing the five protesters. In order to develop these two series, the film's directors interweave a rich, heterogeneous array of documentary components. There are interviews with attorneys of the accused, activists from an NGO's fact investigation committee, and a media activist of Color TV, a guerrilla-type internet broadcasting group that originated in the New Progressive Party (Chinbo shindang) in 2008, all of whom offer different—juridical, political, and humanitarian—accounts of and perspectives on the issues surrounding the incident, including what really happened on the day, what was witnessed at the street, what was problematic in the police's operations of suppressing the demonstration, and how the trials went on. These accounts are juxtaposed with voice reenactments and transcripts of the testimonies by the SWAT agents who were involved in the police operations, voice recordings of interrogations of the team's agents as witnesses by prosecutors and defense attorneys, the agents' statements, and, most significantly, CCTV records of the street where the incident took place, live footage taken from distance by Color TV and another guerrilla broadcasting group Sajahoo TV, and video evidence produced and submitted by the police. Applying those heterogeneous materials to its fact-finding process, the film develops the two series into a kind of storytelling that is unfamiliar to the traditional activist documentaries, one reminiscent of Errol Morris's *The Thin Blue Line* (1988), which dexterously blends thriller-style dramatic reenactments with a quasi-forensic investigation into the trial of a murder case of a police officer in 1976. The film's reconstruction of the trials mobilizes its investigative approach, situating spectators in the position of the jurors who were indeed absent in the trials.[48] Its reconstruction of the incident itself, coupled with dreary music and recurrent images of the fire in the lookout at 7:20 a.m., creates the dramatic atmosphere that encourages viewers to feel engrossed in its scenes in real time. Critic Maeng Soo-Jin comments on the immersive thriller effect of the film's storytelling as follows: "It is hard for viewers to escape the nightmare of witnessing where even breathing becomes difficult as if putting a stone on the chest."[49] Indeed, this spectatorial experience produced by the film's subjunctive reconstruction of the past is what its production team intended, as Lee Hyuk-sang, a member of PINKS who would later codirect *The Remnants* (2016, see epilogue), a sequel to *Two Doors*, remarks: "What we considered crucial to the film was that viewers have *the impression of experiencing the incident*, which we might call *reality of the senses*. So we needed several cinematic devices, such as sound mix, reenactments, visual effects through CGI, and intertexts, *for they were used in different ways than the realistic use of the videos.*"[50]

The Digital Turn   **243**

Digital technologies play a central role in the investigative and dramatic reconstructions of the incident and its trials. The directors' extensive appropriation and juxtaposition of the disparate materials distinct in source and media (printed, video, audio) must have been owed to the digital nonlinear editing system that allows for nonsequential and random access to a film being made. For Martin Lefebvre and Marc Furstenau, the technological transition of editing from the celluloid-based to the digital-based system enables both filmmakers and viewers to have more analytical and manipulative relationships to a film's details: "The non-linearity of digital editing systems that is reproduced in DVD players and other domestic technologies that allow viewers to view and manipulate images suggests the possibility of resurrecting other traditions of analysis, which are based on fragmentation and recombination."[51] Seen in this light, a key consequence of digital imaging systems for the filmmaker is to encourage viewers to have an analytical relationship to the film in a manner similar to the manipulation, fragmentation, and recombination of it that are effected by the advent of postfilmic viewing devices or applications. In the case of *Two Doors*, digital editing tools allow the videos taken by both Color TV and Sajahoo TV and the police's evidence collection team to be played in slow motion or freeze frame at certain moments, so viewers are invited to take a closer look at them from the standpoint of either the juror who judges their juridical value in dialogue with the written or recorded testimonies of the SWAT agents (in the light of the second series), or of the distant witness who encounters the indexical record of the past from which she was absent (the first series). Besides these two effects, the film's codirectors capitalize on nonlinear digital editing to process and combine all the heterogeneous materials, which leads to the third, final series aimed at offering the viewer larger political and socioeconomic contexts of the incident: digitized newspaper articles and video clips from TV news reports are employed to explain the origin of SWAT, which was founded in 1983 as a special antiterrorist task force in preparation for the 1986 Asian Games and the 1988 Seoul Olympics but later expanded to cope with demonstrations of strike laborers and evictees in 1996, the Yongsan Redevelopment Plan in 2003 as derived from the complicity of state-led developmentalism and corporate capitalism, and the mobsters hired to threaten, terrorize, and evict the residents of the area. By employing the existing media artifacts in this way, *Two Doors* does not abandon documentary film's discursive functions to present its persuasive argumentation on the incident, namely, that what matters most in the incident is the neoliberal capitalism that caused the struggles of the tenants and evictees, and the state power that did not hesitate to exert its violent operations for suppressing their sit-ins, despite its representational strategies to

244 Post-activism

rely on the tropes of courtroom drama and crime thriller films. Thus, the digital editing system applied to the film, in the words of Kim Soyoung, "offers a model for how [Korean] independent documentary can translate other media forms in order to demand social justice."[52]

To elucidate the ways in which digital editing in *Two Doors* is eventually used to "demand for social justice," I would argue that it brings the contestation of the two types of videos, the live broadcast footage of Color TV and Sajahoo TV and the police's video evidence, to the fore in self-reflexive manner to perform what Henry Giroux has called "critical pedagogy." By this, Giroux means a range of educational or informative strategies to allow individuals to seek space for an alternative politics, as it is expected to offer "a discourse of plurality, difference, and multinarratives . . . in order to explain either the mechanics of domination or the dynamic of emancipation."[53] Applying this term to the ways in which YouTube and social media technologies could be used for citizens' self-empowerment and the development of their agencies for social change, Douglas Kellner and Gooyong Kim argue that "emancipatory, politically progressive, and socially transformative uses of the media and technology should thus be informed by a critical pedagogy to produce a viable counter-hegemonic cultural politics and pedagogy of the Internet."[54] From this perspective, *Two Doors* substantiates its operation of critical pedagogy by drawing viewers' attention not merely to each of the two video records themselves, but also to the larger media environment concerned with their production and circulation, an environment that structured the incident. In the case of the footage taken by Color TV and Sajahoo TV on the street where the incident took place, it is the participatory media culture cultivated by the arrival of the Web 2.0 and portable media interfaces such as laptops equipped with recording and internet connection since the late 2000s that it alludes to. During the 2008 Candlelight Protests against the Lee Myung-bak government's agreement to resume US beef imports despite citizens' concern with mad cow disease, "Citizen journalist collectives and live-streaming performers not only produced news stories, but played critical roles . . . to monitor or control the police's violence, to open up live discussion or to mediate each other's actions, and to work for tele-interactions like a computer game."[55] Color TV and Sajahoo TV were two media activist collectives born out of this networked social movement, establishing as their mission to offer spontaneous, real-time coverage of the political and social struggles neglected by mainstream media, such as the protests at Ssangyong Motors and Gangjeong Beach (see chapters 2 and 3). In this sense, the footage of the two collectives reflects the ways in which participatory digital media and the grassroots activist culture offered by it boosted and updated local media activism, including the activist documentary practices aimed at constructing a collective agency of disenfranchised citizens. The footage produced by these two collectives, then, serves as visible evidence of the police's violence on the evictees' sit-in strike, although it was filmed from a distance at a building across Namildang: for it documents undeniable details of the police operation, such as the use of a crane and a container for some SWAT agents' dispatch to Namildang's rooftop, others' entrance into its lookout, and the firing of water cannons toward the lookout. The testimonies of Park Seonghoon, a member of Color TV, validate the capacity of its guerrilla live streaming practice to serve not only as an alternative news agency for the site of people's struggle that the mainstream press neglected to cover, but also as a public watchdog by filming violent attacks of the SWAT agents on the people and disseminating the record instantly through the internet.

In Two Doors, however, the "dynamics of emancipation" activated by the digitally enabled media activism turns out to coincide with the "mechanics of domination" embodied by the police video evidence. Armored with portable video cameras, the police's evidence-collection (*ch'aejǔng*) teams began to monitor and film protesters to control peaceful demonstrations in the new century, including the 2008 Candlelight Protests, in service of collecting visible evidence of their violent behavior and use of illegal means, such as Molotov cocktails. The use of these cameras, then, became one of the most efficient apparatuses for regulating citizens' direct action and their subjectivity, as they partially replaced the tear gas that had widely been used to suppress demonstrations by students and labor workers in the 1980s and 1990s. This type of protest control was indebted to the way that digital technologies made possible what Thomas Matheisen has called "synoptic surveillance." Arguing that Michel Foucault's panoptic model of surveillance is insufficient to explain the pervasiveness of optical and networked devices for monitoring and recording in contemporary society, Matheisen defines synoptic surveillance as allowing the many to capture and monitor the few.[56] This implies that the state apparatus became capable of effecting governmentality on citizens and activists with the same technological means they were able to use: just as the citizens and activists demonstrate their emancipatory power by producing their camera-witness of police violence, so do the police capitalize on the visual power of evidence-collecting cameras to control their protests. This contestation of the two apparatuses in the scenes of mutual surveillance is, I argue, what digital montage in *Two Doors* presents as a key form of critical pedagogy. It can particularly be found in the sequence of reenacting the SWAT agents' preparation for getting into the container at 6:30 a.m. Here the directors alternate broadcast footage of Sajahoo TV and Color TV with police evidence videos, so that viewers are

246 Post-activism

able to recognize their differences and similarities. Because the members of the two media collectives were not allowed to enter Namildang and its neighboring street, their camera perspective was limited to a high angle from the buildings that they temporality inhabited. However, the police videos were taken both on the ground and from above, thus testifying to the police's pervasive power of synoptic surveillance. This difference is further supplemented by the juxtaposition of a video by Color TV and Police Video Evidence No. 59, which share the same referent: several SWAT agents who surrounded the fire caused by Molotov cocktails that the protesters in Namildang might have thrown. Given that without captions it is not possible to identify who filmed them, the director's editing that underlines the similarity of the two videos presents the complicated coexistence of digital media activism and the police's multidimensional technologies of control as fundamental to understanding a major condition of contemporary power and resistance. This also explains why the directors intermittently insert fragments of CCTV taken from the street of Yongsan on the day of the incident in their reconstruction of its progress, so that they function as establishing shots of its events.

It is also here that *Two Doors* is distinct from *The Intention* and *Ghost Ship* in its reliance on the subjunctive mode of documentary. The film's accumulation and juxtaposition of the videos and testimonies remind one of Morris's *Standard Operating Procedure* (2008), which attests to the capacity of the nonlinear editing software to compile, examine, and rearrange a vast collection of the photos that emerged from the Abu Ghraib prison complex in Iraq in April 2004. Morris's digital investigation of the photos via isolating and magnifying them and opening their metadata looks beyond their surface and draws viewers' attention to something hidden or deeper. However, this method does not produce an authoritative truth of what really happened at the prison complex, but instead "highlight[s] the same tension between the extreme legibility of what the images depict and their inability . . . to narrate the story adequately."[57] For the tension suggests that there might be computational or governmental interventions in the gap between the original photos and those that were submitted to the trial as evidence. In the context of *Two Doors*, the videos taken by the guerrilla broadcasters and by the *ch'aejǔng* team of the police squad do not offer any crucial, legible evidence of who caused the fire, much less any witness. For as the attorneys and human rights activists commonly argue, the police headquarters claimed at the trials that there was no footage taken inside Namildang right before or right after the fire: footage that might have demonstrated who was responsible for it. A notable political achievement of *Two Doors*, then, is that it does not plot a conspiracy theory about the legal truth about the fire in the same way as the films of Project Bu;

nor does it employ the testimonies of the experts to present an authoritative version of the truth. While acknowledging the videos' partiality and elusiveness in terms of their legal use, the directors of *Two Doors* draw viewers' attention to what they ineluctably preserve: that is, the trace of the evictee-victims who were dead inside the watchtower. In this sense, the film's reconstruction of the materials via its database method makes a powerful claim on the truth that no one can evade: the video serves as the index of the violence by governmental authority (*konggwŏllyŏk*) that suppressed the demand and voice of the evictees at the site of their sit-in. Here the film's strategy of creating the suspense and suffocating atmosphere of the incident is also justified, as it vividly reconstructs the material and sensory power of the *ch'aejŭng* cameras and noise meters that have been applied to the police's protest surveillance since the beginning of this century. As Kim Eun-sung points out, these devices involve a form of micropower relating to the police's governmentality, a power that is transmitted through protesters' affective experience: "Protesters are daunted by the visual power of cameras, when they see many police cameras surrounding them. [They] perceive the sonic power of noise meters when the police shout with megaphones to turn down volume on their loudspeakers."[58]

Consequently, the film's deliberate digital editing and subjunctive mode innovate the activist tradition's political advocacy for the evictees of urban redevelopment while also signaling a notable liberation from its aesthetic and epistemological grounds. As its directors make clear in their production statement, "the film deals with the mechanism of *konggwŏllyŏk* as an undeniable aspect of truth, which has repeatedly been executed in Korean society."[59] This aspect of truth is ultimately the case with what the film's montage of disparate materials recurrently compels viewers to witness: the image of the burning lookout (figure 7.3). By engendering multiple associations between this haunting image of the traumatic memory and the competing records and accounts, *Two Doors* emblematizes the power of montage that Georges Didi-Huberman highlights in his reflection on how an artwork, including a film, is able to deal with the images of violence despite evidentiary limits that obscure any privileged access to its hidden truth: "Montage is valuable only when it doesn't hasten to conclude or to close: it is valuable when it opens up our apprehension of history and makes it more complex."[60]

The Future of Digital Documentary Cinema

The variety of the digital documentary forms discussed in this chapter testify to the diversification of seeking truths about a range of contested realities

Figure 7.3 *Two Doors* (Kim Il-rhan and Hong Ji-yoo, 2011)

in twenty-first-century Korea: the Park Chung-hee syndrome and the deep-seated persistence of anticommunism in postdocumentary diversions, the spectral presence of postcolonial Cold War violence in the camptown and DMZ in VR documentaries, and the Yongsan Massacre and the Sewol Ferry Disaster in subjunctive documentaries. As in the case of the increased availability of archival footage, digital technologies for postproduction and nontheatrical viewing have allowed directors to develop modes of documentary filmmaking other than the activist method, and this has resulted in the multiple approaches to reality and history that are the hallmark of post-activist documentaries. Challenging the supremacy of *hyŏnjang* aesthetics in the activist tradition of Korean documentary cinema in the 1980s and 1990s, the digital modes also validate the filmmakers' effort to renew the tradition's engagement with state violence, social injustice, and traumatic events despite their formal and aesthetic departure from the tradition's political investment in the immediacy and authenticity of what the camera saw.

Recent filmmaking of younger-generation directors and artists has advanced digital documentary cinema to the point of establishing the digital as more than a tool for imaging and postproduction: that is, they either assert the digital as fundamental to their access to reality and history or consider it constitutive of their reality as such. *Graeae: A Stationed Idea* (*Kŭraiai: Chudunhanŭn shin*, Jeong Yeoreum, 2020, 35 min.) employs the play-mode interface of the augmented-reality game *Pokémon Go*, situating its fictional self as a player who decodes the history of Yongsan Garrison, the site of the headquarters for the US military forces stationed in South Korea. Here the game itself functions as the only means for the investigative self to navigate through the site that Korean citizens are not permitted to enter, as the site's monuments are rendered as hotspots connected via GPS and Google Maps. By aligning the self-as-player with the self-as-explorer who amasses from search engines and YouTube a wide array of photos and documents about the site, clips of archival films about the US Army, and videos that document the site's key areas by its residents and authorized visitors, the film reveals the geopolitical history of the US military policy in South Korea while also decoding media images that serve to portray the US Army as the guardian of world peace. Jeong's film is then remarkable for its digitized innovation of the archival turn that I have discussed in chapter 6. It also demonstrates that for Jeong, the reality and history themselves that she investigates are perceived as fundamentally permeated with the digital image itself and the digital tools that transform and process it. In dialogue with the film, *People in Elancia* (*Naeŏnnijŏnjihyŏn'gwa na*, Park Yun-jin, 2020, 87 min.) offers an intriguing case of how the first-person documentary's participant-observer engages a different kind of subject matter than those of its activist predecessors, or a different type of reality. Park is marked by two coexisting subjectivities that are tied together, a filmmaker-I who investigates a role-playing game called *Elancia* developed by Nexon and a group of devoted players, and a game avatar named "My Sister Jun Ji-hyun (*Naeŏnnijŏnjihyŏn*)" that develops its character by executing the game's missions, acquiring its items helpful for the growth of its ability, and using macros for maximizing the pleasure of gaming. In this sense, the performative documentary's blending of the boundaries between reality and artifice or between filmed fact and the reality affected by the filmmaker's interaction is changed into the fundamental link between the virtual space and the space of reality. Park's journey into the computational logic of the game world and her fellow players' different motivations for gaming goes so far as to change her identity in the course of making the film, as she investigates the transformation of the game industry since the post-IMF crisis, visits Nexon to ask about fixing the game's bugs, and meets with the company's union members who are struggling against its unequal wage system. In this way, the film portrays the game world of Elancia not simply as a self-autonomous ecosystem operated by the interplay of developers, algorithms, and players, but also as one of our contemporary realities in which the virtual is inseparable from the social.

Epilogue

The Remnants

The Remnants (*Kongdongjŏngbŏm*, Kim Il-rhan and Lee Hyuk-sang, 2016, 106 min.) appears to be a response of PINKS to a line of negative critiques of *Two Doors*: that the film does not sufficiently advocate for the evictees who engaged in the sit-in struggles at Yongsan district before and on January 20, 2009, as well as the bereaved family members of the five protesters who perished in the fire at 7:20 a.m. on that day. The film takes as its subject matter five participants who were sentenced to several years in prison for the court's verdict that they were "joint principal offenders" (which is what the film's original Korean title means) guilty of the deaths of the five protesters and a SWAT member. The protagonists, the male survivors of the intense struggle and the massacre, are divided into two categories: there is Lee Chung-yeon, a resident of Yongsan district who was directly been impacted by the redevelopment plan, led the demonstrations, and lost his father due to the fire; the other four were protesters from the Association of National Evictees (ANE: Chŏn'guk chŏlgŏmin yŏnhap'oe), who came from other redevelopment areas in Seoul and Gyeonggi Province to show solidarity with the residents of the district. Tracking each of the five protagonists' everyday lives after release from prison in January 2013 (drinking alone, nurturing plants, becoming a Catholic, etc.), as well as their trauma, loneliness, and alienation, the two directors invite them to recall what they experienced on that day—a process of compelling them to recall what makes each of them painful and to face what each of them does not want to face.

While premised upon the codirectors' intimate interaction with the five social actors involved in the massacre, the film delicately inscribes its post-activist epistemology and political consciousness, so it becomes an example of what Janet Walker calls the "trauma cinema." Walker refers to it as a group of films dealing with "a world-shattering event or events of the past" through "an unusual admixture of emotional effect, metonymic symbolism and cinematic flashbacks,"[1] all of which aim to probe the limits of representing the traumatic events—and, by extension, to express the fundamental indiscernibility of the

---

Activism and Post-activism. Jihoon Kim, Oxford University Press. © Oxford University Press 2024.
DOI: 10.1093/oso/9780197760413.003.0009

public and the private in them. Unlike the investigative approach, digital editing, and reenactments applied to *Two Doors*, *The Remnants* heavily relies on filmed interviews with each of the five participants, a key rhetorical component of the activist tradition. Kim and Lee endeavor to convey not only each of the five social actors' testimonies but also to draw viewers' attention to each of their expressions and surroundings. The codirectors' arrangement of two cameras on the sites of the interviews frames the same participant in two different sizes, in bust or medium shots and in close-ups, propelling the viewers to notice slight discrepancies between the two. Far from stressing their testimonies as the immediate voices of the disenfranchised, this self-reflexive operation of the two cameras establishes two different perspectives on each of the protagonists that in turn allude to his divided subjectivity and his unstable memory of the past. The four participants from the ANE confess their pains and traumas: Kim Chang-soo belatedly learned that his wife was hospitalized due to cancer when he was in prison; Ji Seok-joon suffered from the leg injury he got on January 20; and Kim Joo-hwan lost his temper and drank heavily. When they revisit the moments of the struggle and the fire, the four participants reveal the instability, partiality, and even falsity of their memories, as, for instance, demonstrated by Ji's recollection that two fellow demonstrators escaped from the fire before he fell on the ground, which proves not to be true (the two were found dead in the watchtower).

This divided self is also applied to Lee Chung-yeon, but from a different perspective. The film's early parts foreground Lee as a bereaved family (*yugajok*) member of the massacre, showing his demands for finding its truth, his opening of a beer pub near the district, and his negative attitude toward the others, who he thinks do not actively join in his activism. As the codirectors ask what he did and remembers, his evasions, made visible by the two cameras, signal the shift of perspective from Lee as *yugajok* to a survivor (*saengjonja*) who stands on the same page as the rest. Here the footage taken by Sajahoo TV and Color TV or by the police's *ch'aejŭng* team returns less as data with which to reconstruct the incident, as in the case of *Two Doors*, than as a dominant image that recurs in each of their psyches (like the image of the fire that started at 7:20 a.m.). Or it functions as a kind of visible evidence against which each memory of the five protagonists is tested, and which lays bare what each of them does not remember or eschews to do so. This is particularly true of the scenes associated with the nightmare of Lee, a quasi-reenactment vignette that serves as a substitute for a dramatic restaging of the event. Again, the codirectors' digital editing plays a key role in reconstructing the painful return of his psyche to the unresolved past and Lee's sense of guilt for having survived the fire. For instance, Lee's determination to fight

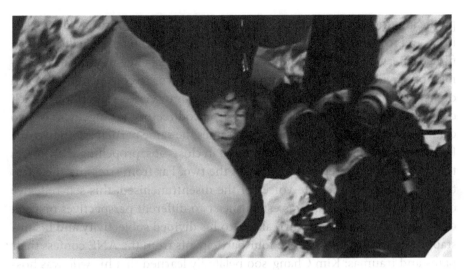

Figure E.1 *The Remnants* (Kim Il-rhan and Lee Hyuk-sang, 2016)

for the truth as a way of consoling himself for the loss of his father, revealed in an interview with the codirectors, is followed by the footage in which Lee is lying on a stretcher after the fire had been extinguished (figure E.1). Here the codirectors magnify the footage while also adding a cosmic zoom derived from the digital intermediate process, revealing that Lee did not lose consciousness. These two techniques create a stereoscopic effect on the original two-dimensional footage that invokes the experimental films of Ken Jacobs. It adds the sensory power to Lee's ethical predicament marked by the oscillation between his will to survive the trauma and his sense of guilt.

Another post-activist aspect of *The Remnants* lies in its revisionist view of the idea of the community of *minjung* that the traditional activist documentaries aspired to construct through stressing the images of collective action and solidarity. The film's orchestration of the interviews with the observational records of the lives of the five survivors highlights the ongoing tension between Lee Chung-yeon and the other four after the traumatic failure of the struggles at the Yongsan redevelopment district. Lee's demand that authorities investigate the disaster does not match the other survivors' desire to draw public attention to their emotional pain and solitude. The clash between the two parties culminates in a private meeting in October 2015, filmed with handheld cinematography that contrasts with the stationary cameras applied to the interviews. This clash suggests a "post-*minjung*" or "postcommunity" assumption that underlies some documentarians affiliated with activism in the twenty-first century: namely, that the idea of the community of disenfranchised people as a political group united by a single cause or unquestioned solidarity has become difficult. As Kim Il-rhan remarked, this assumption relates to the gradual dissolution of the communities that hitherto formed the basis of the people's political enlightenment and communal solidarity in the 1980s and 1990s: "I realized that nowadays there are few communities that support me and the value of my life and that ground grassroots movements. It was hard for me to feel the sense of community even when I visited this or that community screening."[2] Despite this sense of disillusionment, however, *The Remnants* also seems to suggest a different idea of community, that is, a kind of *post*community that reconciles the demand for the collective struggle for a common will with the singularity of each person's trauma and pain. In the words of philosopher Jean-Luc Nancy, the community in question could be an "inoperative community" in the sense that "there is no being without another singular being," and in the sense that it is based on "communication" as the act of "sharing . . . to be constitutive of being-in-common."[3] After the clash between the two parties, the film shows the five survivors' second meeting, in which they share their memories while watching footage of the incident together. The possibility for that type of community based on the sharing of singularities standing on the common—the memories of neoliberal redevelopment and the disaster that it caused—is suggested in the film's end: it loosely juxtaposes the five survivors' participation in a rally aimed to demand *jinsan ggyumyŏng* with the aerial view of the district under construction, on which the intertitles "The site of the Yongsan Massacre will be the large-scale complex of high-rise buildings" are overlaid.

Consequently, the pair of *Two Doors* and *The Remnants* emblematizes post-activism's two directions that dialectically complement each other: *Two Doors* incorporates the technical, aesthetic, and rhetorical innovations that makes the twenty-first-century Korean documentary cinema distinct from its activist predecessors; and then, this is complemented by *The Remnants* that represents the politically and ethically renewed maneuvers of the activist tradition. The interplay of the two directions in close dialogue with the shifting sociopolitical and cultural conditions of the twenty-first century Korean society add up to a larger critical map of the documentary cinema that I have drawn in this book.

Korean Documentary as Transnational Cinema

How can the Korean documentary cinema from its activist origin to its post-activist divergences be viewed in light of Korean national cinema, or, more broadly, of national cinema as a unifying yet contestable concept? It

254 Epilogue

undeniably problematizes what Andrew Higson has called the "limiting imagination" of national cinema, according to which the idea of national cinema "can offer coherent images of the nation, sustaining the nation at an ideological level."[4] Added to this is that the "imagined community" argument premised on a common identity and sense of belonging tends to reinforce the idea of national cinema as sharing not only the specific culture and history of the nation but also a limited set of genres, styles, and industrial practices. In this regard, this book suggests that documentary cinema in nongovernmental and noncorporate sectors of cinematic activities has lent itself to questioning the idea of Korean national cinema in terms of its politics and aesthetics since the early 1980s. On one side, having emerged as an agent of grassroots social movements during the military dictatorship, the activist tradition has produced audiovisual discourses for advocating the rights of marginalized subjects and demanding progressive social change while monitoring the state and other powerful institutions. In so doing, it has made significant political contributions to cultivating democratic citizenship against the dominant public ideologies of anticommunism, authoritarianism, neoliberalism, and existing and new types of discrimination and hate.[5] On the other side, by departing from the epistemological and aesthetic assumptions of the activist tradition, the post-activist Korean documentary films and videos of the twenty-first century have formed the most vibrant screenscape for cinematic experimentations that challenge the widespread awareness of Korean national cinema as represented either by the action-melodrama-blockbuster complex of its mainstream strain or by several internationally well-known commercial or arthouse auteurs. These experimentations have also meaningfully renewed the activist tradition's political and ethical commitment to Korean society and history by profoundly investigating the bodies and voices of individuals excluded from the ideological, cultural, and historical interpellation of the state apparatus, as well as the spatial and temporal complexity of their memories and traumas. Bifurcating in these two directions, which also have converged with each other in the form of the double helix, South Korean documentary cinema in its forty-year processes of evolution and diversification has become *a national cinema within Korean national cinema with its independent, defiant, and disruptive forces that nonetheless promote a set of shared social values, such as democracy, equity, justice, and progress.*

Still, is this really the endpoint of a historiography of Korean documentary cinema? Thinking of documentary cinema of a given nation-state as a variant or component of a national cinema has largely been taken for granted due to its inherent link to the society that its films and videos address and engage, to the social actors as both their subjects and audiences, and to the historical, cultural, and geopolitical contexts within which they are produced and circulated. Bearing in mind the processes by which its formal, aesthetic, technical, epistemological, and thematic boundaries have been redrawn and expanded during the last two decades, however, I would also leave it for future research to refigure Korean documentary cinema from transnational perspectives. For that task, some could perhaps start with exploring such border-crossing filmmakers as Yang Yonghi and Zhang Lu, whom I have discussed in chapters 4 and 5.[6] A sequel to her two *Pyongyang* films, Yang's latest documentary, *Soup and Ideology* (*Sup'ŭwa ideollogi*, 2021), expands Yang's intertwinement of transborder family narrative with Cold War history beyond the scope of Zainichi's liminal, drifting identity between Japan and North Korea—into South Korea's still-persisting geopolitical and ideological tragedy. This 118-minute film tells the story of Yang's mother, who has lived alone in Osaka after her father passed away in 2009. While the film's first part presents the mother's everyday life, which Yang films on her monthly visit from Tokyo with her Japanese boyfriend (and later husband), its second part focuses on what the mother has never told her before being diagnosed with senile dementia: the mother experienced the April Third Incident after she emigrated from Osaka to escape from US air raids in 1945, losing her relatives and even her fiancé. Accordingly, the latter half tracks the family's travel to Jeju Island, their attendance at the commemoration ceremony of the incident, and their visits to the April Third Research Institute and places where the atrocities committed by the South Korean army took place, as efforts to recall the mother's memories that are becoming lost as her condition worsens. Unlike the first half, where she primarily stands behind her camera, Yang enters the frame in the second half as a character, realizing that her mother's deep-seated affiliation with North Korea, which Yang did not totally understand in her filming of the two *Pyongyang* films, was deeply engrained in what she had witnessed in the island. More than embodying this history lesson, however, Yang's presence profoundly alludes to the insurmountable gap between the public commemoration of the state and ideological violence and its impacts on the mnemonic and psychic dimensions of the individuals who experienced it: for the ceremony in Jeju April Third Peace Park and its monuments paradoxically stress the gradual and irreversible loss of the memories of her mother. Yang's shift of her position to the filmmaker-in-the-text in the second half, then, does more than assert how difficult it is to bridge the gap: her presence further suggests that it is a key motivation of the post-activist documentarians to elaborate on documentary modes of storytelling in service of minimizing the gap, or making rich yet multiplied negotiations between the personal and the public.

256 Epilogue

While the films of Zhang and Yang undoubtedly call into question the idea of Korean national cinema as premised upon and consolidating a shared ethnicity or community, I would briefly sketch out two categories of recent nonfiction films that help us to expand the scope of Korean documentary cinema into concepts of transnational cinema.

The first category includes films and videos made by Korean diasporas based in foreign countries. Their makers are either adoptees to the United States, the Netherlands, and Denmark, to name just a few, in their childhood, or filmmakers or artists who have been living overseas for study, job, or marriage, traversing national borders between their home and current countries. Certain films are built upon a more conventional mode of documentary storytelling or a humanitarian approach to their subject matter, as evidenced by French-Korean Lyang Kim's two films—*Dream House by the Border* (*Kyŏnggyeesŏ kkumkkunŭn chip*, 2013, 78 min.) and *Forbidden Fatherland* (*Padaro kaja*, 2018, 71 min.)—about North Korean displaced persons' (including her own father's) memories of the Korean War and its aftermath and about the precarious lives of their second and third generations in a borderland village of the DMZ. Others are more experimental in form, technique, and enunciation, demonstrating that the personal and archival turns of twenty-first-century Korean documentary cinema can also be applied to the nonfiction practices of Korean diaspora filmmakers and artists. *Overseas* (*Haeoero*, 2019, 90 min.), a film by French-Korean Sung-a Yoon, expands her experience of international adoption into the issue of global child care and household labor. The footage that she shot in Manila's training center for domestic work for four years exemplifies a balanced combination of straight observational and more stylized documentary records. *Songs from the North* (*Pungnyŏkkesŏ on norae*, 2014, 72 min.), by a US-based filmmaker, Soon-mi Yoo, is a nonnarrative travelogue to North Korea composed of a wide variety of North Korean films and TV clips meant to integrate North Korean people in shared ideas of sacrifice, honor, and patriotism. *Yukiko* (*Yuk'ik'o*, Young Sun Noh, 2018, 70 min.) is a richly layered, contemplative personal documentary that interweaves elusive memories of three border-crossing women—the director herself (based in France), her mother (who was born in Pyongyang and still lives in South Korea), and her Japanese grandmother (who returned to Okinawa after Korea's liberation)—through the intersection of the director's distancing, disembodied voice (it calls her mother "she" and her grandmother "Yukiko") and evocative landscape images. *Community of Parting* (*Ibyŏrŭi kongdongch'e*, 2019, 72 min.), a feature-length film by artist-filmmaker Jane Jin Kaisen, who was born on Jeju Island and raised in Denmark, exhibits many traits of post-activist nonfiction films, including subjective camerawork and polyphonic sound-image disjunction.[7] Here Kaisen invites about a dozen of female narrators, including folklorist, religious scholar, cultural anthropologist, historian, and activist, so that they offer their overlapping views on the Bari myth, a traditional story whose myriad versions have been orally transmitted on the Korean Peninsula, in terms of how it can be read in relation to Korea's geopolitical and historical contexts. In so doing, she also blends these different voices with her doubled quest for shamanism: shamanism as an indigenous ritual in Jeju Island for commemorating and comforting the victims of the April Third Incident, and shamanism in favor of her self-therapy of the traumas and fatigues that she underwent throughout her diasporic life. The shaman's ritual chants, then, address and echo the stories of other women who were dislocated, excluded, or traumatized in the official history of modern and contemporary Korea: North Korean defectors, comfort women, deceased sex workers in *kijich'on*, female migrants in Japan and Kazakhstan, and the victims of Sewol Ferry Disaster. Attempting to renew the cinematic representation of cultural identities in flux, the films of all the diaspora directors connect their negotiations with national, ideological, or historical borders to their endeavors to dismantle the formal and rhetorical boundaries of documentary.

The second category is akin to what Hamid Naficy has termed "independent transnational cinema." By this Naficy means a set of films practiced by filmmakers who straddle multiple ethnic cultures to explore dislocation, loss, longing, or nostalgia and who "not only inhabit interstitial spaces of the host society but also work on the margins of the mainstream film industry."[8] Although she is not a diaspora director, filmmaker and scholar Kim Soyoung has illustrated this type of documentary cinema with her "Exile" trilogy (2014–2017), which investigates the history and present of the Soviet/Russian Korean diaspora, or, Koryŏ people (*koryŏ saram*), who include the generations of Koreans who emigrated to Russia around the 1860s and who were deported by the Stalin regime to Central Asia in 1937.[9] In *Heart of Snow: Heart of Blood* (*Nunŭi maŭm: Sŭlp'ŭmi urirŭl teryŏganŭn kot*, 2014, 98 min.), Kim focuses on Alex Kim, a Uzbekistan-born Koryŏ who survives by running a small restaurant in the biggest multiethnic town in Gyeonggi-do. Through her transborder location shooting, Kim also compiles testimonies of two Koryŏ diaspora groups: first, elderly people who have had the traumatic experience of enforced migration and exclusion; and second, their descendants, whose liminal identities hover between Russian, Central Asian, and Korean and who seek to settle down in Korea for better economic opportunities. The second film, *Sound of Nomad: Koryo Arirang* (*Koryŏ Arirang: Chŏnsanŭi tiba*, 2016, 97 min.), continues Kim's recounting of the story of the enforced displacement and survival of Koryŏ people through two female divas—one is

258 Epilogue

still living, and the other is dead—who sang and danced in the Koryŏ theater, a nomadic form of theater that aimed to comfort Koryŏ people across the
former Soviet Union. In the trilogy's finale, *Goodbye My Love, NK* (*Kutpai mai
rŏbŭ NK: Pulgŭn chŏngch'un*, 2017, 80 min.), Kim reconstructs the drifting
trajectories of eight North Korean filmmakers who were sent to study at the
Gerasimov Institute of Cinematography in 1952 and sought political asylum
in 1958 after criticizing the Kim Il-sung regime. More than conveying the
sentiments of loss, longing, and nostalgia common to many exilic or diasporic
cinemas across different genres or modes of production, the trilogy attests to
Kim's keen awareness of what Will Higbee and Song Hwee Lim consider crucial in independent transnational cinema: "power relations between center/
margin, insider/outsider, as well as the continual negotiation between the
global and local that often extends beyond the host/home binary."[10] Kim indeed expresses this awareness in her statement regarding how she became
fascinated with the history of Koryŏ people: "The dispersion and dissemination [of the people] might trigger a productive re-orientation of a geopolitical
sense of sovereignty centered on the peninsula, which has been the stage of
a protracted turf war between the big powers of China, Russian, Japan, and
the US."[11] Ran Ma explains Kim's diasporic filmmaking based on her cross-
border journey in and across Central Asia, and between the region and South
Korea, as "a place-based methodology," which intends "to shift away from a
macro-chronology revolving around the axis of 'origin and return' and to pay
attention to the rhizomatic trajectories of migration and mobility."[12] I would
add that Kim's methodology, attuned to the mobility of the Koryŏ diaspora,
has entailed not only the mobility of filmmaking but also *a filmmaking of
mobility* that renders the aesthetic and formal boundaries of documentary
cinema open and in flux. Based on the testimonies of the displaced people as
their common primary material, Kim's shift from one mode of filmmaking to
another throughout the three films demonstrates this point: from the observational ethnography in *Heart of Snow*, to the retrieving of archival films from
Central Asia and the Soviet Union and the divas' performances in *Sound of
Nomad*, and to the rich deployment of archival footage (often mediated by the
three-channel split-screen technique, dramatic reenactments, and readings
or intertitles of poetry and prose) in *Goodbye My Love, NK*.

Another type of independent transnational documentary is built upon what
Mette Hjort has called "affirmative transnationalism," a mode of transnational
filmmaking that involves cross-border collaboration inspired by the concept
of cultural affinity or similarity. Affirmative transnationalism, as Hjort further specifies, need not uniquely be predicated upon the correspondence of
ethnicity, language, or culture shared by multiple nations: for it "can also rise

in connection with shared problems or commitments in a punctual now, or with the discovery of features of other national contexts that are deemed to be relevant to key problems experienced within a home context."[13] Oh Minwook, who has delved into the untold memories and spectral remainders of post-colonial modernity under the urban or geographical strata of Busan with his experimental documentary approach (see chapter 5), expands his scope into the transnational impacts of Cold War violence on East Asian regions—Busan, Taiwan, and Japan—in *Letters to Buriram* (*Haehyŏp*, 2019, 127 min.). Combining the poetic travelogue reminiscent of Chris Marker's *Sans Soleil* (1982) with the epistolary mode of narration embodied by Taiwanese female artist named Hsiao (who is also Oh's collaborator), the film complicates the "distance, separation, absence, and loss" invoked by the ghosts of the wars in East Asia (including a Korean journalist who was killed during his reporting on the Second Taiwan Strait Crisis in the Kinmen Islands in 1958) while also manifesting the "desire to bridge the multiple gaps"[14] that they left. By inviting the ethnographic images of spiritual or ceremonial cultures in the three countries, the haunted images of their historical places, and the memories of recent regional or transregional crises (such as the Hualien earthquake in 2018, and the rise of Japanese far-right organizations), the letter lays the groundwork for *Letters to Buriram* as an epistolary essay film that "radically mixes and merges private notations and commentary on public matters, [and] the record of both everyday life and momentous events."[15] Im Heung-soon's recent film *Good Light, Good Air* (*Choŭn pit, choŭn konggi*, 2020, 111 min.), extended from his multichannel installation of the same title in 2018, is a documentary based on an affirmative transnationalism, as his statement clarifies: "The history of Argentina and South Korea (Gwangju), two countries on the opposite side of the earth from each other, are very similar like a reflection on a mirror—the history of brutality and massacre of human done by human at the age of military rule during the similar era of 1970s and 80s."[16] This idea is reflected in the film's parallel storytelling, which connects the two groups of female subjects who have survived the pain and loss of their struggle against each country's military dictatorship: a group of grandmothers who lost their children or other family members amid Gwangju Uprising and are still demanding the preservation of its evidence; and women who suffered from abduction, imprisonment, torture, and the disappearance of their relatives during Argentina's military dictatorship era (1977–1982). Im does more than collect the women's testimonies to construct the affinities of lingering trauma and aspiration for democracy between the two social movements: his montage of the two stories across their national border and beyond their geographical distance constitutes a rich set of parallelisms—between the ruins

260 Epilogue

of violence (prisons in Argentina and the army hospital used to care for the injured citizens in Gwangju), between the relics (photos, tombs, and skeletons) charged with the spectral persistence of the dead, and the efforts to preserve and investigate the material traces of the violence and missing (the archaeological method applied in Gwangju, and the forensic analysis of the skeletons in Buenos Aires). These multiple parallels, then, create mutual understanding and solidarity between younger generations of the women, evidenced by the tele-workshop that invites female teenagers in the two cities to make media artifacts that blend 2D and 3D (VR works that transform two-dimensional images of the historical places in the two cities into 360-degree spherical videos), based on studying what happened to the other.

The Politics and Aesthetics of Korean Documentary Cinema

South Korean documentary cinema from its birth in the early 1980s to the year 2022 deserves to have its own history, which this book offers for the first time in English. My survey of its evolution from its activist tradition to its post-activist diversification aims to construct its history in light of the continual negotiation between aesthetics and politics, or between "actuality" and the ways in which documentarians have dealt with it in favor of "creative treatments" of it, from the regionalization of Third Cinema in the early 1980s to the personal, audiovisual, archival, and digital turns in the twenty-first century. The negotiation resonates with the way in which Jacques Rancière considers documentary film in terms of the intersection of politics and aesthetics and of the transition to the "aesthetic regime" in the twentieth century. For Rancière, documentary is a cinematic form concerned with articulating the real, or, what is common to the community, and with the "distribution of the sensible," as other arts and even narrative film do. In this context, documentary emblematizes "aesthetics as politics" in the sense that politics is understood as intervening in the social hierarchies that determine what can be seen and heard, and whose parts are said and made visible or sensible. "Like forms of knowledge," documentary is then read as constructing " 'fictions,' that is to say material rearrangements of signs and images, relationships between what is seen and what is said, between what is done and what can be done."[17] Here what Rancière calls "fiction" is not opposed to the real: nor he does argue that documentary as a mode of film practice or genre is totally indistinguishable from narrative film. Rancière refers to "fiction" as creative production of sensible knowledge in ways freed from "treating the real as effect to be produced," or of "treating it as a fact to be understood."[18] In this regard, what Rancière calls "documentary fiction" does not exclusively contain docudrama or docufiction but rather encompasses different strategies of nonfiction filmmaking to blur the boundaries between fact and fiction, and between art and life, and to forge exchanges between the two, in favor of making facts and knowledge of the real legible and sensible.

As Nico Baumbach brilliantly writes of Rancière's ideas, "Documentary film is then a more radical starting point for the aesthetic regime of art than so-called fiction film because it starts with non-art as its raw material and can play directly with the capacity of heterogeneous signs to be linked or delinked, to construct or withhold meaning."[19] Creating both harmony and cacophony with the main melody of social change documentaries, twenty-first-century post-activist films and videos, I assert, have demonstrated a capacity to embrace formal strategies and aesthetic components different from those of the activist tradition and to organize heterogeneous elements in protean manner. The capacity has been realized with a basso continuo that echoes the sociopolitical shifts in Korea, in the hope of refashioning Korean documentary cinema's initial aspiration to redistribute the sensible of marginalized or excluded subjects—or to render their bodies visible, their voices heard, their spaces inhabitable, and their memories and affects indelible.

This historiography and critical mapping of the Korean documentary films and videos in the nongovernmental and noncorporate sectors during the last four decades ends with a brief note on *The 2nd Repatriation* (*2ch'a songhwan*,

Figure E.2 *The 2nd Repatriation* (Kim Dong-won, 2022)

262 Epilogue

2022), Kim Dong-won's latest film as well as a sequel to *Repatriation* (see chapter 2), in terms of how the activist tradition has also renewed its form and aesthetics in dialogue with the sociopolitical changes while striving to fulfill its commitments to making the disenfranchised sensible and to articulating their bodies and voices. This 156-minute film is based on video footage that Gong Mi-yeon, a member of Docu Purn, filmed from 2003 to 2006 for her own documentary about Kim Young-shik, who had been imprisoned for twenty-seven years and appeared in *Repatriation*. After Gong's unexpected termination of her filmmaking, Kim Dong-won completed this sequel by editing her footage and adding his voice-over and another series of shots that he has taken since 2013. The bumpy production processes are reflected in the film: Kim Dong-won's plan to shoot still-alive, unconverted, long-term prisoners who had been sent to North Korea, and the hometowns of his parents (they were displaced persons, as they had left North Korea during the postliberation era), was promoted but not realized due to the rapid cooling of North-South relations after the failure of the Hanoi summit of Donald Trump and Kim Jong-eun in 2019. More than inscribing those processes, the film deepens Kim Dong-won's directorial effort for *Repatriation* to negotiate the storytelling of the effable yet intrepid man (Kim Young-shik) who has been fighting against the National Security Law and for the second repatriation of other long-term prisoners (nine as of 2023, including Kim), with Kim's own perspective on how his parents had been affected by the division of North and South and how his understanding of the United States shifted from a dream country to the cause of wars, including the Korean War, and violence across the globe. Acknowledging the temporal and epistemological distance between Gong's footage and his own commentary, Kim's editing places the spaces and activities of Kim Young-shik within the larger geopolitical and ideological contexts of North-South relations in the twenty-first century while also presenting him, other fellow longtime prisoners, and their supporters as subjects who have increasingly become invisible in contemporary Korean society but still insist upon their utopian belief in unification. The last long shot of the film, in which Kim Young-shik stages a one-man protest in front of the Blue House (figure E.2), encapsulates Kim Dong-won's humanitarian and aesthetic endeavor to render this conviction sensible with the interplay of distance and visibility.

Notes

Introduction

1. For the women's labor movement in this industrial sector of the 1970s, see Minkyong Kim, "Gender, Work and Resistance: South Korean Textile Industry in the 1970s," *Journal of Contemporary Asia* 41.3 (2011): 411–430.
2. Nam Inyoung, "Fifteen Years of Committed Documentaries in Korea: From *Sanggye-dong Olympics* to *Repatriation*," *Documentary* Box 25 (2005), http://www.yidff.jp/docbox/25/box25-3-e.html (accessed December 14, 2016).
3. Chris Berry, "The Documentary Production Process as a Counter-public: Notes on an Inter-Asian Mode and the Example of Kim Dong-Won," *Inter-Asia Cultural Studies* 4.1 (2003): 139–144.
4. Thomas Waugh, "Introduction: Why Documentary Filmmakers Keep Trying to Change the World, or Why People Changing the World Keep Making Documentaries," in *"Show Us Life": Toward a History and Aesthetics of the Committed Documentary*, ed. Thomas Waugh (London: Scarecrow Press, 1984), xiv.
5. For a revisionist history of Korea's labor movements with a focus on gender politics, see Hwasook Nam, *Women in the Sky: Gender and Labor in the Making of Modern Korea* (Ithaca, NY: Cornell University Press, 2021).
6. Im's emphasis upon women workers as *individuals* in *Factory Complex* is paralleled in *Sewing Sisters* (*Misingt'anŭn yŏjadŭl*, Kim Jung-young and Lee Hyukrae, 2020, 109 min.), a documentary that attends to three former sewing workers who joined the struggle for protecting the Cheonggye Clothing Labor Union at Pyounghwa Market and a night school for textile workers in the 1970s, a struggle inspired by the self-immolation of Chun Tae-il in 1970, a symbolic martyr of Korea's labor movement history. In lieu of narrating the three women's stories from the perspective of the collective working class, the film privileges each of their oral testimonies, which are performed against the backdrop of personal and archival photos projected on the screen, positioning the struggle within their personal feelings and awareness of the grueling working conditions (including working fifteen to sixteen hours a day). For an account of the struggle at Pyounghwa Market, see Hagen Koo, *Korean Workers: The Culture and Politics of Class Formation* (Ithaca, NY: Cornell University Press, 2001), chapter 4.
7. It was in February 2022 that Kim eventually had the company's honorary reinstatement and retirement after her thirty-seven-year fight.
8. For Im's documentary installation works, which I do not delve into due to limits of space, see my "Testimonies, Landscapes, and Reenactments in Im Heung-Soon's Documentary Works," *Interventions* 23.5 (2021): 729–753.
9. For a comprehensive overview of *minjung* art in English, see Sohl Lee, ed., *Being Political Popular: South Korean Art as the Intersection of Popular Culture and Democracy, 1980–2010* (Seattle: University of Washington Press, 2012).

264 Notes

10. Park Chan-kyong, "'Minjungmisul'gwaŭi taehwa" [Dialogue with *minjung* art], *Munhwa gwahak* [Culture science] 60 (2009): 155.

11. Quoted in Im Heung-soon and Park Chan-kyong, "Samgwa nodongŭi chogak moŭm" [Collecting fragments of life and work], *Cine 21*, August 20, 2015, http://www.cine21.com/news/view/?mag_id=80934 (accessed April 1, 2022).

12. Young-a Park, *Unexpected Alliances: Independent Filmmakers, the State, and the Film Industry in Postauthoritarian South Korea* (Stanford, CA: Stanford University Press, 2014).

13. Hye Seung Chung and David Scott Diffrient, *Movie Minorities: Transnational Rights Advocacy and South Korean Cinema* (New Brunswick, NJ: Rutgers University Press, 2021), 4.

14. Nam Inyoung, Lee Seung-min, Jung Min-ah, and Cho Heyyoung, *Han'guk tak'yumentŏri yŏnghwaŭi onŭl: Changnŭ, yŏksa, maech'e* [Today's Korean documentary cinema: Genre, history, media] (Seoul: Buonbooks, 2016), 10.

15. See, for instance, Chris Atton, *Alternative Media* (London: Sage, 2001); Leah A. Lievrouw, *Alternative and Activist New Media* (New York: Polity, 2011); Chris Robé and Stephen Charbonneau, eds., *Insurgent Media from the Front: A Media Activism Reader* (Bloomington: Indiana University Press, 2020).

16. Michael Warner, *Publics and Counterpublics* (New York: Zone Books, 2002), 111–112. See also Nancy Fraser, "Rethinking the Public Sphere: A Contribution to the Critique of Actually Existing Democracy," *Social Text* 25/26 (1990): 56–80.

17. Lee Seung-min, "Tongshidae aekt'ibijŭm tak'yumentŏri yŏnghwa" [Contemporary activist documentary films], *Tongnip yŏnghwa* [Independent film] 47 (2018): 94.

18. Namhee Lee, "The South Korean Student Movement: *Undongkwŏn* as a Counterpublic Sphere," in *Korean Society: Civil Society, Democracy and the State*, ed. Charles K. Armstrong (New York: Routledge, 2002), 133. For a collection of documents (manifestos, columns, etc.) relating to the 1980s democratization movement, see Namhee Lee and Kim Won, eds., *The South Korean Democratization Movement: A Sourcebook* (Seongnam: Academy of Korean Studies Press, 2016).

19. Cho Jung-kwan, "The Kwangju Uprising as a Vehicle of Democratization: A Comparative Perspective," in *Contentious Kwangju: The May 18 Uprising in Korea's Past and Present*, ed. Gi-wook Shin and Kyung Moon Hwang (Lanham, MD: Rowman and Littlefield, 2003), 72.

20. Cho Hee-yeon, "Changes in Social Movements in the Post-dictatorship Context in South Korea—Focused on Three Dimensions," in *Contemporary Korean Society: A Critical Perspective*, ed. Hee-yeon Cho, Lawrence Surendra and Hyo-je Cho (New York: Routledge, 2013), 68.

21. Kim Sunhyuk, "Civil Society and Democratization," in Armstrong, *Korean Society*, 99.

22. For the history of the social movements for comfort women, see Lee Na Young, "Women's Redress Movement for Japanese Military Sexual Slavery: Decolonizing History, Reconstituting Subjects," in *Korean Memories and Psycho-historical Fragmentation*, ed. Minkyoung Kim (London: Palgrave Macmillan, 2019), 51–71; Pyong Gap Min, *Korean "Comfort Women": Military Brothels, Brutality, and the Redress Movement* (New Brunswick, NJ: Rutgers University Press, 2021).

23. For the historical context of the commission and its activities, see Kim Dong-choon, "The Long Road toward Truth and Reconciliation: Unwavering Attempts to Achieve Justice in South Korea," *Critical Asian Studies* 42.4 (2010): 525–552.

Notes 265

24. For an account of the Park Chung-hee syndrome in twenty-first-century Korea, see Youngju Ryu, "Conclusion: From Yusin Redux to *Yuch'eit'al*," in *Cultures of Yushin: South Korea in the 1970s*, ed. Youngju Ryu (Ann Arbor: University of Michigan Press, 2018), 279–292.

25. Namhee Lee, *Memory Construction and the Politics of Time in Neoliberal South Korea* (Durham, NC: Duke University Press, 2022), 15

26. For a detailed account of the *sonyŏsang* activism, see Kim Joohee, "Faces of Korean Women in Two Mass Movements," *Positions Politics* (2020), http://positionspolitics.org/faces-of-korean-women-in-two-mass-movements/ (accessed January 15, 2021). For a study on how the statue evokes surviving grandmothers' fight for peace and justice and how its materiality elicits embodied engagements, see Elizabeth W. Son, *Embodied Reckonings: 'Comfort Women,' Performance, and Transpacific Redress* (Ann Arbor: University of Michigan Press, 2018). The activism was reignited after the Park Geun-hye government's "comfort women" agreement with Japan in December 2015, which was not based on the surviving grandmothers' consent. It promoted the popularity of the films on comfort women, including Miki Dezaki's documentary *Shusenjo: The Main Battleground of the Comfort Women Issue* (2018) and *My Name Is Kim Bok-dong* (*Kim Boktong*, Song Won-geun, 2019, 102 min.), in both theaters and community screenings. A biopic documentary on Kim Bok-dong (1926–2019) who broke her silence in 1992, the latter depicts her as a human rights activist who shared her experiences and called for women's justice in her campaigns around the world in collaboration with the Korean Council.

27. Lim Jie-hyun, *Kiŏk chŏnjaeng: Kahaejanŭn ŏttŏk'e p'ihaejaga toeŏnnŭn'ga* [Memory war: How perpetrators have become victims] (Seoul: Humanist, 2019), 295.

28. Lee, *Memory Construction*, 31.

29. See, for instance, Hagen Koo, "The Changing Faces of Inequality in South Korea in the Age of Globalization," *Korean Studies* 31 (2007): 1–18; Ji Joo-hyoung, *Han'guk shinjayujuŭiŭi hyŏngsŏnggwa kiwŏn* [The origin and formation of Korean neoliberalism] (Seoul: Book World Publication, 2011), 411–465.

30. Hagen Koo, "Rising Inequality and Shifting Class Boundaries in South Korea in the Neo-Liberal Era," *Journal of Contemporary Asia* 51 (2021): 1–19; Shin Kwang-yeong, "Globalization and Social Inequality in South Korea," in *New Millennium South Korea: Neoliberal Capitalism and Transnational Movements*, ed. Jesook Song (New York: Routledge, 2011), 11–28.

31. Yoonkyung Lee, "Labor Movements in Neoliberal Korea: Organizing Precarious Workers and Inventing New Repertoires of Contention," *Korea Journal* 61.4 (2021): 44–74.

32. Shin Kwang-yeong, "Economic Crisis, Neoliberal Reforms, and the Rise of Precarious Work in South Korea," *American Behavioral Scientist* 57.3 (2013): 335–353.

33. For a recent edited collection of these various rights-claiming movements, see Celeste L. Arrington and Patricia Goedde, eds., *Rights Claiming in South Korea* (Cambridge: Cambridge University Press, 2021).

34. Sun-chul Kim, "The Paradox of the Social Movement Society," *Korea Journal* 61.4 (2021): 5–19.

35. Shin Jin-wook, "New Waves of Civic Participation and Social Movements in South Korea in the 21st Century: Organization, Configuration and Agency," *Korea Europe Review* 1 (2021), https://doi.org/10.48770/ker.2021.no1.3.

36. Yoonkyung Lee, *Between the Streets and the Assembly: Social Movements, Political Parties, and Democracy in Korea* (Honolulu: University of Hawai'i Press, 2022), 2.

266 Notes

37. Michael Hardt and Antonio Negri, *Multitude: War and Democracy in the Age of Empire* (New York: Penguin Press, 2004), xiv (emphasis added).
38. Hardt and Negri, *Multitude*, xv.
39. For a detailed account of the scandal in relation to the Park government's cultural policy, see Yuk Joowon, "Cultural Censorship in Defective Democracy: The South Korean Blacklist Case," *International Journal of Cultural Policy* 25.1 (2019): 33–47.
40. See, for instance, Nan Kim, "The Color of Dissent and a Vital Politics of Fragility in South Korea," *Journal of Asian Studies* 77.4 (2018): 971–990; Hyunjin Seo, *Networked Collective Actions: The Making of an Impeachment* (New York: Oxford University Press, 2021), 59–72.
41. Angela J. Aguayo, *Documentary Resistance: Social Change and Participatory Media* (New York: Oxford University Press, 2019), 58–59.
42. Shin Eun-sil, "The 21st-Century 'Independent' Film," in *Movements on Screens 2*, ed. Korean Film Archive (Seoul: Korean Film Archive, 2019), 37. For an account of this transformation of the cultural policy connected to liberal democracy, see Hye-kyung Lee, *Cultural Policy in South Korea: Making a New Patron State* (New York: Routledge, 2019), 63–86.
43. Kim Ji-hyun, "Han'guk chamyŏ yŏngsang munhwaŭi hyŏngsŏnggwa t'ŭkching: Yŏngsang midiŏundongŭl chungshimŭro" [The formation and aesthetics of participatory visual media culture in South Korea from the late 1980s to the 2010s], PhD dissertation, Graduate School of Film and Media, Chung-ang University (2013), 73–74.
44. See, for instance, Martin Jay, "That Visual Turn," *Journal of Visual Culture* 1.1 (2002): 87–92; Fredric Jameson, *The Cultural Turn: Selected Writings on the Postmodern, 1983–1998* (New York: Verso, 1998).
45. Kim Sunah, "Tak'yumentŏri, hyŏnjae: Taehang yŏksakisul, chŏnt'ongjŏk imijiŭi p'agoe, hŏgu yŏnghwaŭi chŏnyu" [Documentary now: Alternative historiography, destruction of the traditional image, and the appropriation of fiction film], *Tongnip yŏnghwa* 7 (2000): 13.
46. Nam Inyoung, "Chŏngch'ijŏk riŏllijŭm: Han'guk tongnip tak'yummentŏriesŏ riŏllit'i kuch'uk pangshik" [Political realism: Ways of constructing reality in Korean independent documentary), in *Han'guk tongniptak'yumentŏri* [Korean independent documentary], ed. Independent Documentary Study Group (Seoul: Yedam, 2003), 132.
47. Michael Renov, "New Subjectivities: Documentary and Self-Representation in the Post-verité Age," in Renov, *The Subject of Documentary* (Minneapolis: University of Minnesota Press, 2004), 171–181.
48. Linda Williams, "Mirrors without Memories: Truth, History, and the New Documentary," *Film Quarterly* 46.3 (1993): 12.
49. Bill Nichols's *Introduction to Documentary* (Bloomington: Indiana University Press, 2001) was published in Korean in 2005.
50. Lee Hyun-jung, Kim Hee-young, and Hwang Yoon, "The Camera of the 'I': Han'guk tongnip tak'yumentŏriesŏ 'na'ŭi wich'iwa sŏnggyŏk" [The camera of the "I": The positions and characters of "I" in Korean independent documentary]," in Independent Documentary Study Group, *Han'guk tongniptak'yumentŏri*, 177–178.
51. Lee Seung-min, *Yŏnghwawa konggan: Tongshidae han'guk tak'yumentŏriyŏnghwaŭi mihakchŏk shilch'ŏn* [Cinema and space: Spatiality in Korean documentary films] (Seoul: Kalmuri, 2017), 30–31.
52. Park, *Unexpected Alliances*, 72.
53. Kim Dong-ryung and Park Kyoung-tae, "Tale Where Inside and Outside Are Divided," https://pregnantgoblin.notion.site/ (accessed April 1, 2022).

Notes **267**

54. Kim Seong-nae summarizes these imperatives as follows: "The testimonies of the comfort women had the effect of creating open discourse on the shameful past of the colonial era by verbalizing the wounds of women that were invisible in the patriarchal historical space. While risking being branded as an impure woman with their exposure to the public space, they acquire the gendered identity of the 'victim women (*p'ihaeja yŏsŏng*)'" ("Yŏsŏngjuŭi kusulsaŭi pangbŏmnonjŏk sŏngch'al [A methodological reflection on the feminist oral history], in Lee Jae-kyung et al., *Yŏsŏngjuŭi yŏksassŭgi: Kusulsa yŏn'gu bangbŏp* [Feminist oral history: Deconstructing institutional knowledge] [Hongcheon, Gangwondo: Arke, 2012], 42).

55. Heonik Kwon, "Legacies of the Korean War: Transforming Ancestral Rituals in South Korea," *Memory Studies* 6.2 (2013): 172.

56. For a couple of recent studies on the works of the artists and writers, see Chungmoo Choi, *Healing Historical Trauma in South Korean Film and Literature* (New York: Routledge, 2021); Koh Dong-yeon, *The Korean War and Postmemory Generation: Contemporary Korean Arts and Films* (New York: Routledge, 2022).

57. For the works on the monuments, museums, and geopolitical sites in Korean studies, see Sheila Miyoshi Jager and Jiyul Kim, "The Korean War after the Cold War: Commemorating the Armistice Agreement in South Korea," in *Ruptured Histories: War, Memory, and the Post–Cold War in Asia*, ed. Sheila Miyoshi Jager and Rana Mitter (Cambridge, MA: Harvard University Press, 2007), 233–265; Suk-young Kim, *DMZ Crossing: Performing Emotional Citizenship along the Korean Border* (New York: Columbia University Press, 2014); Daniel Kim, "Nationalist Technologies of Cultural Memory and the Korean War: Militarism and Neo-liberalism in 'The Price of Freedom' and the War Memorial of Korea," *Cross-Currents: East Asian History and Culture Review* 14 (2015): 91–123; Jung Keunsik, "On the Ruins: Forgetting and Awakening Korean War Memories at Cheorwon," *Development and Society* 46.3 (2017): 523–555; Suhi Choi, *Right to Mourn: Trauma, Empathy, and Korean War Memorials* (New York: Oxford University Press, 2019).

58. A recent example of the rise of the archival document as crucial to the public discourse on state violence is the rare footage showing US and Chinese forces rescuing Korean survivors of sexual slavery, including Park Yeong-sim, who was pregnant, in September 1944, discovered and aired by the Korean Broadcasting System (KBS) on May 28, 2020. See Moon Hyun-sook, "KBS Shows Rare Footage of Comfort Women Survivors Being Rescued by Allies," *The Hankyoreh*, May 29, 2020, https://english.hani.co.kr/arti/english_edition/e_international/947130.html (accessed April 1, 2022).

59. For a polemical yet lucid summary of the constructivist epistemology of those strategies, see Erika Balsom, "The Reality-Based Community," *e-flux Journal* 83 (June 2017), https://www.e-flux.com/journal/83/142332/the-reality-based-community (accessed March 1, 2022).

60. For a study on the role of film festivals as producer, including IFFR, see, for instance, Miriam Ross, "The Film Festival as Producer: Latin American Films and Rotterdam's Hubert Bals Fund," *Screen* 52.2 (2011): 261–267.

61. Thomas Elsaesser, "Film Festival Networks: The New Topographies of Cinema in Europe," in *The Film Festival Reader*, ed. Dina Iordanova (Andrews, Scotland: St. Andrews Film Studies, 2013), 74.

62. For more details on the incident, see Darae Kim, Dina Iordanova, and Chris Berry, "The Busan International Film Festival in Crisis or, What Should a Film Festival Be?," *Film Quarterly* 69.1 (2015): 80–89.

268 Notes

63. For the two films' distribution strategies, see Nam Inyoung, Kim Il-rhan, and Lee Seung-min, *Hanʾguk takʾyumentʾŏri yŏnghwaŭi paegŭpkwa haeoe shijang kaebarŭl wihan yŏnʾgu* [A study of the distribution and foreign market development of Korean documentary films] (Seoul: Korean Film Commission, 2010), 51–61.

64. Lee, former TV producer, benefited from the postproduction facilities of MediAct. The film's character-led plot and Lee's manipulation of sound effects contradict the camera's observational approach to the life of its protagonists in favor of the appeal to the general public.

65. Prominent cases of the popular documentary are the theatrical releases of *Tears in Arctic* (*Pukkŭgŭi nunmul*, Munhwa Broadcasting Corporation, 2009), *Tears in Amazon* (*Amajonŭi nunmul*, MBC, 2010), and the KBS-sponsored *Don't Cry for Me, Sudan* (*Ulchima tʾonjŭ*, Koo Soo-hwan, 2010), a film that pays tribute to doctor and priest Lee Tae-seok (1962–2010) who was active as a missionary in a Sudanese village.

66. For a summary of the bereaved families' acts of resistance, see Hyeon Jung Lee, "From Passive Citizens to Resistant Subjects: The Sewol Families Stand Up to the State," in *Challenges of Modernization and Governance in South Korea: The Sinking of the Sewol and Its Causes*, ed. Jae-Jung Suh and Mikyoung Kim (New York: Palgrave Macmillan, 2017), 49–73.

67. Kim, "The Color of Dissent," 986.

68. "What Went Wrong in the South Korean Ferry Disaster?," *New Yorker*, April 17, 2019, https://www.youtube.com/watch?v=5_A8dq2fA5o (accessed February 9, 2021). Indeed, the impacts of digital technologies on Korean documentary cinema have resulted in the diversifications of its screens and platforms and made them irreducible to community screenings and movie theaters. The Internet Protocol Television (IPTV) service since the late 2000s and the over-the-top (OTT) platforms since the late 2010s, such as Naver SeriesOn, Wavve, and Watcha Play, as well as Purplay, an independent OTT platform dedicated to offering women's independent shorts and feature-length films, have also propelled the multiplication of documentary screens, so that viewers are able to experience documentary films on small screens and on the move. This diversification of the screens and accesses has also encouraged independent film professionals, from individuals to collectives, to harness social media (Facebook and Twitter) and video-sharing platforms (YouTube and Vimeo) for archiving and publishing their content, and for their activities of publicity and consciousness-raising.

69. Quoted in June Jennings, "Yi Seung-jun and Gary Byung-seok Kam on *In the Absence*," *Field of Vision* website, August 13, 2019, https://fieldofvision.org/in-the-absence-interview (accessed February 9, 2021).

70. Jennings, "Yi Seung-jun." Yi said that the major broadcasting services declined his request to provide their news footage, and that a congressman, a former human rights lawyer who had represented the families, was of great help in securing footage from the Coast Guard and the rescue patrol, as well as government recordings of conversations.

71. Quoted in Anon., "The AFI DOCS Interview: IN THE ABSENCE With Director Yi Seung-Jun," *American Film Institute* website, June 12, 2019, https://www.afi.com/news/the-afi-docs-interview-in-the-absence-with-director-yi-seung-jun/ (accessed February 9, 2021).

Chapter 1

1. Here I leave the historical origins and conceptual refractions of the term *kirok yŏnghwa* in the history of Korean cinema for future study. One thing I remark here, however, is that the term was already used in the writings of left-wing critics involved in the Korea Artista Proleta Federatio (KAPF, K'ap'ŭ) in the early 1930s, that is, during the Japanese Occupation period when there were only educational and propaganda newsreels supported by the Japanese government. In their newspaper articles in 1931, the critics discussed Dziga Vertov's *Man with a Movie Camera* (1929) and Oleksandr Dovzhenko's *Earth* (1930), characterizing them as *kirok yŏnghwa* and appreciating their strategic use of montage for educational and propagandistic effects.

2. After changing its name several times, the institution now exists as KTV (Kungmin bangsong), a cable television channel managed by the Ministry of Culture, Sports, and Tourism.

3. In the local studies on Korean film history, *munhwa yŏnghwa* has gained increased attention since the early 2010s. For a valuable edited collection on this topic, see *Chiwŏjin han'guk yŏnghwasa: Munhwa yŏngwaŭi an'gwa pakk* [An erased history of Korean cinema: Inside and outside of culture film], ed. Korean Film Archive (Seoul: Korean Film Archive, 2014).

4. For a recent English-language study on the feminist implications of Khaidu's films and performances in the 1970s, see Hieyoon Kim, *Celluloid Democracy: Cinema and Politics in Cold War South Korea* (Berkeley: University of California Press, 2023), chap. 4.

5. Tom Gunning, "Before Documentary: Early Nonfiction Films and the 'View' Aesthetic" (1997), in *The Documentary Film Reader: History, Theory, Criticism*, ed. Jonathan Kahana (New York: Oxford University Press, 2016), 52–63.

6. Park, *Unexpected Alliances*, 33.

7. Kim Hong-joon, "Wae yŏnghwain'ga?" [Why cinema?], in *Yallasyŏngŭi chŏt pŏntchae yŏnghwamadang p'amp'ŭllet* [Yalashung's first film screening pamphlet] (Seoul: Yalashung, November 7–8, 1980), quoted in *Pyŏnbangesŏ chungshimŭro: Han'guk tongnip yŏnghwaŭi yŏksa* [From margin to center: A history of Korean independent film], ed. Seoul Visual Collective (Seoul: Shigakkwaŏnŏ, 1996), 21–22.

8. Namhee Lee, *The Making of Minjung: Democracy and the Politics of Representation in South Korea* (Ithaca, NY: Cornell University Press, 2007), 6.

9. Quoted in Seoul Visual Collective, *Pyŏnbangesŏ chungshimŭro*, 26.

10. The prints of both films were lost. My description of the two relies on the following: Nam Tae-je and Lee Jin-pil, "Kyŏktongŭi hyŏnshiresŏ p'iŏnan tongnip tak'yumentŏri: 1980nyŏndae-90nyŏndae ch'obanŭi yŏngsang undonggwa tak'yumentŏri" [Independent documentary in turbulent reality: Visual movement and documentary in the 1980s and early 1990s], in Independent Documentary Study Group, *Han'guk tongnip tak'yumentŏri*, 22.

11. Ibid., 20.

12. Ibid., 21 (emphasis added).

13. Film historian Lee Hyo-in rightly describes SFC as a collective in which "aspiration to the new cinema, which had been cultivated by experience at the French Institute and the Goethe Institute, and demands for democratization movement, were unstably mixed" (*Han'guk nyu weibŭ yŏnghwa 1975–1995* [Korean new wave cinema 1975–1995], [Seoul: PJBook, 2020], 220).

270 Notes

14. Kim Yong-tae, "*Pannori Arirang*," in *Maehogŭi kiŏk, tongnip yŏnghwa* [Enchanted memory, Korean independent film], ed. Cho Young-gak et al. (Seoul: Association of Korean Independent Film and Video, 1999), 49.
15. Lee, *The Making of Minjung*, 11.
16. Chungmoo Choi, "The Minjung Culture Movement and the Construction of Popular Culture in Korea," in *South Korea's Minjung Movement: The Culture and Politics of Dissidence*, ed. Kenneth M. Wells (Honolulu: University of Hawai'i Press, 1995), 108.
17. For an anthropological survey of the farmers' movements in the 1980s in terms of a *minjung* movement, see Nancy Abelmann, "Minjung Movements and the Minjung: Organizers and Farmers in a 1980s Farmers' Movement," in Wells, *South Korea's Minjung Movement*, 119–154.
18. Quoted in Hong Man, "Yŏnghwa sojiptan undong" [Small film collective movement], in *Yŏnghwa undongnon* [Theory of film movement], ed. Seoul Film Collective (Seoul: Hwada, 1985), 224.
19. Ibid.
20. Critic Yoo Un-seong, a former member of Yalrashung in the 1990s, considers *Water Utilization Tax* a political pamphlet film that "takes on contemporaneity," a specific type of the essay film distinct from the "first-person and autobiographical documentary" (quoted in Seoul Independent Film Festival, "171203 shinet'ok'ŭ 1: *Surise, P'arangsae*" [December 3, 2017, Cinetalk 1: *Water Utilization Tax* and *Bluebird*], http://indienow.kr/?p=3741 [accessed February 1, 2021]).
21. Fernando Solanas and Octavio Getino, "Towards a Third Cinema: Notes and Experiences for the Development of a Cinema of Liberation in the Third World" (1969), in *New Latin American Cinema*, vol. 1, ed. Michael T. Martin (Detroit: Wayne State University Press, 1997), 56.
22. Kim, *Celluloid Democracy*, 107.
23. Park, *Unexpected Alliances*, 41.
24. Jang Sun-woo, "Yŏllyŏjin yŏnghwarŭl wihayŏ" [Toward an opened cinema], in *Saeroun yŏnghwarŭl wihayŏ* [Toward a new cinema], ed. Seoul Film Collective (Seoul: Hakmin, 1983), 320.
25. Park, *Unexpected Alliances*, 36.
26. As Lee Hae-young writes, "We need to be aware that the key movements of the Third World have been done with small film. This is a necessary consequence since film does not function as commodity" ("Taehak yŏnghwaron" [Theory of college film], in Seoul Film Collective, *Yŏnghwa undongnon*, 241).
27. The Ukamau Group's collective production of *The Courage of the People* (1971) inspired the members of SFC. The group's book, *Theory and Practice of a Cinema with the People* (Spanish in 1979 and English in 1989), was indeed translated in Korean (*Hyŏngmyŏng yŏnghwaŭi ch'angjo* [Seoul, Hankyoreh, 1988]) from its Japanese edition (1981).
28. Hong, "Yŏnghwa sojiptan undong," 219.
29. Erik Barnouw, *Documentary: A History of the Non-fiction Film* (New York: Oxford University Press, 1974), 229–294. SFC's translation of excerpts was included in Seoul Film Collective, *Saeroun yŏnghwarŭl wihayŏ*, 137–180.
30. Quoted in Seoul Film Collective, "T'oron: Han'guk yŏnghwaŭi pansŏng" [Roundtable: reflections on Korean cinema], in *Saeroun yŏnghwarŭl wihayŏ*, 329.
31. Anon., "Ch'am munhwarŭl kakkunŭn saramdŭl: 'Sŏul yŏngsang jiptan' sae yŏnghwa undonge apchang" [People who cultivate true culture: "Seoul Visual Collective" leads

the way in a new film movement], *The Hankyoreh*, May 15, 1988, quoted in Seoul Visual Collective, *Pyŏnbangesŏ chungshimŭro*, 70.

32. For a helpful study of the video, see Park Nohchool, "Gwangju Video and the Tradition of South Korean Independent Documentaries," *Review of Korean Studies* 13.2 (2010): 191–193. A recent documentary, *Gwangju Video: The Missing* (*Kwangju pidio: Sarajin 4shigan*, Lee Jo-hoon, 2020), revisits the videos and the people who were involved in production, dissemination, and screening.

33. In fact, *Sanggye-dong Olympics* is part 3 of a series of videos that Kim made during the period. Part 1 is a newsreel-style documentation of the three-day demolition of the area in October 1986. While taking the same event as its subject, part 2 focuses upon the process of forced eviction and the violence of hired gangsters against the residents who protested it. Kim completed *Sanggye-dong Olympics* by selecting the footage from parts 1 and 2 and adding new footage that captured their life and struggle after leaving Sanggye-dong.

34. Nam, "Fifteen Years."

35. Quoted in Kang Seong-ryul and Maeng Soo-jin, "Kamdokkwaŭi intŏbyu" [Interview with the director], in *Han'guk tongnip tak'yuŭi taebu Kim Dongwŏn chŏn* [Retrospective on Kim Dong-won, godfather of Korean independent documentary], ed. Kang Seong-ryul and Maeng Soo-jin (Paju, Gyeonggi-do: Booksea, 2010), 136, 138.

36. Kim Dong-won, "Kananhan sarami sesangŭi chuiniranŭn himang: *Sanggye-dong ollimp'ik*" [A hope that the poor are owners of the world: *Sanggye-dong Olympics*], in Cho et al., *Maehogŭi kiŏk*, 28.

37. Koo, *Korean Workers*, 153–187; Lee Won-bo, *Han'guk nodong undongsa 100nyŏnŭi kirok* [A hundred-year history of Korean labor movements] (Seoul: Korea Labor & Society Institute, 2013), 291–309.

38. Quoted in Song Joon-ho, "Nodongja nyusŭ jejaktan 30nyŏn: T'ujaenghanŭn nodongjaŭi pŏt" [Thirty years of Labor News Production: A friend of workers in struggle], jinbo.net, November 4, 2019, http://rp.jinbo.net/change/63420 (accessed February 1, 2021).

39. See Seoul Film Collective, *Yŏnghwa undongnon*, 253–278. An English translation, "French Radical Documentary after May 1968," is found in Waugh, "*Show Us Life*", 168–191. Hence it can be surmised that SFC used the translation for the article's publication in Korean. For a detailed historiography of the French militant cinema after May 1968, see Paul Douglas Grant, *Cinéma Militant: Political Filmmaking and May 1968* (New York: Wallflower Press, 2016).

40. Nam and Lee, "Kyŏktongŭi hyŏnshiresŏ p'iŏnan tongnip tak'yumentŏri," 45.

41. Bae has explained her fascination with video as follows: "This was the first time that SVC filmed the Great Struggle of Workers with a video camera, not with a film camera. We were shocked by the fact that we were able to contain two hours of footage in a VHS tape and to change it for another hour, and we could play what we filmed on the night of the day with a video player. It was in no way possible with film. . . . For me, *Labor News No. 1* was the opportunity to say goodbye to film." Quoted in Todaki, "Kutpai p'illŭm, 1988nyŏn chŏn'guk nodongja daehoe" [Goodbye, film! 1988 National Workers' Rallies], jinbo.net, July 15, 2016, http://rp.jinbo.net/change/26669 (accessed January 10, 2021).

42. For the helpful accounts of the US video guerrillas, see Deidre Boyle, *Subject to Change: Guerilla Television Revisited* (New York: Oxford University Press, 1995) and Chris Robé, *Breaking the Spell: A History of Anarchist Filmmakers, Videotape Guerrillas, and Digital Ninjas* (Oakland, CA: PM Press, 2017), 67–120.

272 Notes

43. For an account of the film's central status in the film movement of the late 1980s and early 1990s, see Nam Lee, "*The Night before the Strike* (1990): The Legendary *Minjung* Realist Film," in *Rediscovering Korean Cinema*, ed. Sangjoon Lee (Ann Arbor: University of Michigan Press, 2019), 246–259. For the nontheatrical screenings of the film (produced in 16 mm) at rallies, activist gatherings, and unions, see Park, *Unexpected Alliances*, 44–45. The film's restored version was finally released in theaters on May 1, 2019.

44. The documents produced by the NFI related to such activities were recently compiled in an edited collection: *Yŏnghwa undongŭi ch'oejŏnsŏn* [At the forefront of the film movement], ed. Han Sang-eon (Namyangju-si, Gyeonggi-do: Han Sang-eon Film Institute, 2022).

45. National Film Institute, "Yŏnghwa yesulgwa minjok minju undong" [Film Art and the National Democratic Movement], in *Minjok yŏnghwa 1* [National film 1], ed. National Film Institute (Seoul: Chingu, 1989), 4. The journal *National Film* ceased publication after its second issue in 1990.

46. Lee Hyo-in, "Minjok yŏnghwaŭi tangmyŏn'gwajewa immu" [The urgent task and mission of national film], in National Film Institute, *Minjok yŏnghwa 1*, 16.

47. Min Byung-jin, "Kihoek podo yŏnghwaŭi hwalsŏnghwarŭl wihayŏ" [For invigorating the planned report film], in *Minjok yŏnghwa 1*, 96.

48. The film's director of photography was Byun Young-joo, and it was mainly screened in university festivals. Bariteo made its second film, *Our Children* (*Urine aidŭl*, Do Sung-hee, 1990), in collaboration with women's organizations concerned with the issues of the urban poor and their children. It is a forty-minute video about the structural lack of day care that left the children neglected. The film was inspired by a real-life incident in which children of a urban poor family burned to death in March 1990 because their parents, with no financial capacity to pay for day care, locked them in a semi-basement house.

49. Even the 16 mm film *The Workers Advancing from 87 to 89* was rephotographed with a video camera and copied onto videotapes for distribution. See Heo Nam-woong, "Yi Ŭn, Ch'oe Yongbae kamdok int'ŏbyu" [Interview with Lee Eun and Choi Yong-bae], in *Tashi mannan tongnip yŏnghwa vol. 3* [Meeting independent cinema again, vol. 3], ed. Seoul Independent Film Festival (Seoul: Seoul Independent Film Festival, 2020), 55.

50. Lee Chang-won, quoted in Kim Hyung-seok, "Yi Sangin, Yi Ch'angwŏn kamdok int'ŏbyu" [Interview with Lee Sang-in and Lee Chang-won], in Seoul Independent Film Festival, *Tashi mannan tongnip yŏnghwa vol. 3*, 101.

51. Lee Sang-in, "Kihoek kirok yŏnghwa *Kkangsuni*, *Syuŏp'ŭrodŏkch'ŭ nodongja* chejak pogosŏ" [Production report of planned documentary *Kkangsuni*], in National Film Institute, *Minjok yŏnghwa 1*, 106.

52. Lee Sang-in, quoted in Kim, "Yi Sangin, Yi Ch'angwŏn kamdok int'ŏbyu," 102.

53. *Sanggye-dong Olympics* had been screened at the "Young Forum" section of the Berlin International Film festival in 1989.

54. Abé Marcus Nornes, *Forest of Pressure: Ogawa Shinsuke and Postwar Japanese Documentary* (Minneapolis: University of Minnesota Press, 2007), 234.

55. Ibid., 232. In Kim Dong-won's own words, "I was excited to know that the films of the Sanrizuka Series deal with evictees like *Sanggye-dong Olympics*, and that [Ogawa] filmed them so perfectly about twenty years before I did" (quoted in Lee Jong-eun, "Kim Dongwŏn int'ŏbyu" [Interview with Kim Dong-won], *KINO* 40 [May 1998]: 97).

56. Kim I-chan, Kim Hwa-beom, and Lee In-sook, "Mosaegŭi shigirŭl nŏmŏ pyŏnhwaŭi umjigimŭro sesangŭl tchikta: 1990nyŏndae tongnip tak'yument'ŏriŭi mosaekkwa pyŏnhwa" [Filming the world in the wind of change, beyond the age of endeavors: Endeavors and

changes in 1990s independent documentary], in Independent Documentary Study Group, *Han'guk tongniptak'yumentŏri*, 66–70.

57. This was partly due to the situation that many practitioners of the 1980s were put on the police's wanted list or tried to avoid arrest under the public security regime of the time (author's phone conversation with Lee Sang-in, October 15, 2020).

58. Quoted in Seoul Visual Collective, *Pyŏnbangesŏ chungshimŭro*, 52.

59. Kim, Kim, and Lee, "Mosaegŭi shigirŭl nŏmŏ," 61.

60. Maeng Soo-jin, "Movements on Screen," in *Movements on Screen*, ed. Korean Film Archive (Seoul: Korean Film Archive, 2018), 153.

61. Park, "Gwangju Video," 205–206.

62. Paul Y. Chang and Gi-wook Shin, "Democratization and the Evolution of Social Movements in Korea: Institutionalization and Diffusion," in *South Korean Social Movements: From Democracy to Civil Society*, ed. Paul Y. Chang and Gi-wook Shin (New York: Routledge, 2011), 6–7.

63. Nam, "Fifteen Years."

64. Kim Dong-won, "Chejak not'ŭ: *Tto hanaŭi Sesang: Haengdang-dong saramdŭl 2*" [Production note: *Another World We Are Making*], in *Han'guk tongnip tak'yuŭi taebu*, 69.

65. Kim has said that the association "wanted him to make a documentary about victory" and he "did not want it to go that way." Quoted in Kang and Maeng, "Kamdokkwaŭi int'ŏbyu," 180.

66. Quoted in Kim, Kim, and Lee, "Mosaegŭi shigirŭl nŏmŏ," 71.

67. Quoted in Park Hye-kyong and Lee Jong-eun, "Saeroun tongnip yŏnghwarŭl wihayŏ: *Tumilli: Saeroun hakkyoga yŏllinda*" [For a new independent film: *Doomealee: A New School Is Opening*], *KINO* 3 (July 1995): 206.

68. Byun Young-joo, "A Letter from Byun Young-joo, the director of *The Murmuring* series," in *50 Viewpoints of Korean Documentary Film*, ed. DMZ International Documentary Film Festival (Goyang, Gyeonggi-do: DMZ Docs, 2019), 56.

69. Kim Soon-young and Seo Jung-eun, "*Najŭn moksori 2*ŭi kihoekkwa hongboŭi modŭn kŏt" [All about the planning and publicity of *Habitual Sadness*], in *Najŭn moksori2 chejak not'ŭ* (Production note on *Habitual Sadness*), ed. Docu-factory Vista (Seoul: Docu-factory Vista, 1997), 45–52.

70. David Whiteman, "Out of the Theaters and into the Streets: A Coalition Model of the Political Impact of Documentary Film and Video," *Political Communication* 21 (2004): 51.

71. Byun's interested in the sexual slavery issue from her feminist perspective was anticipated in her *Women Being in Asia* (*Asiaesŏ yŏsŏngŭro sandanŭn kŏt*, 1993, 59 min.), a video documentary about Pan-Asian prostitution that she made in Docu Purn.

72. Byun, "7nyŏn tonganŭi chinshil ch'atki, ije tashi shijagida" [Seven years of seeking truth, now starting it over], *Cine 21*, March 14, 2000, http://www.cine21.com/news/view/?idx=0&mag_id=31361 (accessed January 15, 2021).

73. Chung Hye Jean, "The *Murmuring* Trilogy (1995–99): Documentary Film as Testimony," in Lee, *Rediscovering Korean Cinema*, 287.

74. The organization was later reformed into the Association of Korean Independent Film and Video (KIFV, 1998–present).

75. Anon., "Chŏlmŭn yŏnghwaindŭl sae kigu kyŏlssŏng" [Young film professionals organized a new association], *The Hankyoreh*, February 3, 1990.

76. Park, *Unexpected Alliances*, 50.

274   Notes

77. Yi Hyo-in, "Han'guk tongnip yŏnghwa, sunan'gwa ŭijiŭi hŭnjŏk" [Korean independent film, vestiges of suffering and will], in Cho et al., *Maehogŭi kiŏk*, 128.

78. The latter festival was meaningful to the institutionalization of independent documentary as its first edition gave the Best Documentary Award to *Doomealee: A New School Is Opening*.

79. Kim Myung-joon, "1980nyŏndae ihu chinbojŏk yŏnghwa undongŭi chŏn'gae gwajŏng: Sangsŭng, t'oegak, chaep'yŏn" [The development of the progressive film movement since the 1980s: Rise, fall, reform], in *Yŏnghwa undongŭi yŏksa: Kugyŏnggŏriesŏ haebangŭi mugiro* [A history of film movements: From visual feast to the tool of liberation], ed. Prism (Seoul: Seoul Publishing Media, 2002), 428.

80. Contributors of Seoul Short Film Festival, "To All Film Professionals and Film Lovers," November 15, 1996. Quoted in Song Eun-ji, "Sŏul tanp'yŏn yŏnghwaje k'ŏlleksyŏn haeje" [Comments on the Seoul Short Film Festival Collection], Korean Movie Database (KMDB), December 29, 2022, 36, available at https://www.kmdb.or.kr/collectionlist/det ail/view?colId=442 (accessed October 15, 2023).

81. Kim was arrested because he was a member of the festival's executive committee. His arrest warrant was later dismissed.

82. For a more detailed account of the independent film scene's struggles against censorship in the 1990s, see Park, *Unexpected Alliances*, 65–69.

83. Kim Soyoung, "'Cine-mania,' or Cinephilia: Film Festivals and the Identity Question," *UTS Review* 4.2 (1998): 174.

84. The festival was organized and operated by LNP.

85. After its hiatus in the late 1990s, the festival was resumed in 2001. Since then, it has changed its name three times: Rainbow Film Festival (2001–2006), Seoul LGBT Film Festival (2007–2013), and Korea Queer Film Festival (2008–present). For a study of the festival's history in dialogue with the local queer social movements until the mid-2000s, see Jeongmin Kim, "Queer Cultural Movements and Local Counterpolitics of Visibility: A Case of Seoul Queer Films and Videos Festival," *Inter-Asia Cultural Studies* 8.4 (2007): 617–633.

86. Cindy Hing-Yuk Wong, *Film Festivals: Culture, People, and Power on the Global Screen* (New Brunswick, NJ: Rutgers University Press, 2011), 160.

87. For instance, the only book-length study on BIFF, Ahn Soo Jeong's *The Pusan International Film Festival, South Korean Cinema and Globalization* (Hong Kong: University of Hong Kong Press, 2012), does not delve into the implications of its Wide Angle section.

88. As Young-a Park remarks, many key headquarter members of BIFF were in the circuit of the 1980s *yŏnghwa undong*, whether they were critics, scholars, producers, or filmmakers (*Unexpected Alliances*, 154). Another brief example of this is that Hong Hyo-sook, a former member of SVC, joined BIFF and was involved in the programming of the Wide Angle section until her resignation in 2017.

89. It is also true that not all activist videomakers agreed on this new identity. In a postscreening discussion at BIFF in the late 1990s, Tae Joon-sik, then a member of LNP, "declared himself a *hwaltongga* (activist), not a *kamdok* (director), when a fan in the audience referred to him as such" (Park, *Unexpected Alliances*, 159).

90. Hong Hyung-sook, "A Letter to the Audience," in DMZ International Documentary Film Festival, *50 Viewpoints*, 72.

91. Nam Inyoung, "90nyŏndae han'guk tongnip tak'yumentŏri yŏnghwaŭi iyagi pangshik" [Ways of storytelling in the 1990s Korean independent documentary], *Munhwa gwahak* [Culture science] 21 (2000): 131.

Notes   275

92. See BIFF's statement posted on its SNS account on July 24, 2020, https://www.facebook.com/busanfilmfest/posts/3051107461605444 (accessed July 20, 2021). Yang's rebuttal to that statement was published in December 2020. See Yang, "A Case Involving *Reclaiming Our Names*," https://docs.google.com/document/d/1F4ej30sJOo83nTBDaytMEc5DrdG5zcthvRfmORE-SKY/edit (accessed March 1, 2022).

93. For a summary of Hong's statement and the legal issues surrounding the Hong-Yang conflict, see Kim Seong-hoon, "*Ponmyŏngsŏnŏn* toyong nollan husok ch'wijae (Follow-up report on the plagiarism dispute over *Reclaiming Our Names*)," *Cine 21*, March 12, 2020, http://www.cine21.com/news/view/?mag_id=94788 (accessed July 20, 2021).

94. Kim Sohye, "Questioning Authenticity: On the Documentary Film *Reclaiming Our Names*," *Azalea: Journal of Korean Literature & Culture* 12 (2019): 353.

95. Kim, "Questioning Authenticity," 349.

96. Even KIFV at that time released a statement supporting Hong and criticizing the *Joongang Daily*, which had reported the claim made by Yang, for tarnishing Hong's reputation (Ibid., 351).

97. Kim Dong-ryung, "'Sŏngch'arhanŭn na'e taehan myŏt kaji tansang" [Several thoughts on the 'self-reflexive I'], paper presented at the special forum on documentary's intellectual property rights and production ethics, July 26, 2020, https://docs.google.com/document/d/17oHhOo64prRn-ldla_id4shsG4eeq7dRNSq8kH-B4wU/edit?ts=6095be5d (accessed July 20, 2021).

98. Byun, "7nyŏn tonganŭi chinshil ch'atki."

99. Hwang Miyojo, "*My Own Breathing*," in Korean Film Archive, *Movements on Screen*, 250.

Chapter 2

1. For the background of the first commission and its activities, see Presidential Truth Commission on Suspicious Deaths, *A Hard Journey to Justice: Presidential Truth Commission on Suspicious Deaths* (Seoul: Samin Books, 2004).

2. Hoon Joo Kim, "Local, National, and International Determinants of Truth Commission: The South Korean Experience," *Human Rights Quarterly* 34.3 (2012): 729

3. Youngju Ryu, "Introduction," in *Cultures of Yusin*, 5.

4. For a helpful summary of the history of spy fabrication cases since the Park regime, see Han Hong-goo, "Kukka p'ongnyŏkŭrosŏŭi kanch'ŏp chojak sagŏn" [Spy fabrication cases as state violence], in *Taehanmin'guk in'gwŏn kŭnhyŏndaesa 2* [A modern and contemporary history of human rights in South Korea, vol. 2] (Seoul: National Human Rights Commission, 2020), 153–205. The eight victims were acquitted in 2007, but the issue of the state's compensation for the victims and their families has remained unresolved.

5. Park, *Unexpected Alliances*, 121–125.

6. Kim Hee-chul has validated his long-term commitment to Kim's case with *The Time of Lovelessness* (*Saranghal su ŏmnŭn shigan*, 2011), a sequel to *Gate of Heaven* that reexamines the documents related to it. In September 2017, the ministry recognized Kim's case as a death in the line of duty (*sunjik*) (Yeo Jun-suk, "Army to Investigate 'Mystery Deaths,'" *Korea Herald*, September 1, 2017, http://www.koreaherald.com/view.php?ud=20170901000799 [accessed January 1, 2021]).

276   Notes

7. Kim Dong-choon, "The Truth and Reconciliation Commission of Korea: Uncovering the Hidden Korean War," *Asia-Pacific Journal*, March 1, 2010, https://apjjf.org/-Kim-Dong-choon/3314/article.html (accessed January 1, 2021).

8. Gi-wook Shin, *Ethnic Nationalism in Korea: Genealogy, Politics, Legacy* (Stanford, CA: Stanford University Press, 2006); Paik Nak-chung, "South Korea: Unification and the Democratic Challenge," *New Left Review* 197 (1993): 67–84.

9. Kim Dong-choon, Henry Em, and Christine Hong, "Coda: A Conversation with Kim Dong-choon," *Positions: Asia Critique* 23.4 (2015): 837–849. See also Henry Em, "War Politics, Visuality and Governmentality in South Korea," *North Korean Review* 12.1 (2016): 51–65.

10. As Kim has underlined in an interview, "I was very concerned about the basics of documentary because I could not be a long-term prisoner. The film that takes long-term prisoners as its subject is difficult to make without trust"(quoted in Docu Purn, "*Songhwan* chejak sŭt'ori" [Production story of *Repatriation*], in *Han'guk tongnip tak'yuŭi taebu*, 251).

11. Bill Nichols, *Introduction to Documentary*, 3rd ed. (Bloomington: Indiana University Press, 2017), 139; see also Hye Seung Chung and David Scott Diffrient, *Movie Minorities: Transnational Rights Advocacy and South Korean Cinema* (New Brunswick, NJ: Rutgers University Press, 2021), 148.

12. Markus Nornes, "*Repatriation*: A Very Persona Division," in *Rediscovering Korean Cinema*, 392.

13. Song returned to Germany in 2004 after receiving a suspended sentence of three years imprisonment by Seoul High Court because the court of appeal found him not guilty on the espionage charges except for unauthorized visits to North Korea.

14. Jamie Doucette and Se-Woong Koo, "Distorting Democracy: Politics by Public Security in Contemporary South Korea," *Asia-Pacific Journal*, February 20, 2014, https://apjjf.org/2013/11/48/Jamie-Doucette/4042/article.html (accessed November 1, 2020).

15. Gi-wook Shin and Rennie J. Moon, "South Korea after Impeachment," *Journal of Democracy* 27.4 (2017): 124.

16. Lee, *Han'guk nodong undongsa*, 360. See also Kevin Gray, *Korean Workers and Neoliberal Globalization* (New York: Routledge, 2008), 110–129.

17. Yoonkyung Lee, "Labor Movements in Neoliberal Korea: Organizing Precarious Workers and Inventing New Repertoires of Contention," *Korea Journal* 61.4 (2021): 54.

18. For NLP's account of the three forms, see Bae In-jung, "Ilsangŭi panbok: Nonyudan 30nyŏn" [Repetition of routines: Thirty years of Labor News Production], jinbo.net, January 6, 2020, http://workright.jinbo.net/xe/issue/67657 (accessed January 1, 2021).

19. Lee Ji-young, "Director's Statement," KMDB (Korean Movie Database), https://www.kmdb.or.kr/db/kor/detail/movie/A/03526 (accessed January 1, 2021).

20. Aguayo, *Documentary Resistance*, 54.

21. Ibid., 59.

22. The struggle has been the subject of scholarly works, as well as a feature film (*Cart* [*K'at'ŭ*, Boo Ji-young, 2014]), a webtoon (*Awl* [*Songgot*], 2014), and a TV drama (*Awl*, 2015) based on the webtoon.

23. Jennifer Jihye Chun, "Contesting Legal Liminality: The Gendered Labor Politics of Irregular Workers in South Korea," in *New Millennium South Korea*, 76.

24. As Kim Mi-rye describes in her production note, "Women workers in protests or labor movements make a temporary entry into the public spheres while being loosened from their everyday private spheres. While their relationships with their family members remain

strong enough, another kind of relationship that expanded in the space of struggles widened the scopes of their personal worlds. They started to recognize their identity as workers [*nodongja*]" (Kim Mi-yre, "Production Note: *Stayed Out Overnight*," in *Movements on Screen 2*, 200).

25. Bill Nichols, "Fred Weisman's Documentaries: Theory and Structure," *Film Quarterly* 31.3 (1978): 17.

26. Hyun Bang Shin and Kim Soo-hyun, "The Developmental State, Speculative Urbanisation and the Politics of Displacement in Gentrifying Seoul," *Urban Studies* 53.3 (2016): 556.

27. Quoted in Kim Sohye, "*192-399: Tŏburŏ sanŭn chim iyagi*: Yi Hyŏnjŏng kamdok intŏbyu" [*192-399: A Story about the House Living Together*: Interview with Lee Hyun-jung], *Tongnip yŏnghwa* 32 (2007): 12.

28. Jay Ruby, *Picturing Culture: Explorations of Film and Anthropology* (Chicago: University of Chicago Press, 2000), 266.

29. Oscar Lewis, "Culture of Poverty," in *On Understanding Poverty: Perspectives from the Social Sciences*, ed. Daniel P. Moynihan (New York: Basic Books, 1969), 187–220.

30. Cho Uhn, *Sadang-dong tŏhagi 25* [Sadang-dong plus 25] (Seoul: Ttohanaŭi munhwa, 2012), 314.

31. Lee Seon-young and Yoonai Han, "When Art Meets Monsters: Mapping Art Activism and Anti-gentrification Movements in Seoul," *City, Culture and Society* 21 (2020), https://doi. org/10.1016/j.ccs.2019.100292 (accessed December 1, 2020).

32. Um Ji-won, "Farming, Knitting, Live Music: New Trends in Protesting," *The Hankyoreh*, June 23, 2013, http://m.hani.co.kr/arti/english_edition/e_national/592829.html (accessed December 1, 2020).

33. Ben Jackson, "Former Noodle Restaurant Dooriban Highlights Legal Loopholes Letting Down Evictees," *Yonhap News*, May 18, 2011, https://en.yna.co.kr/view/AEN2011051600 1800315 (accessed December 1, 2020).

34. David E. James, "Film Diary/Diary Film," in *To Free the Cinema: Jonas Mekas & the New York Underground*, ed. David E. James (Princeton, NJ: Princeton University Press, 1992), 164.

35. Lee has occasionally filmed other public demonstrations in Seoul with her Super 8 mm and 16 mm cameras, and the footage was incorporated into her films, including *Optigraph* (which I will discuss in chapter 4).

36. You Dong Chul and Se Kwang Hwang, "Achievements of and Challenges Facing the Korean Disabled People's Movement," *Disability and Society* 33.8 (2018): 1266.

37. Jane M. Gaines, "Political Mimesis," in *Collecting Visible Evidence*, ed. Jane M. Gaines and Michael Renov (Minneapolis: University of Minnesota Press, 1999), 84–102.

38. Choi Sung-kyu, "Pak Chongp'irŭi 6kaeŭi ssin" [Six scenes of Park Jong-pil], *Tongnip yŏnghwa* 47 (2018): 68.

39. Park Han-na, "Demanding to Be Heard, Disability Groups Disrupt Rush-Hour Trains," *Korean Herald*, December 20, 2021, http://www.koreaherald.com/view.php?ud=2021122 0000833 (accessed February 1, 2022). In 2022, Solidarity against Disability Discrimination (Chŏn'guk changaein ch'abyŏl yŏndae, founded in 2007), the association that led the sit-ins and rallies at subway stations for mobility rights, released Park's film on its YouTube channel (https://www.youtube.com/watch?v=g16toHkM1L8).

40. Eunjung Kim, *Curative Violence: Rehabilitating Disability, Gender and Sexuality in Modern Korea* (Durham, NC: Duke University Press, 2017), 79.

278 Notes

41. Pooja Rangan, *Immediations: The Humanitarian Impulse in Documentary* (Durham, NC: Duke University Press, 2017).
42. Chung and Diffrient, *Movie Minorities*, 129–130.
43. Thomas Austin, "Interiority, Identity and the Limits of Knowledge in Documentary Film," *Screen* 57.4 (2016): 415.
44. Laura U. Marks, *The Skin of the Film: Intercultural Cinema, Embodiment, and the Senses* (Durham, NC: Duke University Press, 2000).
45. For the use of this type of voice-over, see Charles Wolfe, "Historicizing the Voice of God: The Place of Vocal Narration in Classical Documentary," *Film History* 9.2 (1997): 149–167.
46. Hwang Yoon, "Ŏnŭ saengt'aejuŭijaŭi yŏnghwa mandŭlgi" [An ecologist's filmmaking], *Tongnip yŏnghwa* 30 (2006): 69.
47. Quoted in Jeong Ji-hye, "Hwang Yun: Yŏgiesŏ, hamkke, chal salgi wihayŏ" [Hwang Yoon: To Live Well, Here, Together], *Cine21*, March 30, 2016, http://www.cine21.com/news/view/?mag_id=83500 (accessed September 10, 2020).
48. Cary Wolfe, *What Is Posthumanism?* (Minneapolis: University of Minnesota Press, 2010), xxii.
49. Hwang, "Ŏnŭ saengt'aejuŭijaŭi yŏnghwa mandŭlgi," 73, 75.
50. Vivian Sobchack, *Carnal Thoughts: Embodiment and Moving Image Culture* (Berkeley: University of California Press, 2004), 251.
51. Hwang Yoon, "Tak'yumentŏri, haengdonggwa sŏngch'al saiesŏ haedabŭl ch'ajaganŭn yŏjŏng" [Documentary, a journey to find an answer between action and reflection], *Tongnip yŏnghwa* 31 (2006): 113.
52. Chung and Diffrient, *Movie Minorities*, 229.

Chapter 3

1. Yoonkyung Lee, *Between the Streets*, 29.
2. Hardt and Negri, *Multitude*, xiv.
3. For an account of the impacts of the inequalities on the protests, see Yoonkyung Lee, "Articulating Inequality in the Candlelight Protests of 2016–2017," *Korea Journal* 59.1 (2019): 16–45.
4. Yi Jin-kyung, "The Flow of the Masses and the Candlelight Demonstrations in South Korea," *Korea Journal* 60.3 (2020): 259.
5. Indeed, *Cleaning* and *The Blue Whale Flies* derived from Kim's *Underground* and Hong's *Junha's Planet*, respectively (see chapter 2).
6. Separated from *Candlelight in the Wave*, *Candlelight Feminists* alone was showcased in many film festivals, including the Seoul International Women's Film Festival. *Blue Butterfly* was extended into a eighty-three-minute documentary, *Blue Butterfly Effect* (*P'aran nabi hyogwa*, 93 min.), which was released in theaters in June 2017.
7. Kim, "Paradox," 12.
8. Kim Soyoung, "The Birth of the Local Feminist Sphere in the Global Era: 'Trans-cinema' and *yosongjang*," *Inter-Asian Cultural Studies* 4.1 (2003): 83.
9. Song-Woo Hur, "Mapping South Korean Women's Movements during and after Democratization: Shifting Identities," in *East Asian Social Movements: Power, Protest, and Change in a Dynamic Region*, ed. Jeffrey Broadbent and Vicky Brockman (New York: Springer, 2011), 182.

Notes 279

10. Cho Jin-hee, "'Pyŏnghaengsŏn'gwa Sogŭmŭlŭl chungshimŭro salp'yŏbon yŏsŏng nodongja tak'yumentŏri" [Parallel and Salt, documentaries on female workers], Ashia yŏsŏng yŏn'gu [Asian women's studies] 44.1 (2005): 303–304.

11. Another key documentary film that takes the struggle as its subject matter is Food, Flower, Scapegoat (Pab, Ggot, Yang, 2001), made by Seo Eun-joo with Im In-ae, who formed LARNET (Labor Reporters' Network). Like Parallel, the film was refused by the labor union and the film festival committee in Ulsan, which did not want to bring the issue of female laborers to the forefront of their agenda. Accordingly, LARNET decided to publish the film's segments on the website sponsored by Jinbonet.

12. Quoted in Park, Unexpected Alliances, 130.

13. Kazuhiko Togo, "Park Yuha and the Uncomfortable Realities of South Korean Democracy," East Asia Forum, November 22, 2017, https://www.eastasiaforum.org/2017/11/22/park-yuha-and-the-uncomfortable-realities-of-south-korean-democracy/ (accessed December 1, 2020). The Comfort Women of the Empire was translated into Japanese in 2014.

14. Park won the defamation case in 2017, as judge in the Eastern District Court in Seoul stipulated that her academic freedom must be protected.

15. Quoted in Shin Eul-sil, "Redŭ maria 2rŭl tullŏssan tamnondŭl" [Interview with Kyung-soon: Discourses surrounding Red Maria 2], Tongnip yŏnghwa 46 (2016): 92.

16. Jinsook Kim, "#iamafeminist as the 'Mother Tag': Feminist Identification and Activism against Misogyny on Twitter in South Korea," Feminist Media Studies 17.5 (2017): 804.

17. Jinsook Kim, "Sticky Feminist Activism: The Gangnam Station Murder Case and Sticky Note Activism against Misogyny and Femicide," JCMS: Journal of Cinema and Media Studies 60.4 (2021): 40.

18. Sohn Hee-jeong, Peminijeum ributeu [Feminism reboot] (Seoul: Wood Pencil Books, 2017), 86.

19. Sohn, Peminijeum ributeu, 36–37.

20. For a more detailed discussion of the local feminist movement against digital sex crimes, see Kim, "Faces of Korean Women."

21. Euisol Jeong and Jieun Lee, "We Take the Red Pill, We Confront the DickTrix: Online Feminist Activism and the Augmentation of Gendered Realities in South Korea," Feminist Media Studies 18.4 (2018): 708.

22. Hakyung Kate Lee, "Thousands of Women Protest against Spy-Cameras, Gender-Biased Investigations," ABC News, August 5, 2018, https://abcnews.go.com/International/thousands-women-protest-spy-cameras-gender-biased-investigations/story?id=57011255 (accessed December 1, 2020).

23. Thanks to these protests maintained by various feminist groups and participants, the Constitutional Court in April 2019 ruled as unconstitutional the sixty-six-year-old law that made abortion a crime punishable by up to two years in prison, calling for an amendment to the law. But the amendment had not been made as of January 2021.

24. Julia Lesage, "The Political Aesthetics of the Feminist Documentary Film," Quarterly Review of Film Studies 3.4 (1978): 515.

25. Aguayo, Documentary Resistance, 156.

26. Kim Bo-ram has described her interest in menstrual cups as follows: "After gathering more information, I started to wonder why the market in Korea uniformly provides disposable sanitary pads for menstruation and why women just conform to what they are given. I wanted to at least begin a dialogue about the social perception of menstruation and alert women of the options they have other than uncomfortable sanitary pads" (quoted in Jin

280 Notes

Min-ji, "Starting a Public Period Dialogue: *For Vagina's Sake* Director Gets Honest about Menstruation," *Joongang Daily*, January 18, 2018, https://koreajoongangdaily.joins.com/2018/01/18/movies/Starting-a-public-period-dialogue-For-Vaginas-Sake-director-gets-honest-about-menstruation/3043513.html (accessed January 1, 2021)).

27. Janet Walker and Diane Waldman, "Introduction," in *Feminism and Documentary*, ed. Janet Walker and Diane Waldman (Minneapolis: University of Minnesota Press, 1999), 19.

28. For detailed accounts of these movements in the mid-1990s, see Jeongmin Kim, "Queer Cultural Movements and Local Counterpolitics of Visibility: A Case of Seoul Queer Films and Videos Festival," *Inter-Asia Cultural Studies* 8.4 (2007): 617–633; Pil Ho Kim and C. Collins Singer, "Three Periods of Korean Queer Cinema: Invisible, Camouflage, and Blockbuster," *Acta Koreana* 14.1 (2011): 121–122.

29. For a helpful survey of twenty-first-century queer movements, see Joe Philips and Joseph Yi, "Queer Communities and Activism in South Korea: Periphery-Center Currents," *Journal of Homosexuality* 67.2 (2019): 1–26.

30. Ju Hui Judy Han, "The Politics of Postponement and Sexual Minority Rights in South Korea," in *Rights Claiming in South Korea*, ed. Celeste L. Arrington and Patricia Goedde (Cambridge: Cambridge University Press, 2021), 246.

31. For issues regarding sexual minority activism's efforts to legislate the bill, see Han, "The Politics of Postponement"; Young Ran Kim, "Queer Protest! Solidarity and the Formation of Minority Politics in South Korea," *Korea Journal* 61.4 (2021): 20–43.

32. Since 2020 PINKS has been operating its own YouTube channel named Yŏnbunhong TV (https://www.youtube.com/c/%EC%97%B0%EB%B6%84%ED%99%8DTV/v), on which it has been uploading infotainment content for sexual minorities, episodes of its self-produced queer sitcom *Ŭratp'ap'a* (2021), and video documentations of the demonstrations and sit-ins demanding passage of the Ch'abyŏl kŭmji bŏp.

33. Kim Il-rhan once remarked that the protagonists' direct gaze at the camera was based on her scheme of creating the impression that "it's only for you. I value you, so I'll tell you because my relationship with you is special." Quoted in Lee Dong-yoon, "K'wiŏ yŏnghwawa k'wiŏu ndongŭi sanggwan'gwan'gye: Yŏnbunhongch'ima" [The correlation between queer cinema and queer movements: PINKS], in *Han'guk k'wiŏ yŏnghwasa* [A history of Korean queer cinema], ed. Lee Dong-yoon (Seoul: Pictureless, 2019), 244.

34. Ruin, "Mobile Numbers and Gender Transitions: The Resident Registration System, the Nation-State, and Trans/gender Identities," in *Queer Korea*, ed. Todd A. Henry (Durham, NC: Duke University Press, 2020), 366.

35. G-voice, founded in 2003 as part of Chungusai's gay rights movement, is featured in the documentary *Weekends* (*Wik'enjŭ*, Lee Dong-ha, 2016, 98 min.). Interweaving footage of the members' backstage practices for the chorus' tenth-anniversary concert with their testimonies, the film bears witness to how the choir offered a sense of belonging and how its public activities have created the utopian performativity of gay subjects. The film's glossy semi-music video style, which testifies to the aesthetic diversification of local queer documentaries, led to its winning of the Panorama Audience Award at the Sixty-Sixth Berlin International Film Festival.

36. So had gained attention with his queer short film *Auld Lang Syne* (*Oltŭ raeng sain*, 2007), a story of the reunion of a gay couple as seniors in Jongno), and later completed his first feature-length film *REC* (*Arissi*, 2009), a melodrama that foreground two gays who film themselves for the five-year anniversary of their relationship with a videocam. For a concise yet helpful English-language summary of the history of Korean queer cinema, see Kelly

Dong, "Notebook Primer: Queer Korean Cinema," mubi.com, August 12, 2021, https://mubi.com/notebook/posts/notebook-primer-queer-korean-cinema (accessed March 1, 2022).

37. Quoted in Nam, Kim, and Lee, *Han'guk tak'yument'ŏri yŏnghwaŭi paegŭpkwa haeoe shijang kaebarŭl wihan yŏn'gu*, 74.

38. For details of the incident, see Ahn Sung-mi, "Transgender Student Withdraws after Getting Accepted to Sookmyung Women's University," *Korea Herald*, February 7, 2020, http://www.koreaherald.com/view.php?ud=20200207000642 (accessed March 1, 2022).

39. Lee Young, "Sosuja yŏsŏngŭn marhal su innŭn'ga: Yŏsŏng ch'angjak chiptan umŭi yŏnghwa shirhŏm" [Can the minority women speak? Film experiments by women's film collective WOM], *NW4.5*, issue 0 (2018): 17.

40. Thomas Waugh, *The Right to Play Oneself: Looking Back on Documentary Film* (Minneapolis: University of Minnesota Press, 2011), 206.

41. Neither the bill nor the declaration has been enacted thus far.

42. Lee, "Sosuja yŏsŏngŭn marhal su innŭn'ga," 20.

43. The plan to construct Shin-kori 5 and 6 nuclear power plants was later suspended by the Moon Jae-in government, which has pursued a denuclearization policy. See Sin Dong-myeong et al., "Shin-Kori 5 and 6 Construction Suspension Welcomed by Miryang Residents," *The Hankyoreh*, June 28, 2017, http://english.hani.co.kr/arti/english_edition/e_national/800634.html (accessed October 1, 2020).

44. Seungsook Moon, *Militarized Modernity and Gendered Citizenship in South Korea* (Durham, NC: Duke University Press, 2005).

45. For a detailed study of the protests, see Andrew Yeo, "U.S. Military Base Realignment in South Korea," *Peace Review: A Journal of Social Justice* 22.2 (2010): 113–120.

46. Lina Koleilat, "Spaces of Dissent: Everyday Resistance in Gangjeong Village, Jeju Island," *Cross-Current* 33 (2019): 250.

47. Bridget Martin, "Moon Jae-In's THAAD Conundrum: South Korea's 'Candlelight President' Faces Strong Citizen Opposition on Missile Defense," *Asia-Pacific Journal*, September 15, 2017, https://apjjf.org/2017/18/Martin.html (accessed December 1, 2020).

48. Berry, "Documentary Production Process," 143.

49. Al Yeo, "Realism, Critical Theory, and the Politics of Peace and Security: Lessons from Anti-base Protests on Jeju Island," *European Journal of International Security* 3.2 (2017): 243.

50. Su Young Choi, "Protesting Grandmothers as Spatial Resistance in the Neo-developmental Era," *Korean Studies* 43 (2019): 40.

51. Helen Hughes, *Green Documentary: Environmental Documentary in the 21st Century* (London: Intellect, 2014), 42.

52. Caty Borum Chatoo, *Story Movements: How Documentaries Empower People and Inspire Social Change* (New York: Oxford University Press, 2020), 167.

53. Lee Seung-min, "Chŏnŏllijŭm tak'yumentŏ-ri yŏnghwa: T'ibi chŏnŏllijŭmgwa tongnip tak'yumentŏriŭi nach'ikŭn chou" [Journalism documentary films: A familiar encounter of TV journalism and independent documentary], *Docking Magazine*, December 23, 2019, http://dockingmagazine.com/contents/17/123/?bk=menu&cc=&ci=&stype=&stext=&npg=1

54. Evan Ramstad, "In South Korea, Journalists Protest Government," *Wall Street Journal*, March 6, 2012, https://www.wsj.com/articles/SB100014240529702033706045772648515 43837924 (accessed December 1, 2020).

282 Notes

55. *Criminal Conspiracy* (theatrical release date, August 17, 2017) and *Spy Nation* (October 13, 2016) garnered 260,512 and 143,648 attendances, respectively.
56. For a detailed account of this negative attitude toward the press, see Shin Wooyeol, Kim Changwook, and Joo Jaewon, "Hating Journalism: Anti-press Discourse and Negative Emotions toward Journalism in South Korea," *Journalism* 22.5 (2021): 1239–1255.
57. The accused of this case received a sentence of innocence in 2012 through the Truth and Reconciliation Commission.
58. Brant Houston, "The Future of Investigative Journalism," *Daedalus* 139.2 (2010): 45.
59. Bill Nichols, *Speaking Truth with Film: Evidence, Ethics, Politics in Documentary* (Berkeley: University of California Press, 2016), 86.
60. Lee Sang-ho once admitted that he did not make the film for its cinematic value and said that he did not deny his inadequacy as a filmmaker.
61. Patricia Aufderheide, *Dangerous Documentaries: Reducing Risk When Telling Truth to Power* (Washington, DC: Center for Media and Social Impact, 2015), 23.
62. Jung Sooyoung, "The Korea Center for Investigative Journalism Newstapa: *The Removal of Accumulated Evils in the Press* and the Construction of a Democratic Media System, Walking That Long Road Together," in *The Emerging Investigative Journalism Movement in Japan and Asia*, ed. Tatsuro Hanada and Makoto Watanabe (Tokyo: Waseda Chronicle, 2020), 43.
63. Whiteman, "Out of the Theaters."
64. Yoon Hye-ji, "Mogŭmaek 4ŏk3427ma6ch'ŏnwŏn kirok'an *Chabaek* sŭt'ori p'ŏnding" [Story funding for *Spy Nation* garnered approx. $393,236], *Cine 21*, October 19, 2016, http://m.cine21.com/news/view/?mag_id=85424 (accessed December 1, 2020).
65. Chuck Tryon, "Digital Distribution, Participatory Culture, and the Transmedia Documentary," *Jump Cut* 53 (2011), https://www.ejumpcut.org/archive/jc53.2011/TryonWebDoc/text.html (accessed December 1, 2020).
66. The project's outcome, *Act with Media in Chungju*, was later extended into a feature-length labor documentary *For Dear Life* (*Sasu*, Kim Seol-hae, Jo Yeongeun, Jeong Jong-min, 2018, 103 min.).
67. *Act with Media in Miryang* (*Midiŏ-ro haengdonghara Miryang*, 2015, 54 min.), for instance, comprises seven videos, five audio recordings, and a magazine that documents the three-day struggle of the residents against the transmission tower.
68. Kevin Howley, "Introduction," in *Understanding Community Media*, ed. Kevin Howley (London: Sage, 2010), 2.
69. David Scott Diffrient, "*If You Were Me*: Human Rights Discourses and Transnational Crossings in South Korean Omnibus Films," *Transnational Cinemas* 3.1 (2012): 111.
70. For a detailed report of the committee's activities, see *Kirogi t'ujaengida: Sewŏrlo ch'amsa midiŏ hwaltong 4nyŏnŭi kirok* [To document is to struggle: Four-year record of the media activities of the Sewol Ferry Disaster] (Seoul: 4.16 Solidarity Media Committee, 2019), https://drive.google.com/file/d/19UosnEsE9XCZPXIGXMGOO4CWQELGDVlW/view?fbclid=IwAR3cclMGW2xFFUMzczdYGllpM98ZmKnzhauCT4vrPD6_f6v6Fwxe IFHXfRo (accessed December 1, 2020).
71. For instance, *Forgetting and Remembering* had sixty-one community screenings and was introduced in the Sixteenth Seoul Independent Documentary Film Festival and the Twenty-First Seoul Human Rights Film Festival in 2016. After garnering KRW 41,600,000 via crowdfunding, *Forgetting and Remembering 2* received 286 community screenings (including two overseas) and was shown at seven film festivals in 2017, and some of its shorts

were aired on TBS (Traffic Broadcasting System) and EBS (Educational Broadcasting System).

72. For a detailed account of the relationship between the Sewol Ferry Disaster and the 2016–2017 Candlelight Protests, see Nan Kim, "Candlelight and the Yellow Ribbon: Catalyzing Re-democratization in South Korea," *Asia-Pacific Journal*, July 15, 2017, https://apjjf.org/2017/14/Kim.html (accessed December 1, 2020).

73. Sewol Ferry Documentation Team, *Sewŏlho, kŭnarŭi kirok* [Sewol Ferry, the record of the day] (Seoul: Chinshirŭihim), 2016.

74. For an investigation of the performances that take the disaster as their subject, see Areum Jeong, "Beyond the Sewol: Performing Acts of Activism in South Korea," *Performance Research* 24.5 (2019): 33–43.

75. Lee, "Tongshidae aekt'ibijŭm tak'yumentŏri yŏnghwa," 99.

76. Joo Hyun-sook and Hoyeon, "Tashi nonjaengŭl shijak'aja: Midiŏ hwaltongŭi chaehyŏn bangshikkwa midiŏ yulli" [Let's resume the debate: The Media Committee's ways of representation and media ethics], in *Kirogi t'ujaengida*, 56.

77. For the trend of archiving of citizens' amateur videos that document the global protests, see my *Documentary's Expanded Fields: New Media and the Twenty-First-Century Documentary* (New York: Oxford University Press, 2022), chapter 5.

78. Lille Chouliaraki, *The Spectatorship of Suffering* (London: Sage, 2006), 44.

79. Hardt and Negri, *Multitude*, 100.

80. See Jo He-rim, "Female Prosecutor Opens Up about Sexual Harassment," *Korea Herald*, January 30, 2018, http://www.koreaherald.com/view.php?ud=20180130000855 (accessed March 1, 2022).

Chapter 4

1. Quoted in Scott Macdonald, "Interview with Gina Kim," in Macdonald, *Adventures of Perception: Cinema as Exploration, Essays/Interviews* (Berkeley: University of California Press, 2009), 85.

2. Kim Sunah, "P'osŭt'ŭ kojŏn tak'yumentŏriŭi kiŏkkwa chŏngch'ihak" [The memory and politics of the postclassical documentary], *Tongnip yŏnghwa* 11 (2001): 14–15.

3. Alisa Lebow, "Introduction," in *The Cinema of Me: The Self and Subjectivity in First Person Documentary*, ed. Alisa Lebow (New York: Wallflower Press, 2012), 1.

4. Lee Do-hoon, "Ip'yŏn'gwa chŏp'yŏn, tangsinŭn ŏdie?" [Here and there, where are you?], *Reverse*, March 10, 2019, http://reversemedia.co.kr/article/133 (accessed April 5, 2021).

5. Jeong Su-eun, "Tu pŏntchae yŏnghwa, tchikŭl su issŭlkka?" [Second film, can we shoot it?], posted on March 17, 2017, https://www.facebook.com/docufemi/posts/1081661225312966/ (emphasis added, accessed April 1, 2021).

6. Jim Lane, *The Autobiographical Documentary in America* (Madison: University of Wisconsin Press, 2002), 8.

7. Kiki Tianqi Yu, *"My" Self on Camera: First Person Documentary Practice in an Individualising China* (Edinburgh: Edinburgh University Press, 2019).

8. Nam Inyoung, "Han'guk tongnip tak'yumentŏri yŏnghwaŭi chaehyŏn yangshik yŏn'gu" [A study of the modes of representation in Korean independent documentary films], PhD dissertation, Graduate Program of Film Studies, Chung-ang University, 2004, 174–175.

9. Lane, *Autobiographical Documentary in America*, 95.

284 Notes

10. Michael Renov, *The Subject of Documentary* (Minneapolis: University of Minnesota Press, 2004), 219.
11. Nam, "Han'guk tongnip tak'yument'ŏri yŏnghwaŭi chaehyŏn yangshik yŏn'gu," 120.
12. Jinhee Park, "Departure and Repatriation as Cold War Dissensus: Domestic Ethnography in Korean Documentary," *Journal of Korean Studies* 22.2 (2017): 433–457; Koh, *Korean War*.
13. Marianne Hirsch, *The Generation of Postmemory: Writing and Visual Culture after the Holocaust* (New York: Columbia University Press, 2012), 5.
14. See, for instance, Timothy Corrigan, *The Essay Film: From Montaigne to Marker* (New York: Oxford University Press, 2011); Laura Rascaroli, "The Essay Film: Problems, Definitions, and Textual Commitments," *Frameworks* 49.2 (2008): 24–47; Rascaroli, *How the Essay Film Thinks* (New York: Oxford University Press, 2017); Nora M. Alter, *The Essay Film after Fact and Fiction* (New York: Columbia University Press, 2018).
15. Renov, *The Subject of Documentary*, 109.
16. Bill Nichols, *Blurred Boundaries: Questions of Meaning in Contemporary Culture* (Bloomington: Indiana University Press, 1994), 96–97.
17. Nichols, *Blurred Boundaries*, 99.
18. Cho Han Haejoang, "'You Are Entrapped in an Imaginary Well': The Formation of Subjectivity within Compressed Development—a Feminist Critique of Modernity and Korean Culture," *Inter-Asia Cultural Studies* 1.1 (2000): 57.
19. James R. Raymo, Hyunjoon Park, Yu Xie, and Wei-jun Jean Yeung, "Marriage and Family in East Asia: Continuity and Change," *Annual Review of Sociology* 41 (2015): 473.
20. Chang Kyung-sup, "Individualization without Individualism: Compressed Modernity and Obfuscated Family Crisis in East Asia," in *Transformation of the Intimate and the Public in Asian Modernity*, ed. Emiko Ochiai and Leo Aoi Hosoya (Leiden: Brill, 2014), 39–62.
21. Heonik Kwon, *After the Korean War: An Intimate History* (Cambridge: Cambridge University Press, 2020), 20.
22. Jager and Kim, "Korean War."
23. Hyangjin Lee, *Contemporary Korean Cinema: Identity, Culture and Politics* (Manchester: Manchester University Press, 2000), 139.
24. Annette Kuhn, *Women's Pictures: Feminism and Cinema* (London: Routledge & Kegan Paul, 1982), 186.
25. Nam Inyoung and Nam Lee, "Construction of the Female Self in South Korean Feminist Documentaries *Family Project: House of a Father* (2001) and *The Two Lines* (2011)," *Journal of Japanese and Korean Cinema* 12.2 (2020): 124.
26. Quoted in Nam Inyoung, Lee In-sook, and Kim Jin-yeol, "Yŏsŏng yŏnghwa, kŭ yŏndaeŭi yŏksarŭl ch'ajasŏ: Yŏsŏngjuŭi aekt'ibijŭm pidioŭi yŏksawa hyŏnjae" [Women's film, finding the history of its solidarity: The history and present of feminist video activism], in Independent Documentary Study Group, *Han'guk tongnip tak'yument'ŏri*, 203.
27. Hwang Miyojo, "Kong/saŭi kwan'gyerŭl haech'ehagi: Han'guk yŏsŏng tak'yument'ŏriwa 'kaeinjŏgin kŏt'" [Deconstructing the public/personal relationship: Korean women's documentaries and "the individual"], in *21segi tongnip yŏnghwa* [The twenty-first-century independent film], ed. Seoul Independent Film Festival (Seoul: Association of Korean Independent Film and Video, 2014), 144.
28. Quoted in Kim Soo-jeong, "Ryu Mirye, 'Mosŏng ideollogie pan'gyŏk kahanŭn yŏnghwa mandŭlgo shipta' (Ryu Mi-rye, 'I Want to Make Films That Counterattack the Ideology of Maternity')," *Nocutnews*, April 11, 2019, https://www.nocutnews.co.kr/news/5133319 (accessed April 1, 2021).

Notes 285

29. The film was made available for streaming by the *New York Times*: "The Secret My Mom Told Me Never to Tell," February 9, 2021, https://www.nytimes.com/2021/02/09/opinion/tiger-and-ox-single-mom-korea.html (accessed April 1, 2021).

30. Park, " Departure and Repatriation," 437–438.

31. Yang Yonghi, *Kamerarŭl kkŭgo ssŭmnida* [I turn off the camera and write], trans. In Yeni (Seoul: Maumsanchaek, 2022), 31.

32. Renov, *The Subject of Documentary*, 219.

33. Park, "Departure and Repatriation," 446.

34. Near the end of the film, Yang remarks that she is permanently forbidden to enter North Korea because *Dear Pyongyang*, which contains her critique on its system, was screened in South Korea.

35. Stella Bruzzi, *Approximation: Documentary, History and the Staging of Reality* (New York: Routledge, 2020), 4.

36. Hirsch, *The Generation of Postmemory*, 6.

37. Jaimie Baron, *The Archive Effect: Found Footage and the Audiovisual Experience of History* (New York: Routledge, 2014), 86.

38. For a valuable interdisciplinary study on the apartment boom and its construction of middle-class subjectivity since Korea's economic modernization, see Park Hae-cheon, *Konk'ŭrit'ŭ yut'op'ia* [Concrete utopia] (Seoul: Vowels and Consonants, 2011).

39. Myungji Yang, *From Miracle to Mirage: The Making and Unmaking of the Korean Middle Class, 1960–2015* (Ithaca, NY: Cornell University Press, 2018), 86.

40. For an influential socioanthropological study of the debt crisis since Korea's neoliberal drive, see Jesook Song, *South Koreans in the Debt Crisis: The Creation of a Neoliberal Welfare Society* (Durham, NC: Duke University Press, 2009).

41. Stella Bruzzi, *New Documentary: A Critical Introduction* (New York: Routledge, 2000), 101.

42. Quoted in Kim Haery, "Han'guk yŏnghwae pach'inŭn tu p'yŏnŭi p'illŭm esei" [Two film essays dedicated to Korean cinema], *Cine 21*, January 11, 2003, http://m.cine21.com/news/view/?mag_id=16396 (accessed April 1, 2021).

43. Alexandre Astruc, "The Future of Cinema" (1948), in *Essays on the Essay Film*, ed. Nora M. Alter and Timothy Corrigan (New York: Columbia University Press, 2017), 96.

44. The film is the first work of Kim's "Women's History" trilogy. Its second installment, *I'll Be Seeing Her* (*Hwangholgyŏng*, 2003, 52 min.) explores the changing images of women in Korean cinema from the 1950s to the 1970s as viewed by women filmmakers and moviegoers. The final film, *New Woman: Her First Song* (*Wŏllae, yŏsŏngŭn t'aeyangiŏtta: Shinnyŏsŏngŭi p'ŏsŭt'ŭ song*, 2004, 63 min.) interweaves animation, historical footage, and interviews to investigate Na Haesuk (1896–1948), the first female painter who emerged in the Japanese Occupation period. The rest of the two films are also built upon an essayistic approach that activates Kim's subjective mode of inquiry, though their textual organization is less digressive and fragmentary than that of *Koryu*.

45. As Kim has written regarding her production experience of *Kokyu*, "What fascinates me in digital filmmaking is that its field monitor on *hyŏnjang* allows me to make scenes that are closest to my vision." Quoted in Kim Soyoung, "Kim Soyŏng kamdogŭi *Kŏryu* chejakki" [Director Kim Soyoung's production note, *Koryu*], *Cine 21*, April 6, 2001, http://www.cine21.com/news/view/?mag_id=1345 (accessed April 1, 2021).

46. Corrigan, *The Essay Film*, 32.

47. Lee Do-hoon, "Kim Eungsuŭi esei yŏnghwadŭre taehan tansang" [Reflection on Kim Eung-su's essay films], *Tongnip yŏnghwa* 45 (2015): 78.

286 Notes

48. Rascaroli, "The Essay Film," 37.
49. Quoted in Lee Do-hoon, "Kim Eungsuǔi *O!saranggwa Ch'ohyǒnshil*" [Kim Eung-su's *Oh! Love* and *Surreal*], okulo.kr, April 16, 2018, http://www.okulo.kr/2018/04/okulo-news.html (accessed April 1, 2021).
50. Rascaroli, *How the Essay Film Thinks*, 17.
51. For the accounts of the debates surrounding the Cheonggyecheon restoration project, see Ryu Jeh-hong, "Naturalizing Landscapes and the Politics of Hybridity: Gwanghuamun to Cheonggyecheon," *Korean Journal* 44.3 (2004): 8–33.
52. Quoted in "Kelvin Kyung Kun Park: Artist Talk" at the Reclaiming the City Conference (November 12–13, 2021) organized by the Nam Center for Korean Studies, University of Michigan. I was the moderator of Park's talk.
53. Rascaroli, *How the Essay Film Thinks*, 146.
54. Nicolas Abraham, "Notes on the Phantom: A Complement to Freud's Metapsychology," trans. Nicholas Rand, *Critical Inquiry* 13 (1987): 287.
55. Kelvin Kyung Kun Park, "Director's Statement," Press Kit of *Cheonggyecheon Medley* for the 2011 Berlin International Film Festival Forum section, unpaginated, http://www.kelvink yungkunpark.com/projects/cgc/110207CGCM_presskit.pdf (accessed April 1, 2021).
56. Quoted in Pierce Conran, "Kelvin Kyung Kun Park: Director of *A Dream of Iron*," Korean Film Biz Zone, May 10, 2014, http://www.koreanfilm.or.kr/eng/news/interview.jsp?blbdCo mCd=601019&seq=85&mode=INTERVIEW_VIEW (accessed January 2, 2019).
57. Alter, *Essay Film*, 5.
58. Williams, "Mirrors without Memories," 13.
59. Vanessa Agnew, "Introduction: What Is Reenactment?," *Criticism* 46.3 (2004): 327.
60. Vanessa Agnew, "History's Affective Turn: Historical Reenactment and Its Work in the Present," *Rethinking History* 11.3 (2007): 299
61. Joram ten Brink, "Reenactment, the History of Violence and Documentary Film," in *Killer Images: Documentary Film, Memory, and the Performance of Violence*, ed. Joram ten Brink and Joshua Oppenheimer (London: Wallflower Press, 2012), 176–189; Deirdre Boyle, "Trauma, Memory, Documentary: Reenactment in Two Films by Rithy Panh (Cambodia) and Garin Nugroho (Indonesia)," in *Documentary Testimonies: Global Archives of Suffering*, ed. Bhaskar Sarkar and Janet Walker (New York: Routledge, 2012), 155–172.
62. Bruzzi, *Approximation*, 4.
63. Bill Nichols, "Documentary Reenactment and the Fantasmatic Subject," *Critical Inquiry* 35 (2008): 84.
64. Park Jecheol, "Korean Shamanic Experience in the Age of Digital Intermediality: Park Chan-kyong's *Manshin*," *Concentric: Literary and Cultural Studies* 43.2 (2017): 122.
65. Quoted in Son Si-nae, "Pich'amhan sayǒn? pijanghan unmyǒng: *Imshinhan namuwa tokkaebi*, Kim Dongnyǒng, Pak Kyǒngt'ae" [Pitiable story? heroic destiny: *The Pregnant Tree and the Goblin*, Kim Dong-ryung, Park Kyoung-tae], *Reverse*, October 3, 2019, http://reversemedia.co.kr/article/248 (accessed February 28, 2021).
66. Kim Dong-ryung, quoted in Son, "Pich'amhan sayǒn?"
67. Grace Kyungwon Hong, "Ghosts of Camptown," *MELUS* 39.3 (2014): 51.
68. Nichols, *Blurred Boundaries*, 100.
69. Annabelle Honess Roe, *Animated Documentary* (New York: Palgrave Macmillan, 2013), 25.
70. Jennifer Allen, "'Einmal ist keinmal': Observations on Re-enactment," in *RE:akt! Reconstruction, Re-enactment, Re-reporting*, ed. Antonio Caronia, Janez Janša, and Domenico Quaranta (Brescia, Spain: LINK Editions, 2014), 22.

Notes 287

71. Renov, *The Subject of Documentary*, 181.
72. Alisa Lebow, "First-Person Political," in *The Documentary Film Book*, ed. Brian Winston (London: British Film Institute, 2013), 258.

Chapter 5

1. Nichols, *Introduction to Documentary*, 102–105.
2. For the multiple histories of these intersections that suggest documentary and avant-garde cinema are not two sharply distinct modes of film practice, see Bill Nichols, "Documentary and the Modernist Avant-garde," *Critical Inquiry* 27.4 (2001): 580–610.
3. Lucas Hildebrand, "Experiments in Documentary: Contradiction, Uncertainty, Change," *Millennium Film Journal* 51 (2009): 2–10; Scott MacDonald, *Avant-Doc: Intersections of Documentary and Avant-Garde Cinema* (New York: Oxford University Press, 2015).
4. See, for instance, Kendall R. Philips and G. Michell Reyes, eds., *Global Memoryscapes: Contesting Remembrance in a Transnational Age* (Tuscaloosa: University of Alabama Press, 2011); Miguel Cardina and Inês Nascimento Rodrigues, "The Mnemonic Transition: The Rise of an Anti-anticolonial Memoryscape in Cape Verde," *Memory Studies* 14.2 (2021): 380–394.
5. Stephanie Kappler, "Sarajevo's Ambivalent Memoryscape: Spatial Stories of Peace and Conflict," *Memory Studies* 10.2 (2017): 132.
6. Kwon's debut feature-length documentary, *Homeground* (*Homgŭraundŭ*, 90 min.), had its premier at DMZDocs in 2022. The film explores the history of lesbian bars in Seoul, including the first lesbian pub, Lesbos, opened in 1996.
7. For a helpful study that illustrates these aspects of home for queer subjects, see Andrew Gorman-Murray, "Gay and Lesbian Couples at Home: Identity Work in Domestic Space," *Home Cultures* 3.2 (2006): 145–167.
8. For an intersection of the governmental, community, and artistic agents involved in the urban regeneration projects of twenty-first-century South Korea, see, for instance, U-seok Seo, "Urban Regeneration Governance, Community Organizing, and Artists' Commitment: A Case Study of Seongbuk-dong in Seoul," *City, Culture and Society* 21 (2020), https://doi.org/10.1016/j.ccs.2019.100328
9. Ross King, *Seoul: Memory, Reinvention, and the Korean Wave* (Honolulu: University of Hawai'i Press, 2018), 13.
10. As Youngshik D. Bong summarizes, "The Pagoda movie theater located in a back alley of the Jongno commercial area in downtown Seoul has long been known as a place for gay people to 'socialize.' Many heterosexual Koreans tended to regard the place as symbolizing the reclusive, ghetto-like lifestyle of homosexuals" ("The Gay Rights Movement in Democratizing Korea," *Korean Studies* 32 [2008]: 100).
11. Ungsan Kim, "Cruising the Art Museum: On the Migration of Queer Experimental Cinema in South Korea," *JCMS: Journal of Cinema and Media Studies* 62.3 (2023): 194.
12. For a masterful book-length study of the state violence and human rights advocacy relating to the incident, see Hun Joon Kim, *The Massacres at Mt. Halla: Sixty Years of Truth Seeking in South Korea* (Ithaca, NY: Cornell University Press, 2014).
13. For the process of the construction of *kijich'on*, see Lee Na Young, "The Construction of Military Prostitution in South Korea during the U.S. Military Rule, 1945–1948," *Feminist Studies* 33.3 (2007): 453–481.

288 Notes

14. See, for instance, Katherine H. S. Moon, *Sex among Allies: Military Prostitution in US-Korea Relations* (New York: Columbia University Press, 1997); Seungsook Moon, "Regulating Desire, Managing the Empire: US Military Prostitution in South Korea, 1945–1970," in *Over There: Living with the US Military Empire from World War to the Present*, ed. Maria Höhn and Seungsook Moon (Durham, NC: Duke University Press, 2010), 39–77.

15. For the feminist-oriented activist fieldwork and ethnography on the sex workers, see Lee Na Young, "Un/forgettable Histories of US Camptown Prostitution in South Korea: Women's Experiences of Sexual Labor and Government Policies," *Sexualities* 21.5–6 (2018): 751–775.

16. In 2017, the Korean court ordered the government to pay fifty-seven plaintiffs the equivalent of $4,240 each in compensation for the sex workers' physical and psychological damage (Choi Sang-hun, "South Korea Illegally Held Prostitutes Who Catered to G.I.s Decades Ago, Court Says," *New York Times*, January 20, 2017, https://www.nytimes.com/2017/01/20/world/asia/south-korea-court-comfort-women.html [accessed May 1, 2022]).

17. For influential studies on the memorials and exhibitions associated with the Korean War and the DMZ, see Sheila Miyoshi Jager, "The Construction of Military Prostitution in South Korea during the U.S. Military Rule, 1945–1948," *Public Culture* 14.2 (2002): 387–409; Kim, *DMZ Crossing*, chapter 5. The April Third Incident became a national commemoration day in 2014.

18. Choi, *Right to Mourn*, 32.

19. Lee Do-hoon, "Han'guk tongnip yŏnghwaŭi 'kongganjŏk sŏnhoe': 2008 nyŏn ihu han'guk tongnip yŏnghwaŭi konggansŏng yŏn'gu" [A "spatial turn" in Korean independent films: A study of spatial representation since 2008], *Munhakkwa yŏngsang* [Literature and film] 14.4 (2013): 1086.

20. Lee Seung-min, "Han'guk tak'yumentŏri yŏnghwaŭi saeroun kyŏnghyang: 'Konggan-imiji'ŭi tŭngjang'" [A new tendency of Korean documentary films: The emergence of the 'space-image'], *Tongnip yŏnghwa* 45 (2015): 55.

21. Pierre Nora, "Between Memory and History: *Les Lieux de Mémorie*," *Representations* 26 (1989): 7. These three topological categories of the new spaces portrayed and studied by the documentaries of the "audiovisual turn" are indebted to Lee Seung-min's informative monograph on the aesthetics of spaces in recent Korean independent documentary. See her *Yŏnghwawa konggan*, 46–62.

22. Gilles Deleuze, *Cinema 2: The Time-Image*, trans. Hugh Tomlinson and Robert Galeta (Minneapolis: University of Minnesota Press, 1989), 19.

23. Deleuze, *Cinema 2*, 17.

24. Deleuze, *Cinema 1: The Movement-Image*, trans. Hugh Tomlinson and Barbara Habberjam (Minneapolis: University of Minnesota Press, 1985), 109.

25. Deleuze, *Cinema 2*, ix.

26. Deleuze, *Cinema 2*, 243.

27. Deleuze, *Cinema 2*, 244 (emphasis added).

28. Elizabeth Cowie, *Recording Reality, Desiring the Real* (Minneapolis: University of Minnesota Press, 2011), 169–170.

29. Elizabeth Cowie, "Documentary Space, Place, and Landscape," *Media Fields Journal* 3 (2011): 1.

30. D. N. Rodowick, *Gilles Deleuze's Time Machine* (Durham, NC: Duke University Press, 1997), 148.

31. Lee, "Han'guk tak'yumentŏri yŏnghwaŭi saeroun kyŏnghyang," 62.

Notes 289

32. For the national and local commemorations of the incident, see Seong-nae Kim, "Mourning Korean Modernity in the Memory of the Cheju April Third Incident," *Inter-Asia Cultural Studies* 1.3 (2000): 461–476.

33. Achille Mbembe, "Necropoltics," *Public Culture* 15.1 (2003): 15–40.

34. Yoo Un-seong, "Yŏksa, purhwahanŭn malgwa p'unggyŏng saiesŏ: Im Hŭngsunŭi yŏngsang jagŏbe taehan not'ŭ" [History, between the dissensus of speech and landscape: Notes on Im Heung-soon's films and videos], okulo.kr, October 2016, http://www.okulo.kr/2016/10/critique-002.html (accessed February 1, 2022).

35. Frances Guerin and Roger Hallas, "Introduction," in *The Image and the Witness: Trauma, Memory, and Visual Culture*, ed. Frances Guerin and Roger Hallas (New York: Wallflower Press, 2007), 7.

36. Deleuze, *Cinema 2*, 243.

37. Choi, *Right to Mourn*, 49.

38. Clarence Tsui, "*Tour of Duty* (*Geomi-eo ttang*): Yamagata Review," *Hollywood Reporter*, October 17, 2013, https://www.hollywoodreporter.com/review/tour-duty-geomi-eo-ttang-649372 (accessed February 1, 2022).

39. Jeehey Kim, "Wandering Ghosts of the Cold War: Military Sex Workers in the Film *Tour of Duty*," *Journal of Korean Studies* 22.2 (2017): 417.

40. Walter Benjamin, *The Origin of German Tragic Drama*, trans. John Osborne (New York: Verso, 1977).

41. Hilderbrand, "Experiments in Documentary," 5–6.

42. Hilderbrand, "Experiments in Documentary," 3.

43. Iván Villarmea Álvarez, *Documenting Cityscapes: Urban Changes in Contemporary Non-fiction Film* (New York: Wallflower Press, 2015), 63.

44. Quoted in Oh Minwook and Lee Do-hoon, "104pŏntchae tongnip yŏnghwa syok'eisŭ: *Pŏmjŏn*" [104th Independent Film Showcase: *A Roar of the Prairie*], in 2015 *tongnibyŏnghwa syok'eisŭ* [2015 independent film showcase], ed. Association of Korean Independent Film and Video (Seoul: Association of Korean Independent Film and Video, 2016), 192.

45. Choi, *Right to Mourn*, 32.

46. Quoted in Kim Na-hyun, "Tak'yu *Kŏmiŭi ttang* . . . kijich'on, kŭ kot'ongŭi kiŏk" [Documentary *Tour of Duty* . . . camptowns, their memories of pain], *Joongang Daily*, January 18, https://news.joins.com/article/19432774 (accessed March 1, 2022).

47. Quoted in Kim Heejin, "Appreciating Im Heung-soon," in *Im Heung-soon: Toward a Poetics of Opacity and Hauntology*, ed. National Museum of Modern and Contemporary Art (Seoul: National Museum of Modern and Contemporary Art, 2018), 345.

48. Benjamin, *Origin*, 178.

Chapter 6

1. In 2018, the conservative Liberty Korea Party (LKP [Chayu han'guk tang], now People's Power Party [Kungminŭi him]) recommended Ji for membership on the Gwangju Democratization Movement Truth-Finding Commission, but the Moon Jae-in government declined to appoint. Even several extreme right-wing congressmen of LKP invited Ji as a guest speaker at a national assembly conference in December 2018, which was designed to condemn as *chongbuk chwap'a* the people of the Democratic Party (Tŏburŏ minju dang)

290 Notes

who endorsed the uprising as a prodemocracy movement. For this recent political controversy on the uprising, see Elizabeth Shim, "South Korea Conservatives Clash with Gwangju Uprising Activists," *UPI News*, February 8, 2019, https://www.upi.com/Top_News/World-News/2019/02/08/South-Korea-conservatives-clash-with-Gwangju-Uprising-activists/1751549636800/ (accessed June 1, 2019).

2. Williams, "Mirrors without Memories." Indeed, Kang confessed that he had watched *Thin Blue Line* along with *Citizen Kane* (1941) and *The Velvet Goldmine* (1998) during his postproduction period. This attests to the influence of the investigative form on the narrative of *Kim-gun*. See Lee Hwa-jung, "*Kim-gun*: 518ŭl kyŏnghŏmhaji anŭn sedaega tŏnjinŭn chilmun" [*Kim-gun*: Questions posed by the generation that has not experienced 5.18], *Cine 21*, May 23, 2019, http://www.cine21.com/news/view/?mag_id=93050 (accessed June 1, 2019).

3. Quoted in Jung Dae-ha, "A Face Symbolizing the Gwangju Democratization Movement," *The Hankyoreh*, May 8, 2019, http://english.hani.co.kr/arti/english_edition/e_national/893111.html (accessed May 15, 2019).

4. For the definition and history of compilation filmmaking, see Jay Leyda, *Film Begets Film* (New York: Hill and Wang, 1964); Keith Beattle, *Documentary Screens: Non-fiction Film and Television* (London: Palgrave Macmillan, 2004), 125–145.

5. For the influences of the Soviet montage directors on the development of compilation filmmaking, see Leyda, *Film Begets Film*; Paul Arthur, "The Status of Found Footage," *Spectator* 20.1 (1999): 57–69.

6. For the history of the compilation films in postwar North American experimental cinema, as well as their aspiration to devise a nonlinear and fragmentary historiography with disjunctive editing, see William C. Wees, *Recycled Images: The Art and Politics of Found Footage Films* (New York: Anthology Film Archives, 1993), 32–57; Catherine Russell, *Experimental Ethnography: The Work of Art in the Age of Video* (Durham, NC: Duke University Press, 1999), 238–272.

7. Bill Nichols, "Remaking History: Jay Leyda and the Compilation Film," *Film History* 26.4 (2014): 146.

8. Michel Foucault, *The Archaeology of Knowledge*, trans. Alan Sheridan (London: Pantheon Books, 1972), 1–2.

9. Jacques Derrida, *Archive Fever: A Freudian Impression*, trans. Eric Prenowitz (Chicago: University of Chicago Press, 1995), 4.

10. Hal Foster, "An Archival Impulse," *October* 110 (2004): 5.

11. Foster, "An Archival Impulse," 22.

12. Bruzzi, *New Documentary*, 12.

13. William C. Wees, "From Compilation to Collage: The Found Footage Films of Arthur Lipsett," *Canadian Journal of Film Studies* 16.2 (2007): 20.

14. Walter Benjamin, *The Arcades Project*, trans. Howard Eiland and Kevin McLaughlin (Cambridge, MA: Harvard University Press, 1999), 462.

15. Scott MacKenzie, "Flowers in the Dustbin: Termite Culture and Detritus Cinema," *Cineaction* 47 (1998): 28. See also Jeffrey Skoller, *Shadows, Specters, Shards: Making History in Avant-Garde Film* (Minneapolis: University of Minnesota Press, 2005), 28.

16. Russell, *Experimental Ethnography*, 252.

17. Benjamin writes, "The destructive or critical momentum of materialist historiography is registered in that blasting of historical continuity with which the historical object first constitutes itself" (*The Arcades Project*, 475).

Notes   291

18. Catherine Russell, "The Restoration of *The Exiles*: The Untimeliness of Archival Cinema," *Screening the Past* 34 (2012), http://www.screeningthepast.com/2012/08/the-restoration-of-the-exiles-the-untimeliness-of-archival-cinema/ (accessed November 15, 2016). See also her "New Media and Film History: Walter Benjamin and the Awakening of Cinema," *Cinema Journal* 43.3 (2004), 81–85.

19. Walter Benjamin, "On the Concept of History," in *Selected Writings*, vol. 4: *1938–1940*, ed. Howard Eiland and Michael W. Jennings, trans. Edmund Jephcott et al. (Cambridge, MA: Harvard University Press, 2003), 391.

20. Hyun Ok Park, "The Politics of Time: The Sewŏl Ferry Disaster and the Disaster of Democracy," *Journal of Asian Studies* 81.1 (2022): 141.

21. Hirsch, *The Generation of Postmemory*.

22. Quoted in Lee Hwa-jung, "*Kim-gun*." The "86 generation (86 *sedae*)" refers to the generation of Koreans born in the 1960s who attended colleges and universities in the 1980s. It was used as a catchword to indicate the generation's pivotal role in the democratization movement.

23. Koh, *Korean War*, 3.

24. Catherine Russell, *Archivelogy: Walter Benjamin and Archival Film Practices* (Durham, NC: Duke University Press, 2018), 48.

25. Chung Cheol-woong, "Int'ŏbyu: Younghwa *Miguk'ŭi baramgwa bul* Kimgyŏngman kamdok" [An interview with Kim Kyung-man, director of *An Escalator in World Order*], *Midiŏonŭl* [Media today], July 30, 2012, http://www.mediatoday.co.kr/?mod=news&act=articleView&idxno=104025 (accessed January 15, 2017).

26. Benjamin, *The Arcades Project*, 209.

27. Russell, *Experimental Ethnography*, 238.

28. Baron, *The Archive Effect*, 24.

29. Paul Virilio, *War and Cinema: The Logistics of Perception*, trans. Patrick Camiller (New York: Verso, 2009).

30. Sven Spieker, *The Big Archive: Art from Bureaucracy* (Cambridge, MA: MIT Press, 2008), 173–174.

31. Lee Sang-hyun, "The ROK-US Relations in Lee Myung-bak Government: Toward a Vision of a '21st-Century Strategic Alliance,'" *Journal of East Asian Affairs* 22.1 (2008): 7.

32. Jamie Shinhee Lee, "Globalization and Language Education: *English Village* in South Korea," *Language Research* 47.1 (2011): 123.

33. Corrigan, *The Essay Film*, 155.

34. Rascaroli, "The Essay Film," 35.

35. Renov, *The Subject of Documentary*, 110.

36. Corrigan, *The Essay Film*, 175. See also Benjamin, *The Arcades Project*, 463.

37. Sun-chul Kim, "The Trajectory of Protest Suicide in South Korea, 1970–2015," *Journal of Contemporary Asia* 51.1 (2021): 38.

38. Hieyoon Kim, "On *1987*: South Korean Cinema in the Era of Re-democratization," *Korea Journal* 60.3 (2020): 287.

39. Chang Kyung-sup, "Compressed Modernity and Its Discontents: South Korean Society in Transition," *Economy and Society* 28.1 (1999): 48.

40. Quoted in Stefen Steinberg, "A Serious Approach to History: *Non-fiction Diary* by South Korea's Jung Yoon-suk," *World Socialist Web Site*, February 24, 2014, https://www.wsws.org/en/articles/2014/02/24/berl-f24.html (accessed February 15, 2017).

41. Benjamin, *The Arcades Project*, 462.

292 Notes

42. Russell, *Experimental Ethnography*, 245.
43. Russell, *Experimental Ethnography*, 240. For Craig Owens's original concept of the allegory that Russell develops in her work on found footage filmmaking and alternative historiography, see his "The Allegorical Impulse: Toward a Theory of Postmodernism," *October* 12 (1980): 67–86.
44. Wees, MacKenzie, and Russell have all underlined this aesthetic effect of the collage-style editing in found footage filmmaking.
45. Michael Zyrd, "Found Footage Film as Discursive Metahistory: Craig Baldwin's *Tribulation 99*," *Moving Image* 3.2 (2003): 42.
46. Baron, *The Archive Effect*, 23.
47. Olaf Möller, "As Times Go By," *Film Comment* 50.3 (2014), https://www.filmcomment. com/article/berlin-film-festival-2014/ (accessed January 15, 2017).
48. For the English information on the series, visit https://modernkorea.wordpress.com/.
49. For an overview of the enactment of the Special Act, see Shim Young-hee, "Feminism and the Discourse of Sexuality in Korea: Continuities and Changes," *Human Studies* 24 (2001): 133–148.
50. For more details on the Nth Room scandal, see Nicole de Souza, "The Nth Room Case and Modern Slavery in the Digital Space," *The Interpreter*, April 20, 2020, https://www.lowyin stitute.org/the-interpreter/nth-room-case-and-modern-slavery-digital-space (accessed March 10, 2022).
51. Quoted in KBS, "Chŏng Jaeŭn kamdok, *Modŏn k'oriae* tamŭn shidaejŏk ŏnŏ 'chimsŭng' " [Director Jeong Jae-eun, 'Beast,' a language of the time in *Modern Korea*], *K-Star News*, March 30, 2021, https://kstar.kbs.co.kr/list_view.html?idx=43527 (accessed March 10, 2022).
52. Hilderbrand, "Experiments in Documentary," 6.
53. Hito Steyerl, "In Defense of Poor Images," in *The Wretched of the Screen* (Berlin: Sternberg, 2012), 38.

Chapter 7

1. Choi Jin-sung, "Tijit'ŏl, tak'yument'ŏri p'yohyŏn yangshigŭi hwakchang tongnyŏk" [Digital, a driving force of expanding documentary's mode of expression], in Independent Documentary Study Group, *Han'guk tongniptak'yument'ŏri*, 215.
2. Igong, catalog for a special screening program "Saeroun shido: P'osŭt'ŭ tak'yument'ŏri chŏn" [New attempts: Postdocumentary showcase] (Seoul: Igong, 2001), unpaginated.
3. Renov, *The Subject of Documentary*, 138.
4. John Corner, "Performing the Real: Documentary Diversions," *Television and New Media* 3.3 (2002): 259.
5. For an insightful account of the syndrome, see Lee, *Memory Construction*, chapter 3.
6. For a helpful account of *Saemaul undong*, see Seung-mi Han, "The New Community Movement: Park Chung Hee and the Making of State Populism in Korea," *Pacific Affairs* 77.1 (2004): 69–93.
7. Choi, "Tijit'ŏl," 215.
8. As Seungsook Moon summarizes, the plan of the Park memorial stirred a tug of war between progressive and conservative forces: "The plan generated strong opposition,

organized by progressive social groups. In 2000, these opposition groups formed the National Solidarity against the Park Chung-hee Memorial Hall and published a white paper on Park's erroneous policies and tyrannical rule" ("The Cultural Politics of Remembering Park Chung Hee," *Asia-Pacific Journal*, May 9, 2009, https://apjjf.org/-Seungsook-Moon/3140/article.html [accessed October 1, 2020]). The construction of the museum was completed in 2012.

9. Youngju Ryu, "Introduction," in *Cultures of Yushin: South Korea in the 1970s*, ed. Youngju Ryu (Ann Arbor: University of Michigan Press, 2018), 11.

10. Maeng Soo-jin and Mo Eun-young, *Chinshil hokŭn hŏgu, kyŏnggyee sŏn tak'yumentŏri: Han'guk tongnip tak'yumentŏrirŭl chungshimŭro* [Truth or fiction, documentary on the border: Korean independent documentary] (Seoul: Sodo, 2008), 49.

11. Quoted in Han Sunhee, "Chilmunhanŭn yesulga, shimin: kamdok Chŏng Yunsŏk" [Citizen, artist who asks questions: director Jung Yoon-suk], *Docking Magazine*, May 28, 2017, http://dockingmagazine.com/contents/6/20 (accessed October 1, 2020).

12. Alexandra Juhasz and Jesse Lehner, "Introduction: Phony Definitions and Troubling Taxonomies of the Fake Documentary," in *F Is for Phony: Fake Documentary and Truth's Undoing*, ed. Alexandra Juhasz and Jesse Lehner (Minneapolis: University of Minnesota Press, 2006), 2.

13. Ahn Kearn-hyung, in his e-mail conversation with the author, September 17, 2020.

14. Following the trend of international film festivals to embrace VR, such as the Venice International Film Festival's launching of the VR competition section and the Tribeca Film Festival's Virtual Arcade Program, BIFF featured thirty-six VR films in its first VR Cinema program in 2017.

15. Quoted in Sonia Kil, "Virtual Reality Comes to Mainstream Cinema in South Korea," *Variety*, May 9, 2018, https://variety.com/2018/biz/news/vr-virtual-reality-gina-kim-1202801584-1202801584/ (accessed December 1, 2020).

16. Chris Milk, "How Virtual Reality Can Create the Ultimate Empathy Machine," TED Talk, March 2015, https://www.ted.com/talks/chris_milk_how_virtual_reality_can_create_the_ultimate_empathy_machine (accessed July 1, 2018).

17. Nonny de la Peña et al., "Immersive Journalism: Immersive Virtual Reality for the First-Person Experience of News," *Presence* 19.4 (2010): 291.

18. For more detailed accounts of this negotiation that I conceptualize as "synthetic vision," see my *Documentary's Expanded Fields: New Media and the Twenty-First-Century Documentary* (New York: Oxford University Press, 2022), 92–105.

19. *Meeting You* has produced four other episodes besides the one on Nayeon, based on the VR recreation of social actors. Its fifth episode (2021) features the last moment of the worker Kim Yong-kyun (see chapter 2), reconstructing the dangerous thermal power plant that led to his death.

20. Violet Kim, "Virtual Reality, Real Grief," *Slate Magazine*, May 27, 2020, https://slate.com/technology/2020/05/meeting-you-virtual-reality-documentary-mbc.html (accessed December 1, 2020).

21. Lee Gyu-lee, "*Meeting You* Creator on His Controversial Show: 'I Hope It Opens Up Dialogue,'" *Korea Times*, April 10, 2020, https://www.koreatimes.co.kr/www/art/2020/04/688_287372.html (accessed December 1, 2020).

22. Jonathan Kahana, "Introduction: What Now? Presenting Reenactment," *Framework* 50.1–2 (2009): 50.

294 Notes

23. Bill Nichols, "Documentary Reenactment and the Fantasmatic Subject," *Critical Inquiry* 35 (2008): 86 (emphasis added).

24. Bill Nichols, *Introduction to Documentary* (Bloomington: Indiana University Press, 2001), 131 (emphasis added).

25. Brian Winston, "The Tradition of the Victim in Griersonian Documentary," in *New Challenges for Documentary*, ed. Alan Rosenthal (Berkeley: University of California Press, 1988), 269–287.

26. Gina Kim, "Director's Statement: *Bloodless*," http://www.ginakimfilms.com/bloodless-2017 (accessed December 1, 2020, emphasis added).

27. Quoted in "*Tongduchŏn*, Kim China kamdok intŏbyu" [Interview with Gina Kim on *Bloodless*], Seoul International Women's Film Festival website, November 29, 2017, https://siwff.tistory.com/786 (accessed December 1, 2020).

28. Kate Nash, "Virtual Reality Witness: Exploring the Ethics of Mediated Presence," *Studies in Documentary Film* 12.2 (2018): 128.

29. Kim, *DMZ Crossing*, 104.

30. Quoted in Amelia Seely, "Interview: Hayoun Kwon, *489 Years* Director," Glasgow Short Film Festival website, February 28, 2017, https://glasgowshort.org/latest/news/interview-hayoun-kwon-489-years-director (accessed December 1, 2020).

31. *The Intention* has garnered 540,658 audiences since its theatrical release on April, 12, 2018. This is the thirteenth highest-grossing Korean independent and arthouse film of all time.

32. Mark J. P. Wolf, "Subjunctive Documentary: Computer Imaging and Simulation," in *Collecting Visible Evidence*, ed. Jane M. Gaines and Michael Renov (Minneapolis: University of Minnesota Press, 1999), 274.

33. Wolf, "Subjunctive Documentary," 281.

34. Williams, "Mirrors without Memories," 10.

35. Craig Hight, "Primetime Digital Documentary Animation: The Photographic and the Graphic with Play," *Studies in Documentary Film* 2.1 (2008): 10.

36. Hight, "Primetime Digital Documentary Animation," 23.

37. José van Dijck, "Picturizing Science: The Science Documentary as Multimedia Spectacle," *International Journal of Cultural Studies* 9.1 (2006): 11.

38. Honess Roe, *Animated Documentary*, 23.

39. Quoted in "*Yuryŏngsŏn*, Kim Jiyŏng kamdok: Tongnip tak'yumentŏrinŭn chŏehuŭi poru (Kim Ji-yeong, Director of *Ghost Ship*: "Independent documentary is the last stand")," *Cine 21*, April 23, 2020, http://www.cine21.com/news/view/?mag_id=95239 (accessed September 1, 2020).

40. Michael Nitsche, *Video Game Spaces: Image, Play, and Structure in 3D Game Worlds* (Cambridge, MA: MIT Press, 2008), 73.

41. Winston, *Claiming the Real: The Documentary Film Revisited* (London: British Film Institute, 1995), 135.

42. Edward Tufte, *Beautiful Evidence* (Cheshire, CT: Graphics Press, 2006), 9.

43. For instance, Galloway argues that visualizations of data as clouds, networks, and maps paradoxically suggest that "something is happening behind and beyond the visible," and that "there are some things that are unrepresentable" (*The Interface Effect* [London: Polity, 2012], 86), namely, the algorithmic and the computational. This accords with Chun's claim on the paradoxical coincidence of visibility and invisibility in the computer: "This notion of the computer as rendering everything transparent, however, is remarkably at odds

Notes 295

with the actual operations of computation, for computers—their hardware, software, and the voltage differences on which they rely—are anything but transparent" (*Programmed Vision: Software and Memory* [Cambridge. MA: MIT Press, 2011], 17).

44. Leon Gurevitch, "The Documentary Attraction: Animation, Simulation, and the Rhetoric of Expertise," in *Drawn from Life: Issues and Themes in Animated Documentary Cinema*, ed. Jonathan Murray and Nea Ehrlich (Edinburgh: Edinburgh University Press, 2019), 90.

45. Gurevitch, "The Documentary Attraction," 98.

46. Quoted in Kim Seong-hoon, "*Kŭnal, pada*, Kim Jiyŏng kamdok: 'Teit'ŏro chŏpkŭnhae sashire tagagaya haetta'" [Kim Ji-yeong, director of *The Intention*, "I had to approach facts with data"], *Cine21*, April 25, 2018, http://www.cine21.com/news/view/?mag_id=89973 (accessed September 1, 2020).

47. Quoted in Kim Dong-won and Hong Hyung-sook, "*Tu kaeŭi mun*, yongsanŭi chaegusŏng: Mosaegin'ga hut'oein'ga" [*Two Doors*' reconstruction of Yongsan: Seeking or retreat], *Cine21*, no. 859 (June 19, 2012): 90.

48. The attorneys of the accused applied citizen participation in the criminal case to the court of the trials, but it dismissed that request on March 26, 2009.

49. Maeng Soo-jin, "*Tu kaeŭi mun*" [*Two Doors*], kmdb.or.kr, February 17, 2012, https://www.kmdb.or.kr/story/12/2214 (accessed September 1, 2020).

50. Quoted in Yoo Un-seong, "Poiji annŭn mangnu" [The invisible lookout], okulo.kr, http://www.okulo.kr/2018/01/interview-001.html (accessed September 1, 2020, emphasis added).

51. Martin Lefebvre and Marc Furstenau, "Digital Editing and Montage: The Vanishing Celluloid and Beyond," *Cinémas: Journal of Film Studies* 13.1–2 (2002): 76.

52. Kim Soyoung, "Towards a Technology of the Dead: Kim Soyoung on Her 'Exile' Documentary Trilogy," *Senses of Cinema* 78 (2016), https://www.sensesofcinema.com/2016/feature-articles/kim-soyoung-exile-trilogy (accessed June 1, 2020).

53. Henry A. Giroux, *Border Crossings: Cultural Workers and the Politics of Education* (New York: Routledge, 1992), 51.

54. Douglas Kellner and Gooyong Kim, "YouTube, Critical Pedagogy, and Media Activism," *Review of Education, Pedagogy, and Cultural Studies* 32.1 (2010): 6.

55. Jo Dongwon, "Real-Time Networked Media Activism in the 2008 *Chotbul* Protest," *Interface: A Journal for and about Social Movements* 2.2 (2010): 94.

56. Thomas Matheisen, "The Viewer Society: Michel Foucault's 'Panopticon' Revisited," *Theoretical Criminology* 1.2 (1997): 215–234.

57. Kris Fallon, "Archives Analog and Digital: Errol Morris and Documentary Film in the Digital Age," *Screen* 54.1 (2013): 40.

58. Kim Eun-sung, "The Sensory Power of Cameras and Noise Meters for Protest Surveillance in South Korea," *Social Studies of Science* 46.3 (2016): 400.

59. Quoted in Byun Sung-chan, Kim Il-rhan, and Hong Ji-yoo, "*Tu kaeŭi mun*" [*Two Doors*], in *Han'guk tongnibyŏnghwahyŏp'oe kit'a ganhaengmul 2012* [The Association of Korean Independent Film and Video's supplementary publication 2012], ed. Association of Korean Independent Film and Video (Seoul: Association of Korean Independent Film and Video, 2012), 147.

60. Georges Didi-Huberman, *Images in Spite of All: Four Photographs from Auschwitz*, trans. Shane B. Lillis (Chicago: University of Chicago Press, 2008), 121.

296 Notes

Epilogue

1. Janet Walker, "False Memories and True Experience," *Screen* 42.2 (2001): 214.
2. Quoted in Yoo Un-seong, "Poiji annŭn mangnu."
3. Jean-Luc Nancy, *The Inoperative Community*, ed. Peter Connor, trans. Peter Connor et al. (Minneapolis: University of Minnesota Press, 1991), 28–29.
4. Andrew Higson, "The Limiting Imagination of National Cinema," in *Cinema and Nation*, ed. Mette Hjort and Scott Mackenzie (New York: Routledge, 2000), 69.
5. For a comprehensive account of the shifting notion of citizenship from modern to contemporary Korea, see Seungsook Moon, "The Idea and Practice of Citizenship in South Korea," in *Citizenship and Migration in the Era of Globalization: The Flow of Migrants and the Perception of Citizenship in Asia and Europe*, ed. Markus Pohlmann, Jonghoe Yang, and Jong-hee Lee (New York: Springer, 2013), 9–38.
6. For another helpful take on *Scenery*, see Ran Ma, "A Landscape over There: Rethinking Translocality in Zhang Lu's Border-Crossing Films," *Verge: Studies in Global Asias* 4.1 (2018): 111–132.
7. The work was commissioned for *History Has Failed Us, but No Matter* (*Yŏksaga urirŭl mangch'yŏ nwatchiman kŭraedo sanggwan ŏpta*), the Korean Pavilion exhibition for the Fifty-Eighth Venice International Biennale in 2019, curated by Kim Hyunjin. For more detailed discussions of the work, see *Community of Parting*, exhibition catalog, ed. Anne Kølbæk Iversen and Jane Jin Kaisen (Berlin: Archive Books, 2020).
8. Hamid Naficy, "Phobic Spaces and Liminal Panics: Independent Transnational Film Genre," in *Global/Local: Cultural Production and the Transnational Imaginary*, ed. Rob Wilson and Wimal Dissanayake (Durham, NC: Duke University Press, 1996), 125.
9. For a couple of influential studies on the migration of Koryŏ people and the formation of their community in Central Asia, see German N. Kim, "Koryo Saram, or Koreans of the Former Soviet Union: In the Past and Present," *Amerasia Journal* 29.3 (2003–2004): 23–29; Alexander Kim, "The Repression of Soviet Koreans during the 1930s," *The Historian* 74.2 (2012): 267–285.
10. Will Higbee and Song Hwee Lim, "Concepts of Transnational Cinema: Towards a Critical Transnationalism in Film Studies," *Transnational Cinemas* 1.1 (2010): 9–10.
11. Kim, "Towards a Technology." For her more detailed theoretical reflection on the trilogy, see Soyoung Kim, "On Exile Trilogy: Trans-Asia Trajectory," in *Trans-Asia as Method: Theory and Practices*, ed. Jeroen de Kloet, Yiu Fai Chow, and Gladys Pak Lei Chong (Lanham, MD: Rowman & Littlefield, 2019), 99–114.
12. Ran Ma, *Independent Filmmaking across Borders in Contemporary Asia* (Amsterdam: Amsterdam University Press, 2020), 95.
13. Mette Hjort, "On the Plurality of Cinematic Transnationalism," in *World Cinemas, Transnational Perspectives*, ed. Nataša Durovicová and Kathleen E. Newman (New York: Routledge, 2009), 17.
14. Hamid Naficy, *An Accented Cinema: Exilic and Diasporic Filmmaking* (Princeton, NJ: Princeton University Press, 2001), 101.
15. Rascaroli, *How the Essay Film Thinks*, 146.
16. Quoted in Im's website, http://imheungsoon.com/2020-good-light-good-air/ (accessed July 20, 2021). The film's title, *Good Light, Good Air*, originates from Im's effort to explore

the affinities of the two cities, as "good light" refers to Gwangju ("Gwang" means "light") while "good air" is the English translation of "Buenos Aires."

17. Jacques Rancière, *The Politics of Aesthetics: The Distribution of the Sensible*, trans. Gabriel Rockhill (New York: Continuum, 2006), 39.

18. Jacques Rancière, *Film Fables*, trans. Emiliano Battista (New York: Berg, 2006), 158. As he further elaborates, "It is not a matter of claiming that everything is fiction. The fiction of the aesthetic age defined models for connecting the presentation of facts and forms of intelligibility that blurred the border between the logic of facts and the logic of fiction" (*The Politics of Aesthetics*, 38).

19. Nico Baumbach, "Jacques Rancière and the Fictional Capacity of Documentary," *New Review of Film and Television Studies* 8.1 (2010): 67.

Index

For the benefit of digital users, indexed terms that span two pages (e.g., 52–53) may, on occasion, appear on only one of those pages.

#metoo (*mit'u*), 123–24, 215–16
1988 Seoul Olympics, 41–42, 243–44
4.16 Solidarity Media Committee (4.16 yŏndae midiŏ wiwŏnhoe), 28–29, 120

Abelmann, Nancy, 270n.17
Abraham, Nicolas, 155–56
Act with Media (Midiŏro haengdonghara), 117–19
activism, 7–17, 24–30, 35–36, 41–42, 44–45, 54–55, 61–62, 66–67, 79–80, 88, 205–6
 archive activism, 120–21
 environmental activism, 13, 86–87, 91, 106–7, 110, 111–12, 119–20
 feminist activism, 95–96
 migratory-grassroots media activism, 91–92, 117–18, 119
activist film (*undong yŏnghwa*), 52–53
activist mode, 15–17, 66–67, 120–21, 220–22
activist (*hwaltongga*), 5, 19–20, 130, 274n.89
aesthetic period (*mihakchŏk shigi*), 6–7
affective turn, 159
affirmative transnationalism, 258–60
agitprop (*sŏndong*), 72–73
Agnew, Vanessa, 159
Aguayo, Angela J. 15
Ahn, Kearn-hyung, 225–26
 How to Stop Being Korean (*Han'guginŭl kwandunŭn pŏp*, 2018), 225–26
Ahn, Soo-jeong, 274n.87
Ahn, Sung-mi, 281n.38
allegory, 213, 292n.43
Allen, Jennifer, 163–64
Alter, Nora M. 284n.14
alternative journalism documentary, 14–15, 91–92, 113–17
alternative media (*taean maech'e*), 7–8, 15–17, 42–44, 72–73, 86–87, 110–11, 116–17, 119–20
Álvarez, Iván Villarmea, 289n.43

Andersen, Thom, 193–95
animal rights (*tongmulgwŏn*), 13, 61–62, 83–87, 89–90, 99–100
Antiabortion Law (Nakt'ae gŭmji pŏp), 96–97
anticommunism (*pan'gongjuŭi*), 64–66, 224–25
anticommunist, 10–12, 33–34, 66–70, 105–6, 114–15, 135, 145–46, 179, 192
 anticommunist policy (*pan'gong gukshi*), 223–24
Antidiscrimination Law (Ch'abyŏl gŭmji pŏp), 101–2
Antonio, Emile de, 193–95
any-space-whatever, 176–78, 184
 See also Deleuze, Gill
approximation, 160
 See also Bruzzi, Stella
Apted, Michael, 78–79
 7 Up (1964), 78–79
 63 Up (2019), 78–79
archival footage, 17–18, 23–24, 49–50, 64–65, 139–40, 149–50, 152–53, 156–57, 160–61, 165, 171–72, 179–80, 193–96, 202–3, 209–10, 222–23, 247–48, 257–58
archival impulse, 197–98, 203–4, 210–11
 See also Foster, Hal
archival turn, 23–24, 196–99, 200–1, 214–15, 216, 217, 248–49, 256–57
Association of Korean Independent Film and Video (KIFV), 56–57, 275n.96
Association of National Evictees (ANE: Chŏn'guk chŏlgŏmin yŏnhap'oe), 250
Astruc, Alexandre, 150–51
Atton, Chris, 264n.15
audiovisual turn, 22–24, 29–30, 168–71, 175–76, 178, 190, 191
Aufderheide, Patricia, 116
Austin, Thomas, 82–83
auteurism, 99–100, 111–12, 130

300 Index

authoritarianism, 114–15, 253–54
avant-doc, 168, 170–71

Bae, In-jung, 42–44, 276n.18
Baldwin, Craig, 193–95
Bang, Eun-jin, 57–58
Barnouw, Erik, 40, 46–47
Baron, Jaimie, 202–3, 285n.37
Baumbach, Nico, 261
Beattle, Keith, 290n.4
Beck, Ulrich, 211–12
Benjamin, Walter, 17–18, 23–24, 184, 191,
    196–97, 198–207, 209–10, 212–13, 216
bereaved families (*yugajok*), 9–10, 14–15,
    27–29, 58–60, 63–64, 89–90, 105–6,
    120–22, 139–40, 169, 173–74, 190,
    199–200, 207–8, 240, 241
Berlin International Film Festival, 51–52,
    266n.52, 280n.35, 286n.55
Berry, Chris, 1–2, 9–10, 109–10
Blacklist Scandal, 14–15
Bolivian Ukamau Film, 39–40
Bong, Joon-ho, 227
    Parasite (2019), 227
Bong, Youngshik D. 287n.10
Boyle, Deidre, 159, 271n.42
Brazilian Cinema Novo, 39–40
Brecht, Bertolt, 37–38, 152–53
Brink, Joram ten, 159
broadcast documentary (*pangsong
    tak'yument'ŏri*), 33–34
Bruzzi, Stella, 148–49, 160, 197–98
Busan International Film Festival(BIFF),
    25–26, 55–57, 169–70, 274n.87,
    274n.88, 274n.89, 275n.92
Bush, George W. 204–5
Byun, Gyu-ri, 102–3
    Coming to You (*Nŏege kanŭn kil*,
    2021), 102–3
Byun, Sung-chan, 295n.59
Byun, Young-joo, 1–2, 24–25, 26–27, 46–47,
    51–52, 92–93, 179
    The Murmuring (*Najŭn moksori*, 1995),
    51–52, 55–56
    Habitual Sadness (*Najŭn moksori 2*, 1997),
    51–52, 55–56
    My Own Breathing (*Najŭn moksori 3:
    Sumgyŏl*, 1999), 51–52, 59–60

candlelight protest (*chotbul siwi*), 13–15, 91–92,
    107–8, 120, 149, 160–61, 244–46

Cardina, Miguel, 287n.4
Chang, Kyung-sup, 134–35, 211–12
    See also compressed modernity
Chang, Paul Y. 48–49
Chatoo, Caty Borum, 281n.52
Chingusai (Ch'in'gusai), 100–1, 102–3
Cho, Gab-je, 222–23
Cho, Hee-yeon, 9–10
Cho, Heyyoung, 264n.14
Cho, Jin-hee, 93–94
Cho, Jung-kwan, 264n.19
Cho, Sung-bong, 53–54, 110, 195–96
    Red Hunt (*Redŭ hŏnt'ŭ*, 1997), 53–54,
    55–56, 110
    Red Hunt 2: State Crime (*Redŭ hŏnt'ŭ 2:
    Kukka pŏmjoe*, 1999), 110
    Gureombi: The Wind Is Blowing (*Gureombi:
    Parami punda*, 2013), 110, 181–82
Cho, Uhn, 78–79
    Sadang-dong Plus 22 (*Sadang-dong tŏhagi
    22*, 2009), 78–79
    Sadang-dong Plus 33 (*Sadang-dong tŏhagi
    33*, 2020), 78–79
Choi, Chungmoo, 267n.56, 270n.16
Choi, In-hoon, 225–26
Choi, Jin-sung, 113–14, 220–21, 222–23
    Fuckumentary (*Ppŏkk'yument'ŏri: Pakt'ong
    jilligyo*, 2001), 222–24
    The Reservoir Game (*Chŏsuji keim*,
    2017), 113–14
Choi, Seung-ho, 113–14
    *Seven Years: Journalism without
    Journalists* (*7nyŏn: Kŭdŭri ŏmnŭn ŏllon*,
    2016), 113–14
    Spy Nation (*Chabaek*, 2016), 113–15, 116–17
    Criminal Conspiracy (*Kongbŏmjadŭl*,
    2017), 113–14
Choi, Su Young, 281n.50
Choi, Suhi, 174–75
Choi, Sung-kyu, 277n.38
Chopin, Frederic, 206–7
Chouliaraki, Lille, 122–23
Chun, Doo-hwan, 8–9, 202–3
Chun, Jennifer Jihye, 75
Chun, Tae-il, 58–59
Chun, Wendy Hui Kyong, 239–40
Chung, Cheol-woong, 291n.25
Chung, Hye Jean, 273n.73
Chung, Hye Seung, 5–6, 66–67
Chungmuro, 34, 37–38, 39–40, 41–42, 47–48,
    52–53, 150–51

Index **301**

Cinemadal, 26–27, 88, 116–17, 120
Cinéma militant, 42–44
Cinéma verité, 9–10, 29–30, 38–39, 40, 46,
  58–59, 74, 91, 96–97, 118–20, 161–62,
  168, 181–82, 220
cinephiles, 8–9, 34–35, 37–38, 55–56,
  150–51
citizen (*simin*), 48–49
civilian government (*munmin jŏngbu*), 9–10,
  212–13, 217–19
civil movement (*shimin undong*), 9–12, 61–62
civil society (*simin sahoe*), 34–35, 48–49,
  51–52, 88–89
classical cinema, 176–77
Coexistence of Animal Rights on Earth
  (CARE, Tongmulgwŏn danch'e
  k'ŏ), 83–84
Cold War, 9–12, 62–70, 135, 139–41, 142–48,
  258–60
  Cold War ideology, 69–70, 131–32
collective (*chiptan*), 5, 8–9, 34–36, 42–44,
  47–49, 51–53, 244–45
comfort women (*wianbu*), 9–12, 26–27, 46–47,
  51–52, 59–60, 88–89, 92–95, 163, 179,
  256–57, 265n.26
committed documentary, 1–2, 41–42, 46–47,
  51–52, 216
common, 14–15
  See also multitude (tajung)
communal production (*kongdong chejak*),
  8–9, 35–37, 39–40, 47–48
community (*kongdongch'e*), 35–36, 37–38,
  39–40, 42–44, 50–51, 55–56, 105, 106–7,
  109–11, 117–19, 252–53
community screening (*kongdongch'e
  sangyŏng*), 8–9, 26–27, 28–29, 47–48,
  72–73, 84–86, 88, 102–3, 116–17, 119–20,
  252–53, 268n.68, 282–83n.71
compilation documentary, 23–24, 196, 201,
  206–7, 215–16
compressed modernity, 211–12
conglomerates (chaebol), 12–13, 52–53, 77
Conner, Bruce, 193–95
conservative (*posu*), 10–12, 68–69, 90, 105–6,
  289–90n.1, 292–93n.8
conspiracy theory, 192, 235–36, 239–40,
  246–47
Corner, John, 222
Corrigan, Timothy, 152, 208, 209–10
counterdiscourse, 195–96
counterhistory, 98–100

counternarrative, 198–99, 213
counterpublics, 7–8, 54–55, 91–92, 95–96,
  108–11, 195–96
Cowie, Elizabeth, 177–78
critical pedagogy, 244–46
cultural blacklist, 53–54
cultural turn, 18
culture film (*munhwa yŏnghwa*), 33–34,
  205–6
Curtis, Adam, 193–95

Daechuri, 107–10, 119–20
Daehan News, 64–65
data visualization, 72–73, 238–39
Defense Security Command (Kukkun gimu
  saryŏngbu), 171–72
Deleuze, Gilles, 17–18, 22–23, 175–78,
  180–81, 187–88
Democratic Labor Party (Minju nodong
  dang), 75
Democratic Republican Party (Minju
  gonghwa dang), 64–65
democratization (*minjuhwa*), 1–2, 4–5, 8–9,
  10–13, 15–17, 36–37, 65–66
Derrida, Jacque, 197–98
developmental dictatorship (*kaebal
  tokchae*), 223–24
developmentalism, 106–7, 149–50, 222–23,
  243–44
Dezaki, Miki, 265n.26
  *Shusenjo: The Main Battleground Of
  Comfort Women Issue* (2018), 265n.26
dialectical image, 198–200, 205–7, 209–10
  See also Benjamin, Walter
diary film, 61–62, 80, 136–37
diaspora, 30, 151, 256–58
Didi-Huberman, Georges, 247
Diffrient, David Scott, 5–6, 66–67, 282n.69
digital turn, 24, 260–61
Dijck, José van, 236–37
direct cinema, 9–10, 18–19, 40, 77–78,
  118–19, 238–39
director (*kamdok*), 6–7, 9–10, 19–20, 21–22,
  24–25, 34–35, 46–48, 55–56, 61–62,
  122–23, 124, 128, 130, 178, 196–97
disabled people (*changaein*), 80–81
discrimination (*ch'abyŏl*), 95–96, 101–2
distanciation effect, 37–38, 162–63
  See also Brecht, Bertolt
distribution of the sensible, 260–61
  See also Rancière, Jacques

302 Index

DMZ (Demilitarized Zone), 24, 173–74, 247–48, 256–57, 288n.17
DMZ International Documentary Film Festival (DMZdocs), 25–26, 129, 178–79, 231–33, 287n.6
Do, Sung-hee, 272n.48
   Our Children (Urine aidŭl, 1990), 272n.48
Docu-Factory Vista (Kirok yŏnghwa jejakso Poim), 46–47
docufiction, 24, 152–53, 161–63, 260–61
Docu Purn (P'urŭn yŏngsang), 26–27, 46–48, 49–50, 53–55, 63–64, 74, 109–10, 136–37, 220, 261–62
document visual (kirok yŏngsang), 8–9, 34–35
documentary (kirok yŏnghwa or tak'yumentŏri), 33–35, 44–46
documentary as diversion, 222
documentary disavowal, 221–22
Documentary Film and Videomakers' Council (Tak'yumentŏri jakka hoeŭi), 44–45
   For Our Song that will Echo through the Oakpo Bay (Okp'omane mearich'il uridŭrŭi noraerŭl wihayŏ, 1991), 44–45
   Battle Line (Chŏnyŏl, 1991), 44–45
domestic ethnography, 130–33, 143–49, 170–71
Dong, Kelly, 280–81n.36
Dooriban protest, 80
Doucette, Jamie, 276n.14
Dovzhenko, Oleksandr, 269n.1
   Earth (1930), 269n.1

Elsaesser, Thomas, 267n.61
Em, Henry, 276n.9
enlightenment period (kyemongchŏk shigi), 6–7
essay film, 18–19, 21–22, 23–24, 25–26, 38–39, 133, 150–58, 165, 170–71, 196, 201, 208–11, 216, 258–60
everyday (ilsang), 48–49, 59–60
evictee (chŏlgŏmin), 4–5, 8–9, 10–13, 34–35, 36–37, 41–42, 48–50, 66–67, 77–80, 109–10, 207–8, 241–42, 243–44, 246–47, 250
evidence-collection (ch'aejŭng), 245–46
experimental documentary, 17–18, 22–23, 34, 111–12, 159, 168, 169–70, 172–73, 177–79, 186–88, 189, 258–60

Fallon, Kris, 295n.57
family (kajok), 131–32, 134–35

Femidangdang, 96–97, 99–100
film movement (yŏnghwa undong), 8–9, 34–36, 39–53, 70–72, 103–5
first-person (irinch'ing), 18, 19–20, 21–22, 46, 57–58, 67–68, 74, 82–83, 86, 128, 130–31, 136–37, 139, 140–41, 143, 147–48, 165, 208–9, 227, 231–32, 238
Forgács, Péter, 193–95
Foster, Hal, 197–99, 203–4
Foucault, Michel, 197, 245–46
found footage, 23–24, 193–201, 202–4, 205–6, 216
Fraser, Nancy, 270n.16
Furstenau, Marc, 243–44

Gabriel, Teshome, 39–40
Gaines, Jane, 80–81
Galloway, Alexander R. 239–40
Gangjeong, 107–10, 119–20, 244–45
gender change (sŏngbyŏl chŏnhwan), 101–2
gentrification, 12–13, 61–62, 77, 79–80, 154–55
Getino, Octavio, 38–40
girl statue (sonyŏsang), 10–12
Giroux, Henry, 244–45
Gitai, Amos, 51–52
globalization (segyehwa), 12–13, 55–56, 134–35, 211–13
Gobalnews (Koballyusŭ), 113–14
Godard, Jean-Luc, 50–51
   Numéro deux (co-directed with Anne-Marie Miéville, 1975), 50–51
Goo, Ja-hwan, 64–65
   Red Tomb (Redŭ t'um, 2013), 64–65
Gorman-Murray, Andrew, 287n.7
governmental authority (konggwŏllyŏk), 246–47
Grand narrative, 130
Grant, Paul Douglas, 271n.39
Green Korea (Noksaek yŏnhap), 83–86
Green Party (Noksaek tang), 83–84
Guerin, Frances, 180–81
guerrilla cinema, 38–39
Gunning, Tom, 34
Gurevitch, Leon, 240
Gwangju Uprising (Kwangju minjuhwa hangjaeng), 10–12, 23–24, 34–36, 40–41, 44–45, 107–8, 160–61, 173–74, 192–97, 199–201, 203–4, 210–11, 258–60
Gwangju Video, 40–41

Index **303**

Gye, Woon-gyeong, 81–82
  Pansy and Ivy (*P'aenjiwa tamjaengi,*
    2000), 81–82

Hallas, Roger, 289n.35
Han, Hong-goo, 275n.4
Han, Ju Hui Judy, 101–2
Han, Ok-hee, 34
  2 Minutes 40 Seconds (*2pun 40ch'o,*
    1975), 34
  Colors of Korea (*Saekdong,* 1976), 34
  See also Khaidu (K'aitu)
Han, Sang-eon, 272n.44
Han, Seung-mi, 292n.6
Han, Sunhee, 293n.11
Han, Tae-ee, 141–42
  Welcome to X-World (*Welkŏm t'u X-wŏltŭ,*
    2019), 141–42
Han, Yoonai, 79–80
Hardt, Michael, 14, 88–89
hate (*hyŏmo*), 95–97, 105–6, 123–24, 135,
  139, 253–54
Hennnebelle, Guy, 42–44
Heo, Nam-woong, 272n.49
Higbee, Will, 257–58
Higson, Andrew, 253–54
Hildebrand, Lucas, 168
Hirsch, Marianne, 17–18, 132–33, 200
historic sites (*sajŏkchi*), 174–75
history documentary, 49–50, 53–54, 63–64,
  99–100
Hjort, Mette, 258–60
homecoming (*kwiguk*), 143
homeland (*choguk*), 143
homosexuality (*iban*), 101,–5
Hong, Christine, 276n.9
Hong, Grace Kyungwon, 162–63
Hong, Hyo-sook, 274n.88
Hong, Hyung-sook, 1–2, 24–25, 50–51, 55–57,
  61–62, 67–68, 89–90, 119–20, 130–31, 241
  Doomealee: A New School Is Opening (*Tumilli:*
    Saeroun hakkyoga yŏllinda, 1995), 50–51
  On-Line: An Inside View Of Korean
    Independent Film (*Pyŏnbangesŏ*
    chungshimŭro: Tongnip yŏnghwae
    taehan t'ŭkpyŏrhan shisŏn, 1997), 50–51
  Reclaiming Our Names (*Ponmyŏng sŏnŏn,*
    1998), 56–58
  Doomealee, The Very First Step
    (*Shijak'anŭn sun'gan: Tumilli tu pŏntchae*
    iyagi, 2000), 50–51

The Border City (*Kyŏnggye doshi,* 2002),
  67–68, 130–31
The Border City 2 (*Kyŏnggye doshi 2,*
  2009), 68–69
The Blue Whale Flies (*P'urŭn korae nalta,*
  in *Candlelight in the Wave,* 2017), 89–90
  Junha's Planet (*Chunhaŭi haengsŏng,*
    2018), 81–82, 278n.5
Hong, Jae-hee, 142–43, 145–46
  My Father's Emails (*Abŏjiŭi imeil,* 2012),
    142–43, 145–46
Hong, Jin-hwon, 217
  melting icecream (*Melt'ing aisŭk'ŭrim,*
    2021), 217
Hong, Ki-seon, 38–39
  Water Utilization Tax (*Surise,* 1983), 38–40,
    270n.20
Hong, Man, 270n.18
HOPE (*Hŭimang*), 93–94
Houston, Brant, 282n.58
Howley, Kevin, 282n.68
Hoyeon, 283n.76
Hughes, Helen, 281n.51
human rights (*in'gwŏn*), 9–10, 20–21, 40–41,
  50, 62–68, 100–6
Human Rights Movement Sarangbang
  (*In'gwŏn undong sarangbang*), 9–10,
  50, 53–54
human trafficking (*inshin maemae*), 215–16
Hur, Song-Woo, 92–93
Hwang, Miyojo, 59, 284n.27
Hwang, Yoon, 83–87, 89–90
  Farewell (*Chakpyŏl,* 2001), 83–86
  One Day on the Road (*Ŏnŭnal kŭ kiresŏ,*
    2006), 84–86
  An Omnivorous Family's Dilemma
    (*Chapshik kajogŭi tillema,* 2014), 86
  Chicken in the Plaza (*Kwangjangŭi tak,* in
    Candlelight in the Wave, 2017), 89–90
  Sura: A Love Song (*Sura,* 2022), 86–87
hyŏnjang (on-the-spot), 1–2, 7–10, 15, 18,
  19–20, 22–23, 24–25, 27–28, 29–30,
  38–40, 41–44, 46–47, 51–52, 58–59, 64,
  69–70, 72–74, 80–81, 94, 105–6, 110,
  111–12, 120–22, 130–31, 165, 168, 169,
  195–96, 205–6, 208–9, 211, 220, 241

ideological conversion system (*sasang*
  chŏnhyang jedo), 66–67
Im, Cheol-min, 172–73
  Glow Job (*Yagwang,* 2018), 172–73

304 Index

Im, Heung-soon, 3–4, 18–19, 166, 169, 178–79, 258–60, 269n.8
  Jeju Prayer (*Pinyŏm*, 2012), 169, 178–82, 190–91
  Factory Complex (*Wirogongdan*, 2014/2015), 3–7, 166, 263n.6
  Good Light, Good Air (*Choŭn pit, choŭn konggi*, 2020), 258–60
Im, Kwon-taek, 150–51
imagined community, 253–54
IMF (International Monetary Fund), 12–13, 17, 70–72, 211–12
immediations, 81–82
immersion, 227–28, 230–31
immersive journalism, 227
independent documentary (*tongnip tak'yumentŏri*), 1–2, 9–10, 18, 34–35, 38–39, 46–48, 50–51, 52–54, 56–57, 59–60, 66–67, 83–84, 108–9, 113–14, 115–18, 128, 129–30, 141–42, 166–67, 169–70, 181–82, 190–91, 195–96, 208, 211, 220–21, 243–44
independent film (*tongnip yŏnghwa*), 15–17, 18–20, 25–26, 41–42, 52–54, 55–56, 220
independent transnational cinema, 257–58
Indie Forum, 25–26, 53–55
Indiespace, 15–17
Indiestory, 26–27
individual (*kaein*), 9–10, 19–22, 24–25, 48–49, 59–60, 61–62, 70–72, 130, 133–34, 160, 165, 178
individual film (*kaein yŏnghwa*), 19–20
individualization, 134–35
industrialization (*sanŏp'wa*), 3, 10–12, 21–22, 134–35, 147–48, 149–50
inoperative community, 252–53
  See also Nancy, Jean-Luc
Institute of Social Photography (Sahoe sajin yŏn'guhoe), 217
International Documentary Film Festival Amsterdam (IDFA), 25–26
International Film Festival Rotterdam (IFFR), 25–26, 214–15
investigative documentary, 23–24, 64, 201, 216
Iordanova, Dina, 267n.62
irregular job (*pijŏnggyujik*), 12–13, 217–19
Irregular Workers Protection Act (*Pijŏnggyujik poho pŏp*), 217–19
Ivens, Joris, 111–12
  The Bridge (1928), 111–12

Jackson, Ben, 277n.33
Jager, Sheila Miyoshi, 135, 267n.57
James, David E. 277n.34
Jameson, Fredric, 266n.44
Jang, Sunwoo, 39–40
Jang, Yun-mi, 75–76, 149–50, 157–58
  Anxiety of Concrete (*K'onk'ŭrit'ŭŭi puran*, 2017), 157–58
  Under Construction (*Kongsaŭi hiroaerak*, 2018), 149–50
  Flag, Blue Sky, Party (*Kitpal, ch'anggong, p'at'i*, 2019), 75–76
Jangsangotmae, 44–45, 52–53
  O Dreamland (*O! Kkumŭi nara*, 1989), 44–45
  The Workers Advancing from 87 to 89 (*87esŏ 89ro chŏnjinhanŭn nodongja*, 1989), 44–45, 272n.49
  The Night before the Strike (*P'aŏp chŏnya*, 1990), 44–45
Japanese-Korean (Zainichi), 56–57, 94–95, 142–43
Japanese Occupation, 145–46, 155–56, 160–61, 167–68, 225–26, 269n.1, 285n.44
Jay, Martin, 266n.44
Jeju April Third Incident (Sasam sagŏn), 10–12, 62–63, 173–74
Jennings, June, 268n.69, 268n.70
Jeon, Sung-yeon, 96–97
  The Fearless and Vulnerable (*Haeil ap'esŏ*, 2019), 96–97
Jeong, Areum, 283n.74
Jeong, Euisol, 279n.21
Jeong, Jae-eun, 214–15, 216
  Take Care of My Cat (*Koyangirŭl put'ak'ae*, 2001), 214–15
  Talking Architect (*Malhanŭn kŏnch'ukka*, 2011), 214–15
  Talking Architecture, City: Hall (*Malhanŭn kŏnch'uk: Sit'i hor*, 2012), 214–15
  Ecology in Concrete (*Ap'at'ŭ saengt'aegye*, 2017), 214–15
Jeong, Ji-hye, 278n.47
Jeong, Su-eun, 129
  One Warm Spring Day (*Kŭ nal*, 2016), 129
Jeong, Yeo-reum, 248–49
  Graeae: A Stationed Idea (*Kŭraiai: Chudunhanŭn shin*, 2020), 248–49
Jeonju International Film Festival (JIFF), 25–26, 102–3, 178–79, 214–15
Ji, Joo-hyoung, 265n.29

Ji, Man-won, 192, 199–200
Jijon Clan (Jijonpa), 211–14
Jinbo.net, 72–73
Jo, Dongwon, 295n.55
Jo, He-rim, 283n.80
Jo, Se-young, 97–98
  Let's Dance (*Cha ije taensŭt'aim*,
    2013), 97–98
Jo, Yun-kyung, 136–37
  Family Project: House of a Father (*Kajok
    p'ŭrojekt'ŭ: Abŏjiŭi chip*, 2001), 136–39
job insecurity (*koyong buran*), 12–13, 61–62
Joo, Hyun-sook, 122–23
  Yellow Ribbons (*Tangshinŭi sawŏl*,
    2019), 122–23
Joo, Jaewon, 282n.56
Joung, Ho-hyun, 136–37
  Umma (*Mother*) (*Ŏmmarŭl ch'ajasŏ*,
    2005), 136–39
Juhasz, Alexandra, 293n.12
June Democratic Struggle (Yuwŏl minjuhwa
  hangjaeng), 9–10
Jung, Dae-ha, 290n.3
Jung, Geum-sun, 78–79
Jung, Il-gun, 109–10
  Daechuri War (*Daechuri chŏnjaeng*,
    2006), 109–10
  Memories of Daechuri (*Daechurie salta*,
    2009), 109–10
Jung, Jae-hoon, 186–87
  Hosu-gil (*Hosugil*, 2009), 186–87
  Turbulence at Dodol Hill (*Todori ŏndŏge
    nan'giryu*, 2017), 186–87
Jung, Keunsik, 267n.57
Jung, Min-ah, 264n.14
Jung, Sooyoung, 116–17
Jung, Yong-taek, 80
  Party 51 (*p'at'i51*, 2013), 80
Jung, Yoon-suk, 201, 211, 216, 224–25,
  291n.40
  Bamseom Pirates Seoul Inferno
    (*Pamsŏmhaejŏktan sŏul bulbada*,
    2017), 224–25
  Non-fiction Diary (*Nonp'iksyŏn taiŏri*,
    2013), 291n.40
juridical murder (*sabŏp sarin*), 63–64
Juvenile Protection Act (Ch'ŏngsonyŏn
  boho bŏp), 101–2

Kahana, Jonathan, 263n.5, 293n.22
Kaisen, Jane Jin, 256–57

Community of Parting (*Ibyŏrŭi
  kongdongch'e*, 2019), 256–57
Kang, Dae-jin, 140–41
  Before Sunset (*Haettŏrŏjigi chŏne*,
    1960), 140–41
Kang, Sang-woo, 192–95
  Kim-gun (*Kimgun*, 2018), 192–95, 199–201,
    216, 217
Kang, Seong-ryul, 271n.35
KangYu, Garam, 90, 91, 98–101, 123–24
  My Father's House (*Morae*, 2011), 98–99
  Itaewon (*It'aewŏn*, 2016), 98–99
  Candlelight Feminists (*Shigukp'emi*, in
    Candlelight in the Wave, 2017), 90, 99–100
  Us, Day by Day (*Urinŭn maeilmaeil*,
    2019), 99–100
KAPF (Korea Artista Proleta Federatio,
  K'ap'ŭ), 269n.1
Kappler, Stephanie, 287n.5
KBS (Korean Broadcasting System), 113–14,
  200–1, 214–16
Kellner, Douglas, 244–45
Khaidu (K'aitu), 34
Kil, Sonia, 293n.15
Kim, Alexander, 296n.9
Kim, Bo-ram (a), 98
  For Vagina's Sake (*P'iŭi yŏndaegi*, 2017), 98
Kim, Bo-ram (b), 158
  Baek-gu (*Kaeŭi yŏksa*, 2017), 158
Kim, Changwook, 282n.56
Kim, Dae-jung, 10–13, 15–17, 58–59, 61–62,
  65–67, 70–72, 173–74, 202–3, 223–24
Kim, Daniel, 267n.57
Kim, Darae, 267n.62
Kim, Dong-choon, 64–66, 264n.23
Kim, Dong-ryung, 20–21, 57–58, 161–62,
  169, 182
  American Alley (*Amerik'an aelli*, 2008), 182
  Tour of Duty (*Kŏmiŭi ttang*, co-directed
    with Park Kyoung-tae, 2013), 161–62,
    169, 178, 182, 190–91
  The Pregnant Tree and the Goblin (*Imshinhan
    namuwa tokkaebi*, co-directed with Park
    Kyoung-tae, 2019), 20–21, 161–62
Kim, Dong-won, 5–6, 18–19, 24–25, 41–42,
  46–47, 48, 49–50, 53–54, 61–62, 66–67,
  77, 78–79, 130–31, 163–64, 167–68, 208,
  241, 261–62, 272n.55
  Sanggye-dong Olympics (*Sanggye-dong
    ollimp'ik*, 1988), 41–42, 46–47, 78–79,
    167–68, 208, 271n.33

306 Index

Kim, Dong-won (*cont.*)
  Haengdang-Dong People (*Haengdang-dong saramdŭl*, 1994), 49–50, 77–79, 208
  The Six-Day Fight In Myong-dong Cathedral (*Myŏngsŏng, kŭ 6ilŭi kirok*, 1997), 49–50, 55–56
  Another World We Are Making: Haengdang-Dong People 2 (*Tto hanaŭi sesang: Haengdang-dong saramdŭl 2*, 1999), 49–50, 77–78
  Repatriation (*Songhwan*, 2003), 5–6, 26–27, 66–67, 130–31, 143, 261–62
  My Friend Jung Il-woo (*Nae ch'in'gu Chŏng Iru*, 2017), 163–64
  2nd Repatriation (*2ch'a songhwan*, 2022), 261–62
Kim, Eo-jun, 233–34, 240
Kim, Eun-sung, 246–47
Kim, Eung-su, 21–22, 133, 152–53
  The Past is A Strange Country (*Kwagŏnŭn natsŏn narada*, 2007), 152–53
  Without Father (*Abŏji ŏmnŭn sam*, 2012), 152–53
  The City in the Water (*Mul sogŭi toshi*, 2014), 152–53
  Oh! Love (*Oh! Sarang*, 2017), 153
  Surreal (*Ch'ohyŏnshil*, 2017), 153, 154
Kim, Eunjung, 81–82
Kim, German N. 296n.9
Kim, Gina, 127–28, 130–31, 136–37, 228–29
  Gina Kim's Video Diary (*Kim Jinaŭi pidio ilgi*, 2002), 127–28, 130–31
  Bloodless (*Tongduch'ŏn*, 2017), 229–31
  Tearless (*Soyosan*, 2021), 229
Kim, Gooyong, 244–45
Kim, Haery, 285n.42
Kim, Hee-chul, 64, 128, 139
  My Father (*Naŭi abŏji*, 2001), 128, 139
  The Gate of Truth (*Chinshirŭi mun*, 2004), 64
  The Time of Lovelessness (*Saranghal su ŏmnŭn shigan*, 2011), 275n.6
Kim, Heejin, 289n.47
Kim, Hieyoon, 210–11, 269n.4
Kim, Hong-joon, 34, 35–36, 150–51
  Seoul 7000 (*Sŏul 7000*, co-directed with Hwang Joo-ho, 1976), 34
  Smoking Women (*Tambae p'iunŭn yŏja(tŭl*), 2003), 150–51
  My Chungmuro (*Mai Chungmuro*, 2003), 150–51

My Korean Cinema (*Naŭi han'guk yŏnghwa*, 2003-2006), 150–51
A Short Film about Joseon Cinema (*Chosŏn yŏnghwarŭl marham*, 2006), 150–51
Kim, Hoon-Joo, 275n.2
Kim, Hwa-beom, 269n.5
Kim, Hwan-Tae, 121–22
  Five Enemies of Sewol (*Sewŏl ojŏk*, in *Forgetting and Remembering 2*, 2017), 121–22
Kim, Hyung-seok, 272n.50
Kim, I-chan, 272–73n.56
Kim, Il-rhan, 102, 120, 240, 250, 252–53
  3xFTM (2008), 102–3
  Two Doors (*Tu kaeŭi mun*, co-directed with Hong Ji-yoo, 2011), 240, 241–47, 250–53
  The Remnants (*Kongdongjŏngbŏm*, co-directed with Lee Hyuk-sang, 2016), 161–62, 185–86, 200, 241–42, 250–53
Kim, Il-sung, 143, 144–45, 257–58
Kim, Jeehey, 182–83
Kim, Jeongmin, 274n.85, 280n.28
Kim, Ji-gon, 169–70
Kim, Ji-hyun, 15–17
Kim, Ji-yeong, 233–34, 238
  The Intention (*Kŭnal, pada*, 2018), 233–34, 235–40, 246–47
  Ghost Ship (*Yuryŏngsŏn*, 2020), 233–34, 235–40, 246–47
Kim, Jin-suk, 3–4
Kim, Jin-yeol, 63–64
  Forgotten Warriors (*It'yŏjin yŏjŏnsa*, 2004), 63–64
Kim, Jinsook, 95–96
Kim, Jiyul, 135, 267n.57
Kim, Jong-eun, 261–62
Kim, Jong-il, 66–67
Kim, Joohee, 265n.26
Kim, Jung-geun, 76–77, 89–90, 169–70, 224–25
  The Island of Shadows (*Kŭrimjadŭrŭi sŏm*, 2014), 76–77
  Cleaning (*Chŏngso*, 2017, in *Candlelight in the Wave*, 2017), 89–90
  Underground (*Ŏndŏgŭraundŭ*, 2019), 76–77
Kim, Jung-young, 263n.6
  Sewing Sisters (*Misingt'anŭn yŏjadŭl*, co-directed with Lee Hyukrae, 2020), 263n.6

Kim, Ki-choon, 114–15
Kim, Kiseong, 170–71
 Land and Housing (Pongmyŏngjugong, 2020), 170–71
Kim, Kyung-man, 201, 202, 206–7, 213–14
 An Escalator in World Order (Miguk'ŭi baramgwa bul, 2011), 201, 202–7
 People Passing By (Chinaganŭn saramdŭl, 2014), 201, 206–7
Kim, Lee-jin, 128, 136–37
 Kaleidoscope (Chumadŭng, 2001), 128
Kim, Lyang, 256–57
 Dream House by the Border (Kyŏnggyeesŏ kkumkkunŭn chip, 2013), 256–57
 Forbidden Fatherland (Padaro kaja, 2018), 256–57
Kim, Mi-rye, 74
 Nogada (Nogada, 2005), 74
 Stayed Out Overnight (Oebak, 2009), 75
Kim, Mikyoung, 268n.66
Kim, Minkyong, 263n.1
Kim, Myung-joon, 26–27, 52–53
 Our School (Uri hakkyo, 2006), 26–27
Kim, Nan, 266n.40, 283n.72
Kim, Pil Ho, 280n.28
Kim, Sae-ron, 160–61
Kim, Sang-kyu, 69–70
 Killing Alice (Aellisŭ chugigi, 2017), 69–70
Kim, Seol-hae, 282n.66
 For Dear Life (Sasu, co-directed with Jo Yeongeun and Jeong Jong-min, 2018), 282n.66
Kim, Seong-hoon, 275n.93, 295n.46
Kim, Seong-nae, 272n.55, 289n.32
Kim, Seung-hee, 141–42
 Tiger and Ox (Horangiwa so, 2019), 141–42
Kim, Sohye, 57, 277n.27
Kim, Soo-hyun, 277n.26
Kim, Soo-jeong, 284n.28
Kim, Soon-ak, 163
Kim, Soon-young, 273n.69
Kim, Soyoung, 44–45, 54–55, 92–93, 243–44, 257–58
 Every Little Grass Has Its Own Name (Chakŭn p'uredo irŭm issŭni, 1990), 44–45
 Koryu: Southern Women, Southern Korea (Kŏryu, 2000), 151
 Heart of Snow: Heart of Blood (Nunŭi maŭm: Sŭlp'ŭmi urirŭl teryŏganŭn kot, 2014), 257–58

Sound of Nomad: Koryo Arirang (Koryŏ Arirang: Chŏnsanŭi tiba, 2016), 257–58
 Goodbye My Love, NK (Kutpai mai rŏbŭ NK: Pulgŭn chŏngch'un, 2017), 257–58
Kim, Suk-young, 267n.57
Kim, Sun-chul, 90, 265n.34, 291n.37
Kim, Sunah, 18, 128
Kim, Sunhyuk, 264n.21
Kim, Swoo-geun, 171–72
Kim, Tae-il, 50, 63–64, 119–20, 195–96
 A Purple Handkerchief (Ŏmŏniŭi poratpin sonsugŏn, 1995), 50, 55–56
 People Who Transcended Division (Pundanŭl nŏmŏsŏn saramdŭl, 1995), 50
 Making the Spy (22ilganŭi kobaek, 1998), 50
 April 9 (4wŏl 9il, 2000), 63–64
Kim, Ungsan, 172–73
Kim, Violet, 228
Kim, Yong-tae, 270n.14
Kim, Young-ran, 280n.31
Kim, Young-sam, 9–10, 12–13, 48, 212–13
Koh, Dong-yeon, 267n.56
Koleilat, Lina, 107–8
Koo, Hagen, 42–44, 263n.6, 265n.29, 265n.30
Koo, Se-Woong, 276n.14
Koo, Soo-hwan, 268n.65
 Don't Cry for Me Sudan (Ulchima t'onjŭ, 2010), 268n.65
Korea-US Free Trade Agreement (FTA), 119–20
Korea Creative Content Agency (KOCCA), 227
Korea Queer Film Festival, 274n.85
Korea's US military camptowns (kijich'ŏn), 20–21, 161–63, 173–74, 182–84, 230–31
Korean-style democracy, 223–24
Korean Animal Rights Advocates (KARA, Tongmulgwŏn haengdong k'ara), 83–84, 86
Korean Association of Bereaved Families for Democracy (KABFD, Minjuhwa shilch'ŏn gajok undong hyŏbŭihoe), 58–60
Korean Broadcasting System (KBS), 33–34, 113–14, 200–1, 214–16
Korean Central Intelligence Agency (KCIA, Chungang jŏngbobu), 114–15
Korean Christian Association, 204–5
Korean Confederation of Trade Unions (KCTU, Chŏn'guk minju nodong johap ch'ongyŏnmaeng), 70–72

308 Index

Korean Council and the Sexual Violence Counseling Center (Sŏngp'ongnyŏk sandamso), 92–93
Korean Council for Justice and Remembrance (Chŏngŭi kiŏk yŏndae), 9–10, 92–93
Korean Cyber Sexual Violence Response Center (KCSVRC, Han'guk saibŏ sŏngp'ongnyŏk taeŭng sent'ŏ), 96–97
Korean documentary cinema, 1, 5–8, 15–17, 19–20, 23–30, 33–35, 58, 91–93, 100–1, 113, 116–17, 124, 129, 133–34, 160, 166–67, 168–69, 175, 178–79, 181–82, 191, 193–97, 199, 200–1, 214–15, 217, 220–21, 222–23, 238–39, 247–48, 253–57, 260–62
Korean Film Council (KOFIC: Yŏnghwa jinhŭng wiwŏnhoe), 15–17
See also Korean Motion Picture Promotion Corporation
Korean flag (*taegeukgi*) Rallies, 225–26
Korean Homosexual Human Rights Association (Tonginhyeop), 100–1
Korean Independent Filmmakers Association (KIFA: Han'guk tongnip yŏnghwa hyŏp'oe), 52–53
See also Association of Korean Independent Film and Video (KIFV)
Korean Metal Workers' Union (Kŭmsok nodong johap), 75–76
Korean Motion Picture Promotion Corporation (Yŏnghwa jinhŭng gongsa), 15–17
See also Korean Film Council (KOFIC)
Korean New Wave, 37–38, 39–40
Korean War, 8–9, 10–12, 20–21, 63–64, 111–12, 128, 129, 134–36, 139–41, 145–46, 148–49, 160–61, 173–75, 187–89, 199–200, 206–7, 230–31, 256–57, 261–62
Koryŏ people (*koryŏ saram*), 257–58
KTV (Kungmin bangsong), 200–1, 269n.2
Ku, Bon-hwan, 139–40
To Find Tiger Kim (Paektusan horangirŭl ch'ajasŏ, 2006), 139–41
Kuhn, Annette, 136–37
Kwon, Aram, 170–71
Queer Room (k'wiŏŭi pang, 2018), 170–71
Homeground (Homgŭraundŭ, 2022), 287n.6
Kwon, Hayoun, 228–29, 231–32
489 Years (489nyŏn, 2016), 231–33

Kwon, Heonik, 21–22, 284n.21
Kyung-soon, 58–59, 62–63, 69–70, 94–95
Dandelion (Mindŭlle, co-directed with ChoiHa Dong-ha, 1999), 58–60
Patriot Game (Aegukcha keim, co-directed with ChoiHa Dong-ha, 2001), 222–23
What Do People Live For (Saramŭn muŏsŭro sanŭn'ga, 2004), 62–63
Red Maria (Redŭ maria, 2011), 94–95
Red Maria 2 (Redŭ maria t'u, 2015), 94–95
Patriot Game 2: To Call a Dear a Horse (Aegukcha keim 2: Chirogwima, 2019), 69–70

Labor News Production (LNP: Nodongja nyusŭ jejaktan), 42–46, 52–53, 54–55, 72–74, 93–94
Labor News No. 1(Nodongja nyusŭ 1ho, 1989), 42–44
Hundred-year Record of the History of Labor Movements in Korea (Nodongja yŏksa, paengnyŏnŭi kirok, 2013), 72–73
I Am Kim Yong-kyun (Naega Kim Yonggyunida, 2018), 72–73
Lane, Jim, 130–32
Lanzmann, Claude, 177–78
Shoah (1985), 177–78
law-abiding covenant (*chunbŏp sŏyaksŏ*), 67–68
Lebow, Alisa, 165, 283n.3
Lee, Chang-jae, 26–27
Our President (No Muhyŏnyipnida, 2017), 26–27
Lee, Chang-won, 44–45
Lee, Chung-ryoul, 26–27
Old Partner (Wŏnangsori, 2008), 26–27
Lee, Do-hoon, 129, 152–53, 175–76
Lee, Dong-ha, 280n.34
Weekends (Wik'enjŭ, 2016), 280n.34
Lee, Dong-yoon, 280n.33
Lee, Gyu-lee, 293n.21
Lee, Hae-young, 270n.26
Lee, Hakyung Kate, 279n.22
Lee, Han-yeol, 58–59, 207–8, 210–11
Lee, Hwa-jung, 290n.2, 291n.22
Lee, Hyangjin, 135
Lee, Hye-kyung, 266n.42
Lee, Hye-ran, 1, 93–94, 103–5
Parallel (P'yŏnghaengsŏn, co-directed with Seo Eun-joo, 2000), 93–94
We Are Not Defeated (Uridŭrŭn chŏngŭip'ada, 2006), 1, 3–5, 103–5

Lee, Hyeon-Jung, 268n.66
Lee, Hyo-in, 44–45, 269n.13
Lee, Hyuk-sang, 102–3, 241–42, 250
  The Miracle on Jongno Street (Chongnoŭi kijŏk, 2010), 102–3
Lee, Hyun-jung, 77–78
  192-399: A Story about the House Living Together (192-399: Tŏburŏ sanŭn chim iyagi, 2006), 77–78
Lee, In-sook, 272–73n.56, 284n.26
Lee, Jae-kyung, 267n.54
Lee, Jamie Shinhee, 291n.32
Lee, Ji-young, 73–74
  On the Right Track: First Episode (Chŏllo wiŭi saramdŭl: Ch'ŏk pŏntchae iyagi, 2001), 73–74
Lee, Jieun, 279n.21
Lee, Jin-pil, 269n.10
Lee, Jo-hoon, 64–65, 271n.32
  Land of Sorrow (Sŏsan gaechŏktan, 2018), 64–65
  Gwangju Video: The Missing (Kwangju pidio: Sarajin 4shigan, 2020), 271n.32
Lee, Jong-eun, 272n.55
Lee, Jong-in, 116
Lee, Jung-ha, 44–45
Lee, Kang-hyun, 17, 166–67
  The Description of Bankruptcy (P'asanŭi kisul, 2006), 17–18
  The Color of Pain (Bora, 2010), 166–67
Lee, Mario, 119–20
Lee, Muk, 105–6
Lee, Myung-bak, 10–12, 61–62, 65–66, 106–7, 113–14, 154–55, 204–5, 207–8, 244–45
Lee, Na Young, 264n.22, 287n.13, 288n.15
Lee, Nam, 137, 272n.43
Lee, Namhee, 10–13, 35–36
Lee, Sang-ho, 113–14
  The Truth Shall Not Sink with Sewol (Daibingbel, co-directed with Ahn Hae-ryong, 2014), 25–26, 116–17
  President's Seven Hours (Taet'ongnyŏngŭi 7shigan, 2019), 113–14
Lee, Sang-hyun, 291n.31
Lee, Sang-in, 44–45
  Kkangsuni (Kkangsuni, Syuŏp'ŭrodŏkch'ŭ nodongja, co-directed with Lee Chang-won, 1989), 44–45, 46
Lee, Seok-ki, 69–70
Lee, Seon-young, 79–80

Lee, Seung-min, 7–8, 19–20, 113, 120–21, 175–76, 288n.21
Lee, Sohyun, 121–22
  The Talent Show (Changgi jarang, 2022), 121–22
Lee, Sun-hee, 96–97
  Face, the Other Side (Ŏlgul, kŭ majŭn p'yŏn, 2018), 96–97
Lee, Tae-seok, 268n.65
Lee, Won-bo, 42–44
Lee, Won-woo, 80, 148–49
  Generator of Dooriban (Turiban palchŏn'gi, 2012), 80
  Optigraph (Opt'igŭraep'ŭ, 2017), 148–49, 277n.35
Lee, Yong-soo, 59
Lee, Yoonkyung, 70–72, 265n.31, 265n.36, 278n.1, 278n.3
Lee, Young, 103–6
  Lesbian Censorship in School (Iban'gŏmyŏl, 2005), 103–5
  Out: Smashing Homophobia Project (Iban'gŏmyŏl: Tu pŏntchae iyagi, 2007), 103–5
  Troublers (Puronhan tangshin, 2017), 105
LeeKil, Bo-ra, 141–42
  Glittering Hands (Pantchaginŭn paksu sori, 2013), 141–42
Lefebvre, Henri, 175
Lefebvre, Martin, 243–44
Lehner, Jesse, 293n.12
Lesage, Julia, 279n.24
Lewis, Oscar, 78–79
Leyda, Jay, 290n.4, 290n.5, 290n.7
Liberty Korea Party (LKP ,Chayu han'guk tang), 289–90n.1
Liberty News, 202–3
Lievrouw, Leah A. 264n.15
Lim, Jie-hyun, 10–12
Lipsett, Arthur, 193–95

Ma, Min-ji, 147–48
  Family in the Bubble (Pŏbŭl p'aemilli, 2017), 147–48
Ma, Ran, 257–58, 296n.6
Macdonald, Scott, 168, 283n.1
Mackenzie, Scott, 290n.15, 296n.4
Maeng, Soo-jin, 48–49, 241–42, 271n.35, 293n.10
mainstream media, 7–9, 37–38, 83–84, 110–11, 113–14, 116, 244–45

310 Index

Marker, Chris, 154–55, 258–60
   Sans Soleil (1982), 258–60
Marks, Laura U. 82–83
Martin, Bridget, 108–9
Massey, Doreen, 175
materialist historiography, 17–18, 23–24,
   198–99, 206–7, 210–11
Matheisen, Thomas, 245–46
Mbembe, Achille, 179
Mediact (Midiaekt'ŭ), 15–17, 268n.64
Megalia, 96–97
Mekas, Jonas, 80, 148–49
memory war (*kiŏk chŏnjaeng*), 10–12, 23–24,
   192, 196–97, 199–200, 210–11, 215–16,
   217
memoryscape, 22–23, 29–30, 169, 170–71,
   172–75, 178, 180–81, 190, 191
menstruation (*saengni*), 98
military culture (*kunsa munhwa*), 223–24
military dictatorship, 1–2, 4–6, 8–12, 22–23,
   34–35, 61–62, 192, 202–3, 207–8,
   211–13, 253–54, 258–60
Milk, Chris, 227
Min, Byung-jin, 272n.47
Min, Pyong-Gap, 9–10
minjung (people), 4–5, 6–7, 8–10, 12–13,
   14–15, 34–53, 58, 61–62, 77–79, 88–89,
   90, 107–8, 130, 133–34, 138–39, 160–61,
   208–9, 217–19, 252–53
minjung art (*minjung misul*), 4–5, 217
Miryang, 106–7, 110–12, 117–18
misogyny, 14, 95–97, 99–100, 123–24, 215–16
Mo, Eun-young, 293n.10
mobility rights (*idonggwŏn*), 80–81
modern cinema, 176–77
modernization, 22–23, 33–34, 133, 134–35,
   147–48, 149–50, 154–55, 160–61,
   171–72, 175–76, 204–5, 211–12, 213
Möller, Olaf, 292n.47
montage, 17, 34, 42–44, 50–51, 72–74, 93–94,
   110, 121–22, 160–61, 168, 172–73,
   185–86, 196, 198–99, 206–7, 213,
   215–16, 223–24, 245–46, 247, 258–60
Moon, Chang-hyun, 110–11
Moon, Hyun-sook, 267n.58
Moon, Jae-in, 10–12, 88–89, 101–2, 113–14,
   281n.43, 289–90n.1
Moon, Katherine H. S. 288n.14
Moon, Rennie J. 69–70
Moon, Seung-wook, 166–67
   Watchtower (*Mangdae*, 2014), 166–68

Moon, Seungsook, 107–8, 288n.14,
   292–93n.8, 296n.5
Moon, So-ri, 160–61
Moon, Sung-joon, 121–22
   Touch of Memory (*Kiŏgŭi son'gil*, in
   Forgetting and Remembering 2,
   2017), 121–22
Moore, Michael, 91–92, 115–16
Morris, Errol, 193, 241–42
   The Thin Red Line (1988), 193
movement-image, 22–23, 177–78, 187–88
   See also Deleuze, Gilles
movement sphere (*undongkwŏn*), 8–9
multitude (*tajung*), 14–15, 88–90, 122–23
Mun, Jeong-hyun, 119–20, 201, 207–8
   Grandmother's Flower (*Halmae kkot*,
   2007), 139–41, 207–8
   Yongsan (*Yongsan*, 2010), 201, 207–9, 216

Na, Haesuk, 285n.44
Naficy, Hamid, 257–58
Nam, Hwasook, 263n.5
Nam, Inyoung, 1–2, 9–10, 18, 55–56, 130,
   137, 268n.63
Nancy, Jean-Luc, 252–53
Nash, Kate, 294n.28
National cinema, 30, 253–56
National Film Institute (NFI: Minjok
   yŏnghwa yŏn'guso), 44–45
National Film Production Agency (NFPA:
   Kungnib yŏnghwa jejakso), 33–34
national film (*minjok yŏnghwa*), 52–53
National Guidance League Massacre
   (Podoyŏnmaeng haksal), 64–65
National Human Rights Commission
   of Korea (NHRCK, Kukka in'gwŏn
   wiwŏnhoe), 101–2
National Intelligence Service (Kukka
   jŏngbowŏn), 67–68
national liberation (*minjok haebang*), 44–45,
   222–23
national liberationists (*chusap'a*), 222–23
National Photography Institute (Minjok
   sajin yŏn'guso), 217
National Security Law (Kukka boan bŏp), 50,
   63–64, 65–66, 67–70, 224–25, 261–62
necropolitics, 179
Negri, Antonio, 14, 88–89
neoliberalization, 12–13, 61–62, 77, 119–20,
   134–35, 147–48
New Documentary, 18–19, 234–35

New German Cinema, 37–38
New Korea (*sin Han'guk*), 12–13, 212–13
New Military (Sin'gunbu), 34–35
New Progressive Party (Chinbo shin dang), 241–42
New Right, 10–12, 90, 222–23
news bulletins (*sokpo*), 42–44
Newstapa (Nyusŭt'ap'a), 113–14, 116–17
   A Story of Confession (*Chabaek-iyagi*, 2013), 116–17
Nichols, Bill, 18–19, 66–67, 133–34, 163, 168, 193–96, 228–29
NIMBY (Not in My Backyard), 109–11
Nitsche, Michael, 294n.40
Noh, Young-sun, 256–57
   Yukiko (*Yuk'ik'o*, 2018), 256–57
Nonhuman, 83–86, 186–87, 189, 190–91
Nora, Pierre, 175–76
Nornes, Abé Marcus, 272n.54
Nouvelle vague, 37–38
Nth room (Np'ŏn bang), 215–16

observational mode, 50–51, 69–70, 75–76, 78–79, 81–83, 105–6
Ogawa, Shinsuke, 18–19, 46–47, 51–52, 109–10
Oh, Minwook, 169–70, 187–88, 258–60
   Ash: Re (*Chae*, 2013), 187–89
   A Roar of the Prairie (*Pŏmjŏn*, 2015), 188–90
   Letters to Buriram (*Haehyŏp*, 2019), 258–60
omnibus documentary, 91–92, 119, 120
one-person production system (*irin jejak shisŭt'em*), 47–48, 73–74, 119, 220
open cinema (*yŏllin yŏnghwa*), 35–36, 39–40
opportunism (*kihoejuŭi*), 225–26
oral history (*kusulsa*), 21, 179
Owens, Craig, 292n.43
Ozi Film (Ojip'illŭm), 110–11

Paik, Nak-chung, 65–66
pamphlet film, 38–39
Parents and Families of LGBTAIQ People in Korea (PFLAG Korea, Sŏngsosuja pumomoim), 102–3
Park, Bae-il, 110–11
   Legend of Miryang (*Miryangjŏn*, 2013), 110–11
   Miryang Arirang (*Miryang arirang*, 2014), 110–12
   Sosungri (*Sosŏngni*, 2017), 111–12

Park, Chan-kyong, 4–5, 160–61
   Manshin: Ten Thousand Spirits (*Manshin*, 2013), 160–63
Park, Chung-hee, 10–12, 33–34, 63–65, 114–15, 145–46, 147–48, 156–57, 160–62, 199–200, 202–3, 206–7, 222–24, 225–26, 247–48
Park Chung-hee Syndrome, 222–24, 247–48, 265n.24
Park, Dong-hyun, 171–72
   Kimu: The Strange Dance (*Kiihan ch'um: Kimu*, 2009), 171–72
Park, Geun-hye, 10–12, 13, 14–15, 25–26, 28–29, 53–54, 61–62, 65–66, 69–70, 88, 105–6, 108–9, 113–15, 120, 225–26, 235–36
Park, Hae-cheon, 285n.38
Park, Han-na, 277n.39
Park, Hong, 222–23
Park, Hye-kyong, 273n.67
Park, Hyun-Ok, 199–200
Park, Hyunjoon, 284n.19
Park, Insun, 161–62, 182, 184, 185–86
Park, Jecheol, 160–61
Park, Jinhee, 142–43
Park, Jong-pil, 80–81, 120, 121–22
   Diver (*Chamsusa*, in *Forgetting and Remembering 2*, 2017), 121–22
   Report on the Stripe of the Disabled (*Pŏsŭrŭl t'aja: Changaein idonggwŏn t'ujaeng bogosŏ*, 2002), 80–81
   Salvage (*Inyang*, in *Forgetting and Remembering*, 2016), 121–22
Park, Kelvin Kyung Kun, 18–19, 21–22, 133, 152, 154–55
   Cheonggyecheon Medley (*Ch'ŏnggyech'ŏn medŭlli*, 2010), 154–56
   A Dream of Iron (*Ch'rŭi kkum*, 2014), 154–55, 156–57
   Army (*Kundae*, 2018), 157–58
Park, Kwang-soo, 37–38
Park, Kyoung-tae, 20–21, 161–62, 182, 190–91
   Me and the Owl (*Nawa puŏngi*, 2003), 182
   See also Kim, Dong-ryung
Park, Moon-chil, 90, 163
   Blue Butterfly Effect (*P'aran nabi hyogwa*, 2017), 90
   Comfort (*Podŭrapke*, 2020), 163
Park, Nohchool, 48–49, 271n.32
Park, So-hyun, 123–24

312 Index

Park, Young-a 5–6, 19–20, 39–40, 52–53, 274n.88
Park, Yuha, 94–95
Park, Yun-jin, 248–49
  People in Elancia (*Naeŏnnijŏnjihyŏn'gwa na*, 2020), 248–49
ParkGang, Areum, 141–42
  Areum Married (*Pakkang Arŭm kyŏrhonhada*, 2019), 141–42
participatory documentary, 66–67
participatory mode, 6–7, 23–24, 66–67, 70–72, 75–76, 78–79, 82–83, 89–90, 195–96, 211, 216
patriotic martyr (*aeguk yŏlsa*), 209–11
Peña, Nonny de la, 227
People's Action for Immediate Resignation of President Park Geun-hye (Pak Kŭnhye jŏnggwŏn t'oejin pisang gungmin haengdong), 88
people's film (*minjung yŏnghwa*), 52–53
People's Power (Kungminŭi him), 289–90n.1
People's Revolutionary Party Incident (Inmin hyŏngmyŏng dang sagŏn), 63–64
performative documentary, 18–19, 133–34, 163, 221–22, 248–49
performative mode, 98, 133–34, 228–29, 230–31
personal (*sajŏk*), 129–32, 165
personal documentary (*sajŏk tak'yument'ŏri*), 21–22, 128, 129–32, 141–42
personal turn, 21–22, 59, 165
personal film (*sajŏk yŏnghwa*), 19–20
Philips, Joe, 280n.29
PINKS: Solidarity for Sexually Minor Cultures and Human Rights (Yŏnbunhongch'ima), 102–3, 120, 241–42, 250
planned report film (*kihoek podo yŏnghwa*), 44–45
poetic mode, 155–56, 206–7
polarization (*yanggŭk'wa*), 12–13, 88–89, 211–13
political (*chŏngch'ijŏk*), 129–31
politics of kinship, 135
politics of pity, 122–23
poor hillside village (*taltongne*), 78–79, 157–58
poor image, 217–19
post-1987 48–49, 54–55
post-activism, 5–7, 17–18, 21, 24–25, 27–29, 253
post-Age-of-Resistance, 48–49

postclassical documentary, 128
post-Cold War, 108–9
postcommunity, 252–53
postdictatorship, 9–10
postdocumentary, 18–19, 220–22, 223–26, 247–48
Post-IMF, 17, 77, 93–94, 147–48, 222–23, 248–49
post-liberation Korea, 22–23
post-*minjung*, 4–5, 252–53
post-verité, 18–19
posthumanism, 83–84
postmemory, 17–18, 21–22, 25–26, 132–33, 145–47, 148–49, 155–56, 200
  See also Hirsch, Marianne
postmodern documentary, 193
prisoner of war, 63–64, 66–67, 149
Presidential Truth Commission on Suspicious Deaths (PTCSD: Ŭimunsa jinsang gyumyŏng wiwŏnhoe), 62–63
press (*ŏllon*), 40–41, 69–70, 91–92, 113–14, 116–17, 121–22, 217, 241, 244–45
privatization (*minyŏnghwa*), 12–13, 70–72
pro-leftist (*chwap'a*), 65–66
pro-North (*chongbuk*), 61–62, 69–70, 143
pro-US ideology, 201, 202–3, 204–6
progressive (*chinbo*), 7–8, 10–12, 36–37, 48–49, 61–62, 63–64, 67–70, 75, 90, 92–93, 99–100, 175, 189–90, 244–45, 253–54, 292–93n.8
Project Bu (P'ŭrojekt'ŭ pu), 233–34, 246–47
propaganda film, 41–42, 72–73, 203–4, 224–25
public (*kongjŏk*), 129–34
pure optical and sound situation, 176–78, 180–81, 184

Ramstad, Evan, 281n.54
Rancière, Jacques, 260–61
Rangan, Pooja, 81–82
Rascaroli, Laura, 152–53, 155–56
Raya, 170–71
  A Long Farewell (*Chibŭi shigandŭl*, 2018), 170–71
Raymo, James R. 284n.19
rebuilding (*chaegŏnch'uk*), 170–71
Record and Video Law (Ŭmban bidio pŏp), 46–47, 53–54
redevelopment (*chaegaebal*), 8–9, 22–23, 77–78, 79–80, 157–58, 166–68, 170–72, 173–74, 175–76, 182–83, 184, 187–89, 201, 207–9, 241, 243–44, 250, 252–53

Index **313**

reenactment, 3–5, 17–19, 21–22, 24, 38–39, 49–50, 64–65, 97–98, 133–34, 139–40, 145–47, 159–64, 165, 179–80, 211, 222, 228–29, 231–32, 234–35, 241–42, 250–52, 257–58
reflexive period (*sŏngch'alchŏk shigi*), 6–7
reflexive mode, 133–34, 142–43
Renov, Michael, 18–19, 23–24, 130–32, 133, 221–22
Resident Registration (Chumin tŭngnok), 102
Rhee, Syngman, 36–37, 64–65, 139–40, 202–3, 225–26
right to survive (*saengjon'gwŏn*), 106–7, 110, 241
riot (*p'oktong*), 10–12, 53–54, 173–74, 192, 199–200
rioter (*p'okto*), 173–74, 241
risk society, 211–12
ritual (*gut*), 38–39, 156–57, 160–61, 179–80, 256–57
Robé, Chris, 264n.15, 271n.42
Rodowick, D. N. 177–78
Rodrigues, Inês Nascimento, 287n.4
Roe, Annabelle Honess, 236–37
Roh, Moo-hyun, 10–12, 26–27, 61–62, 65–66, 69–72, 101–2, 149, 173–74, 217–19
Roh, Tae-woo, 8–9
Ross, Miriam, 267n.60
Ruby, Jay, 78–79
Ruin, 182–86, 187–90, 191
Russell, Catherine, 198–99, 200–1, 202–3
Ryu, Hyun-kyung, 160–61
Ryu, Mi-rye, 136–37, 141–42
   Life Goes On (*Ŏmma*, 2004), 136–37, 138–39, 141–42
Ryu, Youngju, 265n.24, 275n.3, 293n.9

Saemangeum, 86–87
Saemaul undong (New Village Movement), 222–23
Sampoong Department Store (Samp'oong baekhwajŏm), 211–12
Sanrizuka series, 46–47, 109–10
   See also Ogawa, Shinsuke
Sekula, Allan, 154–55
self-consciousness, 9–10, 17, 19–20, 51–52, 55–56, 57–60, 61–62, 97–98, 124, 130–31, 140–41, 196–97
Seo, Hyun-suk, 171–72
   The Lost Voyage (*Irŏbŏrin hanghae*, co-directed with An Chang-mo, 2012-17), 171–72

Seo, Hyunjin, 266n.40
Seo, Ji-hyun, 123–24
Seo, Joon-sik, 53–54
Seo, Jung-eun, 273n.69
Seo, U-seok, 287n.8
Seongsu Bridge (Sŏngsu daegyo), 211–12
Seoul Film Collective (SFC: Sŏur yŏnghwa chiptan), 35–36
   Pannori Arirang (*P'annori arirang*, 1982), 37–38, 39–40
   See also Seoul Visual Collective (SVC)
Seoul Human Rights Film Festival, 53–54, 282–83n.71
Seoul Independent Documentary Film Festival (SIDOF), 25–26, 128, 282–83n.71
Seoul Independent Film Festival (SIFF), 25–26
Seoul International Labor Film Festival, 54–55
Seoul International New Media Festival (NeMaf), 25–26
Seoul International Women's Film Festival (SIWFF), 25–26, 54–55, 92–93, 100–1
Seoul Queer Films and Videos Festival, 100–1
Seoul Queer Pride Parade, 105–6
Seoul Visual Collective (SVC: Sŏul yŏngsang chiptan), 40, 220
   See also Seoul Film Collective (SFC)
Severe Workplace Disaster Punishment Law (Chungdae jaehae giŏp chŏbŏl bŏp), 72–73
Sewol Ferry disaster, 14–15, 24, 27–28, 89–90, 91–92, 102, 105–6, 116, 120–21, 133, 149, 153, 160–61, 199–200, 212–13, 221–22, 234–35, 256–57
sex labor, 94–95
sexual harassment (*song hŭirong*), 123–24, 163–64, 173–74, 215–16
sexual minorities (*song sosuja*), 7–8, 13, 95–96, 100–2, 105–6, 170–71
Shin, Eun-sil, 266n.42
Shim, Young-hee, 292n.49
Shin, Eun-mi, 69–70
Shin, Gi-wook, 48–49, 65–66, 69–70
Shin, Hyun-Bang, 77
Shin, Jin-wook, 13
Shin, Kwang-yeong, 265n.32
Shin, Wooyeol, 282n.56
Shub, Esfir, 193–95

314 Index

Singer, C. Collins, 280n.28
sit-in (*nongsŏng*), 1, 27–28, 46, 58–59, 63–64, 75–76, 96–97, 111–12, 208, 217–19, 243–44
small film (*chakŭn yŏnghwa*), 35–36, 39–40, 53–54
Sobchack, Vivian, 84–86
social change documentary, 7–8, 15–17, 24, 50–51, 61–63, 73–74, 80–81, 91, 113, 220, 244–45, 261
socially engaged documentary, 1–2, 46–47
social media, 13, 56–57, 69–70, 88, 95–96, 116–18, 244–45, 268n.68
social movement (*sahoe undong*), 1–2, 4–6, 7–13, 24–25, 26–28, 34–35, 41–42, 48–50, 51–52, 55–56, 58–60, 61–64, 69–70, 77, 81–82, 86–87, 88–92, 100–1, 102–3, 105–6, 117–18, 120–21, 129–30, 161–62, 163–64, 181–82, 190, 195–96, 199–200, 210–11, 215–16, 244–45, 253–54, 258–60
social reform (*sahoe byŏnhyŏk*), 8–9, 36–37, 44–45
Sohn, Hee-jeong, 95–96
Soja, Edward W. 175
Solanas, Fernando, 38–40
solidarity (*yŏndae*), 1–2, 7–8, 15, 18, 20–21, 24–26, 27–29, 38–39, 42–44, 50–51, 58–59, 61–62, 72–73, 74, 75, 76–77, 78–79, 92–94, 99–100, 103–5, 107–8, 110–11, 118–23, 132–33, 149, 215–16, 250, 252–53, 258–60
Solidarity Committee of the Disabled to Obtain Mobility Rights (SDOMOR), 80–81
Son, Si-nae, 286n.65
Song, Du-yul, 67–70
Song, Hwee-lim, 257–58
Song, Jesook, 265n.30, 285n.40
Song, Joon-ho, 271n.38
Song, Won-geun, 265n.26
  My Name is Kim Bok-dong (*Kim Boktong*, 2019), 265n.26
SoP (sense of presence), 227, 229, 230–31, 232
Souza, Nicole de, 292n.50
space documentary (*konggan tak'yumentŏri*), 175
spatial turn (*kongganjŏk sŏnhoe*), 175–76
Special Act for Sexual Violence (Sŏng p'ongnyŏk t'ŭkpyŏ lbŏp), 214–15
Spieker, Sven, 203–4

Steinberg, Stefen, 291n.40
Steyerl, Hito, 217–19
streaming video, 116–17
struggle (*t'ujaeng*), 1–4, 6–7, 8–10, 15, 36–37, 38–39, 41–44, 45–46, 50–51, 53–54, 58–59, 70–73, 74, 80–81, 83–84, 90, 97–98, 99–100, 106–12, 117–18, 120–21, 139–40, 166, 169, 178–79, 206–8, 215–16, 217, 224–25, 241, 243–45, 250, 252–53
subcontracting (*hach'ŏng*), 74
subjectivization, 21, 109–10
subjunctive documentary, 24, 221–22, 234–35, 238–39, 247–48
subjunctive mode, 234–35, 239–40, 241–42, 246–47
sublime, 154–55, 156–57
Suh, Jae-Jung, 268n.66
Sundance Film Festival, 26–27
synoptic surveillance, 245–46
synthetic vision, 293n.18

Tae, Joon-sik, 121–22, 274n.89
  Classroom (*Kyoshil*, in *Forgetting and Remembering*, 2016), 121–22
  Days of Human (*In'ganŭi shigan*, 2000), 73–74
  The War Waged by You and Me (*Tangshin'gwa naŭi chŏnjaeng*, 2010), 73–74
Takju Cooperative (T'akchu johap), 169–70
testimony, 3–4, 67–68, 74, 103–5, 109–10, 111–12, 114–15, 121–22, 139–40, 145–46, 149–50, 160, 161–62, 163, 177–78, 180–82, 189–90, 228–29, 231, 232–33
THAAD, 90, 108–9, 111–12
the 38th parallel (*samp'alsŏn*), 145–46
Theory of Film Movement (*Yŏnghwa undongnon*), 39–40, 42–44
  See also Seoul Film Collective (SFC)
Third Cinema, 37–40, 260–61
time-image, 17–18, 22–23, 175–78, 180–81, 184, 185–86, 187–88, 190, 191
  See also Deleuze, Gilles
Togo, Kazuhiko, 279n.13
Toward a New Cinema (*Saeroun yŏnghwarŭl wihayŏ*), 39–40
  See also Seoul Film Collective (SFC)
transmedia documentary, 116–17
transnational cinema, 256, 257–58
trauma cinema, 250–51

Trump, Donald, 261–62
truth claim, 1–2, 18, 217–19, 220–21, 238–40
truth-finding (*jinsang gyumyŏng*), 10–12,
  24–25, 28–29, 61–62, 173–74
Truth and Reconciliation Commission
  (Chinshilgwa hwahae wiwŏnhoe),
  10–12, 173–74
Tryon, Chuck, 282n.65
Tsui, Clarence, 182
Tuan, Yi-Fu, 175
Tufte, Edward, 238–39

Um, Ji-won, 277n.32
unconverted long-term prisoners
  (*pijŏnhyang changgisu*), 66–67
Unified Progressive Party (UPP: t'onghap
  chinbo dang), 69–70
unrepresentability, 159
urban poor (*toshi pinmin*), 7–8, 9–13, 35–36,
  41–42, 44–45, 48–50, 61–62, 77–80,
  163–64, 241
urban regeneration (*toshi jaesaeng*), 171

Varda, Agnès, 151
  The Gleaners and I (2000), 151
Venice Biennale, 3, 171–72
Vertov, Dziga, 193–95, 269n.1
  Man with a Movie Camera (1929), 269n.1
victim women (*p'ihaeja yŏsŏng*), 267n.54
victimhood (*hisaengjasŏng*), 20–21
victim (*hisaengja*), 9–13, 20–21, 28–30, 50,
  51–52, 53–54, 58–59, 61–65, 81–83,
  84–86, 92–93, 94–95, 96–97, 113, 114–16,
  120–22, 132–33, 139–40, 149, 153, 154,
  159, 161–62, 169, 173–75, 178, 179–81,
  190–91, 195–96, 207–12, 215–16, 223–24,
  235–37, 240, 241, 246–47, 256–57
video guerrilla, 42–44, 118–19
Virilio, Paul, 202–3
virtual reality (VR) documentary, 221–22
Vivacqua, Paolo, 155–56

Wagner, Richard, 153
Waldman, Diane, 280n.27
Walker, Janet, 250–51
Warner, Michael, 264n.16
war politics (*chŏnjaeng jŏngch'i*), 50, 61–62,
  65–66, 173–74
Waugh, Thomas, 1–2, 103–5
we (*uri*), 1
Wees, William C. 290n.6, 290n.13

Western princess (*yanggongu*), 173–74
Western whore (*yanggalbo*), 173–74
Whiteman, David, 273n.70, 282n.63
Williams, Linda, 18–19, 193, 234–35
Winston, Brian, 229, 238–39
Wiseman, Frederick, 75–77
Wolf, Mark J. P. 234
Wolfe, Cary, 83–84
Wolfe, Charles, 278n.45
WOM (Yŏsŏng yŏngsang chiptan Um), 1, 103–5
women worker (*yŏgong*), 1
women's sphere (*yŏsongjang*), 92–93, 131–32
Women's Visual Collective Bariteo (Yŏsŏng
  yŏngsang jiptan Paritŏ), 44–45, 46–47,
  103–5
Womenlink (Han'guk yŏsŏng
  minuhoe), 44–45
Wong, Cindy Hing-Yuk, 274n.86
worker (*nodongja*), 1–5, 42–46, 70–77, 92–95,
  161–62, 173–74, 206–7
Worker's Party of Korea (WPK, Chosŏn
  nodong dang), 68–69
workplace (*chagŏpchang*), 3–4, 17, 22–23,
  42–45, 61–62, 70–77, 149–50, 163–64,
  166–67, 179–80, 186–87, 190, 206–7,
  217–19, 231

Yalrashung (Yallasyŏng), 35–37, 270n.20
  Galileans of This Land (*I ttangŭi kallilli
    saramdŭl*, 1984), 36–37
  Kukpung (*kukp'ung*, 1981), 36–38
  *Twenty-Five Years of Democratization
    Struggles* (*Minjuhwa t'ujaeng 25nyŏn*,
    1984), 36–37
Yamagata International Documentary Film
  Festival (YIDFF), 46–47
Yang, Myungji, 285n.39
Yang, Yonghi, 56–57, 142–43, 254–55
  The Swaying Spirit (*Yureru kokoro*,
    1996), 56–57
  Dear Pyongyang (*Tiŏ p'yŏngyang*,
    2005), 142–45
  Goodbye Pyongyang (*Kutpai p'yŏngyang*,
    2009), 142–43, 145
  Soup and Ideology (*Sup'ŭwa ideollogi*,
    2021), 254–55
Yellow Ribbon (Noran ribon), 121–22
Yeo, Andrew, 281n.45
Yeonpyeong Incident, 160–61
Yeosu-Suncheon Incident (Yŏsuns
  agŏn), 139–40

316 Index

Yi, Jin-kyung, 88–89
Yi, Joseph, 280n.29
Yi, Seung-jun, 5–6, 28–29, 82–83
    Planet of Snail (*Talp'aengiŭi pyŏl*, 2010), 5–6, 28–29, 82–83
    In the Absence (*Pujaeŭi kiŏk*, 2018), 28–30
    Shadow of Flowers (*Kŭrimja kkot*, 2019), 28–29
Yongsan Massacre (Yongsan ch'amsa), 24, 102, 149, 207–8, 221–22, 240, 241, 247–48, 252–53
Yoo, Soon-mi, 256–57
    Songs from the North (*Pungnyŏkk'esŏ on norae*, 2014), 256–57
Yoo, Un-seong, 180–81, 270n.20, 295n.50, 296n.2

Yoo, Young-gun, 227
Yoon, Hye-ji, 282n.64
Yoon, Keum-yi, 229
Yoon, Sung-a 256–57
    Overseas (*Haeoero*, 2019), 256–57
Yoon, Yi-sang, 67–68
You, Dong-chul, 277n.36
Yu, Ga-ryeo, 114–15, 116–17
Yu, Kiki Tianqi, 130
Yu, Woo-sung, 114–15, 116–17
Yuk, Joowon, 266n.39
Yusin regime, 223–24
    See also Park, Chung-hee

Zhang, Lu, 166, 254–55, 256
    Scenery (*P'unggyŏng*, 2013), 166, 296n.6
Zyrd, Michael, 213–14